MASTER AND MADMAN

The Surprising Rise and Disastrous Fall of the Hon Anthony Lockwood RN

by

Peter Thomas & Nicholas Tracy

Farewell, a long farewell, to all my greatness!
This is the state of man; to-day he puts forth
the tender leaves of hope, to-morrow blossoms,
and bears his blushing honours thick upon him;
the third day, comes a frost, a killing frost;
and – when he thinks, good easy man, full surely
his greatness is a ripening – nips his root,
and then he falls, as I do.

Wolsey, *Henry VIII*, III.ii

Seaforth
PUBLISHING

Copyright © Peter Thomas & Nicholas Tracy 2012

First published in Great Britain in 2012 by
Seaforth Publishing,
Pen & Sword Books Ltd,
47 Church Street,
Barnsley S70 2AS

www.seaforthpublishing.com

British Library Cataloguing in Publication Data
A catalogue record for this book is available from the British Library

ISBN 978 1 84832 121 2

Typeset and designed by MATS Typesetting, Leigh-on-Sea, Essex
Printed and bound by CPI Group (UK) Ltd, Croydon, CR0 4YY

Contents

Preface

THIS ACCOUNT OF the life of the Honourable Anthony Lockwood, who rose from obscurity at the bottom of the social scale, and the life of a common seaman, to high office in colonial New Brunswick, was the last great scholarly labour undertaken by Peter Thomas, late Professor of English at the University of New Brunswick (UNB). When he found that he was dying he asked me to finish his work, writing the chapters on Lockwood's madness and fall from the height he had reached, and finishing his draft of the rest of the book for publication. Our paths had crossed a number of times while Peter was undertaking his monumental research work, but his selection of me for this honour was also based on his suspicion that my own life and tenuous connection with the establishment at UNB resonated with Lockwood's experience as an 'outsider' in the Loyalist culture of New Brunswick. Apart from the effects of organic disease, Lockwood's mad attempt at mounting a *coup d'état* in New Brunswick, in Peter's assessment, was a response to the rottenness at the monarchical core of colonial society, and to the example of the successful rebellions taking place in the Spanish empire. For my part, the acceptance of Peter's invitation was an act of friendship: Peter was an intelligent, generous and humane man, and almost my last words to him were that I wished we had known each other better – a sentiment he reciprocated. At the same time, my own background made me an obvious choice to complete the study of Lockwood. My scholarly career is in naval history, with some time spent studying colonial New Brunswick history, I have experience of naval life, as a yachtsman I am familiar with some of the coast Lockwood surveyed, and my home has been in New Brunswick and Nova Scotia for much of my life. My part in this project has been both a logical extension of my scholarly life, and a journey with my departed friend.

I am grateful for the assistance of archivists in Canada and Britain who assisted me in confirming, and in some instances correcting, references to material unearthed by Peter Thomas during his two-decade-long research work. I am particularly indebted to Gary Shutlak at the Public Archives of Nova Scotia, Robert Fellows and Rob Gilmore at the Public Archives of New Brunswick, Daryl Johnson at the Museum of New Brunswick, Daniel Somers at the Public Archives of Canada, and Tom Catherall and Guy Hannaford at the United Kingdom Hydrographic Office. In addition I have been greatly assisted by Robert W Hoge, Curator of North American Coins and Currency for the American Numismatic Society, and Joanne Smyth, reference librarian at the University of New Brunswick. While responsibility for any errors of commission or omission must be shared by Peter Thomas, who was unable to finish his manuscript, and myself, who arrived late on the scene, I am grateful indeed for the willingness shown by Dr William Acheson, historian of Saint John, New Brunswick, to read the manuscript before publication.

Nicholas Tracy
Fredericton, 21 April 2011

Illustrations

Provincial Archives of New Brunswick, H Series Maps: H2-203.29-1818.

10 *A View of the City & Harbour of St John, New Brunswick, NA, taken from the Hills WSW of Fort Howe*, Charles Turner, British (1774–1857), after Ralph Stennett, active 1812–1815. Hand-coloured etching and aquatint on wove paper, laid down on canvas support: 58.0 x 69.0cm (trimmed within plate mark at top and bottom), publication: London, England. New Brunswick Museum, William B Tennant Collection, 21183.1.

11 *View of Saint John, New Brunswick*, Joseph Brown Comingo, Canadian, 1784–after 1821, watercolour, with pen and ink on wove paper support: 34.7 x 51.6cm. New Brunswick Museum, Webster Museum Foundation purchase, 1966.100a.

12 *On the Kenibeckasis near St John* by Lady Mary (Heaviside) Love, lithograph by Day and Haghe, London, 1831, from *The British Dominions in North America; or a Topographical and Statistical Description of the Provinces of Lower and Upper Canada, New Brunswick, Nova Scotia, the Islands of Newfoundland, Prince Edward, and Cape Breton*, by Joseph Bouchette, published by Henry Colburn and Richard Bentley, London, 1831. Provincial Archives of New Brunswick, J Leonard O'Brien fonds: MC299-4.

13 *General Smyth, 1816*, by Allison Montrose Colwell, Canadian, 1889–1963, apparently on the basis of research and consultation provided by Captain Charles Coburn Taylor (1868–1941) who was a riverboat captain. Pen and ink drawing with wash on wove paper *c.*1935–1941, sight: 17.8 x 38.2cm, support: 27.8 x 48.3cm, New Brunswick Museum, X5184.[1]

14 *View of Province Hall and Public Offices, Fredericton, New Brunswick*, after George Neilson Smith, lithograph by Ephraim W Bouvé, Boston, *c.*1850. Provincial Archives of New Brunswick Assorted Photo Acquisitions #4: P37-162.

15 *Governor's Residence, Fredericton, New Brunswick*, oil on canvas, painter unknown. New Brunswick Museum, William Francis Ganong Collection, X16488.

16 *Barracks and Market House, Frederickston [sic] N*, John Elliott Woolford (attributed) in Joseph Bouchette, Day and Haghe, Lithographers to the King, 17 Gate St, Lincolns Inn Fields, *British Dominions in North America*, 1832, p. 110, vol 2.

17 *Officers' Barracks at Fredericton, Winter, 1834*, by John Campbell and W P Kay, lithograph by S Russell of Day and Haghe Lithographers, London. Campbell was the son of Sir Archibald Campbell, Lieutenant Governor of New Brunswick, 1831–1837. Provincial Archives of New

Brunswick Assorted Photo Acquisitions #4: P37-345.

18 *Sleighing Party*, Fredericton, New Brunswick, attributed to John Elliott Woolford, British (1778–1866) (titled and dated on the back in what is apparently Woolford's hand). Oil on paper applied to canvas, 1830, support: 46.5 x 87.5cm, frame: 57.6 x 98.2cm, New Brunswick Museum, J Delancy and Susan White Robinson Collection, 1964.42.[2]

19 *Survey of Richibucto Reserve Lands*, Anthony Lockwood, signed, Provincial Archives of New Brunswick RS656-KE-19-4-2.

20 Sketch of Robert C Minette's proposed route for Chignecto Canal, surveyed in 1825. Provincial Archives of New Brunswick, H4-203-12.

1823 . 5. 30 . 9 (14)
Steam Boat

Sir

I respectfully beg your Honor
to relieve me from the weighty
and responsable duty in Council
my present ailment being
subject to increase by confinement
I have the honor to be
Sir your devoted
Servant
Rockwood
Rec R Sur Gen

His Honor
The President

MASTER AND MADMAN

Introduction

BY PETER THOMAS

THE EVENTS OF 1 June 1823 were only the culmination of a series of public 'outrages' over the previous two weeks. During that time Anthony Lockwood had moved about the province of New Brunswick, brawling, threatening the lives of sundry individuals, and otherwise behaving in an eccentric, not to say insane, fashion. By 5 June a commission *De Lunatico Inquirendo* had determined that he was indeed mad and a committee was appointed to manage his affairs. It was quickly established that his accounts as Receiver General were short by nearly £2,000; within the year Lockwood's house and most of its contents were offered at auction to replenish these funds. Though he was removed from jail by September 1823, he was kept under house-arrest and watched over by a constable, while continually petitioning to be examined for sanity until November 1825, at which time he was at last officially removed from his offices – only six years after his arrival in the province. He left for England almost immediately, never to return, and died nearly thirty years later after periods in the private madhouses of Peckham and Bethnal Green.

Even this spare outline is fuller and more accurate than the few references to Lockwood which appear in existing histories of New Brunswick. In W S MacNutt's *History of New Brunswick, 1784–1867*, Lilian Mary Beckwith Maxwell's *History of Central New Brunswick*, and James Hannay's *History of New Brunswick*, Lockwood's madness merits a paragraph or so. There are briefer references to his New Brunswick career elsewhere. He is sometimes confused with his son; dates are often wrong. Nor is his much longer career as a naval hydrographer (1800–1818) better served. There is a shrewd but sparsely-informed entry in L S Dawson's *Memoirs of Hydrography* (1885) – shrewd because it detected the sarcastic streak in Lockwood's character – but the two references in Sir Archibald Day's *The Admiralty Hydrographic Service* (1967) hardly glance as they pass. The fullest accounts of Lockwood's life to date are mine in the *Dictionary of Canadian Biography* and *passim* in *Strangers from a Secret Land* (1986).

This neglect is not surprising and has both particular and general causes. Despite the singularity of what might be viewed as an attempted one-man *coup d'état* in Fredericton, it occurred in one of the most dimly-lit corners of empire. New Brunswick does not loom large in the imagination of colonialism. The doings of obscure madmen from the early days of remote outposts do not demand much attention from any but local historians.

The province had no provincial archives until 1968 and to write any ranging account of its history required heroic persistence in consulting scattered and often unsorted materials. In addition, Lockwood poses a peculiar problem to the historian. During his madness he apparently attempted self-consciously to erase himself from the public record. Within days of his imprisonment it was discovered that he had destroyed or 'mutilated' the maps, surveys, grant and timber licence books of the Surveyor General's office. It took his three immediate successors, with the assistance of two extra clerks, more than five years to partially reconstruct what was missing. It is therefore impossible to offer anything but an approximate account of what Anthony Lockwood did as Surveyor General. Of his service as Receiver General only fragments remain. Even the contemporary investigators put their faith in a mysterious 'black box' secured at the Bank of New Brunswick in Saint John which proved to contain few answers. As to Lockwood's personal papers: there is first the evidence of a letter he wrote to the Admiralty on 30 January 1818 asking for confirmation of his naval service, the original documents having been lost, he stated, when 'a Merchant Brig, having on board my books and papers, from Barbadoes bound for St John's [*sic*], New Brunswick, in November 1815, suffered wreck upon Partridge Island, in the Bay of Fundy.'[1] Then, in 1833, he was unable to provide the Admiralty with accurate dates for a memorandum of service, 'my Journals and Certificates being destroyed in my dwelling house in Fredericton in North America in 1824.'[2]

Thus it was by shipwreck, fire, and his own hand, that many of the accumulated materials of Anthony Lockwood's life were eliminated. Any biographical enquiry must be nurtured by specialised forms of hope.

From another perspective, though, there is a kind of wild propriety to these visitations of fire and water, the self-murder of an official identity, the antics of a loony dictator-manqué attempting to save New Brunswick from itself. As a romantic gesture, Lockwood's performance on 1 June 1823 does have resounding cultural resonance, and to dismiss his actions as mad, and therefore meaningless, is to miss an important insight into New Brunswick history. Every generation has its models, its styles in madness. Moreover, perhaps at no time in history was madness more compellingly eloquent. Kings, poets, politicians went mad, while the spirit of revolution was widely understood as collective unreason, the dark storm of misrule, afflicting the psyches of whole nations. The greatest English poet to be accused of madness claimed that reason itself imposed 'mind forg'd manacles' upon the liberating imagination. Madness, from this viewpoint, was supremely radical, the most absolute form of anti-conservatism – as the Marquis de Sade understood when he presented the play-acting of asylum inmates as the subversion of social decorum and restraint. In short, madness at all times is implicitly political, as it is also existential. Madness always has more than one context.

The purpose of this book is to show that Anthony Lockwood's attempt to seize the day on 1 June 1823 was both mad and meaningful and that he acted out of complex and concealed circumstances which made what he did, though extreme, logical. But this great crisis of Lockwood's life – there were others – can only be fully appreciated if elements of his biography are known. His story is a kind of fable. Even his catastrophe proved less absolutely devastating than appears and his life had a surprising end to go along with the peculiar middle. As for the beginnings, they were not exactly what might be expected in a Receiver General of the King's Casual Revenues.

Despite the destruction of records, there is no need to reconstruct Lockwood's fable simply from scraps and shadows. The man who went spectacularly mad was of course a particular person who left many marks. What remains of the documentary evidence is substantial. Lockwood's naval career – described by himself as 'twenty five years' incessant peregrination' – can be reached principally through the files of the Admiralty, the Navy Board, and the Hydrographical Office. This wanderer's somewhat erratic course almost exactly spanned the period of the French wars and the war of 1812. Lockwood was commended for bravery in action against the French; was present at the Spithead Mutiny; shipwrecked and imprisoned in France; appointed master attendant of the naval yard at Bridgetown, Barbados, during the year the slave trade was abolished; served as an hydrographer on the coast of Spain, in the Channel Islands, the Spanish Main, and elsewhere – before beginning his three-year marine survey of Nova Scotia and the Bay of Fundy. He produced a new land map of Nova Scotia. In 1818 he published his *Description* of that province. His had not been a trivial story by the time he reached New Brunswick in the summer of 1819.

Furthermore, there is also a considerable body of material touching on Lockwood's search for a civilian position (1818–1819) to be found in the same main sources, with the addition of that of the Treasury Office. From his arrival in New Brunswick, Lockwood necessarily entered directly into the political and social life of the province. He was the first true outsider to be appointed to the Executive Council of the province, a factor which may have contributed to the events of 1 June 1823. The direct source materials of this phase of his life are widely dispersed, mainly in New Brunswick, until the onset of his madness. But that episode, the immediate political context in which it took place, its legal and personal consequences, are substantially recorded. Most particularly, a group of Lockwood's letters from jail have survived. In short, while Lockwood remains a case, and not a life, a vivification is possible.

Even partial biographers must justify their subjects, most fully to themselves. This is obviously most true when the subject is little known, despite the paradox that the very purpose of biography is to make a life known. I was first drawn to this study by the absurd dramatic performance of Lockwood's last fateful ride. It seemed to me questionable from the beginning that this was a mere aberration. Is there any such thing? My scepticism was fuelled by the odd circumstance that no surviving unguarded comment by a New Brunswick contemporary on the events of that day has come to light. What remains is the official record of the Executive Council enquiry. Even the two issues of the *Royal Gazette* which may have contained a report are missing – as are copies of the Saint John newspapers of the period. This is not the preface to a conspiracy-theory, except perhaps a conspiracy of embarrassed silence. Yet it remains curious. The spectacle of the Surveyor General – his face the worse for earlier fights – brandishing pistols on horseback must surely have been an attention-grabbing event in a village of 1,700 persons, a veritable feast for gossip. It is worth recalling Sherlock Holmes' wisdom in *The Dog That Didn't Bark*. Silence can indeed be eloquent. What does it speak of here?

Lockwood is one of those figures from the past who appear to represent essential elements of their times by failure rather than success. In his downfall he presented questions which concerned both the thinkers and men of action of his day – questions concerning the nature of political authority, the limits of reason, and the rights of the individual. From this perspective, Fredericton was not an obscure and ill-lit stage at all. Lockwood's great performance took place in the capital of a new land in a time of change, where individual will and political order contended more nakedly than in more established societies. Properly approached, the case of Lockwood is thus of significance in a much larger context than that of New Brunswick.

PART ONE

Lockwood, Master RN

1

Dead Man's Cloaths

THE ICARUS OF GREEK myth, son of Daedalus who was a renowned smith and artificer, fashioned for himself wings of feathers stuck on with wax. Together they took to the air, but Icarus came to disaster when he flew too close to the sun. Lockwood's is an Icarus story, made possible by the opportunities that a brave man could make for himself in wartime. His spectacular end came when the thin atmosphere of colonial New Brunswick high society ceased to support his wings, and he spiralled in despair to his destruction. He did not recognise himself as an Icarus figure, but he did identify himself with the less well known myth about Icarus's cousin Acalus. Otherwise known as Talos, Calus, Perdix and Taliris, at the age of twelve Acalus was sent to Daedalus as an apprentice. He had inherited the family's gift of inventiveness, and this led to his ruin. His remarkable creativity inspired furious jealousy in Daedalus, who flung the boy from the Acropolis to his death. Lockwood rose from obscurity because of his creativity, although his reach did exceed his grasp; he scaled the heights of colonial society, but fell to his ruin in the streets of Saint John and Fredericton armed with a pair of sawn-off pocket pistols.

His first documented appearance on the stage of life was when his name was entered into the books of HMS *Iphigenia* on 18 April 1795 at Port Royal, Jamaica. He gave his age as twenty-two, but possibly he lied, as he was to give the same age over a year later when he joined HMS *Duke*. Lockwood is a Yorkshire name, but Anthony was probably born in London. When entered into the muster book of *Iphigenia* he stated his place of birth as being Northumberland, but altered the record to London when joining *Duke*. His baptismal certificate has not been found, but it is likely he was the son of Richard Lockwood, who had been baptised at St Botolph Without Aldgate in 1732, one of the sons of Benjamin and Mary Lockwood who baptised nine children. Richard had joined Captain William McLeod's company as a matross, and served at Onondago Falls (1760), and Albany, before joining the garrison at Fort Edward in 1762, where he remained until his return to England in 1765 as a sergeant, seven years before Anthony's birth. It may be supposed that Rachel, Anthony's mother, was a Steed or Stead, because an older sister had been baptised Elizabeth Steed Lockwood at St Mary, Whitechapel, in November 1768.[1]

As the son of a Royal Artillery sergeant, Anthony may have received some instruction from his father, or more formally, in the mathematics of gunnery targeting, basic geometrical training from which his surveying skills were perhaps derived. He undoubtedly had mathematical aptitude and it was encouraged somewhere. There were also schools of navigation, usually run by retired mariners, though sometimes even by women, in dockside communities all round the British Isles, and Lockwood certainly picked up marine navigation somewhere. But nothing is known of his formal schooling. Apart from mathematics, he evidently had musical abilities. His surviving writings are literate, showing some range of allusion, if not elegant.

But what was he doing in Jamaica? The evidence is at best circumstantial. When Lockwood was temporarily invalided out of the Navy in 1801 his place of residence became Whitehaven in Cumberland, seemingly an odd choice for a convalescent London East Ender, unless he knew the town already and was returning there. Was this his home port during a career as a merchant seaman, at least in the period immediately before the Navy seized him and war possessed him for six years? If he had gone to sea out of Whitehaven, it is possible Anthony worked in the 'Blackberry' or slave trade. There was a highly profitable commerce in general merchandise and slaves between Whitehaven and Jamaica, via Africa. It would be a fine irony if Lockwood's capture by a press gang in Jamaica in the spring of 1795 was a result of his having worked in the slave trade.

The wars with France transformed the Royal Navy. Between 1792 and 1802 the number of men authorised by Parliament for the naval service grew eightfold, from 16,000 to 135,000, with a comparable increase in vessels. The need for men was voracious and unrelenting. The year 1795 was one of particularly desperate and unscrupulous recruitment, as the government administration of William Pitt the Younger scrambled to meet the French threat. Five Quota Acts were passed requiring every English, Scottish and Welsh county to raise a specific number of men for the Navy.[2] Inevitably, these were largely landsmen, and the Navy needed experienced seamen. These it could only obtain through a 'hot press' of sailors. The Admiralty could be asked to provide certificates protecting particular seamen from impressment, but rarely did so for any but a few key crewmen working in vital trades. Assuming that Lockwood's ship had delivered her cargo, whatever it was, he was fair game. In colonial ports the press gangs scoured every public garden, grog-shop, and brothel. The naval class of '95 was not an elite body of men.

The Navy's record keeping does not make it possible to know for certain that Lockwood was pressed. He was listed as a volunteer on the *Iphigenia*'s muster, and in receipt of the bounty for volunteering. But this is weak evidence. The muster-rolls of naval vessels listed a pressed man as a volunteer if he accepted his fate, and allowed himself to collect the £5 bounty for signing on.

A ship's committee, consisting of the first lieutenant, master, boatswain, gunner, carpenter, purser, and sometimes chaired by the captain himself, assessed the capabilities of each new man. In Lockwood's case, had he been a true volunteer his seafaring record would presumably have been available, but pressed men, carrying nothing but themselves to the assessment committee, had to have their claims checked. The fact that he was signed on as able seaman, and was upgraded to master's mate two days later, suggests that Lockwood's status on his previous ship had been confirmed, perhaps by enquiries at dockside.

Along with the bounty, the Navy provided new men with clothing, known as slops, the cost of which was later deducted from their pay. For Lockwood, again strongly implying that he came unprepared and ill-equipped, the muster answers its question 'How dressed?' with the cryptic 'Dead Mans Cloaths'. Lockwood entered the service beholden to an anonymous corpse, probably purchased when a late shipmate's clothes were auctioned according to custom by the purser.

It would be a long, long journey to his transfiguration as the Honourable Anthony Lockwood, gentleman. Few people began their flight of Icarus from so lowly a position. But in the conditions of wartime, a master's mate was firmly on the bottom rung of a ladder that could lead to promotion and social privilege. Lockwood's story illustrates wonderfully the 'upward mobility' possible in the Royal Navy during this time of extreme turbulence and change.

A Royal Navy master was not a commissioned officer, and most never succeeded in crossing that line from 'tarpaulin' to 'gentleman'. But below that line, masters were superior beings. They were the most important of the warrant officers who were appointed by the Navy Board to permanent positions in warships. With the purser, the surgeon and the chaplain, if one were appointed to a ship, the master was of 'wardroom rank', living with the commission officers. The other warrant officers, the gunner, bosun, carpenter, sailmaker, cook, and master-at-arms did not use the wardroom. As one of the ship's 'permanent' officers, masters retained their position even when a ship was laid up 'in ordinary' during a period of peace. When on active service, a master was inferior only to the ship's commissioned captain. Promotion for a warrant officer meant being transferred to a larger ship, when he received more pay for a higher rate.

The status and work of a ship's master came out of the earliest years of the Royal Navy, when it owned few or none of its own ships. Merchant ships were 'taken up' for naval service, and with them came their own officers. The king would commission a military captain to take the ship to war, but still needed the master to manage the ship and navigate it. This division of responsibility became less clear once the Navy began to acquire its own ships, and once commissioned, captains began to learn how to navigate them. But at the end of the eighteenth century the master continued to have charge of navigating the ship, and to be responsible for the stowage of stores both to ensure their adequacy, and also that their placement, and the placement of ballast, did not compromise the seaworthiness of the ship. For two centuries the Navy had also relied upon its masters to be hydrographers, or chartmakers, a role which would prove to be crucial to Lockwood's future.

Lockwood entered the service on a track which led quickly, if fortune conspired successfully with ambition, to a master's position. Among his other duties, a master's mate was responsible for the log board (a slate), marking up navigational observations during the day from which the master's log was compiled.[3] In addition, a master's mate would be expected to assist where needed, and to serve as an apprentice in all the work of the master – the best training any sailor on active duty could receive in practical seamanship and ship's management. The insatiable demand for replacement warrant officers during this phase of the wars meant that fast promotion was the rule rather than the exception.

If he had been employed on a slave ship, Lockwood would have found himself entirely at home during his first period of service in the Royal Navy in the West Indies. It was to be a terrifying encounter with the politics of power and 'liberty', both wearing the masks of principle, and neither giving quarter. On 28 March 1790 the French National Assembly had decreed that the franchise be extended to 'persons of colour', and on 15 May 1791 that such persons, born to free parents, could serve in colonial governing assemblies. But the Republic failed at first to establish its own rule over the decayed aristocrats of Sainte-Domingue, who feared that emancipation of the slaves would soon be imposed. What followed was a vile brew of racial self-interests. French Royalist planters plotted with the British and with the Spaniards of adjacent Santo Domingo, the modern Dominican Republic, against French republican commissioners who attempted to enforce the law of Paris. A revolt of mixed race 'mulattos' in defence of their new rights was suppressed, in part because they refused to invite slaves to join them. Many of them were slave-owners themselves, and they were determined to defend their status in a colonial regime which recognised 128 degrees of negritude.

The suppression of the first mulatto revolt was followed five months later by an uprising of slaves led by Boukman, a ferocious voodoo priest, vowing death to all 'blancs'. Mutilation and rape were commonplace. One rampaging war party carried the body of a dead white baby on a pike as its standard. Some sense of the depth of racial fear inspired by the events in Sainte-Domingue can be gauged by the language of a contemporary white Jamaican, Bryan Edwards: 'Upwards of one hundred thousand savage people, habituated to barbarities, avail themselves of the silence and obscurity of the night, and fall upon the peaceful and unsuspicious planters, like so many famished tigers, thirsty for human blood.' Edwards estimated that ten thousand slaves and two thousand whites were killed, with hundreds more executed afterwards. Over a thousand plantations of sugar, coffee, indigo, and cotton were destroyed. As the confused fighting continued, the republican commissioners increasingly took sides with the blacks in the name of liberty, equality, and fraternity.[4]

On 20 September 1793 a British expedition landed at Jeremie to the sound of church bells and a royal salute to George III. Two days later they were at Môle St Nicolas – important in defending approaches to Jamaica – which they 'received' with its fortifications and two hundred guns. But this early success was grimly deceptive.

General Adam Williamson, Governor General of Jamaica, had assured the British cabinet that he needed no more than the 877 troops he had at hand to secure Sainte-Domingue. Just three weeks before the British landng, however, an army of six hundred slaves, led by a former coachman, skinny, ugly, ascetic, and calling himself Toussaint L'Ouverture, allied with the Spaniards and issued a proclamation, addressed to 'Brothers and Friends': 'I am Toussaint L'Ouverture. My name has perhaps become known to you. I am bent on vengeance. I desire the establishment of Liberty and Equality in St Domingue. I strive to bring them into being. Unite with us, brothers, and fight with us in the common cause.'[5] He was a slave-owner's nightmare – a black leader with military skills and organisational flair whose perceived nobility of character would challenge by heroic actions all the presiding notions of white superiority. On 6 May 1794 he switched sides, massacred the Spanish garrison at Marmelade, raised the Tricolour, and went on to conquer the region known as the Artibonite in the name of the Republic.

The British army occupied the capital, Port-au-Prince, on 4 June, and thus controlled the ports of Sainte-Domingue. The Royal Navy patrolled the coasts. But there was an enemy more formidable even than Toussaint. In the cane fields, in the misty valleys, on the ships at watch, 'Yellow Jack' took a far higher toll than rebellious Africans. The British died by the hundreds. Each vessel in which they sailed, wrote Edwards, 'became a house of pestilence.'[6] In the West Indies as a whole, yellow fever killed about a third of all new arrivals within a year of arrival. They died in agony.

Bryan Edwards was again the bard of horror: 'In a climate where every gale was fraught with poison and in a contest with uncounted hosts of barbarians, what could the best efforts of our countrymen effect? Their enemies indeed fled before them, but the arrows of pestilence pursued and arrested the victors in their career of conquest.' By the end of 1797, out of a total of fifteen thousand British troops landed since 1794 on Sainte-Domingue, no more than three thousand were alive and in a condition for service.[7] So many dead men's cloaths!

It was to assist in this dread and futile exercise that Lockwood was held to have volunteered. The *Iphigenia*, commanded by Captain J J Gardner, had been moored at Port Royal since 10 February gathering supplies and crew, for which a press gang was sent to Kingston as late as 20 April. Sailing again on 3 May, she was employed ferrying soldiers from the 81st and 96th regiments to Sainte-Domingue as reinforcements. By the 19th she anchored off St Marc awaiting a convoy. After taking on board Governor Williamson himself, Port au Prince was reached on the 26th. According to Edwards, the 96th 'perished to a man!'[8]

For the next fifteen months *Iphigenia* sailed in the waters between Jamaica and Sainte-Domingue, often in convoy, generally in port for only a few days, though she was moored at Port-au-Prince during November. She boarded many vessels. Most were West Indian and American neutrals, but she occasionally made a prize. It took the firing of a 12-pounder to bring to the schooner *Polly* off St Marc on 30 May 1795, and there was a more serious engagement on 8 August at Bay des Irois when *Iphigenia* captured a French national privateer of three guns and twenty-three men. She was taken into Port-au-Prince for sale and the prize money distributed on the 29th of the month. Putting out again on 8 December, *Iphigenia* continued her patrols, and transported troops from Port-au-Prince to Petit Riviere between 20–22 March, providing covering fire with other ships for an aborted landing at Leogane, and returned to Port-au-Prince on the 24th with cavalry and infantrymen. There she joined the rest of the Fleet, her crew reduced by many who had died of fever.[9]

Three years later L'Ouverture was to expel the British from Sainte-Domingue, but long before then Lockwood found himself returning to England when *Iphigenia* was given orders to escort the homeward trade. Joining a convoy off Havana in June, she reached Plymouth Sound on 1 September. But so desperate was the Navy for experienced seamen that Lockwood's homecoming led only to his being 'turned over' to another ship. On 20 September, Captain Gardner 'Put the People on HMS *Duke* by order'. It was while serving in *Duke* that Lockwood was to witness one of the most remarkable events in British naval, and labour, history. The great mutiny at Spithead and its violent sequel at the Nore both mirrored, and contrasted with, the slave revolt in Haiti.

Commanded by Captain John Holloway, the *Duke* was a 'second rate' line-of-battle ship of 1,943 tons.[10] Lockwood entered her on 11 September at Hamoaze as a 'master mariner', being provided with slops by the Navy Board to the value of 16s 6d.[11] Eleven days later he was rated as a master's mate. Re-fitting and taking on further crew took until 23 October, but by the 28th the *Duke* was 12 leagues off Ushant, where she joined her squadron patrolling the 'chops' or approaches to the Channel. Until mid-December she sailed between the French coast and the Scillies, enforcing the British blockade of continental Europe. Then, at the turn of the year, she tracked from the Lizard to moor off Spithead on 2 January 1797. Five days later, she set off on the same triangular patrol, returning to Spithead via waters off Ushant and the Lizard by 4 February.[12]

The Spithead Mutiny of 1797 was to demonstrate to the astonished eyes of the British public that working men, even in the Navy where there was scant privacy, where discipline was enforced with the cat-o'-nine-tails, and where men lived separated from the family networks of civilian life, were capable of organising in secret a collective negotiation with their employers and oppressors. For the people of the *Duke* the drama could be said to have begun on 9 February when George Thomas, a seaman, was given a dozen lashes for 'mutinous expressions.' *Duke* sailed her patrol route once more in March, reaching Spithead on the 31st, where she was still lying on 16 April when it was recorded in her log that 'much Cheering was heard most of the afternoon, at 6 Lord Bridport [ie, Admiral Sir Alexander Hood, Viscount Bridport who had assumed command of the Channel Fleet on the 8th] made the signal for all Lieutenants, the Officer returned with an Order which was read to the Ships Company. AM rec'd Beer & Water came on board 9 shipwrights . . . found the Fleet had refused going out to Sea came on board 2 men from the *Queen Charlotte* to the Ships Company about encrease of Wages & Provisions.'[13]

The cheering was a way for the men to indicate their solidarity: British sailors cheered as they went into battle, from deck to deck and ship to ship, and the use of cheering in the great mutiny drew upon that tradition. The strike would last for a month. The sailors had abundant cause. Some ships had been without pay for eight, ten or twelve years, and their nominal rates of pay had not changed for 150 years, since the time of Samuel Pepys' naval reforms. Unscrupulous pursers habitually gave short rations. One of the Admiralty Board said to Lord Spencer, the First Lord of the Admiralty, 'the event forms the most awful crisis that these kingdoms ever saw.'[14] The ruling classes were in despair. Many believed that Britain was on the verge of a Jacobin uprising.

The Spithead mutiny was remarkable for its unanimity, its discipline and moderation. Its code of loyalty never broke and its planners were never identified. As early as 7 March eleven separate petitions from crews had been simultaneously dispatched to the popular Admiral Richard Lord Howe, old 'Black Dick', still nominally the Channel Fleet commander but at the time seeking a cure for gout at Bath. Howe referred them to the Lords Commissioners of the Admiralty, who failed to act. As a result, thirty-two 'Delegates' – the name had a revolutionary ring – two from each ship of the line at Spithead, met in the Great Cabin of the flagship *Queen Charlotte* on 17 April. According to Captain Holloway's log on the *Duke*: 'Boats from each Ship with 2 men went on board the *Queen Charlotte*. AM loosed sails rec[eive]d some Provisions & Stores. People cheered twice a day at 8 o'clock forenoon and sunset with determination not to go to Sea till they received satisfactory answers about their Wages & Provisions.'[15] The delegates met each day on *Queen Charlotte*, drawing up a formal petition to Parliament. They instructed seamen to obey all orders from their officers except that to weigh anchor. But they were so far from seeking a Jacobin revolution, that they made an exception: they were clear that they would take the fleet to sea should the French battle fleet come out of harbour, or should a homeward convoy be expected.

Lord Spencer and other members of the Admiralty Board journeyed to Portsmouth, conferring on 18 April with Lord Bridport and other serving admirals, after which a ludicrously small pay increase was offered, with no response to other grievances. When the offer reached *Duke*, according to Hollway, 'the men cheered as before', and then on 19 April petitioned the Lords Commissioners, complaining that the ship's company had been 'cruelly and unmercifully treated by the following officers, namely – Mr Curtis Lieutenant at Arms, Mr Shanks Boatswain, Messrs Belchier, Baker, Gordon, Stacey and James masters mates and Mr Neales Surgeon.' They wished to have them dismissed the ship and replaced 'by officers possessed of more Humanity.'[16] That same day the delegates repeated their original petition with an additional demand for pay of a shilling a day for all able seamen.

Spencer made concessions which were conveyed to ships' crews directly by their captains on the 21st. The scene on *Duke* was one of the turning points of the whole affair. Holloway had seemed to persuade his 'People' of the merits of the new offer when a voice from the back shouted: 'Wait and see what is done on the *Queen Charlotte*.' The *Duke*'s delegates, Michael Adams and William Anderson, made their way back to the *Queen Charlotte*'s Great Cabin.[17]

Tempers were ragged. Admiral Sir Alen Gardner was rowed to the *Queen Charlotte*, where he harangued the delegates before threatening them with violence. He was shown off the ship. The *Duke*'s seaman passed a letter to the *Queen Charlotte*: 'You may rely upon the *Duke*'s Ship's Company and shall never leave the *Queen Charlotte*.'[18] The delegates now decided that only an Act of Parliament would be acceptable – with a formal royal pardon for the mutineers. This latter was granted and Holloway read the proclamation to his crew at 1.30pm on 24 April. At 6pm the crews of all the ships at anchor gave three cheers, the men returned to their duties, and the vessels were unmoored.

Peace apparently restored, the *Duke* anchored off St Helens on the Isle of Wight on the 25th. But bad weather kept them in and suspicions festered. Holloway's log omits much. A rumour ran through the fleet that Parliament would reject the Seamen's Bill and the *Duke*'s crew was convinced that Holloway had received a secret order from the Admiralty. He temporised, saying that any such order, if received, had been destroyed. Unpersuaded, on May Day seamen broke into Holloway's cabin and threatened him first with a flogging and then with ducking.

Three cheers rang out from the *Queen Charlotte* at 9.30am on 7 May, answered by all the ships of the fleet, once more signalling a refusal to put to sea. Delegates again conferred. Next day, according to Holloway's log, the *Duke* 'received Beer & Water the Delegates went to Spithead. About 1/2 past 4 observed some firing aboard the *London*: at 7 the Delegates returned & said some Blood has been spiled on board the *London*.' This happened when Admiral Sir John Colpoys addressed the mutineers, and a Lieutenant Peter Bover shot down a seaman who appeared to threaten him.[19] More shots were fired; three men were killed and others wounded. Bover's life was in the balance and he, Colpoys, and Captain Griffith (*London*) faced trial by the mutineers, who, however, acquitted them.

On the 9th delegates visited each ship in turn. On the *Duke* they presented Holloway with a list, compiled by the crew: 'Gentlemen, you are desired upon receipt of this that the undermentioned persons quit the ship never to return again, except the persons with a mark against their names, who is to return when everything is settled to the satisfaction of the fleet.' Holloway's name topped the list. He and the *Duke*'s officers were required to depart. 'AM from the hours of eight to twelve the Captain, Eight Lieutenants & 2 Lieutenants of Marines with all the Mates and most of the Midshipmen quitted the Ship: the People having taken the Ship and Mutinied.'[20] Despite this humiliation, it is stated in his log that Captain Holloway 'served Tobacco' to the delegates before going ashore.[21]

At last the Seamen's Act was passed, but the suspicious Fleet insisted on a second Royal Pardon. Lord Howe, still trusted by the mutineers, visited each ship in turn, holding 'a Conference with the Ships Company on the Quarter Deck' of the *Duke*. On the 13th a meeting was held on the *Royal William* at which a blacklist of seventy-five names, headed by that of

Colpoys – who never went to sea again – was presented to Howe, who was forced to accede.

All was not quite over. The crews of the *Duke* and *Mars* were believed to have been communicating with people ashore during the negotiations by their delegates. When the delegates returned to their ships they were repudiated by their comrades, who refused to join the general submission. They toured the fleet, seeking support from other ship's companies, but no other crew would allow them on board. Instead they were hissed, and the delegates, who insisted on an unwavering loyalty to the Crown, sent guard boats to cordon off the *Duke* and *Mars*.[22]

This served, after further reassurances. Captain Ross Donnelly came on board on the 14th to inform three crew members that the Admiralty had withdrawn a court martial order against them.[23] But this had to be authenticated by a visit from a delegate next day, who, according to the Captain's log: 'read His Majesty's Pardon to the Ships Company ... all returned to their Duty.'[24] After some pageantry and symbolic deference to Lord and Lady Howe, all delegates returned to their ships and their old identities. The fleet began to work its way out to sea on 17 May. Holloway resumed command of the *Duke* and she weighed anchor on the 18th. A week later she was off Ushant once more guarding against the French menace.

Given the particularly mutinous zeal of the *Duke* it seems probable that Lockwood signed the *Duke*'s round robin oath, especially as he was not named among the petty officers, including master's mates, the seaman wished to have removed. Circumstances, however, suggest that he did not play a very prominent role. Sometime during the period 13–20 April, and thus perhaps during the very time when the *Duke* and *Mars* crews were rejecting the settlement, Lockwood was examined by Trinity House and found competent to 'take charge as Master of any of His Majesty's Sloops or Cutters from the Downs thro' the Channel to the Westward, and Pilot into Spithead thro' the Needles, and into Plymouth Sound.'[25] Unless the examination took place on board the *Duke*, Lockwood was ashore during the final stage of the mutiny. Nevertheless, it may be supposed that the more than nine-day wonder of the Spithead mutiny opened Lockwood's eyes to the possible heights to which he might fly. If simple seamen could compel King and Parliament, why should not one of their number rise to the status of a gentleman, and even an Honourable?

If the mutiny later had an influence on Lockwood's attitude to authority, the more immediate sequel was to be hot action, and military honour. On 27 May 1797 Admiral Bridport ordered Lockwood to join the *Jason* as master.[26] Commanded by Captain Charles Sterling, and commissioned as recently as 1794, *Jason* carried 38 guns and a complement of 380 men.[27] The date when Bridport's order reached Lockwood is uncertain – the *Duke* was at sea for most of that summer – but he joined *Jason* at Spithead before 28 September.[28]

Like the *Duke*, *Jason* had patrolled the Channel approaches in the weeks before the mutiny, as far south as the Tagus, and the mutiny had left her temporarily unable to proceed to sea. Captain Sterling's log noted that on 21 April 'the Gunner and Boatswain were turned off by the crew', and, as late as 16 May, that 'so many people were on shore that the Fleet could not move. We lost 16 men.'[29] When a crew was assembled, *Jason* showed that she was a highly pugnacious vessel, capturing four privateers between mid-November and mid-April 1798 when on the 19th *Jason* captured the gun-vessel *L'Arrogante* of 6 guns off Brest.[30] It was in these same waters that the *Jason* achieved her greatest triumph, bloody and shattering enough to meet even the demanding contemporary craving for martial heroics.

On 29 June, at 7am, when in company with the 36-gun frigates *Picque* and *Mermaid*, *Jason* fought a nasty action with the 40-gun French frigate *Seine*. *Seine* and *Jason* went aground and the latter swung as the tide rose so that her stern was exposed to French gunnery. But *Jason* got some guns run out through the stern windows where they could open fire, and the *Picque* which had also run aground, managed to slide forward enough to direct a fire at the *Seine*, which accordingly surrendered. *Jason*'s second lieutenant, a corporal of marines, and five seamen were killed, and Captain Sterling, two midshipmen and nine seamen were wounded.[31] In his dispatch reporting the action, Sterling stated that after his wounds had forced him to leave the deck, 'Lieutenant Riboleau commanded the Main Deck ... and behaved with great spirit, as did Mr Lockwood, the Master.'[32] This account was published in the London *Gazette* for 10–14 July 1798. Lockwood thus became one of three officers 'gazetted', the public confirmation of conspicuous gallantry. No one could doubt that he had met a most searching test.

The action left *Jason* unfit for service, but Captain Sterling stayed at sea. He informed the Admiralty on 20 July that *Jason*'s masts were 'so much wounded that they would be endangered by a fresh breeze, and the main yard is so bad that it will barely bear the weight' of a sail.[33] After some repairs at Portsmouth in late August, she returned to sea, and off Le Havre on 11 September Sterling reported picking up 'in a boat three Frenchmen who left Caen two days ago, and say they have despatches of consequence for Lord Grenville and some confidential communication.' These he sent into Portsmouth in the *Trial* cutter, and then was forced by the weather to run for Spithead, but he soon returned to the Brittany coast, and on 13 October had the bad luck to strike on an uncharted rock, and having to put *Jason* ashore on the French coast, there was no avoiding being taken prisoner.

Lockwood was amongst those sent to Valenciennes where so many British officers languished in conditions which seem remarkably benign to modern readers. The worst problem was that the prisoners were encouraged by their hosts to while away the tedium of a small provincial town by gambling more than they could afford. Sterling was apparently the first to make his way back to Britain, exchanged at Paris for a Captain Menseret, and reaching London by 6 December. Lockwood was paired with Captain La Roche, aide-de-camp to General Humbert, commanding officer of the French invading forces in Ireland, both of whom had been captured at Ballinamuck on 8 September.[34] Lockwood was brought to Dover in the *Union* in late January 1799.[35]

It was mandatory that a court martial should be held on *Jason*'s officers for the loss of their ship, but the questioning when the court convened on board the *Gladiator* at Portsmouth on 25 February, presided over by Vice Admiral Sir Roger Curtis, was pro forma and perfunctory. Sterling declared that the *Jason* had sailed those waters for the past four years, that the rock was uncharted, and that the French government itself acknowledged that a survey was needed. Sterling, his officers, and his men were asked if they had complaints about each other. There were none. As *Jason*'s master, Lockwood's evidence was important, and could also affect his own career. He swore that Sterling spoke truly in all respects, that there had been no misconduct, and that a coast pilot had been on board the *Jason*. The latter, said Lockwood, 'was sitting on the barricadoes piloting the Ship at the time and seemed quite confident she was in safety.' Everything had been done to save the ship. The verdict stated that it was absolutely necessary the ship be run ashore and that her crew did their utmost to preserve her and her stores.[36]

Following his release by the court, Lockwood was appointed master of the *Crescent* at the request of her captain, William Granville Lobb.[37] He joined his new ship at Deptford on the Thames on 25 April 1799, where she was moored alongside the sheer hulk.[38] She had begun sea-victualling three days earlier, and Lockwood's log, the first of his to survive, opens on the 22nd. It demonstrates the range and intricacy of a master's many tasks, which clearly required a detailed shipboard knowledge and competence. There were no personal touches here. The master's log for *Crescent* is a strictly professional record of the management of the ship, from preparations for sailing to her daily locations at sea and the details of her navigation, written in precise, terse English. It notes that twenty-seven Greenwich pensioners were employed in the fitting out, and in stowing iron, 58 tons of shingle ballast, coals, fresh beef, and sundry stores. Officers and men joined the *Crescent* on 18 May. She dropped down to Purfleet on 6 June and took on fifty men from HMS *Valiant*, before proceeding to the

Great Nore on the 26th, where she continued victualling, painting, and acquired new barrels.³⁹

Meanwhile, Lockwood found time to request that the Lords Commissioners reimburse him for the loss of his mathematical instruments, lost with the *Jason*. They refused.⁴⁰ It was to be years before the Navy recognised an obligation to provide any compensation for officers and men who lost their ship, to the enemy or to bad weather.

The *Crescent* was a brutal ship even by the standards of the day. Perhaps the continuing fear of mutiny drove Lobb to impose a harsh regime, and he immediately established his rule by giving one man seventeen lashes and another twenty-eight for theft and mutiny. During the next two years, until Lockwood's departure in July 1801, 6,382 lashes were reported on the *Crescent*. They were given for mutiny, theft, fighting, 'contempt', disobedience, drunkenness, quarrelling, desertion, uncleanliness, neglect of duty, insolence, rioting, gambling, swearing, and variants of the above. *Crescent* was at sea almost continuously for twenty-one months, with the briefest, most necessary stays in port, and frequently engaged with the enemy. Later in this period the floggings increased in severity and frequency, while 'scandalous actions' and 'improper professions' were added cause for punishment. On 12 April 1801 Lobb ordered sixty lashes for scandalous actions, and sixty-six for drunkenness early in May, the most severe sentences of the voyage. Lockwood's own log also refers to his punishing men, but gives no details.

Crescent sailed from Spithead on 11 September 1799 for the West Indies, anchoring at Carlisle Bay, Barbados, on 10 November, where she became the flagship of Lord Hugh Seymour, Vice Admiral of the Blue and commander-in-chief. After taking on fresh water she put out almost immediately and was twelve to fourteen leagues northwest of Puerto Rico by the 14th. Next morning she chased a Danish schooner which proved to have been plundered already by a French privateer. That evening, however, the *Calipso* signalled two strange sail and Lobb in pursuit 'saw the Chace were Enemy ships of war.' He prepared for action at 8.10pm and, after a brief engagement, *Crescent* captured the *Galgo*, a 16-gun Spanish brig of war, with ninety-six men. The prisoners were brought on board and a skeleton crew put on the prize. *Crescent* was chasing again on the 18th, when she 'fir'd several musquets' and captured the schooner *La Durad* from Curaçao. Next day she escorted her prizes and a convoy into Port Royal, Jamaica.

This set the pattern for *Crescent*'s service and for Lockwood's return to the West Indies. She patrolled sea lanes, conducted convoys, and harassed the enemy. And once more, Yellow Jack took his toll. After a short stay at Port Royal, Daniel Howard, master-at-arms, was buried at sea on 14 December. By the end of the month seven other crewmen joined him.

Off Cartagena on 10 January 1800 a cutter was sent ashore under flag of truce. Two boats at anchor inshore were boarded but proved to be British privateers. Then on 2 February *Crescent* chased and captured the schooner *Nostra Signeora del Carmen*. Only a single shot was fired. On the 11th she took a Spanish privateer schooner after 'several shots' and by the 20th was at Port Royal again, her prizes secured. More success followed. Patrolling in the Loggerhead Bay/Cape Catouche waters she took a Spanish brig of 4 guns and thirty-five men on 22 March. 'Several shots' were fired during the capture of a felucca from Havana bound for Vera Cruz. Another similar vessel was taken next day. On 13 May, off Puerto Rico, the *Crescent* chased a ship which then hoisted French colours. 'Bow chace guns & musquets' were enough to bring in the corvette *Diligent*, of 12 guns and 124 men. By the 30th of that month *Crescent* was back at Port Royal, her prisoners transferred to a prison ship (offering more bounty for Yellow Jack). In the Loggerhead Bay area again in late June, in company with HMS *Nimrod*, she took another prize on the 31st.

Although the action in *Jason* might have established Lockwood on the rungs of a conventional career as a fighting man, a fortunate event during his service on *Crescent* was to start him down the quite different road as a naval hydrographer that ultimately led to his appointment as Surveyor General of New Brunswick. During the hurricane season *Crescent* made her first protracted stay in Port Royal, and Vice Admiral Lord Hugh Seymour came aboard on 24 July. In November and December 1800 *Crescent* returned to sea to patrol off the Dutch island of Curaçao, and when a French force attacked the Dutch garrison, Captain Frederick Barlow Watkins commanding the frigate *La Nereide* intervened, with the result that the Dutch surrendered to Britain. Vice Admiral Seymour sent four frigates in support, including *Crescent,* and Lockwood was ordered to survey the harbour. The result was so satisfactory that Seymour forwarded it to the secretary of the Admiralty. 'Their Lordships,' he wrote, 'by it will be enabled to form a just idea of that Anchorage, the survey having been made with great Care by the officer charged with that Duty, and with a degree of accuracy I could hardly have expected from his having only had six Days to complete it.'[41]

A memo overleaf reads: 'Convey to his Lordship,' ie, Lord Seymour, 'that my Lords [Commissioners] are pleased with Mr Lockwood's exertions on this occasion. Send the chart to A Dalrymple.' Unfortunately Seymour, the first of Lockwood's professional patrons, was not able to provide Lockwood with any direct advancement because he died of yellow fever off Jamaica on 11 September 1801, aged forty-two. His commendation, however, and that of the Lords Commissioners, started a chain of preferment that ultimately was to lead to Lockwood's appointment as

Surveyor General. The six days surveying the harbour of Curaçao would prove to have been particularly well spent. Alexander Dalrymple was Hydrographer to the Admiralty, heading the Hydrographic Office that had been established as recently as 1795.

All the same, the road ahead was to be a rough one. Lockwood was to continue onboard *Crescent* until 30 June 1802, during which several prizes were taken, and forty-five seamen were rescued from the wreck of HMS *Meleager*. To the accompaniment of sundry lashes for neglect of duty, contempt, theft, and disobedience, *Crescent* made her way back to Jamaica, anchoring at Port Royal on 23 July. For the 30th, Captain Lobb's log contains this unadorned entry: 'Joined the ship as Master W[illia]m Baker in room of Mr Ant[hon]y Lockwood Invalided.' Six years after entering the Navy at Port Royal, Lockwood left the service there, too sick to continue.

He was to carry those brutal years with him, as any man would. As a naval master, Lockwood had risen in social station, but not enough to be considered a gentleman. While class distinctions on a ship of war might bulge and blur in the heat of action, on land, society could be unyielding. There was no comfortable place for a man like Lockwood in the England of Jane Austen. Returning to the Icarus image, Lockwood was still earthbound with marginal prospects.

2

A Saucy Young Puppy

BEING INVALIDED HOME may have been important in creating circumstances that enabled Lockwood move up in the world, taking advantage of Vice Admiral Seymour's recommendation of his ability as a hydrographic surveyor. But paradoxically, his illness may also have sown the seeds of his eventual downfall. The brutality of his experiences in the West Indies probably contributed to personality qualities that impelled his advancement, but also set him against the system in which he had to live.

When Lockwood arrived back across the Atlantic in England there was little immediate hope of naval employment. A peace treaty had been arranged at Amiens in March 1802, and the fleet was immediately reduced from its wartime establishment. The peace only lasted until May 1803, but in the meantime, Lockwood headed north to Whitehaven in Cumberland. The suggestion that he may have been returning to a home he had made for himself before 1795 is based on tenuous evidence, but the attraction of Whitehaven would have been considerable. The Lockwood name was certainly present in the Whitehaven district by the mid eighteenth century. The baptism of John, the son of Anthony's uncle John, was entered in the Crossthwaite parish register 9 June 1747, while a John Lockwood married Bella Jefferson at St James, Whitehaven, on 17 November 1798. Meanwhile, Mary, wife of Thomas Lockwood, parish of Cleator, was buried at Holy Trinity, Whitehaven, on 17 February 1795.[1] Were they close kin to Anthony? Whitehaven would have had professional attractions for a seaman. Surprising as it now seems, Whitehaven claimed to be second only to London in the tonnage of its exports by sea, exceeding Liverpool, Bristol, and Liverpool. Largely this was a result of the coal exports of the Lowthers, the greatest local family, who were massively expanding the port during the time of Lockwood's association with that place.[2]

Just when Anthony first came to Whitehaven is unclear, but in the muster book of the *Examiner*, Lockwood's vessel for his North America survey in 1815–1817, Anthony Lockwood's son, Anthony junior, was entered on 1

January 1816 as aged 18, with his birthplace given as Whitehaven.[3] Although his age may have been falsified in order to increase his pay, there is a possibility that Anthony senior had lived for some years in Whitehaven in the 1790s. There is no possibility, however, that he was there when his son was born, if that was in 1798. All the same, if he was married to Anthony junior's mother, he would by law have been deemed to be the father. No record of his marriage has been discovered, but in 1812, while living on Barbados whence he had taken his family, Lockwood assigned a slave called William 'for the use and Behoof of Martha McKenzie of the County of Cumberland . . . widow.'[4] It is not improbable that this Martha was the mother of his Whitehaven children.

West Indian trade, including the slave trade, was a major feature of the commerce of Whitehaven. The Lowthers had a plantation on Barbados where Robert Lowther became governor. The merchant shipping families of Brocklebank and Jefferson, themselves later linked by marriage, were also constant traders with the Caribbean. Captain Henry Jefferson's marriage on 18 May 1780 at St John's, Antigua, to Miss Anne Tweedie of that island, forged a new commercial link, and John Lockwood's marriage to Bella Jefferson could have led to Anthony sailing on a Jefferson ship to Jamaica, and to his fateful encounter with a Royal Navy press gang.[5]

For Whitehaven, the West Indies were not all profit, as local tombstones eloquently testified. Captain Daniel Brocklebank junior entered Montego Bay, Jamaica, in early July 1798, in the *Alfred*, only to find the anchorage crammed with slave ships rife with Yellow Jack – to which he succumbed. He was buried at Spanish Town on 12 July 1798.[6] The register of the Holy Trinity graveyard at the very centre of Whitehaven contains poignant memorials of similar deaths: of William Hales, son of Captain Jonathan Hales, *Shannon*, who 'died at Salt River, Jamaica, 2 March 1813, aged 17 years'; of Thomas, son of Captain William Christian, who died at Kingston, Jamaica, on 11 August 1822, aged twenty-two; of Captain William Burton, *Hero*, who died 'at the island of St Vincent', 24 April 1816, aged twenty-eight – while the St James churchyard contains stones in memory of Daniel Briggs, who died at Demerara 6 June 1799, aged forty-six; of Joseph Delay, 'lost on his passage to Barbados'; of Thomas Harrison who died at Santo Domingo in 1791, aged thirteen – a mere sampler of the men and boys from the bleak Cumberland coast who perished among the tropic isles.[7]

Anthony's illness, however, whatever it was, appears not to have been a tropical fever, but to have become chronic, and episodic. On 16 March 1803 he wrote to the Navy Board seeking employment, and said that he was 'perfectly recovered of my late indisposition.' As a result, he was warranted to the *Princess Charlotte* in the spring or early summer of 1804. By that time, however, his health had again worsened. On 2 June 1804 he wrote to the Navy Board that he was 'reduced to a condition which renders me for the present incapable either of serving His Majesty or following any Commercial Business.' He asked for half-pay, outlining his service, and noting that 'at the request of Lord Hugh Seymour I surveyed Curaçao, Bonaire, Aruba and islands adjacent and part of the Spanish Main, which service being performed in small Craft and the Fever at that time very prevalent reduced me to a state of debility which caused me to be invalided on the 25th July 1801.' In addition, he enclosed a certificate dated 28 May 1804, signed by Robert Hannay, surgeon, of Whitehaven, and co-signed by Joshua Dixon, MD, stating that Lockwood was 'at present and has long been distressed with severe pains and a tendency to Paralysis and debility in his lower extremities which I am firmly of Opinion has been produced by his long service in a warm Country and the exposure to the Climate which his situation necessarily demanded.' He also enclosed a sworn affidavit by James Steel, JP, that between 31 May 1801 and 31 May 1804 Lockwood 'has not enjoyed any public service on sea or land.'

But the ink was hardly dry before Anthony headed for Plymouth to join his ship, only to find he was too late. On 12 July he informed the Admiralty that he had 'this day joined His Maj[esty's Ship] *Princess Charlotte*, but am acquainted by Captain Gordon that there is another Master appointed but not joined. I used every exertion to join the ship but could not owing to my infirm health, I therefore now wait on the above ship until I know the commissioners pleasure.' The 'turnover' minute on the back of his letter, probably written by the Admiralty Secretary William Marsden, tartly observes: 'he could not suppose that the ship was to wait two months for him – and therefore must now wait till another opportunity offers – which I trust will make him more alert in future.'[8]

Was Lockwood's erratic behaviour a symptom of his condition? Naval service in the West Indies offered so many possibilities of disease. Lime juice against scurvy did not become standard issue in the Navy until 1795, the very year of Lockwood's entry, while the effects of the appalling shipboard victuals, supplemented by gallons of beer and allowances of a pint of wine and half a bottle of rum daily, were dreadful enough. Yellow Jack could destroy a crew within a few days. Malaria and typhus were commonplace – the latter a consequence of overcrowded, unventilated, unhygienic quarters, and known simply as ship fever. All manner of infectious and contagious diseases ran free. In William Turnbull's contemporary *The Naval Surgeon*, he described the West Indies station as 'avowedly the most unhealthy' and advised 'lowering the diet', regular bowel movements, and he considered the occasional bleeding of ten or twelve ounces of blood 'a most useful precaution'. He also observed that 'contagion either from human effluvia, or marshy exhaltation [*sic*], is the most active source of disease in this quarter.' The relatively better living conditions for a senior warrant officer like Lockwood might improve the chances somewhat.

Mental illness was rampant. Insanity was relatively common from early times but not until 1815 was any sort of research work done on the subject, when Dr Sir Gilbert Blane showed that in the Navy the incidence of insanity was seven times as great as in civilian life – one in a thousand compared with one in seven thousand. He suggested that intoxication, leading to men banging their heads violently while clumsily negotiating cramped spaces between decks, was one cause of the high insanity rate. Drunkenness, itself a naval occupational disorder, no doubt produced many cases of temporary insanity, but sheer worry, anxiety and frustration must have driven many a good family man round the bend. There was, however, another unrecognised agency. Venereal disease was epidemic in the Royal Navy. It was often concealed by seamen, since they had to pay fifteen shillings to the ship's doctor, stopped from wages, for an ineffectual 'cure'.[9] The satirical *Advice to Officers of the British Navy* advised surgeons: 'When any libertine comes with a certain fashionable complaint' he should be treated with white vitriol, so that 'he will be apparently cured in a few days.' The inevitable recurrence, within three months, 'you can attribute to his own imprudence' – while pocketing another fifteen shillings.[10]

Were Lockwood's sporadic 'fever,' 'severe pains', and paralysis of the 'lower extremities', symptoms of advancing syphilis? While no definite conclusion can be drawn, it seems distinctly possible that in 1801 Lockwood returned from the West Indies poxed. And he might have contracted the illness before he was pressed into the Navy. Might his illness account to some extent for his son being conceived and born while he was away at sea? One of the effects of the tertiary stage of syphilis is impotence. Martha Lockwood gave birth to another child who was baptised with her mother's name, on 29 October 1805 at St Nicholas, Whitehaven. The baby girl's father's name was entered as Anthony Lockwood, who was described as a former Master RN.[11] But by then Anthony was employed again in the Navy, and had even been promoted. It seems that he was out of touch with his wife, or common-law wife, and possibly that she was compensating for his impotence by finding other fathers for their children.

The tertiary stages of syphilis can also degrade mental function and memory. This medical fact, combined with the emotional stress of his terrible experiences in the West Indies, and the social stress that may have resulted from the fragmented nature of his married life, could well have led to his erratic behaviour. It could also have a direct connection with his tumble from halcyon heights in New Brunswick nineteen years later.

Lockwood did not have too long to wait on the *Princess Charlotte* at Plymouth before he was offered other employment. On the back of his letter to the Navy Board was a second undated scrawl adding: 'app[oin]t[ed] to the *Malta* by Adm[iral] Young.' Soon after 12 July 1804 he was warranted to the *Malta*, but he did not stay with her for long. On 19 August, by an order from Rear Admiral Alexander Cochrane, he was directed 'to survey part of the Spanish coast.'[12] It may safely be presumed that this posting was a result of Sir Hugh Seymour's earlier strong commendation of Lockwood's surveying work.

Cochrane would prove to be the key figure in Lockwood's subsequent career, his essential patron. Son of the Earl of Dundonald, Alexander Cochrane was born into that close-knit web of Scottish grandees who wielded great political and commercial power throughout this period. Closely allied to Henry Dundas, Lord Melville, First Lord of the Admiralty, Cochrane was both militarily and politically influential by the time he noticed Lockwood in 1804. He had entered the Navy himself in 1770 and as a young officer had fought bravely in the West Indies and North American waters during the American Revolutionary War. Severely wounded in 1780, he was promoted to captain three years later. After the peacetime years he returned to the Navy in 1790, fighting many engagements in the Channel, Mediterranean, and West Indies, joining Rear Admiral Sir John Warren at Quiberon and Ferrol, taking part later in the capture of Alexandria. Elected MP for the family borough of Dunfermline in 1802, during the Peace of Amiens, Cochrane was advanced to the rank of Rear Admiral in April 1804. Quickly returning to active service, he sailed to the Spanish coast. There, in the words of James Ralfe, the nearly contemporary naval biographer, he watched 'the proceedings of the Spaniards previous to a declaration of war; and in this situation he was most unjustly accused in some of the daily prints of fabricating accounts, from the most base and sordid motives, which might lead to hostilities with Spain.'[13] Cochrane was defended vigorously enough, but the intense political hostility towards Lord Melville at this time, which led to his impeachment for corruption, spread out to his known allies. Though Cochrane was far too tough to be brought down, in joining him off the Spanish coast, Lockwood was drawing closer to the furnace of power, of great men and their ambitions.

The survey was continued until 25 October and produced a chart of Corunna and Ferrol.[14] By 6 November Lockwood was back in the East End of London, writing to the Lords Commissioners from No 10 Broadway, Rotherhithe. There is no evidence as to whether he had moved his family to London. He reminded their Lordships of his illness and begged 'some compensation' for lost time since he was not one of the limited number entitled to half-pay when not employed. Someone, perhaps the Admiralty Secretary William Marsden, wrote a turnover note asking: 'How much was Mr Geo[rge] Spence paid for survey?' with the answer, '1 guinea [per] day.'

Lockwood, however, was awarded only 15s per diem for the sixty-eight days of the survey and nothing for the time he was invalided.[15]

Meanwhile, at some date between his return from the Spanish survey and 15 November, by order of the Navy Board, Lockwood was examined by Trinity House and found 'qualified to take Charge as Master of any of His Majesty's Ships of the Third Rate from the Downs through the Channel to the Westward, and Pilot into Spithead, through the Needles, and Plymouth Sound.'[16]

Now, for the first time, emboldened by the approval of Seymour and Cochrane, Lockwood put himself forward to the Lords Commissioners by drawing their attention to

> the Imperfect Knowledge yet attained of the soundings NW of Ushant, west of Scilly and southward of Cape Clear, nor has the line of sounding ever yet been ascertained – in consequence, merchant ships, in thick weather, frequently mistake St George's for the English Channel. Part of Ireland, West of England and Scilly I may venture to affirm have never yet been accurately surveyed. I take the liberty further to add, that this service might be performed at very little expense, as the Gun Brigs are well adapted for Surveying, and defending themselves and equally ready for their present intended service.[17]

In response, an anonymous note overleaf directed that Lockwood 'call at the office tomorrow at 2 o'clock' and by 22 November William Marsden was informing him that their Lordships intended to employ him 'on a survey to be made of Bearhaven on the coast of Ireland' for which he was to submit a list of the required materials. This he quickly did, requesting:

> An Astronomical Circle, An Theodolit 7 inches, Brass Sextant 8 Inch, double framed, Quadrant Hadley's 5 Inch, False horizon, case of instruments, Protractor 5 Inch, Station Pointer, 100 feet Measuring Chain, 2 measuring reels, 10 iron pins. A day & night glass. It will be necessary to have two cutters, one not less than Eighty Tons, with two boats, the other not exceeding forty five Tons, of small draft of water, and calculated to take [? the] ground, and one boat, and about Twelve temp Buoys with Ropes.[18]

The survey of Bearhaven was evidently completed during the next six weeks.[19] By 19 January 1805 he had returned to Town, and was awaiting 'their Lordships Pleasure.' Directed 'to come here', he was found another assignment and by 26 January had left for Falmouth to conduct a survey of the harbour, and also to lay moorings.[20] He delivered his reports and surveys to the Lords Commissioners on 23 March, evidently completing his chart by the end of May.[21] But his work did not please the hydrographer, Alexander Dalrymple.

Appointed in 1795, Dalrymple was the first Admiralty Hydrographer, having previously served the East India Company in that capacity. The systematic charting of the English coasts, using a measured base line along the shore, sextant angles, and a station pointer, had been begun by Murdoch Mackenzie junior and his assistant, Graeme Spence, with a survey of the channels and shoals of the Thames Estuary. Mackenzie's 1774 *Treatise on Maritim[e] Surveying* became the basic text for his time.[22] In 1777 Mackenzie applied his technique to the coastline and harbours between Plymouth and Bognor. When he retired in 1788 because of failing eyesight, Spence had succeeded him, and conducted further major surveys off the Scottish coast, of the Goodwin Sands and Downs, and of the Suffolk coast. But there had been no organisation at the Admiralty to oversee the publication of their charts, and those of other surveyors, and technical standards suffered by an apparent attempt to economise on the cost of engraving. Charts were produced by private chartmakers, by naval surveyors on their own initiatives, or by the impulses of the Admiralty or senior officers. Arrangements for printing and disseminating charts were equally chaotic. Some were published by subscription, some financed speculatively by the surveyor, and some purchased and printed by the Navy. There was no body to assess the quality of such work, to set priorities for future surveys, or to encourage the development of better surveying techniques. Sir Archibald Day, author of the official history of the hydrographic service, writes that 'each surveyor after completing his fair sheet was expected to prepare charts, sometimes on a number of different scales, and these were then sent to the engraver for the preparation of copper printing-plates', but 'the meticulous care and attention exercised by Mackenzie and Spence are not apparent' in the published charts.[23]

Dalrymple was a difficult man to work with, as Spence found when in 1804 he accepted a position in the hydrographic office to revise Mackenzie's surveys and be available for consultation.[24] But Dalrymple's task was virtually impossible. He was 'entrusted with the care of such charts etc that are now in office, or may hereafter be deposited and charged with the duty of collecting and compiling all information requisite for improving Navigation, for the guidance of His Majesty's ships.' But he exercised no control over the conduct of hydrographic surveys, and was simply to act as cartographer, leaving the organisation and direction of hydrographic surveys to their Lordships, as had always been the practice. In cases such as Lockwood's, where the order to proceed with a survey came directly from an admiral at sea or from the Lords Commissioners themselves –

thereby excluding the hydrographer completely until the results of the surveys were received by him – feuding was inevitable.

Dalrymple wrote to the Admiralty on 15 June complaining that the 'charts of Falmouth by Lieut Mackenzie, Lt Manderson, and Mr Lockwood show very great disagreement' and proposed that Captain Thomas Hurd, '(having been accustomed to survey with the *Hadley*, in that admirable work of his, the survey of the Bermudas) would in a very few days ascertain the exact position of the Prominent Points of the Banks and principal objects.' In the Hydrographic Office at Taunton is preserved a tracing showing the discrepancies between the three Falmouth surveys.[25] This plan was approved and Hurd's survey became the standard one for many years.[26] The reaction from Dalrymple, however, should not be taken as criticism of Lockwood's work. It was necessary for him to reconcile the differences between three competing surveys.

Lockwood had made his entrée at precisely the right time. Dalrymple recognised the need for new surveys, and repeatedly urged the Admiralty to authorise them. There was plenty of work for competent hydrographic surveyors at the height of the war against the Napoleonic Empire.

His new duties in the infant hydrographic service offered important advantages for a climber such as Lockwood: proximity to influential officers, fewer rigours even when attached to a ship-of-war, far better pay, and the satisfactions of the work itself. The contrast with the lot of a warranted ship's master was striking. For one thing, a contemporary report for the Navy Board made it plain that the plight of Royal Navy masters was scandalous: 'It has become a matter of absolute necessity that Provision should be made to better the condition of this useful class of officers in the Navy . . . considering that no Augmentation to the full Pay of Masters for 1st and 2nd rates has taken place for upwards of 105 Years and for those of inferior rates for upwards of Forty Seven Years.'[27] But Lockwood also faced great perils. By becoming an hydrographer, he became a kind of 'floater', outside the regular pattern of service. Divided loyalties, and confusions about the line of authority, would plague him to the very end of his naval career. And he was not a man to accept quietly the circumstances of his humble birth.

When he was told on 31 May 1805 that their Lordships 'don't have surveying work for him just now' he billed them, on 29 June, for instruments deemed necessary for the completion of earlier work. Officers, however, were expected to provide their own navigational instruments, and unless an undertaking had been made to provide survey instruments, hydrographers were similarly expected to provide for themselves. The Admiralty denied that permission had been give to Lockwood to purchase survey instruments at its expense. Lockwood noted his ineligibility for half-pay and asked to be 'paid the same as other officers' on surveys. On 10 June, however, he claimed 1,666 days, for which the Admiralty directed the Navy Board to pay him 5s a day and at the same rate for his next employment. This ruling conformed to the pattern first established when Lockwood had claimed compensation for the instruments he lost with the shipwreck of the *Jason*, despite it being common knowledge in the Navy that there was no provision for meeting such losses on the part of individuals. He felt that the Navy ought to compensate him, and accordingly made a claim, heedless of the possible effect his attitude might have on his career. It was to become a running battle over the years as Lockwood repeatedly claimed recompense for the loss of the tools of his trade, and continued to be refused.

Again, he was not kept unemployed for long. His earlier suggestion for a survey of the western approaches to the Channel evidently bore fruit, in a modified form, and he was directed by the Admiralty to begin a preliminary survey of the Channel Islands. By 19 August, writing from Guernsey, he reported to Marsden that, after communicating with Rear Admiral Sir James Saumarez who commanded the naval station, he had taken a 'cursory view' of the islands and begun a survey 'of Guernsey and its passages, it being the opinion of Sir James Saumarez that the great and little Russells was of the most importance, the particulars of the Trigometrical operations I have transmitted to A Dalrymple Esq Hydrographer to their Lordships' Office, agreeable to their Lordships instructions.' Indicative of the limitations of Dalrymple's position was Marsden's scribbled turnover note that Lockwood was to be informed 'that he is not in future to address letters intended for me to A Dalrymple.' In effect, the hydrographer was to be kept out of it.

By 7 September Lockwood was reporting to Marsden that, following instructions, he had applied to Saumarez for men and boats and was 'amply supplied' though there were no stores on the islands beyond the station's own needs. 'And as Sweeping Ropes, Leads, Lines, Tallow, a few Poles and Buntin for Station staffs and Flags are requisite for continuing the Survey,' he asked, and received, permission to purchase them at one of the naval dockyards. Saumarez also wrote a supporting letter to the Navy Board. Though Saumarez had provided him with the cutter *Duke of York*, she was too large for fast tides and the 'intricacies of the channels.' Saumarez agreed with him that a vessel of 25–30 tons would suit better. Nevertheless, no time had been lost and the 'chain of triangles' was proceeding. By 6 October they were apparently completed for Guernsey, and since it was too late in the season to continue the chain to other islands, Lockwood proposed 'to take particular plans of the islands Jethon, Erm [ie, Jethou, Herm], and Sark, and also determine the coast-line, the subordinate points, and positions of the Rocks of this Island, as far as the weather will permit.'

He again drew attention to the unsuitability of the *Duke of York*: 'her great draft of water, her doubtfullness of staying, and dullness in sailing' made her dangerous in rocky passages where the tide ran with 'amazing velocity.' There were many small, shallow-drafted vessels available for 'at least one third the expense.' Their Lordships were convinced, and the Navy Board was directed to hire such a vessel. By the 27th Lockwood had obtained the cutter *Charlotte*, which he considered to be 'sound, active and in every respect fit for surveying.'

There were opportunities for him to make a little extra money on the side. He informed the Navy Board on 1 December that he had found four big anchors from HM ships brought on shore by Guernsey pilots and had also taken on board the *Charlotte* 560 12-pound shot and half a ton of pig ballast thrown off HM late cutter *Pygmy* when in distress. Was this material wanted? The turnover note indicated that the Board would determine the salvage value of the jetsam, and the place where it should be delivered.

Lockwood was able to report three days later that 'during the favourable part of last month, I continued the survey of the East side of the Island, and of the Rocks forming the West border of the Little Russells.' Evidently, this work was little enough. He admitted on 13 February that 'the continued Gales of wind during the two preceding months prevented my making any progress' and the Lords Commissioners retorted snappily: 'Let him say what progress *has* been made and when survey will be finished.' Lockwood answered with a summary of his efforts to date on the 27th, referring to his earlier letters and noting that from October to mid-December he 'was employed in taking a particular plan of Sark, the coast line of the East side of Guernsey, ascertaining the position of the Rocks off the North end called the Brays and others extending to the North East of the island of Erm, called Amfrocks, which with the islands of Guernsey and Sark form the entrances of the Russell Passages.' When weather permitted he continued 'the Survey of the Rocks, forming the Little Russell Passage.'

He concurred, diplomatically perhaps, with Saumarez's view of the importance of the Russells. Not having seen Île de Bréhat, Cape Trehal, Roches Douvres, Îsles Chausey, and having only a partial view of Jersey, however, he could not estimate the completion time. He expressed a hope, however, to have finished the work already started by next January and to have the 'whole of the Passages and neighbourhood sounded, and swept, by July following.' Meanwhile, he had swept three sunken rocks 'in the North part of the little Russell passage' which did not appear on charts and had located good passages between the rocks south of Jethou island, between Guernsey and the Brays, 'unknown or never attempted'. In addition, he had tried 'in the latter part of the year to ascertain the extent of Bank de Shole, but was prevented by the Ripple which broke with such violence as to endanger the Vessel.' He would make the attempt again, he wrote, 'the first easterly winds.' Three months later he noted that the survey of Herm, Jethou, and Great Russell passage was continuing, though on 14 May the *Charlotte* 'struck upon a rock near St Sampson's Harbour' and was under repair until the 25th.[28]

But if Lockwood's reference to Saumarez was intended to be diplomatic, it is evident that he did not really know how to handle such great men. For ten months Lockwood had dispatched essentially routine reports back to the Admiralty, conveying the impression of quiet and dutiful industry. But on 18 June 1806 he landed himself in deep trouble. Two admirals had previously shone their light upon him; close now to another, he felt the flames of consuming fire.

The incident that was to resonate so badly for Lockwood suggests that he had taken on too much of the command style of the flogging captain he had served under in *Caroline*, without understanding that he was barred by his birth and rank from treating the sons of gentlemen with contempt. In all its sordid and petty detail the story was described by its apparent victim, Richard Nugent Kelly, a midshipman from *Inconstant*, in a letter to her commanding officer, Captain Edward Stirling Dickson, on 19 June:

> I being yesterday on duty in the Boat with Mr Lockwood the Surveying master having landed him on Island of Herm where we remained from 8 o'clock in the morning till four in the evening. I gave the People liberty all but one to go out of the Boat amongst the Rocks. Mr Toone and the remaining man being in the Boat when Mr Lockwood came down the following conversation took place –

> Question: Where are the People?
> Answer: They are among the Rocks. I will go and call them.
> Mr L: How dare you let them out of the Boat?
> Mr K: I am answerable for the People sir.
> Mr L: Yes sir I will make you answerable for them.
> Mr K: How do you mean sir – in what Manner?
> Mr L: You saucy young Rascal if I have another word of yours I will put you out on a Rock and leave you there.

> When the Business of the day was over on our return to St Sampson's Mr L was going out of the Boat, he asked me my name which I told him –

> Mr L: I shall send a Note on board with you, I recollect sir you were very saucy to me.

Mr K:	I do not conceive sir that I was in the least so. I hope you recollect what you told me. You called me a young rascal and threatened to Put me on a Rock.
Mr L:	I did not call you a young rascal. I called you a saucy young Puppy which you are. You deserved to be put on a Rock. Why did you let the men out of the Boat?
Mr K:	I did not wish to keep them sitting in the Boat all day – The Captain does not wish it to be done.
Mr L:	I don't care what the Captain or any Body else wishes. I wish it to be done and if I wish to keep them in the Boat two days, or three days it shall be done; recollect sir that you and your Boat and your People are under my command.
Mr K:	I shall enquire into that sir.
Mr L:	I will let you know whether you can or not go out of the Boat. Mr Gray will you come with me while I put this Gentleman under the care of the Guard?

Mr Gray went with him and while going up to the Guardhouse Mr Lockwood said Young Gentleman I will cool your courage. I made no answer. When come to the Guardhouse Mr Gray told the Sergeant of the Guard to take Charge of me as a Prisoner, that I was confined by Mr Lockwood for being saucy to him. I remained with the Guard until released by Colonel Ramsey.

I request Sir you will be pleased to represent the Conduct of Mr Lockwood on this occasion to the Admiral that I may not in future when sent on duty as officer of the Boat with Mr Lockwood be subject to be sent Prisoner to a Guard House or put on shore on a Rock just as his Passion may direct him.[29]

Midshipman Kelly was well connected through the Nugents. Vice Admiral Horatio Lord Nelson's old chief, Admiral Sir Peter Parker had married a Nugent girl. What Kelly's relationship was with Earl Nugent, or with Vice Admiral, later Admiral of the Fleet, Sir Charles Edmund Nugent, has not been discovered, but that there was a connection is certain. Lockwood had thus taken on Captain Dickson, who was to end his career as Vice Admiral, and the English and naval establishments. And by asking the army to take charge of Kelly as their prisoner he had taken on the Navy itself. What is more, *Inconstant* was the flagship of Admiral Saumarez, and hence Kelly was one of his followers.

Sir James Saumarez was not merely a commander-in-chief. He was a national hero. His actions against combined French and Spanish squadrons at Algeçiras and the Straits of Gibraltar on 6 and 12–13 July

1801 had been greeted with jubilation in the streets of London. Parliament immediately granted him an annual pension of £1,200. The vote of thanks in the House of Lords was moved by Admiral Sir John Jervis, Earl of St Vincent, who declared that 'this gallant achievement surpasses every thing I have met with in reading or in service.' The vote was seconded by Lord Nelson himself who, generously, insisted that 'a greater action was never fought than that of Sir James Saumarez.' Earlier, as Captain Saumarez, he had commanded the *Orion* at the Battle of Cape St Vincent on 14 February 1797 and been Nelson's second at the Battle of the Nile on 1 August 1798. Algeçiras was hardly a British victory, except in the minds of the ill-informed public. One of the six British ships attacking three French under the Spanish guns of Algeçiras grounded under fire and eventually had to surrender when the rest of the squadron, badly battered, worked its way back to Gibraltar. But the rapidity with which the squadron was repaired at Gibraltar was remarkable, and the subsequent action at sea against the French, reinforced by six Spanish ships, was a triumph of tactics and leadership. The American Admiral Alfred Thayer Mahan would later describe Saumarez's victory as a 'blaze of triumph.' Of Saumarez himself he wrote: 'Eighteen months older than Nelson, not even Nelson saw more or harder fighting than did James Saumarez, nor bore himself more nobly throughout their day and generation.'[30] When Lockwood defied Sir James Saumarez, he challenged a man of immense glamour, authority, and force, at the very height of his powers. This was virtually lunatic recklessness.

And yet there was much more. Saumarez was also the pre-eminent member of a distinguished Guernsey family that traced its arrival there to William the Conqueror. Not only was Lockwood defying the admiral, he was defying one of the great Channel Islands landowners literally within his own demesne, and where he had been received with special honour and reverence after his victories. His appointment to the command at Jersey in 1803, to defend against anticipated French attacks from St Malo and Granville, had been more than a naval matter. Saumarez was a native son guarding the approaches to his ancestral islands. He was not a man to trifle with.[31]

Lockwood provided his own account of the incident in a letter to William Marsden at the Admiralty. With extreme regret, he wrote, he was under the 'painful necessity of troubling there [*sic*] Lordships with a subject of a personal nature', and wrote, that he must 'throw himself upon there Lordship's protection.' 'On the 18th Instant I found the state of the Tide extremely convenient for the purpose of ascertaining the position of some sunken rocks near the islands of Erm and Jethon, in consequence of which a boat was sent at my request from His Majesty's Ship *Inconstant*.' On reaching Herm, he claimed to have left 'orders with the midshipman who had charge of the Boat to keep her afloat and ready to convey me to Jethon', but on returning he found six crewmen missing, whereupon midshipman Kelly insisted 'he was accountable for the Boat's crew . . . in a Tone and manner the most insulting.' Meanwhile, Lockwood went on, the tide was flowing; there was work to be done; he launched the boat 'as best I could.' When they reached St Sampson in the evening, Lockwood claimed he remonstrated with Kelly 'with a view of making him sensible of his error and there letting the matter rest.' However, Kelly was 'as insolent as before' and was therefore put under military guard, 'there being none of His Majesty's ships near St Sampson's harbour.'

Next morning Lockwood reported the matter to both Saumarez and Dickson on board *Inconstant*, at which the former 'thought proper to express himself in very harsh and strong language.' According his own account, Lockwood contented himself by 'observing that whenever [Admiral Saumarez] felt inclined to hear both sides of the question' Lockwood would be vindicated. Saumarez then ordered him to be interviewed in the morning, 'which I did at about 9 o'clock. Here the Admiral recommenced an attack on me in the most furious and violent manner . . . he would not allow me to utter one word in my own justification . . . and insisted [that Lockwood make] a most ample apology' to Kelly. This Lockwood flatly refused to do, whereupon Saumarez 'instantly opened his door and desired me to walk out with every mark of resentment that he could evince.'

With extraordinary rashness, Lockwood chose to complain – at least implicitly – of his treatment by Admiral Saumarez himself. Acknowledging that his instructions directed him to call on Saumarez for assistance, he asserted that 'in the course of this laborious and complicated Service I have had but too much reason to complain of the neglect and inattention with which my requisitions for assistance from the navy have been treated, but by great personal labor and exertions I was able to get forward . . . I forbore making any specific complaint.' Lockwood's strongest evidence was an affidavit of Lieutenant Grey, secretary to Lieutenant General Sir John Doyle, commander of the Channel Islands garrison: 'As to the tone and manner in which this young mans [Kelly's] language was couched, I confess I felt much surprised at it, never having witnessed anything more insolent during the time I have been in the service.'[32] But this evidence was little enough to set against Kelly's family and his situation. Saumarez dispatched to the Admiralty a copy of Kelly's letter, and in addition enclosed a brief formal complaint from Dickson himself concerning Lockwood's conduct. Saumarez would not have troubled them, he wrote, had Lockwood not refused his request to apologise to Kelly.[33]

A week later Saumarez had received from the Admiralty a copy of Lockwood's letter of 20 June. He responded at once. There is no mistaking his anger at Lockwood's enlargement of the issue. It was now definitely a personal matter.

> As the first part of Mr Lockwood's letter more particularly relates to the King's Service, I beg you will please to inform their Lordships that since his arrival here everything that could depend upon me has been done to forward the service on which he is employed, having given the strictest orders that any assistance should be afforded him from His Majesty's Ships in the Road; and [aware of?] the importance of the Service I have taken particular care that my orders were duly complied with, as can be testified by the several Captains on this station, and which Mr Lockwood has acknowledged to me in repeated instances.

This certainly agrees with the evidence of Lockwood's own first reports from Guernsey (as quoted). As for the rest of his 'extraordinary letter', as Saumarez termed it, 'I must assert it to be totally untrue.' His version of events was that 'on the morning of the 19th Mr Lockwood called upon me to inform me that his Chart of this island was nearly completed which he was desirous to submit for my inspection.' 'As he was going away he told me he had been under the necessity of confining one of the midshipmen of the *Inconstant*.' Saumarez said that he then sent for Kelly, Dickson, and Lockwood the following morning. After 'recapitulating the circumstances', Saumarez concluded that Kelly 'had been extremely ill-used' and asked Lockwood to apologise. When he refused, Saumarez informed Lockwood that the incident would be reported to their Lordships. 'Although I may have expressed myself in a strong manner to Mr Lockwood I most truly declare not to have made use of a single expression against which any exception can justly have been made, still less treated him in the manner he so falsely described.' Saumarez concluded by trusting that the Board would not accept baseless accusations against a man of his rank without 'the severest animadversion.'[34]

What on earth was Lockwood up to? He was directed by the Admiralty on 4 July to discontinue the survey.

Apparently on receipt of this order, he prepared a 'general outline' of 'a Report upon the Survey', which contained a technical description of the work carried out to date. He was careful to praise General Doyle for providing horses and 'the most intelligent men' from the garrison, while pointedly excluding mention of naval assistance.[35] Saumarez contented himself, for the time being, with the observation that 'I shall make him a passage to England whenever he makes application to me for that purpose.'[36] Banished from the

Channel Islands, Lockwood preferred to make his own arrangements, returned to London, where he delivered a chart of the Guernsey survey to the Admiralty on 18 July, but requested permission to be allowed to complete the survey according to the original order. He wrote informing their Lordships that 'little more remains to be done at Guernsey than to complete the sea-line rocks and soundings on the west coast which may be effected without any assistance from, or communication with, His Majesty's ship on that Station, and as I am not only in possession of materials that would enable me to go a great way towards the completion of what remains to be done but have also collected a mass of local information from the Pilot and others, relative to the Tides, currents etc which if [not] transferred to others would in a great measure be lost to the service, and . . . the Cutter *Charlotte* hired for the purpose of surveying with two of His Majesty's boats are now lying at St Sampson's Harbor unemployed.'

He enclosed a copy of a letter from General Doyle written in response to Lockwood's request (19 July) for an opinion as to the 'nature and utility' of the survey. Doyle answered the question of 'how far I deem your Efforts upon this duty calculated to carry into Effect the service entrusted to you' with the assurance that the survey was 'of great importance.' 'I can with great truth and justice say that I never saw a more industrious and indefatigable man in my life, nor a person whose zeal appears more likely to do justice to the subject in question.'[37] Given the nature of inter-service rivalry, offering a general's praise to counter an admiral's abuse was not perhaps the best tactic.

Lockwood certainly cut no ice. The Admiralty ordered Saumarez to direct the *Charlotte* to join Lord St Vincent's fleet.[38] Saumarez informed Marsden that the *Charlotte* was 'a small vessel of 21 tons . . . without guns and a complement of ten men', not suitable for redeployment, but he also drew to their Lordships' attention Lockwood's action in discharging seven men from the cutter without permission.[39] Lockwood insisted that he had done so to reduce costs, and two days later, on 18 August, he pressed his case.

As this season of the year is the most favourable for continuing the nautical survey intrusted to me I hope their Lordships will not deem me too importunate, particularly as the remarks, marks and angles, for the rocks and shoals, direction of the tides, leading marks, nature of the bottom etc are in the rough, and field books at Guernsey which while fresh in my memory, are with ease transfer'd to the plan, the chart of that island to be completed, and the Triangles continued to Alderney, Jersey, Rocks Dovre [ie, Roches Douvres], without any assistance than the small vessel, and crew, hired for that purpose.[40]

A memo overleaf to this letter indicates that the Lords Commissioners threw the matter back to Saumarez 'for his consideration.' But he was unyielding. 'Although it would give me real concern to be under the necessity of throwing any obstacle to the Service entrusted to Mr Lockwood, his conduct has been so highly reprehensible that it cannot be passed over without injury to the Public Service, unless he makes proper atonement for it. The very injurious and disrespectful terms made use of in his letter to you of the 20th June and the very unjust and ill-founded charge therein contained of Neglect and inattention paid to his requisitions by the Squadron were of themselves sufficient to have compelled me to request a Court Martial on Mr Lockwood had he been in a different situation.'[41]

Lockwood, meanwhile, unaware of this latest exchange, battered at the Admiralty doors again on 18 August. The 'approaching Equinoctial Tides,' he wrote, were 'extremely favourable' for the survey. 'The whole of my Instruments, and materials for the survey are at Guernsey, and the surveying vessel lying ready.' An unidentified turnover memo dated 1 September requests the Secretary to 'send up every Paper upon this subject – a part only being sent up.' But Lockwood did not wait for a reply. He was insisting to the Lords Commissioners again on 4 September that certain features of the coastline could only be examined at equinoctial tides and noting the 'damages suffered by His Majesty's ships *Alamene*, *Charwell*, *Mercury*, *Constance*, *Pygmy*, *Conquest*, and many others evince the existing errors of the charts extant.' His materials, he reminded them, were still on Guernsey.[42]

It was high time for the Admiralty to conclude the matter. Though the dithering suggests that they really wished the survey to continue, Saumarez would not let them off the hook. At last they laid down clear terms. Overleaf to Lockwood's letter of 4 September, the judgement of the Board was laid down: since 'Mr Lockwood did not appear to be sensible of the impropriety of his conduct and their Lordships having every reason to give full credit to the charges made by Sir James Saumarez [they] do not think proper to continue Mr Lockwood on the service at Guernsey until he shall have made a proper and satisfactory apology to the Rear Admiral for his conduct.'

Lockwood did at last make a pass at an apology to Saumarez, by letter on 6 September: 'My Lords Commissioners of the Admiralty having in a letter of this days date been pleased to signify their determination to me "that I am not to continue the survey of Guernsey untill I have made an apology to you" I do therefore beg to assure you of my being fully sensible of the violence committed upon the service in putting the midshipman of the Boat under military arrest. And any part of my conduct that you have deemed exceptionable I most readily apologise to you for. Should the above prove satisfactory I have to request you will be pleased to make the same known to their Lordships as the approaching Equinoctial Tides are extremely favourable to the revisal of the work.'

The tone of this letter is impertinently offhand. Did Lockwood really expect Admiral Saumarez to accept it? Instead, Saumarez coolly observed that this was not a 'proper apology' – specifically for the general complaints Lockwood had made in his letter of 20 June.[43]

At last Lockwood began to wriggle. He insisted to the Board that his charge of neglect did not refer to Saumarez himself but rather to officers of the *Inconstant* who were not obeying their commander's orders. 'I further beg leave to declare that I never in any one instance behaved with the least disrespect to Sir James Saumarez and hope their Lordships will be pleased to permit my continuing the survey of the islands or employ elsewhere.' Though he had trimmed on the original complaint, the issue of 'disrespect' merely set his word against that of Saumarez once more. Furthermore, any explanation to the Admiralty Board was now irrelevant. It was Saumarez, not them, who required satisfaction. He could only have been infuriated further by Lockwood's constant direct appeals to the Admiralty, especially since this letter was again sent on for his information.[44]

By requesting that he might be employed elsewhere, Lockwood seemed to be finally acknowledging the hopelessness of his position. Nevertheless, he returned to the attack. 'In order to prove my complaints', he sent to Saumarez details of the neglect and inattention of *Inconstant* officers, while making yet another plea directly to the Lords Commissioners. 'Having made an ample apology for the impropriety of placing the midshipman under military arrest', he repeated his request to complete the survey.[45]

When a copy of this letter reached Saumarez he replied with a devastating broadside. Not only did he enclose a copy of his own letter to Lockwood of 30 September, in which he noted that 'you always expressed yourself perfectly satisfied' with the assistance received, but for good measure he included certificates from T Dumaresq commanding *Charwell*, Lewis Shepiard commanding *Thisbe*, and Captain Dickson of *Inconstant*, testifying to their ready assistance to Lockwood. Shepiard also observed that when Lockwood 'had occasion to make application for assistance, it was always done in a very *ungracious manner* which the officers repeatedly complained of,' while Dickson added: 'I cannot help remarking that his conduct has been ungracious to the Officers and Men employed on the Boats and often Contemptuous to me.' Saumarez also revealed that 'Captain Selby of the *Cerberus* as well as Captain Dickson of the *Inconstant* made repeated complaints to me of the improper conduct of Mr Lockwood to them on various occasions.'[46]

The whole affair had been re-positioned in a wider context of 'ungracious', 'improper', 'contemptuous' behaviour. These officers may have loyally closed ranks with Saumarez, but did they actually lie? It seems very unlikely. Lockwood's haughty language, as reported, his threat to maroon the midshipman on a rock, the rash decision to lock him in the guardhouse, all speak of arrogant and reckless disregard for proprieties. Unstated, though surely active in all this, was the fact that Lockwood was a warrant officer, on the wrong side of a social divide. If he had indeed previously acquired a reputation for 'contemptuous' behaviour, Kelly's attitude towards him may be much better understood.

If Kelly's account is even substantially correct, Lockwood's language and behaviour read like a parody of the self-assertive and class-defining style of the time. 'How dare you sir', 'saucy young rascal', 'saucy young puppy' – these blustery phrases, the stress upon absolute obedience, the formal, almost pedantic exchanges between the two men, the bristling consciousness of manner, create an impression that Lockwood was frantically over-playing his role. Both he and Kelly were clearly 'cutting a figure'. And when Lockwood vowed: 'Young Gentleman I will cool your courage', the emphasis may indeed have been upon the 'gentleman', upon social humiliation as much as military discipline. 'Ungracious' was repeated by Saumarez' captains – collusively? – in describing Lockwood's behaviour. The word suggests boorishness and may well have been intended to convey to their Lordships, with killing effect, that Lockwood was not himself a gentleman.

In short, Lockwood had brought about his own fall by taking an unbearably truculent and high line, though Saumarez had revealed the background to the affair with obvious reluctance. But Lockwood's continued stubbornness gave Saumarez no choice. It had become a matter of honour. Lockwood had certainly overvalued his status on Guernsey, apparently believing that his appointment by the Admiralty Board gave him special powers. At the centre of his actions, however, lay an egotistical refusal to concede that might be interpreted as courage on a fitter occasion. But if he really said 'I don't care what the Captain or any body wishes', he was truly off the scale.

The Board finally closed the door. Lockwood was informed on 22 October that he had been removed from the survey. In reply, three days later, he yet again asserted his innocence – of which 'I have the most unequivocal proof' – and begged to be allowed 'to collect my papers, Instruments etc and to compleat [sic] the Plan as far as the materials in my possession will permit.' There was no further concession. He was directed 'to deliver all the materials still in his possession to the Hydrographical Office' and the Navy Board was informed that he could be appointed master 'of any ship where his services might be wanted.'[47] A decided chill had fallen.

Lockwood tried to obtain payment for lost time, having waited 'upwards of fourteen weeks at great expence, besides the expences of Travelling and those incurred while prosecuting the Survey, in consequence of not being supplied with the requisites necessary for that service. Of the latter I never kept any regular account, as I considered my position as maritime surveyor permanent.' He was paid only to the day of his recall.[48] The scale of Lockwood's calamity can be read into this letter. He had been living for three months in London without pay and now saw a whole career disintegrating. Indeed, his belief in the permanency of his position may suggest he felt himself to be the replacement for Graeme Spence.[49] For Lockwood to be thrown back into the pool of general warrant officers, in wartime, with a serious blot on his record, was appalling to contemplate.

Astonishingly, he now applied to be examined for lieutenant. Their Lordships, however, did not 'think proper' to comply with his request.[50] By thus seeking a commission in the depth of his disgrace was he, again, provocatively insisting on his merits in the face of the naval class structure? Had he been so stung by the refusal of midshipman Kelly to accept his authority that he exposed what he believed to be the real cause of his downfall? His sense of victimisation would be deep and lasting. In his relations with the Admiralty and Navy Board he remained aggrieved, scornful, complaining to the end, and capable of public sarcasm. Lockwood would claim, in the 'Introductory Remarks' to his 1818 *Description of Nova Scotia*, to be 'secured from necessity in age, by the liberality of the Board I have the honor to serve, and enjoying an income exceeding my wants, I disclaim even the slightest wish to derive pecuniary benefit from this humble attempt to be useful.' This sarcastic humbug led Llewellyn Styles Dawson to quote the remark in his 1883 *Memoirs of Hydrography* with the droll observation that Lockwood 'appears to have been a veritable *rara avis*, so contented was his disposition.'[51] The truth is that from the Saumarez affair onward Lockwood's relations with authority were complex and embattled. His status was never legitimised from London; he had been cast outside and remained there. How deeply this distrust of authority extended, how much it provoked Lockwood's aggressive self-assertion, can only be guessed at. But the chip was now fixed as firmly on his shoulder as an admiral's epaulette.

'There is a tide in the affairs of men,' wrote William Shakespeare, 'Which, taken at the flood, leads on to fortune; / Omitted, all the voyage of their life / Is bound in shallows and in miseries.'[52] That sad fortune appeared the inevitable outcome of Lockwood's experiences in the strong tides of the Channel Islands. There was essentially only one way to begin the scramble back. He needed the intercession of a powerful figure. By the spring of 1807 Lockwood had reconnected with Rear Admiral, now Sir

Alexander, Cochrane and was appointed master of Cochrane's flagship the *Belleisle*.[53] Cochrane was by that time commander-in-chief at the Leeward Islands, and had served as Vice Admiral Sir John Duckworth's second-in-command when he defeated a French fleet under Vice Admiral Corentin Leissèques off Sainte-Domingue on 6 February 1806, for which service Cochrane had been knighted. In the circumstances, it was surely the best for which Lockwood could hope. But the knowledge of what he had lost must have been peculiarly galling as the squadron sailed out past the Channel Isles en route once more for the West Indies.

3

Equal to the Task

WHEN IN EARLY July 1807 the *Belleisle* anchored in Carlisle Bay off Bridgetown, and Lockwood re-entered the destructive Caribbean climate, he was still trying to escape. On 12 July he wrote asking the Admiralty Secretary, William Marsden, to remind the new Board headed by Lord Mulgrave that the Channel Islands survey had been entrusted to him. By 'much personal labor, and expence, I was enabled to compleat the Trigonometrical process, over Guernsey, Herm, and Sark ... and as the stasimetric scheme is ready for extension, the work might be compleated with great accuracy, and ease.' Admiral Cochrane, he wrote, 'has been pleased to sanction' this further, and in fact hopeless, appeal.[1] But a week later, on 21 July, Cochrane appointed Lockwood acting Master Attendant of the naval yard on Carlisle Bay: 'It is absolutely necessary ... particularly until the whole Wharf and the Buildings and Breakwater, unfinished, is finished, and ... I have every confidence in your Zeal and Abilities.'[2] Cochrane's patronage was to prove invaluable to Lockwood, who was to live in Barbados for the next seven years, an almost biblical epoch in a colony rife with disease, exploitation, and paranoia.

Bridgetown lay at the northerly end of Carlisle Bay, entered from the sea by a canal-like 'Careenage'. The town straggled along the shore for about two miles, with the garrison of St Ann's Fort on a rise above the southern arm. Its military significance had grown during the war. The barracks, with their covered galleries, were built around a spacious parade ground, the Savannah, which in 1807 was still undrained and a morass in wet weather. The fort itself dated from the beginning of the eighteenth century, although it was not until the French provided military support for the American Revolution that it had come into serious use. A battalion had been established at Barbados in 1780 and a British garrison was thereafter maintained for 125 years, swollen from time to time by troops to be shipped elsewhere.[3] But the naval war in the West Indies against Napoleon's empire was all but over following Duckworth's

victory, after which most of the remaining French navy retreated to
Europe. Privateers and raiding frigates might still be encountered in these
waters, but the Royal Navy was primarily engaged in securing control of
French colonial islands. The most valuable French colony after Sainte-
Domingue was Martinique, and Cochrane's Antilles fleet would soon be
engaged in its capture.

From his earlier experience in the West Indies, Lockwood knew what a
shore posting meant. The situation of the Bridgetown naval yard, now the
site of a Hilton hotel, was a deathtrap. Much of the area was a permanent
swamp alive with mosquitoes, with a pond parallel to and only twenty
yards or so from the sea, and a large mast pond and boat houses to the
south at the naval dockyard. South of that was an open area, part of which
contained a military cemetery, and was also a swamp.[4]

Disease was a persistent, eruptive motif in Lockwood's life to the end. To
understand the significance of disease in his life, and something of
Lockwood's time at Barbados, this subject must be revisited. For it was
much more than the simple threat of death. It was the prime element in the
way lives were lived.

Within days of *Belleisle*'s arrival in Carlisle Bay, Cochrane had written
to Marsden about the 'great want of medicines and stores of every kind at
the naval hospitals at Antigua and Barbadoes, and when Medicines are
demanded for the Squadron, the dispensers are obliged to purchase a great
part of them, at enormous Prices, and most probably of inferior qualities.'
Furthermore, there was 'scarcely a Surgeon's Assistant remaining in the
Squadron, who has past his proper examination.'[5] He further informed
Marsden on 7 August that 'Mr Tidbald the naval storekeeper at
Barbadoes, died of Fever the latter end of last month, which was very soon
after his arrival in the country', while drawing attention later in the year
to the exertions of Duncan McArthur, surgeon of the naval yard at
Barbados. 'The additional duty which he has hitherto had, of attending to
the health of the Prisoners of War has been very great, and sometimes at
not less than four different places.' Apart from the naval hospital itself, he
noted, there were two prison ships in Carlisle Bay, as well as the town jail,
and a prison hospital. And on 10 July 1808 Cochrane would report the
death of Dr Ralph Cumming, surgeon at the Antigua hospital, who 'died
of fever about ten days ago, and had just before lost his wife and child.'
Hard on the heels of this tragedy came the news that 'Doctor Hardy,
whom I had appointed to succeed the late Doctor Cumming, died, after a
residence of Six Weeks.' Writing again from Carlisle Bay to the
Honourable William Wellesley Pole, the Admiralty First Secretary, on 28
August 1808, Cochrane reported that 'great numbers of the Marines which
were landed . . . have died of fever.'[6]

Contemporary writers about the West Indies returned again and again to the subject of disease. Disease was endemic to the whole experience of life on the islands: to the economy, the politics, the social values. Disease destroyed the whites; so blacks were imported by the 'middle passage' from Africa to provide labour – not because they were immune to disease but because they were expendable. Those who survived beyond the first generation, white or black, became 'Creoles', who were 'hardened' to the climate by a process of natural selection of their more robust immune systems.

Disease and slavery were thus wedded from the beginning and the issue of that marriage was a brutal society whose inhumanity was both systematic and casual. The Caribbean had always attracted a floating population of chancers and no-hopers, and on Barbados, even though it was the most stable and settled island, the so-called 'redlegs', or poor whites, were numerous. This kind of colonialism, shadowed always by the threat of sudden death, offered its rewards in the forms of immediate tangible pleasures, not ideals of service. Lockwood had re-entered a society in which moral niceties were elusive and civilised restraints few. How far he was himself conditioned by the practices of that society is questionable. But each of the defining elements in West Indian life – disease, slavery, class, and sex – would directly and demonstrably influence the man who was later the Honourable Anthony Lockwood, Esq.

Sexual imperialism was not confined to the redlegs. In John Poyer's *History of Barbados* published in 1808, he comments on the regime of Governor George Points Ricketts, who had resigned eight years earlier. Poyer was a resident of Speightstown, Barbados, and he expressed political anxiety rather than moral disapproval. Sexual commerce with black and coloured women – especially the favoured mulattos – was a time-honoured practice. But elevating such women socially was another matter. The regular presence of a mulatto woman in the governor's bed at the governor's mansion was deeply disturbing at the very time the slaves in Sainte-Domingue under Toussaint L'Ouverture were carrying the day, and when what Poyer referred to as 'the extraordinary mortality' of British troops had led to the formation of coloured regiments.[7]

Yet the political and commercial elite of the resident Creole population of the islands, while defending to the last their right to own slaves, yearned for acceptance by European genteel society, and tried to maintain their idea of a civilised social life. A versified 'Address to the Island of Barbados' published by 'AZ' in the *Bridgetown Mercury* for 10 October 1809 struck the authentic note of white Creole paranoia.

Dear honor'd Isle! tho' thousands shou'd
Thy soil, thy clime, or manners blame–

And with unsparing censure rude
Attempt to vilefy thy name–

To me thou ever shalt be dear;
Nor will I cease to sing thy praise,
Tho' all the world should scoffing sneer:
And with contempt regard my lays.

West Indian society inevitably raised questions about 'civilisation' and 'savagery', gentility and vulgarity, and all their sub-categories. In all this, the image of the 'English Lady' was definitive. During Lockwood's residence there were balls at the garrison and elsewhere, subscription assemblies, advertised significantly as 'Amusement for the Ladies', musical entertainments by the regimental band, a whist club, a literary society, and interest in ornamental gardening with shrubs and trees imported from the United States.

It was the Bridgetown theatre which best illustrated how far cultivated society was measured by its capacity to provide recreation for respectable women. A theatre, it was believed, would be a fit sphere for civilising female influence. Plays were performed from February 1810 – *The Child of Nature* and *The Irishman in London* followed by *Lovers' Vows* and *Fortune's Frolics* – with such success that a subscription was quickly raised to build a theatre.[8] This was opened as the Theatre Royal on 1 January 1812 with 'the celebrated comedy of *The West Indian* followed by the *Entertainment of the Spoilt Child*.' In its account of the first night, the *Bridgetown Mercury* of 4 January 1812 is quite explicit about the function of the theatre: 'The purpose for which the erection of the Theatre was originally undertaken, that of providing a source of agreeable and rational amusement for the Ladies, has been so far accomplished.'

But from the beginning that purpose was vulnerable. There were those, the *Mercury* warned, who might attend with the intention 'of stirring up what is termed *a row*.' However, the report continued, both the Attorney General and the magistrates shared the same 'sentiments' in the matter: they would punish miscreants 'with the utmost severity.' Under the headline 'Apprehensions for the Ladies', the *Mercury* of 1 February noted that the poor attendance on the previous Thursday was probably the result of female fears that 'a disturbance similar to that of the preceding night of performance would again take place.' The newspaper carried a letter of apology a week later from A F Evans and William Rafter, both lieutenants of the 60th Regiment who admitted to 'having been overtaken by liquor.' But the defence of the Ladies required ceaseless vigilance. A drunken soldiery might be expected, yet even the constant theatrical diet of romance and broad comedy could be subverted by agents of riot on the very stage itself. A letter from 'B', published by the *Mercury* on 11 January 1812, tried to stop the rot quickly. The acting of Mr Francklin, 'as Jeremy Fiddler, in the after-piece on Thursday last, making every allowance for the volatile character he personified ... was disgustingly irregular, and brought to the imagination more of the *merry-andrew*, than that of a chaste *comic* performer.'

Lockwood was to refer to this conviction that feminine society had a civilising effect in the 'Introductory Remarks' to his *Brief Description of Nova Scotia*, when he lamented the coarsening effects of life at sea. 'Deprived of refined female society, which tends to perfection more than any plan of education, and without which the manners are harsh and rude; sailors, who see most, and before whom nature derobes, are seldom gifted with descriptive powers.'[9] But this is the context in which he wrote that the munificence of the Royal Navy had removed him from all financial care or motive, so it would be naive to read much of Lockwood's own attitudes into this expression.

In reality, Lockwood had little need to maintain appearances. Refined English ladies were in short supply for a warrant officer renting a house within the naval yard at Bridgetown. He therefore followed local custom and quickly acquired a mistress. Her name was Harriet Lee, the wife of a Bridgetown tailor. Lockwood set up a seafaring man's ménage, and soon Harriet was pregnant.

His relationship with Harriet née Hannibal was to be a long one, and one eventually honoured with the status of marriage. Described as a spinster of St Michael parish, Bridgetown, Harriet had married Joseph Lee, a tailor, also of St Michael, on 9 October 1805.[10] They already had a child, Sarah, baptised at St Michael's church on 12 July 1802.[11] And in the will Joseph Lee drew up soon after the wedding, on 30 October 1805, he left Cork, an 'African Negro' slave boy, to an illegitimate son James Clarke, 'who is at present absent from this Island.' The slave was to revert to Sarah Lee should James Clarke fail either to reach the age of twenty-one or to lawfully marry. Sarah was herself bequeathed a slave girl 'with her future issue', called Nelly and also 'African'. Harriet was to receive 'a Negro Boy named Joseph to her and her heirs for ever.' The rest of the estate was to be divided share-and-share alike between the above-named beneficiaries.[12]

This was a meagre inheritance. On 10 April 1807, furthermore, Joseph Lee had sold Cork and Nelly for £190 to David and George Hall, merchants of Bridgetown, 'with the issue and increase of the said female Slave Nelly hereafter to be born.'[13] This may have been an attempt to settle his affairs, or a necessity imposed by illness, for he died and was buried at St Michael on 17 August following, the cause of death unknown.[14]

Joseph may well have been a good deal older than Harriet. On a deed sealed and witnessed in Bridgetown on 2 July 1796 he had described himself as 'now of the Parish of St Michael and the Island of Barbados', perhaps implying a recent move there. The deed declared that 'in consideration of the many true and faithful Services done and performed for me by my Mulatto Woman Slave named Becky' she was to be 'released manumitted set free and discharged.'[15] Two years later, on 7 December 1798, he paid in full the manumission fee of £50 for this Rebecca Lee into the parish funds of St Michael, as required by law.[16] Rebecca was probably Joseph's mistress, who had lived with him long enough to have earned manumission. Why did he grant it just then?

Since Harriet Hannibal bore Joseph Lee's child in 1802 their liaison started earlier. Did Harriet replace Becky? The year 1796, when Joseph released Becky, saw the main military build-up on the island and it seems possible that he, she, or both, moved to Barbados at that time. Did Joseph meet Harriet in Bridgetown, or bring her with him? The name Hannibal is suggestive of 'African' origins and she, like Becky, may have been a free woman of colour, but the name Hannibal, Hunnable, Hannable, was not uncommon in Ireland. If she were black, or mulatto, her position later in New Brunswick as Lockwood's wife when he became Surveyor General of the province and a member of His Majesty's Executive Council must have been socially provocative, to say the least. But even a white woman living for several years in an irregular union with a humble Bridgetown tailor would have had an extremely dubious status, especially given the racial double standard of the West Indies.

Whatever the truth of this, about fourteen months after Joseph's death Harriet gave birth to another daughter, Marina, baptised at seven weeks old on 19 December 1808. This was sixteen months after Joseph Lee's death, but Marina was entered into the St Michael register as his child.[17] Clearly she was not, but there must have been some reason for not naming Anthony as her father. However she may have been conceived, Lockwood subsequently acknowledged Marina as his own. Soon after her birth, he also took full responsibility for his Whitehaven children, Martha and Anthony junior, who joined him in Bridgetown. It must have been a terrible blow when the sickly reputation of Barbados was quickly manifested in little Martha Lockwood's death. She was buried at St Michael on 10 November 1809.[18]

After some time, Lockwood made a provision for his extended family. On 12 July 1812 he executed the deed transferring the ownership of the slave named William in trust to John Ironmonger the Elder, 'for the use and Behoof' of Martha Mackenzie, who was described as a widow of Cumberland.[19] On 11 December he deeded another slave boy called George to Sarah Lee, to revert to Marina Lockwood when Sarah reached twenty, or at her death. There would be other slaves in the Lockwood-Lee ménage. Harriet sold 'a certain Negro slave called Clarissa' for £75 to John Tull Thomas of St Michael on 3 October 1814, and after he reached Halifax, Anthony junior would sell two slave boys, 'both tradesmen', for £192 to William Marcher, a mariner, also of St Michaels, on 1 July 1817.[20] On the same date Marcher also bought from Sarah Lee a William, 'alias Bill Lee, now at Barbados', for £82.[21] Slaves were considered an appreciating asset, if bought young and trained, especially after the banning of the slave trade increased the value of existing resident slaves.

By acquiring a mistress and slaves, Lockwood swam unhesitatingly with the West Indian current. But by bringing his children together and providing for Harriet's Sarah, as well as for his former common-law wife Martha, he also demonstrated domestic loyalties to which he would be faithful. The possibility that he was not the biological father of any of the children adds another dimension to Lockwood's character. Lockwood was an energetic, sensual man. The 'passion' which midshipman Kelly feared did not express itself only as anger. But during his madness he would write darkly of 'my amours', and sexual frustration may have been an element.

At the time Lockwood took up the appointment, most of the artisans and labourers employed in the Naval Yard were slaves hired from local owners. But the abolition of the slave trade took place in those very weeks. Whereas on 4 July the *Barbados Mercury* could advertise the auction of two sets of twelve African slaves, from the cargoes of the *Hector* and the *Jane*, by 1 August the same newspaper announced 'THE LAST CARGO. *That will probably be retailed on this island*', being '107 PRIME GOLD COAST SLAVES' imported on the brig *President Ince*. Admiral Cochrane saw both immediate and long-term advantage for the service. Writing to Lord Melville from Barbados on 6 February 1808, he observed:

> The admiralty have now an opportunity of soon getting rid of the black Carpenters at the above Yard [Antigua], and in future employ none but their own people – by the late Slave Act all cargoes condemned cannot be sold as Slaves – they may be put in the Army or Navy or bound apprentices. A slave vessel has been lately taken, and I have sent all the men with His Majesty's Ships except about twenty employed at this yard [Barbados] and at the naval hospital. I strongly recommend that from fifty to one hundred be sent to English Harbour – there to be brought up to different trades, and that they may be allowed to chose wives from the female part of the Cargoes that arrive contrary to the provisions of the Act. The black carpenters being slaves, and having but a small part allowed

by their owners, do but little work, and are often absent, are a heavy expense, without an adequate advantage. By having your own people they will always be on the spot, and by giving them rewards in proportion to their abilities, they will be attached to the place, and having their families they will form a kind of colony of free artificers like the Casts in India, handed down from father to son. These, here, are fed on Rice and Salt Fish with about half an allowance of Rum – they have cloathing similar to the King's negroes at English Harbour. They are quite happy and contented, some work in the blacksmith's shop, and others attend the carpenters, by which in a short time they will become handy fellows.[22]

Many men freed from slave cargoes were thus indentured by the Navy. Meanwhile, locally-owned slaves were still hired. The approximate size and composition of the Barbados yard early in Lockwood's charge can be gauged from the Cheque [Pay] Book for the autumn quarter of 1808, which lists seventy-two employees plus twenty 'extra laborers'. Of these, twenty-seven were white shipwrights. Also white were nine smiths, fourteen sailmakers, two porters, two sawyers, and a labourer, while most of the forty-three others listed as shipwrights, carpenters, and painters carried the jocularly demeaning names of slaves: Cato, Moses, Billey, King, Ben Block, Nat Bobstay, Ant Cable, Tom Tackle, Giles Mizen, Tom Toff, Tom Spanker, Ben Bowsprit, Humphrey Clinker, Peregrine Pickle, and so on. Among the 'extra laborers' were nine 'Negro contr[act] laborers'.[23]

Lockwood may possibly have employed slaves of his own in the yard, but if so he got others to 'accept' their pay so as to keep his name off the pay-sheet, except for recording his own pay as master attendant. By the end of his service at the yard he was certainly employing slaves owned by his mistress and her daughter. From January to June 1813 Harriet 'accepted' the pay for a Henry White, and for Anthony White who was 'a hired Negro sawyer', both employed at the naval yard. Sarah Lee similarly 'accepted' the pay of William Lee.[24]

A dockyard master attendant was essentially the overseer of technical facilities at a naval port. In 1814 Lockwood was to give a detailed account of his duties at Barbados in a letter to the second Lord Melville, who had succeeded his father as First Lord in 1812:

There being no resident commissioner, the order, cleanliness, subordination and safety require the constant care and Exertions of the Master Attendant . . . The Surveying, Sails, Cordage and other Stores returned from His Majesty's Ships and Vessels which refit, or complete at this Port, calls for his especial Care in making the proper conversions, as well as to prevent any unnecessary expenditure of Stores. Duties which are unconnected with those of the Storekeeper and with which they are ever considered to be quite unacquainted.

There being neither Boatswain nor Foreman of Sailmakers to the Yard, their duties fall immediately on the Master Attendant, being in his Department, and require his greatest attention in repairing and making Sails, in order to prevent waste of materials or loss of time.

The Chain Moorings laid down in Carlisle Bay for the use of His Majesty's Ships would without the strictest care and attendance, be considered useless and totally lost to the Service whereas they are now no inconsiderable saving in Anchors and Cables.

In addition to the current Duties of the Yard the occasional unloading of Store Ships requires every exertion of the Master Attendant in order to prevent Loss, Damage, or [?one word]. The last Fleet brought nearly One Thousand Tons of Stores which that officer unassisted had to superintend the landing of, as well as to see that they were properly Housed and to regulate the several Demands sent in.[25]

Like other Lockwood claims, this was a varnished account. During the seven years he undertook the duties of master attendant he spent lengthy periods away from the island, at which time the storekeeper and naval officer appear to have taken over. This was a wartime, temporary appointment. Lockwood remained acting master attendant and spent seven fruitless years attempting to persuade the Navy Board to confirm the position. Meanwhile he polished his grievances. He received 'an allowance of twenty shillings per day, from which sum ten per cent Income Tax, seventy five pounds per annum House rent, sums for stationary and fuel are deducted; which reduces the allowance to an amount no means adequate to the expenses unavoidably incident to my situation in this Country.'[26]

In addition to Lockwood himself, the administrative staff was at first tiny: just two clerks, a master shipwright, the storekeeper. By December 1812, however, the complement of the Barbados Yard would rise to 239, while throughout this period there was a very large turnover of employees.[27] The storekeeper kept a monthly register of 'All Persons entered, dead, or discharged' and for the last two months of 1810, for instance, seventy-six names were entered, almost all 'hired negro laborers'. Among the storekeeper's entries for March of that same year was that of William Jones, an 'Extra Clerk . . . murdered at Bridgetown.'[28] The workforce of the naval yard in Barbados could not have been a consistently ruly body of men.

The conduct of naval yards was notoriously corrupt and the opportunities for routine cheating in the deployment of a large, impermanent workforce, and in the procurement of materials, were immense. Many dubious practices were accepted as perquisites that went with the position; nor could the moral and commercial ethos of the West Indies be expected to restrain a man placed in Lockwood's position. The sheer scale of naval expansion had itself created vast new opportunities for graft. Funding for the Navy climbed from £1,943,882 in 1792 to a peak of £20,096,709 in 1813, and the administrative structure was badly in need of reform.[29]

There were three searching enquiries into the civil affairs of the Navy between 1785 and 1808.[30] The first dealt with the conduct of overseas dockyards, and was full of examples from the West Indies and elsewhere of peculation by storekeepers and others buying supplies from local contractors, inflating the charge to the Navy, and pocketing the difference. Fraudulent wage bills, including the listing of phantom workers, were not unknown either. Dockyard commissioners were supposed to supervise the running of the yards but the most honest of these were hampered by the mesh of patronage appointments made by the Board itself and by corrupt networks which extended to the First Lord himself, in the case of the elder Lord Melville. First Lord of the Admiralty from May 1804 to May 1805, he was a notorious Scottish political fixer, and was accused of tolerating a relaxed use of public funds for private investment. Most of the twelve reports of a commission set up in 1802 to investigate frauds in the Navy Board were delivered to him.[31] The example of his patron, Lord Cochrane, was not calculated to keep Lockwood on a path of exemplary restraint. The lack of a local dockyard commissioner at Barbados increased the possibility of 'irregularities', and would lead to further troubles for Lockwood.

The low esteem in which the Navy Board was held by the Lords Commissioners of the Admiralty added to Lockwood's difficulties, throughout his career. Masters attendant, even when temporary 'acting' appointments, were administratively under the authority of the Navy Board. But Lockwood had been appointed by the local commander-in-chief and confirmed by the Admiralty. The Navy Board's *amour propre* was thus involved and Lockwood remained administratively vulnerable. He would be buffeted between the Board and the Lords Commissioners several times.

In practice, the day-to-day running of the Bridgetown yard was out of Lockwood's hands for weeks on end, since Admiral Cochrane used him for other jobs. The first of these came on the initiative of the governor of Trinidad, Brigadier General Hislop, who reported that there was an 'immense' quantity of wild hemp growing on the island. Cochrane said he would send 'a Ropemaker from this Ship, and a couple of other Hands to assist him, in gathering and making a good sample, both of the dressed Hemp, and a proportion of Rope of different Sizes' for examination by the Admiralty and Navy Board.[32] But it was in fact Lockwood who was sent to Trinidad to examine the hemp 'as well as the trees of that island.' He was there by March, and met with a Mr I P Kingston, who 'cheerfully communicated all particulars' concerning the hemp and 'its importance to the Country at this crisis', after which Lockwood made his own assessment and prepared a report for Cochrane, completed in Trinidad on 30 April 1808.

His report gives some sense of those practical abilities Cochrane prized in Lockwood. 'In order to ascertain the produce a Perch was measured and the Plants gathered amounting to One Thousand Two Hundred' – after which the materials were processed to produce approximately 970lbs of hemp per uncultivated acre. He gave a careful account of the harvesting, which took place in March, and of the method used to separate the bark by soaking in streams. 'Want of machinery' restricted the rope made to two-inch thickness, and this was later tarred. He also noted that 'the Spanish Indians make rope of a species of Aloe, known here by the name of Longue Boeuf, the fibres of this root are dry, harsh, unpleasant to work, resist Tar and appear unfit for any service but the common purposes of the Estates, or gear for small vessels of the Gulf.'

Moving on to the question of Trinidadian timber, Lockwood wrote that 'the Plains between Port Spain and point Teague produce a variety of valuable wood.' The cedar was 'equal both in Magnitude and quality to that used at the Havana for building Spanish Ships of War. Trees in the quarter of Naparima measure in Girth from sixteen to twenty two feet.' There was also a wood called *gris-gris* that he indicated was 'capable of squaring from Twenty inches to three feet, easy wrought, close grained and durable', *balata*, 'a very hard, tough and straight-grained wood', *crapou* or *carapaud*, 'an excellent light wood, generally used for Plank, capable of affording Timbers of a moderate size', *mora*, which was found in great quantities about Point Cedar, 'of much the same nature but considerable larger than Balata', *chypre*, 'light and close grained, fit for both Plank and Timber', *l'angeline*, 'excellent Plank, of great growth and very abundant', *pony* or *green-heart*, 'extremely hard, considered incorruptible, would answer any purpose were strength and durability are requisites', and *guatequero*, 'of the same quality as the English Elm, and equally fit for Gun Carriages, Capstans, etc.' 'There are probably many other useful woods that escaped my notice, but the above are common along the shores of the Gulf of Paria.' On the south side of the island most of the trees grew

contiguous to the beach, and vessels have the advantage of anchoring close in-shore, particularly in Erin or south-west quarter, where the Galba a wood highly esteemed by the Spaniards rises to Eighty and Ninety feet, well adapted for Masts or Spars. The native Indians cut and Square the Timber at a very trifling expence, the greatest difficulty is drawing it from the woods, which might be done with ease by Oxen.

Limited time and the approach of the rainy season hindered further examination. But 'the most intelligent Gentlemen of the island' told him that quantities of 'Crooked Timber' for ship construction were to be found.

And Lockwood also reported the existence of a

> lake of Native Pitch . . . situate three quarters of a mile South East of Point Brea, and at a gradual ascent of about Eighty feet from the level of the sea, the Bitumen taking the appearance of Laver [lava?] covers the surface of the Ground to a considerable distance in all directions, and forms a firm good road. The Lake extends one mile East and West, and about three quarters North and South, intersected by Springs of Pure Water, the non-reflection of the surface generally preserves it sufficiently firm to walk upon. There are two or three spots strongly impregnated by Oily or Unctious propertys nearly liquidated which from its appearance would require very little preparation to answer Naval purposes, if prepared upon the Spot, but its removal with all its impuritys would be attended with great inconvenience and Expence.

Kingston followed up Lockwood's report with a request for naval contracts to cultivate the hemp crop, and on 11 June, at anchor in Carlisle Bay, Cochrane informed the Admiralty that he had sent three parcels of 'small cordage made from the wild hemp of Trinidad, also some of the hemp, and its seed together with parcels of Hemp from the Aloe and Plaintain Trees.' He also ordered the planting of 'a small plot of ground' with hemp.[33]

This diversion during the early months of 1808 illustrates Cochrane's confidence in Lockwood as a handy and reliable officer. The Trinidad report is little more than a preliminary survey but it carried conviction enough to persuade a powerful admiral. Cochrane's continued favour was indeed crucial. It had lifted Lockwood after the Channel Islands debacle; now it gave him opportunity to demonstrate special abilities. Perhaps inspired to further demonstration, at some time during 1808 he also prepared 'A Plan of the Anchorage at Barbados', on a scale of six miles to an inch, with sailing instructions for entering Carlisle Bay, and including the whole sweep from Bridgetown to Needham Point. He also made a signed sketch of part of the Bay, dated 5 October that year, showing Pier Head Battery, on the south side of the Careenage, with the purchases attaching the wreck *Columbia* to the shore and to a vessel named the *Edward*.[34]

Soon Cochrane called on Lockwood again, but this time the mission was to run foul of the disorganised command structure on foreign stations. On 25 February 1809, the day following the surrender of Martinique, Cochrane issued an order for Lockwood to act at Martinique 'as Master Attendant at the Temporary Depot, giving the Naval Stores contained

therein into the charge of Mr Belleville Store-keeper's Clerk, who is
instructed to obey your direction: and as there is a number of wrecks in
the careenage which will require to be cleared away, you are to remain here
on this duty, and that of Master Attendant until I shall judge it necessary
for you to return to your duty at Barbados.' By 1 March Lockwood was
able to send Cochrane 'a list of the public Naval Buildings received from the
Captaine de Port.' But naval protocol then raised an ugly head. Cochrane
had been instructed to transport the Commissioner at English Harbour,
Antigua, Commodore Charles White, to Barbados, and this brought White
into contact with Lockwood. On 2 June Cochrane wrote to the Admiralty
from Martinique that on the sloop carrying Commissioner White

> calling at Fort Royal Martinique, Commissioner White took upon himself
> to find fault with Mr Lockwood's, the Master Attendant at the naval yard
> at Barbadoes, having been employed there, agreeably to the enclosed
> order, and directed him immediately to leave the Duties I had employed
> him upon, and return to Barbadoes, and as Mr Lockwood did not think
> himself justified in abandoning that Service, without orders from me, the
> Commissioner has superceded him from his Appointment, conceiving that
> this was an assumption of Power not warranted by his Instructions which
> were confined to the settling of the storekeeper's accounts, I have resisted
> his being deprived of his situation, and shall direct his being continued in
> office until the pleasure of the Lords Commissioners of the Admiralty is
> conveyed to me.
>
> As the Establishment was to be a temporary one to the Squadron, I ever
> considered it to be under my immediate direction in like measure with
> Yards where there is no resident commissioner.[35]

White, like other naval commissioners, was responsible to the Navy Board,
as were masters attendant. In most instances the Admiralty would dis-
engage from a case of this nature but once again the authority of a
squadron commander was being challenged and the issue was plain enough
from the Admiralty viewpoint. No commissioner could be allowed to
override the order of an admiral at sea, let alone that of Sir Alexander
Cochrane who was promoted to vice admiral following the capture of
Martinique. So the Lords Commissioners found themselves inquiring into
the conduct of the same master, third rate, in irregular circumstances, twice
within three years – the main difference, of course, being Lockwood's
position apropos the local commander.

The protocol question was made more intractable because of a report
that White had been guilty of intemperate language. Cochrane's secretary,
John Tracy, had written to him on 11 May that he had 'heard from

numerous quarters of the Commissioner's having made use of language tending to asperse your conduct.' This conflicted with the friendly tone of White's own correspondence, but such tattling reports can have serious consequences.[36]

John Barrow, second secretary to the Admiralty, seems to have been somewhat confused by Cochrane's scrambling grammar, but lost no time in informing the Navy Board of their Lordships' censure of White's conduct in suspending Lockwood 'from his duties as Master Attendant at Barbadoes.' The Board then despatched to White an extract from this letter of 30 June with its own covering letter of 6 July which supported his basic stand that the commander-in-chief was wrongly interfering in matters concerning the officers of the yards.[37] Such equivocation was typical of relations between the Board and the Admiralty. It led White to attempt to justify himself to the Navy Board, and in the process, widened the scope of his complaint.

It appears that Lockwood was at least in part the one to blame for the service quarrel. White asserted that he had been ordered to Barbados 'for the purpose of Inspecting and correcting the existing abuses at that Yard.' Whatever these abuses were, they clearly reflected upon Lockwood. According to White, on his arrival at Bridgetown, Lockwood had refused to 'attend' him. Explaining that 'motives of delicacy' had made him confine his account of the affair to the strict circumstances, White observed to the Navy Board that the Admiralty had now in effect condoned Lockwood's refusal to account for his management of the dockyard.[38] If the beating of Icarus's wings can be heard, this time Lockwood had a powerful patron.

In a letter of 15 August to Barrow and the Admiralty, enclosed with that above, White insisted that his correspondence with Cochrane would show he had wished to consult with the station commander, but had been prevented by the pursuit of the enemy. Then he went on to say that 'Mr Lockwood was employed at Martinique in the recovering of Prize Goods for the benefits of the Captors for which a 15 per Cent was paid, as I heard, to him.' Whether or not that was the correct figure, 'doubtless he got some profit from it.' White may have wanted the money for himself, but he painted a picture of his concern for the King's business. 'He,' Lockwood, 'was also holding the position of Deputy Harbour Master with an adequate salary, and if he attended to the Duties of that occupation he must necessarily have neglected others.' Again, White insisted that motives of delicacy had led him to omit much from his earlier report of 5 May.[39]

The Navy Board gave some support to White in conveying this letter to the Admiralty, but the outcome could hardly be in doubt as long as Cochrane asserted his rank. White wrote again to the Navy Board on 10 September, whereupon the Board concluded that in 'the peculiar circumstances of the case' Cochrane's orders were 'absolutely necessary.'[40] Nevertheless Barrow dispatched White's letter to Cochrane on 2 December, for his comments, which he did in a very long reply, reminiscent of Sir James Saumarez when roused. Cochrane not only defended Lockwood, he informed the Board that he intended to make further use of this estimable officer: 'When Mr Lockwood has completed the removal of the Hulks, it is my intention he should be employed in surveying the Coast of Guadaloupe which has never been done well, and is much wanted.'[41] This ended the White affair. White himself was too ill to fight anyway. After sinking steadily for four months, he died at Antigua in early April 1810, never having got round to defining the 'abuses' at the Barbados yard.

Cochrane must have known something about the Saumarez episode, but he considered Lockwood to be a valuable officer: 'No man so equal to the task' at Martinique, Lockwood would get the survey 'done well'. Cochrane's response was that of an officer on active service irritated by White's petty 'intermeddling' in the field of action. The fifteen per cent commission Lockwood took for salvaging and selling prizes he saw simply as a pragmatic on-the-spot arrangement to which petty accounting procedures devised at home were irrelevant. In the same way, if Lockwood was 'double-billing' by paying himself for two jobs – then why not? He was doing them both. Good men were dying like flies in the West Indies.

Even before this last letter was dispatched, Lockwood had himself gone on to the attack, clearly knowing the strength of Cochrane's support and perhaps hoping for belated redress from the Admiralty. On 1 December 1809 he wrote to the Admiralty First Secretary, William Wellesley Pole, requesting official confirmation of his appointment as master attendant at Barbados 'or some other of His Majesty's Yards' and also claiming recompense for his house rent and stationary costs from 1 July 1807, from which he dated his order from Cochrane. But the Board refused to alter his salary and passed on his letter to the Navy Board, which in turn failed to see the need for an established position of master attendant at Barbados. Nothing had changed – except to reinforce Lockwood's sense of his own merit scorned.

Returning, presumably happily, to his preferred occupation, Lockwood proceeded to the vicinity of Guadeloupe where he completed his survey later that same year. He subsequently produced a chart of the Saintes, a group of islands between Guadeloupe and Dominica that was regularly used by the French Navy as an operational anchorage.[42] After Guadeloupe, he may well have spent a few months at Bridgetown, but he was then appointed to undertake another survey. By that date Cochrane had been relieved of his command, but the new squadron commander, Rear Admiral Sir Francis Laforey, was happy to make use of Lockwood's

abilities. In answer to a later query by the Lords Commissioners as to
'Why was survey done?' Laforey explained that when in October 1810 he
was taking his leave of the new First Lord, Charles Philip Yorke, who had
succeeded Lord Mulgrave in May of that year, 'he desired that I would
have a survey taken of Tortola in consequence of several Line of Battle
ships that had arrived from the Leeward Island Station having been on
shore at that Anchorage.' At Barbados Laforey had found Lockwood,
'who had been employed by the Lords Commissioners of the Admiralty
in the years 1805 and 1806 in taking a Survey of the Anchorages &
Passages about the Island of Guernsey', and directed him to prepare a
chart of Tortola and the Virgin Islands.[43] It seems likely that Laforey knew
little about the Guernsey survey – mention of it could hardly commend
Lockwood to the Lords Commissioners – and presumably his source was
Lockwood himself. It seems curious that Laforey failed to mention the
much more recent chart of the Saintes.

The main part of the Tortola survey was carried out between 1 April and
3 November 1811. After its completion, and the preparation of a chart,
Lockwood submitted an itemised expenses claim on 7 December amounting to $1,446 dollars divided, unusually, into fifty-sixths. It provides a
useful profile of the working necessities of such a task:

> travelling expenses ascending heights, etc. $109 15/56; 12 foot boat
> purchased at Tortola for landing in shallow Bays $60 48/56; An Anchor
> of 268 lbs for mooring Boats on Banks & fixing their position $47 48/56;
> Grapnel of 84 lbs used same purpose esp. determining the position of
> Snake Bank off Tortola $9 42/56; An Iron Stocked Anchor 125 lbs lost in
> Tortola Roads $12; 32 Log Lines for measuring small distances & 10
> small lead lines $29 8/56; Carpenter paid to repair Boats damaged when
> driven on reefs in the Gale of July 1811 $45 54/56; Men hired as Pilots
> and to assist in Sounding & from the different small islands who would
> not serve unless paid on the spot $197; axes for the purpose of clearing
> station ground $9; stationary $61 37/56; Hire of sloop Lydia 30 Tons
> Burthen coppered and completely equipped from April 1 1811 to
> November 3 following $864.

Lockwood also included sworn statements by Jas Haswell and John
Ironmonger, who he described as 'merchants and owners of vessels trading
in the Leeward Islands', testifying that the rental of the *Lydia* was fair. He
noted that he had made no charge for 'Instruments necessary for a Work
of such Magnitude', an obvious reference to his old complaint about the
Navy's parsimoniousness in the matter of surveyors' tools. Lockwood asked
that the storekeeper at Barbados be authorised by the Navy Board to pay

these expenses and Laforey despatched the claim with a covering letter dated 31 December 1811. The chart itself was sent to London by the *Gloire* soon afterwards, and after some huffing and puffing by the Admiralty concerning authorisation for the survey Lockwood received his money and the Hydrographic Office the chart.[44]

Lockwood's continued absence on these surveys at last brought the Admiralty to share the Navy Board's doubts as to whether the Barbados yard really needed a master attendant. Though 1813 was the peak year for British naval expenditures during the war, Napoleon's disastrous Russian campaign and the battles of Borodino and Leipzig were dragging him down to defeat. Consequently, the Admiralty began to reduce its establishment. The case for Lockwood was not compelling. Laforey defended him as 'being the only professional Officer in that department, independent of the various duties which call him afloat, his attendance is most effective to superintend the reception and delivery of stores, to direct the alteration of Sails, a thing invariably required before they can be used, and to assist at the taking of Surveys.'[45] On 8 December 1813 the Lords Commissioners nevertheless gave him notice that he was discharged as master attendant from the end of that month.[46]

They might have considered that Barbados was becoming central in the new naval war that had commenced with the American declaration on 19 June 1812. But the Board's release of Lockwood was to prove providential for him, by making him available for the survey work needed for the new area of naval operations. The ostensible grounds for the American declaration had cited the Royal Navy's practice of boarding American vessels and pressing seaman it believed to be British subjects, including using armed force against a US warship, and the British response to Napoleon's 'Continental System' by Orders in Council setting up a blockade of European ports that forced neutral American shippers to pay duty in Britain. But the more substantial motive for war was a determination to annex present-day Canada, and it was to Canada that Lockwood was to proceed.

Again, Cochrane was the instrument. He had been very busy in the early months of 1813. Under the overall command of Vice Admiral Sir John Warren, Cochrane had made punitive raids along the eastern seaboard of the United States, to divert American energies from the war in Canada. He had returned to Britain at the time of Lockwood's dismissal, where he was appointed commander-in-chief of the North Atlantic fleet in succession to Warren. His status was never higher and again he weighed in heavily on Lockwood's behalf.

In 1807 the Admiralty had appointed a committee of sea officers headed by Captain Thomas Hurd, 'to make a selection of Charts, etc, for the use of His Majesty's Navy', and its first report, of 27 November 1807, was concerned with the 'Coast of North America from the River St John, in the Bay of Fundy, to Rhode Island.' The committee had noted that the survey that had been made by Joseph Frederick Wallet Desbarres (1722–1824) and published in 1778 as *The Atlantic Neptune* 'extended no further than St John's River' and that there were 'innumerable errors and omissions' when compared to Captain Hurd's own survey of 1775.[47] Now Cochrane took the initiative. In the first days of 1814 he submitted to the Board 'the advantage it would be to the Service if two surveyors were employed, one for the coast south of Rhode Island and the other to correct the numerous errors to be found in the Charts published by Desbarres and others. If this meets with their Lordships concurrence I consider Mr Lockwood the present Master Attendant at Barbadoes to be a person well qualified to perform one of these services.'[48]

The Board sought the advice of Captain Hurd who had succeeded Dalrymple as Admiralty hydrographer, following the latter's violent response to the work of the Hurd committee. Lockwood had already come to Hurd's attention as a result of his having prepared a reduced scale 'Plan' of his Tortola survey. He had sought Laforey's support for its publication, subject to the Board's approval, and written a letter to the Board on 29 October 1812 that had been passed on to Captain Hurd as hydrographer. Hurd's response of 4 January 1813 was distinctly cool: 'Mr Lockwood's Survey of the Virgin Islands was received from Sir Francis Laforey in June last and has a material error in its constitution. The one on a reduced scale alluded to in this Letter has not made its appearance in this office.' However, with apparent disdain for the opinion they sought from their own hydrographer, the Board swiftly approved the printing of the reduced scale chart on its arrival. Engraved by S Stockley, it was published in London less than a month later, on 2 February 1813.[49] With this evidence that the Board was now behind Lockwood, no doubt because of Cochrane's support, Hurd avoided giving an opinion of Lockwood's suitability for the job. Instead, he equivocally begged to 'point out to their Lordships a Mr De Mayne, the Master of His Majesty's Ship *Horatio* as a person equally qualified with Mr Lockwood for such an appointment: as one to whom we are indebted for many valuable surveys . . . acquired during his services in the *Amelia* off the coast of Africa with which he has enriched this office.' But he agreed that two surveying officers should be employed, expressing the hope that this would become policy, and by 11 January 1814 both De Mayne and Lockwood had been approved.[50]

On 19 January 1814, before he received this order, Lockwood had written to the First Lord, now the younger Lord Melville, hoping to retain his position at Barbados: 'So many years having elapsed without receiving a Confirmation to the Appointment with which I was honored by Sir Alexander Cochrane . . . and as that Gentleman is in Town may if your Lordship thinks proper be referred to.'[51] He also formally wrote the Navy Board requesting that his position be made permanent, which as a matter of course it refused to do on 19 April.[52] Before this letter was received at the Admiralty, however, Melville dispatched an order to Lockwood to conduct 'such Surveys of the Coast of America as Vice Admiral Sir Alexander Cochrane . . . shall think fit', with an allowance of one guinea a day and provisions 'in the vessel in which you may be borne.'[53]

Cochrane took over from Warren on 1 April, and on the 25th he ordered the blockade of the United States seaboard to be extended to New England. He nevertheless found time to write on 21 May from Bermuda to Rear Admiral Philip Durham, with the information that the Admiralty had ordered Lockwood 'to put himself under my command for the purpose of his making surveys upon the coast of America.'[54] Durham was to transmit the order, and arrange passage for him to Bermuda, 'to join me there or wherever else I may be by the first vessel of war coming this way.' A copy of the order was enclosed, with the direction to Lockwood: 'you will lose no time in repairing to join me', and the package was dispatched by the *Heron* on 24 May.[55]

Lockwood left Barbados on 25 June and joined Cochrane at Bermuda on 19 July, where he received more detailed instruction concerning his survey before Cochrane departed to direct the naval forces for the assault on Washington in which the Capitol and the White House would be torched.[56] His protégé, meanwhile, sailed north to the cold and rockbound Canadian shores. He was done with coral beaches and mangrove swamps.

4

An Emissary of Light

LOCKWOOD REACHED HALIFAX by late September 1814, four months after the signing of the Peace of Paris bringing an end to the war with France, two months before the Treaty of Ghent on 24 December 1814 concluding the war with the United States, and nine months before the Treaty of Vienna following Napoleon's Hundred Days and defeat at Waterloo. The war was all but over in the waters of Nova Scotia, and Lockwood's employment was peaceful in nature. On the face of it, the survey was a splendid opportunity. It had scope and magnitude; it also set him in distinguished company, since Desbarres's North American coastal charts in *The Atlantic Neptune* had been recognised as a signal achievement. Directed by Cochrane to correct the *Neptune* where necessary, Lockwood's professional competence had been publicly asserted. But there were also problems.

Captain Hurd had approved the work, but grudgingly. He and Desbarres were in dispute about their own respective surveys, and Lockwood's situation was inevitably a difficult one. The Admiralty's willingness to pay for hydrographic survey work had been stimulated by the needs of a navy at war, and the outbreak of peace put the future of Lockwood's employment at risk.

Desbarres was a soldier, commissioned in 1756, who had been seconded to the Navy for the survey work following the Peace of Paris in 1762 when New France and Acadia were permanently ceded to Britain. His vessel, the *Diligent*, was aptly named. He had spent a decade on his surveys, employing small shallops for the inshore work, and sending the measured distances and angles to Castle Frederick, his home near Falmouth, Nova Scotia, for transcription by assistants.[1] He spent two years just on the hydrographic survey of Sable Island. By a happy accident he had been in Britain arranging the printing of his charts when the American Revolutionary War broke out, ensuring that *The Atlantic Neptune* was deemed urgently necessary for naval commanders and merchantmen.

The ad hoc arrangements for his surveys, and for their publication, had led to enormously protracted wrangles with the Admiralty over expenses, and had plainly demonstrated the need for an agency such as the Hydrographic Office. Desbarres had had no settled staff or allocation of funds; he had recruited and paid his assistants personally, sometimes negotiating with naval commanders for the temporary transfer of men. Ownership of the *Neptune* plates was disputed between the Admiralty and Desbarres for thirty-five years. He was still living at Amherst, Nova Scotia, at the age of ninety-three when Lockwood arrived in Halifax, and would survive for eight more years. In 1813 he had sent his son, James Luttrell, to press the case in London concerning unresolved *Neptune* issues, as well as the matter of Desbarres' pension and the complex legal squabble over his vast estate at Memramcook, NB. The Desbarres family, while quarrelling amongst themselves, would carry on this fight for years to come.[2]

The dispute within the ranks of the hydrographic service would impact on Lockwood's work, and prospects. When the younger Desbarres arrived in London, Hurd had been asked by the Admiralty for his opinion concerning the value of reprinting the *Neptune* charts. But Hurd's opinion was deeply tainted. Between 1784 and 1820 Cape Breton Island had been administered independently of Nova Scotia, and in 1785 Hurd had been appointed its Surveyor General. A year later he had been removed from his post by none other than Desbarres who was serving as the colony's first British Lieutenant Governor. Moreover, by the time the Admiralty sought his advice concerning the *Neptune*, Hurd was peddling his own Nova Scotia charts. This was described by one of James Luttrell's friends as 'a bastard work of his in Embryo for which he has already received £12,000 with the prospect of drawing an annuity.'[3] No wonder James Luttrell described Hurd to his father as 'one of your worst enemies' in a letter of 28 January 1814, written at the very time Sir Alexander Cochrane proposed Lockwood to the Admiralty specifically to correct the charts of Desbarres and Hurd.[4] In putting forward Lockwood, Cochrane had thus declared a plague on both houses and held out the prospect of a set of charts which would be up to date and incontestably owned by the Navy.

It is little wonder therefore that Hurd approved of Lockwood's appointment only grudgingly, though, in fairness, he may have felt genuine professional misgivings, having found Lockwood's 1805 survey of Falmouth to be seriously at fault, and believing there to be a 'material error' in Lockwood's 1809 survey of the Saintes. None of Lockwood's hydrographic work, furthermore, had been directed by the Hydrographic Office, and for the last eight years he had operated at a great distance from the Admiralty itself, under warrants from Cochrane and Laforey. So the hydrographer might have reasonable reservations about the man now engaged, in part, ostensibly to correct or supersede not only Desbarres' charts but also Hurd's own. For the moment, Hurd prudently bowed to Cochrane, but the hydrographer was a serious enemy for a naval surveyor.

The circumstances were to escalate Lockwood's almost perpetual search for stable employment that was consistent with his abilities, not his humble birth. He evidently found Nova Scotia and New Brunswick to his liking, and much of his energy was to be directed towards finding a way to make a future there for himself and his family. On 13 October he began to muster a sloop, which he named the *Examiner*, and would command for the next three years.[5] The name was of course perfectly appropriate for a surveying vessel, but their might have been a political, and seditious, implication. *The Examiner* was also the title of Leigh Hunt's reformist weekly London newspaper, notoriously hostile to government policy. For scathing criticism in *The Examiner* in March 1812 of the Prince of Wales, the Prince Regent and future King George IV, Hunt and his brother were sentenced to two years in separate prisons, though *The Examiner* continued to appear and Leigh Hunt continued to contribute to it. He was released in February 1815, not long after Lockwood had set up ship.

The province of Nova Scotia had extended to the Quebec border before the influx of Loyalist refugees in 1783–4, after which New Brunswick was carved out of the territory to the west of the Bay of Fundy. Halifax was by far the largest centre of population in the region, with about twelve thousand people in 1812. The port had been the operating base for both the British Army and Navy during the Revolutionary War. The Royal Navy still maintained its North American squadron there each year from June to the end of the hurricane season in November, when it sailed for Bermuda. Nova Scotian ports had also been notable privateering centres for harassing New England commerce. Lockwood's patron, Sir Alexander Cochrane, while commanding the squadron, had acquired extensive estates in Nova Scotia.

For some years in the 1790s Halifax acquired a certain social cachet. Two royal princes, the carousing naval officer William, known popularly as 'Sailor Billy' or 'Silly Billy', later Duke of Clarence, and eventually succeeding to the throne as William IV, and his brother Edward, later Duke of Kent, who would command land forces in British North America. Their exploits, drunken or amatory, were fresh in the communal memory. William had installed his mistress, a Madame St Laurent, in the summer house known as Friar Lawrence's Cell on the shore of the Bedford Basin, owned by the Surveyor General of Woods, John Wentworth. William also built an Italianate villa for himself in the vicinity. Wentworth assisted William further by allowing Wentworth's wife, Frances, to supplant or supplement Madame St Laurent. His reward came in 1792 when the now Duke of Clarence obtained his elevation by a knighthood, and the office of

Governor of Nova Scotia.[6] Edward, meanwhile, permitted Wentworth to use his Bedford Basin lodge after his departure for England in 1798. The shores of the Basin became fashionable. The well-to-do built their own villas there, and after his dismissal as governor in 1808, Wentworth withdrew there. In his very person, however, he kept alive the shameful connivings of past years, a living tribute to the merits of royal service. Old and withdrawn though he was, he would play a part in Lockwood's story.

By 1814 the princes were long gone, and, as a result of demobilisation and the dispersal of manpower to the citadel at Quebec and to other garrisons in British North America, the fortress built by the Duke of Kent on Citadel Hill was sparsely manned. Though many troops passed through in transit, the garrison, according to Governor Sir John Sherbrooke in 1811, 'was barely enough to fill St Paul's at a church parade.'[7] Halifax was still a great port. Its fine natural harbour, largely ice-free, and positioned as first port-of-call for many vessels bound for British North America or the United States, meant that it also attracted a merchant fleet. This was particularly true after 1813, with the need for protection against hostile American warships and privateers.[8] This was a short-lived boom-time, with the dockyards fully-employed and seamen ashore with pay in their pockets. But it was a violent town, and a filthy one, with the incidence of disease high despite the cool climate.

Lockwood's first months in Halifax during that winter of 1814–15 coincided with a severe outbreak of smallpox, and after peace was belatedly proclaimed in Halifax on 3 March 1815, the immediate post-war period was especially violent.[9] Only then were a court, a jail, and a rudimentary police force established in Halifax. Lockwood, however, had grown up in the rougher east end of London, in Whitechapel, and he had lived in docklands or at sea for most of his adult life. He could take care of himself. If Halifax was a rough town there was a lot of expansive optimism about its future and that of the colony.

On his arrival in Nova Scotia, Lockwood had his usual almost pro forma dispute with the Navy Board and Admiralty concerning pay and expenses. He attempted to retain some proportion of his pay as master attendant at Bridgetown while conducting his North America survey, even though a 'Mr Miller master of the flag ship' had been appointed to take his place 'until my return.'[10] Although this claim was not accepted, the Admiralty did query the Navy Board as to what pay Lockwood should be allowed during the survey, and it was set at thirty shillings per diem.[11]

That settled, Lockwood set about making himself comfortable, building a cabin on the west side of the Bedford Basin among the wealthier classes, between the mouth of Salmon River and Indian Island and close to the Hammonds Plains road. Examiner's logs show that she was often to be

moored in the Basin, a short pull on the oars from Lockwood's dwelling.
Sir John Sherbrooke was a neighbour at nearby Birch Cove.[12] Prince's
Lodge, the residence of the Duke of Kent, was still there, though slipping
into disrepair.

Not content with that, Lockwood turned his mind to the future even
before *Examiner* completed her seagoing muster. In a land grant petition to
Sherbrooke dated at the Council Chambers, Halifax, 1 March 1815, he
claimed to be 'a Native of England [who] has served in the Navy since 1791
actively and zealously employed', and he based his claim on the ground
that he 'was called by the Lords Commissioners of the Admiralty to the
difficult and hazardous task of surveying the dangers of this coast.' He said
he was 'desirous of Possessing lands which he may improve and to which
he may retreat after his Hydrographical labors are at an end.' Nobody
apparently checked Lockwood's claim, backdating his naval service by four
years, and he was recommended for five hundred acres three days later,
although the grant was not to be finally authorised until 21 April 1817,
when the Surveyor General of Nova Scotia, Charles Morris or his deputy
was directed to survey the acreage. This was completed by 18 October of
that year, nine hundred acres in total being granted on the east side of
Lochaber Lake to Lockwood and to one John Adam Biswanger 'Late of
the 60th Regiment.' The latter had earlier been given a warrant of survey
on Hammonds Plain, near Lockwood's cabin. Some friendship between
them can be assumed.[13]

Lockwood was taking advantage of the post-war encouragement to
military settlers, but he also had the examples before him of Desbarres,
who had been granted huge estates in New Brunswick and Nova Scotia,
and of Sir Alexander Cochrane himself, who as early as 1796 had been
granted 2,500 acres on Colchester Bay, with title to Pictou Island. In 1814,
the year of Lockwood's arrival in the province, Cochrane purchased
another thousand acres, the old Fort Ellis estate at Stewiacke.[14]

While Lockwood made prudent provision for the future in the spring of
1815, he seems also to have developed some sort of relationship with a
woman by the name of Ann Campbell, who was delivered of a baby boy
in Halifax on 1 December 1815. But it is by no means clear that Ann's
motherhood should be taken as proving Lockwood's virility. The boy was
named Henry Arcade, but he was not baptised until much later, at St
George's Church on 17 July 1821. At that point Lockwood's paternity was
indicated. His rather grand description in the register as Surveyor General
of New Brunswick and 'the author of a treatise on the Bays and Harbours
of N S.' implies a pride of achievement, and suggests that Lockwood was
actually present at the baptism and prompted whoever made the entry. The
choice of names suggests Lockwood's choosing. Henry recurred among the

London Lockwoods, while Arcade echoes the romantic naming of Marina, his daughter of the sea, and reflects Lockwood's new horizons in Acadia, the French name for Nova Scotia. Despite his own insistence in the Introduction to his *Description of Nova Scotia* that 'plain truth must substitute decoration', the names of these natural children speak of something expansively self-defining. But children out of wedlock they were, and the fact that Lockwood's name was given to the boy six years after his birth may mostly reflect Ann's hopes for material support, and with Lockwood's love of children, and possibly also his need to demonstrate a potency that might have been lost years before to disease.[15]

At about the same time that Ann was being delivered of the baby, it appears from admittedly limited evidence that Harriet, Anthony junior, Sarah, and Marina travelled from Barbados to join Lockwood at Halifax. Anthony Lockwood junior had certainly arrived, for he was entered in the *Examiner*'s muster for 1 January 1816.

The narrative of Lockwood's North American survey is buried in the bald statements of activity recorded in the officers' log books, and in the *Examiner*'s musters. The surviving captain's log covers the period 1 July 1815 to 31 December 1816, while those of the second masters William Grant and J Turner extend from 20 March 1815 to 29 September 1817, when the crew was discharged.[16] No logs apparently survive for 14 October 1814 to 20 March 1815, while the captain's is also missing for 1 January to 29 September 1817. The story these documents present is far from complete. For lengthy periods, for instance, neither Grant nor Turner mentions Lockwood by name. The boats go out to survey, *Examiner* continues to sound, but was the commander always on board, in command? His absence might have been explained by the need to take trigonometric sightings, but the masters' logs fail to illuminate this. Lockwood's own log, furthermore, is not in his hand. *Examiner* carried a clerk and though many of the entries are in the first person, substitutions were clearly possible. And what is to be made of the fact that for considerable periods a captain's log does not survive?

The *Examiner* had a nominal complement of twenty-five but the crew was constantly changing. The first muster, on 13 October 1814, listed thirteen names.[17] Two were boys obtained from HMS *Centurion*, and throughout the survey other crewmen were acquired from or exchanged with various naval vessels at Canso, Prince Edward Island, Pictou, or Saint John, but mostly at Halifax. They generally left 'by order' or 'by duty', and their diversity illustrates the fluid and heterogeneous composition of the Royal Navy. During the two month period between 1 September and 31 October 1815, for instance, no fewer than forty-five men were entered into

Examiner's muster. It is probable that the William Lee being paid as an able seaman, birthplace Cape Coast Africa, was the same boy Lockwood sold to William Marcher two years later. If so, and Lockwood concealed his slave status on *Examiner*'s muster, he must himself have collected the pay. Local pilots were taken on every few miles, although none was required for Halifax harbour.[18]

During the earliest period of *Examiner*'s service, the small size of the muster suggests that she spent her time fitting out or confined to Halifax Harbour and Bedford Basin. Lockwood needed some time before setting out to examine the available charts, especially *The Atlantic Neptune*, to take local advice, and to plan the timetable and general strategy of his survey. It is also possible he gave priority to building his cabin during the winter months, establishing his land base. Apart from that, there was his social life with Ann Campbell.

The chronicle of the survey work on the *Examiner* commences with William Grant's log, beginning on 20 March 1815, the day he entered the ship while she rode at single anchor in Halifax Harbour, noting the 'strong Gales and Cloudy Weather.' For the first two months his log provides a fairly detailed summary of the expedition, but it also leaves many questions unanswered. On 21 March *Examiner* started drawing stores from the dockyard and artificers made her ready as she exchanged seamen with *Centurion*. Another nine men joined from *Tenedos* on the 26th, and at 3pm she weighed anchor and worked up into the Bedford Basin where she spent the next two days taking soundings. At 6pm on the 29th she anchored at Herring Cove close outside Halifax, running out in the morning to 'examine the rocks and shoals at the entrance of Halifax harbor', where further soundings were taken. The following day she ran to the careening wharf and took on two tons of iron ballast. They were 'hanging by the [Naval] Commissioner's Yacht' on 5 April before arming themselves by taking on board a 6-pound brass cannon at the ordinance wharf on the 6th, slipping down the harbour at 1.30pm to round Thrumb at four, Jedore Head at eight, and finally anchoring in Jeddore Harbour forty or so miles up the Eastern Shore of Nova Scotia, north of Halifax.

Survey work is hard, and often dangerous, but any account of it is bound to be repetitious. In the morning 'Mr Lockwood [was] away with the Boats measuring a Baseline and Surveying the Harbor.' They continued to survey the harbour for another day, and on the 9th the crew were granted shore leave. The following day *Examiner* made sail through gales and squalls, coasting further up the Eastern Shore, grounding briefly, but reaching Sheet Harbour on the 11th. In the afternoon Lockwood took the boats sounding and surveying four miles up harbour, returning in the evening of the 12th. They surveyed 'Salisbery' Island on the 13th until gales drove them back into Sheet Harbour, where *Examiner* grounded while turning through the Narrows. Next day they ran to Beaver Harbour, at 11am grounding yet again on a spit, and for a time the vessel was 'lashed to the trees.' Freed once more, they waited out 'strong gales and heavy snow' on the morning of 15 April but in the afternoon and evening Lockwood surveyed Newton Quoddy, probably in present day Quoddy Harbour east of Beaver Harbour. Grant's entry for the 16th is starkly eloquent: 'Running along shore among the Rocks and Breakers.' They reached Country Harbour safely, however, and on the following day Lockwood and others examined the head of the harbour.

Most of May was spent in and about Halifax Harbour, and in surveying some back country lakes. Hurd was later 'at a loss to conceive' why, 'as Des Barres charts will answer every purpose.'[19] The weather probably convinced Lockwood that a fuller coastal survey must wait, but there is something decidedly erratic about his choice of surveying sites. Lockwood often spent only a few hours sounding and surveying bays and islands of this highly indented and complex coastline. Was he simply going through the motions? The evidence suggests that very early on he doubted the future of his survey and felt uncertain of its continuance.

In June and early July *Examiner* ran up the Eastern shore again, surveyed Cranberry Island near Canso at the easternmost point of mainland Nova Scotia, and then into the Bras d'Ore Lakes of Cape Breton Island.[20] A few days after returning to Halifax he headed south, rounding Cape Sable Island and crossing the Bay of Fundy to Saint John, New Brunswick.[21] *Examiner* remained there only two days, tied to the wharf, undergoing repairs, and left at 8am on the 21st, 'running among the Wolves Islands' by late morning, and at 3pm rounded the Swallow tail at the north end of Grand Manan Island.

Lockwood and a crew surveyed in boats next day but *Examiner* grounded on the Bar between Cheney and Ross Island southeast of Grand Manan on the 23rd. This is a bad spot to go aground on the ebb, with the tide setting onto a spit of rock. The crew 'threw everything overboard lying about the Decks to lighten her, and all the shot out of the lockers the arm and ammunition chests, [but with the] water leaving her fast, got the Shears out.' Having spent the night aground, kept more or less upright by the shear legs, the next day, after they 'got 2 Brass guns on shore & the Anchors down etc to lighten her', she rose 'gradually with the Tide without the least strain . . . [and] at 1 drew off the Bar.' That evening Lockwood anchored off Edmunds Rock east of Ross Island. By the 26th *Examiner* was standing along the eastern shore of the Bay of Fundy, and next day they surveyed Grand Passage between Brier Island and Long Island, and were off Seal Island at the southwest corner of Nova Scotia on the 29th. Between 30 July and 3 August they rounded Cape Sable to Shelburne. During this time, sometimes by firing shots, they 'brought to and examined several fishing vessels', presumably seeking Americans illegally fishing or carrying contraband. *Examiner*'s muster for the period includes four American prisoners at two-thirds allowance. They were discharged at Shelburne on 4 August.[22]

Returning to Halifax again for repairs, replenishment, and shore leave, on 18th August they 'cleared the run and found an incredible number of young rats. Employed fumigating it with Vinegar.' *Examiner*'s next voyage was a long run up to Pictou and Prince Edward Island, but the time spent on it conducting surveys was even more limited.[23]

On 17 October 1815, while near Ragged Isle Harbour, Lockport, an American schooner was boarded. She proved, Lockwood noted, 'to be the *Henry*, fishing vessel and had been previously boarded, and warned off by the *Jaseur*, left 1 man in charge of her.' Next day 'at 6 sent a party of men alongside the detained Schooner, who were opposed by the Americans.' Lockwood then 'manned and armed the Boats, and sent them.' Finally, 'at 7 succeeded in taking the American Crew out.' He 'sent an officer and 3 men on board the Schooner to conduct her to Shelburne' on the 19th. Having turned his capture over, Lockwood continued along the coast, and on 27 October at Cape Negro suffered a serious misfortune. Lockwood 'sent the Boat away for a Pilot, at 11 came on a tremendous Squall, which upset the Boat, and sunk her.' Two men, Clause [*sic*] Nelson, a Dane, and the American Robert Dunkinson, were drowned. *Examiner* returned to Halifax by the beginning of November, where she would remain until the middle of April 1816, surrounded for some time by drift ice.[24]

The evidence suggests that from the beginning Lockwood was less interested in the immediate task than he was in finding a more certain career, or of ensuring that the one he was in survived the inevitable economies following the end of the war. There is nothing surprising in this: it is the unavoidable consequence of keeping people on short or indefinite contracts. The warrant for Lockwood's survey was at Cochrane's pleasure, and his patron's own commission was for a limited period. The latter sailed from Bermuda for England on 23 April 1815. Rear Admiral Edward Griffith, who took over the command, assumed all standing orders for the station, including both Lockwood's and those of De Mayne who was engaged on a survey of the Bahamas in the cutter *Landrail*.[25] But as Lockwood had learned the hard way, there was no substitute in the Navy for a firm patron.

In the light of this uncertainty, it is not surprising that early in 1815 Lockwood petitioned Sir John Sherbrooke on the subject of the province's lighthouses. He needed a new, and local, patron. Sherbrooke's response was positive. Lockwood was informed that 'his Excellency will with great pleasure receive from you any information . . . likely to be of benefit to the Public', although he was warned not to publish anything on the matter without Sherbrooke's permission.[26] Lockwood acted with despatch. Writing from St Mary's River west of Country Harbour on the Eastern Shore on 26 June 1815 to Michael Wallace, who was a member of the Executive Council, he described a visit to Cranberry Island accompanied by a Mr Lanagan, who 'perfectly concurred' with him on 'the best position for the proposed building' which Lockwood indicated on a beautifully drawn sketch. 'The Light will embrace from Canso Cape to Georges Island.' He would be back in Halifax 'by the 4th of next month if possible,' he wrote, and could then provide further information.[27]

On 30 July 1815, soon after Griffith arrived in Halifax, Lockwood wrote to him a detailed, and highly practical, account of the poor state of the Brier Island lighthouse in the Bay of Fundy: '1. Windows of the lantern repaired with wooden panes, others broken and stuffed with rags. 2. A leaky sea bucket as a lamp, charged with thick train oil. 3. The ventilator or chimney of the lantern clogged and immovable without force, in consequence the glasses inside become smoaked.' 'The light house,' he continued, 'stands immediately over the breakers, and the surf [?] coats the glasses outside with salt, and the person in charge of the light reports that in winter, the snow and sleet together with the sea haze occasioned by the surf form a complete covering to the glasses, which remains until washed off by rain.' Griffith forwarded this letter to Sherbrooke.[28]

Not content to rest there, with a rush of energy Lockwood also wrote to the New Brunswick House of Assembly on 6 November, knocking on all the doors.[29] This appears to be the first evidence of Lockwood's entry into New Brunswick affairs. He justified his approach on the ground that Briar Island was 'of consequence to the shipping interests of your city . . . altho' it is under the jurisdiction of the Nova Scotia government. . . . The Bay of Fundy is conceived by strangers as a dangerous navigation, and approach it with caution that causes delay and frequent danger.' In a typically self-deprecating, if unconvincing, assertion, he added: 'I have no motive but the good of the Province, a motive stimulated by a view of the vast resources which must lift to importance a City so happily situated as St John.' He also called for the establishment of a light on Cape Sable, 'or on one of the islands lying off it; I have minutely examined every part of that neigbour-hood, and am of opinion that the South Seal Island, situated at, or rather forming the elbow, of the Bay of Fundy, deserves a decided preference, and offers an excellent site for a building of that description . . .Vessels bound to and from St John, would particularly feel its advantages, I therefore venture to suggest (should it be determined to place a light on that Island alluded to) that the building be erected at the expense of those concerned in the Shipping Interest at New Brunswick.'

This was a bold suggestion coming as it did from a Navy master, third rate, engaged in survey work. Remarkably, Lockwood's letter did ultimately bear fruit. The New Brunswick House of Assembly voted £100 in 1818 and 1819 to support Brier Island Light. On 2 August 1819 the Nova Scotia government woke up to the fact, and asked the New Brunswick Provincial Secretary for a warrant. The New Brunswick government was still supporting the Brier Island Light in 1830, and was also subsidising the light on Cranberry Island. No decision had yet been made on Lockwood's recommendation of a light on Seal Island, but the New Brunswick Light House Committee reported to the Assembly its recommendation to offer Nova Scotia half the cost of building and maintaining a light house on Cape Sable Island. The Nova Scotia Light House Committee, belatedly following Lockwood's advice, recommended demolishing Brier Island light and constructing a new one.[30]

Lockwood's letter to the New Brunswick House of Assembly concluded by recommending a new survey of Grand Manan, and the Bay of Fundy; making clear his readiness to undertake the work:

> A view of the island of Manan and its extensive ledges, the most dangerous of which are omitted in all the Charts extant, confirmed my opinion that a Survey of the whole Bay of Fundy, would remove or obviate most of its dangers, and thereby save many valuable lives. Should its examination be considered desirable by the Government of New Brunswick, I am willing and ready to execute the task; an application will be necessary, thro' the medium of the Naval Commissioner in Chief, to the Lords Commissioners of the Admiralty, by whom I have the honor to be employed to survey such parts as may be deemed necessary in this quarter of the Globe.

Soon afterwards, at the direction of Sherbrooke, Lockwood prepared a ten-page report on Nova Scotia lighthouses, submitted to the Assembly on 22 January 1816.[31] This contained descriptions and assessments of lights at Halifax, Canso, Liverpool, Shelburne, and Brier Island. Borrowing directly from his letter to the New Brunswick Assembly, he repeated his recommendation of a light on Seal Island, and his suggestion that it might be paid for by New Brunswick. Lockwood was at his best making close observations of this sort, displaying his technical and scientific bent, understanding – as he had in his report on Trinidad for Cochrane – the actual conditions of men at work.

The Ventilator is so very material to the good order of the Light that it merits great care in the construction that its action may be free, and no obstruction given to the smoke.

The fountain lamps upon the improved principle, are simple and preferable to any other, when attended by persons who do not readily adopt improvements; otherwise L'Argand's lamps are very superior.

It would be œconomy even in those who contract to use Spermaceti oil, were they obliged to keep a constant brilliant light. It may perhaps be expedient for the Government to import a quantity equal to the consumption of all the lights on the coast of this Province and thereby ensure its use in the Light houses, supplying the contractors from the public Stores.

It may not be improper here to notice how ill adapted are infirm men to attend the Lights, a duty that requires attention, clear vision, and occasional exertion; the want of which endangers not only property but lives. There are many Tradesmen, such as Shoemakers, Tinmen, Copper-smiths and others, whose occupations are well suited to such solitary posts; having a pursuit they are less subject to lassitude discontent and idleness, and if such a consideration ought to weigh, their Services may be obtained at a cheaper rate than others.

The Halifax light 'is very generally, and very justly complained of, as frequently its faint glimmering was scarcely discernible when close to it: the Glasses of the Lanthorn and the Ventilator were in May last, very much out of order.' Lockwood advised the construction of a small, new light within the harbour: 'Hurst Light at the entrance of the Needles in England is a large Image of what Halifax interior Light House ought to be.' His account of the proposed Canso light drew upon his earlier report on the Cranberry Island site and declares 'it will be of very general benefit, not only to the provinces of Nova Scotia and New Brunswick, but to the trade between Europe and the Northern States of America.' Among other suggestions for the design, he argued that the building should be low: 'In this country where the Fogs are so very prevalent, the lower these buildings are, the less they are subject to be obscured. Besides a low building will admit of a proportionately larger Lanthorn, which indeed can scarcely be too large, the small ones not readily admitting the smoke to escape, besides clogging the glasses, and causing a noxious and unpleasant heat, which the attendant avoids as much as possible and thereby neglects his duty.'

As for the Liverpool light, 'it is to be feared' Lockwood wrote, it 'will prove worse than useless, and ... lamented that its advocates have succeeded in procuring the means of erecting it.' On 'the whole line of coast' no possible site could have 'answered so ill the humane intentions of Government.' Lockwood saw benefit only to the 'limited trade of Liverpool' and claimed the navigational dangers were insufficient to warrant a light in that position. On the other hand, Shelburne harbour and lights were both well maintained and 'generally known and acknowledged' to be valuable. 'Vessels from America run confidently for it, and if caught by a gale of wind on Shore. The Light guides them to a harbour of perfect safety and it requires no alteration or improvement whatever.'

The status of the Brier Island light was perhaps the most politically contentious case, in that it involved both provinces. Lockwood maintained that the lantern must 'be altered' since 'the dangerous and extensive ledges of Manan on which so many valuable Ships have been lost, require that the light on the Eastern Shore should be sufficiently good, to induce the Navigator to run for it, and unless it be improved it had better be totally discontinued.'

He accompanied his report with a letter to Sherbrooke dated from *Examiner*, 22 January 1816, in which he risked a snub by suggesting that work on the lighthouses would reflect well on 'your Excellency's administration'. He also repeated to the Nova Scotia government the suggestion he had previously made to the New Brunswick House of Assembly, that an application should be made to the Admiralty to commission a thorough survey of the bays, harbours, and inlets of the province, with an inspection of the lighthouses, and an assessment of the economic potential each possessed. He unhesitatingly put himself forward: 'In thus volunteering my Services for a task of much labor and some degree of danger, I am activated by the sole desire of effecting a work which the rising importance of the Province seems to demand.'[32] Broadly hinting at Admiral Griffith's approval, he asserted that he had 'no motive but the good of the Province.'[33]

His proposal did bear fruit in the form of a Lighthouse Commission for Nova Scotia, to which James Fraser, John Douglas, and Samuel Cunard were appointed by the Executive Council on 30 March 1816. By 25 November 1818 the new governor, the 9th Earl of Dalhousie, was able to inform the Executive Council that a light had been erected on Cranberry Island.[34] In immediate terms, however, there was nothing in this for Lockwood.

Turner's log records the exceptionally cold spring of 1816, which would become known as 'The Year without a Summer'. *Examiner* spent the first four months anchored in Halifax Harbour, with a skeleton crew. For practically the whole of February there were light winds with 'continual snow'. On the 25th the harbour was 'covered with drift ice' and almost a month later, on 23 March, Turner noted that the sloop was 'surrounded with ice'. *Examiner* did not put out until 29 April. She anchored further down the harbour off McNab's Island, near the entry of the Eastern

Passage, taking on a pilot to navigate the passage on the following day, when she ran on to Jeddore. Between 4 and 10 May seven boats were employed surveying Ship Harbour, and the following day *Examiner* grounded after rounding Tangier Point, 'on the Whale Back Shoal', after which the crew were all 'employed lightening the Sloop' until she floated off. On the 28th *Examiner* 'ran over the Boat', losing more gear, and on the 30th ran aground at St Mary's River 'at Low Water the sloop nearly dry.' She floated free on the 2nd but her rudder irons needed to be replaced and on the 5th the crew hauled *Examiner* onto a beach for careening. They left St Mary's River on the 9th, and returned to Halifax on the 22nd. Still there on 1 July, *Examiner*'s boats were employed salvaging from the wreck of the transport *Archduke Charles* which had gone on Green Island.

On 8 May 1816 Lockwood had offered for sale at Halifax his 'private set' of surveying instruments, 'having received notice from their Lordships [at the Admiralty] that Instruments for that Purpose would be sent by the earliest opportunity.' His set was composed of 'a Portable Transit Instrument purchased only last Winter . . . Jupiter's Satellites, A complete small Theodolite divided on silver, A case of superior Glasses, consisting Night, Day, & Haze Telescopes, A sixteen inch Sextant, divided on Silver, Two Plotting Ivory Scales, An Artificial Quicksilver, An Improved Protractor, 16 Inch Sextant divided on silver.'[35] Selling his instruments and running aground: perhaps these outward events ominously symbolised Lockwood's personal situation.

In London six years later there was to be correspondence concerning a chronometer which Captain George Richard Brooke Pechell commanding the brig-sloop *Bellette* at Halifax from May 1818 had lodged at the office of Commissioner Shield, claiming it to be Lockwood's. The Admiralty Board asked the advice of the hydrographer, Thomas Hurd, who declared that he had supplied Lockwood with two timekeepers, the second in 1817. The Board decided that Lockwood had had his own chronometer and had 'mistakenly' swapped it for the service one.[36]

The Admiralty's apparent generosity in the matter of instruments was misleading. In late June the Board asked for Hurd's opinion of the progress of Lockwood's survey, and his reply began with the complaint that 'nothing has been received from him except . . . an ill defined survey of Halifax Harbour'. He poured scorn on the survey's general misdirection, and followed up on 11 July with the plain assertion that Lockwood's work was useless.[37] As a result, the Admiralty requested Admiral Griffith's opinion of the survey. His reply, dispatched on 23 August 1816, was unequivocal: Lockwood's 'further Labors are not likely to be of any advantage to the Public.' This led to an Admiralty directive of 12 October to Rear Admiral Sir David Milne, who had taken over as commander-in-chief North

America though Griffith remained as senior officer at Halifax, to send Lockwood home, and pay off *Examiner*'s crew.[38]

What prompted these moves? Were there private communications to the Lords Commissioners from Nova Scotia? Griffith's pronouncement has a suspiciously diplomatic suavity. He offers no reasons for his opinion, unless we detect irony in his reference to Lockwood's 'Labors'. There is a sense of something not openly stated here. However it was, Lockwood responded characteristically by fighting a rearguard action.

Although the directive to Admiral Milne had not reached Halifax by this time, Lockwood knew how the wind lay. He could not have known of Hurd's denunciations of his work in letters dated 2 and 11 July in London, which suggests he was aware of troubles much closer to hand, in Halifax itself, where he had clearly lost Griffith's support. He petitioned the Admiralty on 3 August 1816, from *Examiner* at sea: having 'served His Majesty with Zeal to the best of his ability under Officers of first Rank and Character in the Naval Service', of whom Sir Alexander Cochrane, Sir Edward Buller, and Sir William Hargood were still living and could be referred to, 'your Memorialist feeling the effects of long residence in a warm Climate and incessant activity afloat, looks forward to the period of his present Hydrographical Task, as the probable period of his labor.' He asked what would be his pension. He was writing now because of the 'dissolution' of the Barbadoes Yard, 'to which he had conceived himself attached for life.' Though he was willing to continue as maritime surveyor in 'this quarter of the Globe' his present survey was being conducted 'under very uncertain circumstances.'

Lockwood had served under Hargood when the latter commanded Cochrane's flagship, the *Belleisle*, for its voyage to the West Indies in 1807. Hargood had been promoted to vice admiral on 4 June 1814. What Lockwood's connection was with Vice Admiral Sir Edward Buller is not clear, but he was a very well placed reference. James Buller, the Admiral's brother, was private secretary to the Prince Regent.

This petition was received coldly. An unsigned memo overleaf holds a distinct hint of threat: 'Mr Lockwood's servitude and *character* will be considered when his labours (of which he speaks so forcibly) cease.'[39] Was there indeed an underlying issue of 'character'? In its contemporary understanding it meant reputation or moral standing, and the petulant underlining in the memo suggests irritation with Lockwood.

Lockwood's earlier arrogance had infuriated Admiral Saumarez and Commissioner White. Did his newest trouble stem from Griffith's replacement of Cochrane, when Lockwood still carried orders from his naval patron? He may have behaved as if those orders were absolute protection from interference. Griffith had plenty of opportunities to observe

Lockwood, or receive reports, during the disproportionate amount of time the latter spent in Halifax Harbour. Moreover, *Examiner* frequently borrowed men from *Centurion*, Griffith's flagship – the same arrangement that had led to conflict with Saumarez. This is speculative. But there is no question but that by mid 1816 Lockwood was rapidly losing his way. Once again the Lords Commissioners were stirring against him and only the distances and delays of communication gave him respite.

Examiner had sailed again by 24 July, sailing northward through Canso Strait to the Magdalen Islands where on 3 August 'at 10 came on a heavy squall & upset the Boat.'[40] Back in Halifax on 22 August, Lockwood sailed south again on 5 September, conducting surveys en route to Shelburne.[41] After another two-week refit, *Examiner* put out again on 18 October, this time directly to the Bay of Fundy. Reaching Gannet Rock south of Grand Manan by the 21st, Lockwood 'bore up and ran between the ledges and Grand Manan.' After spending a day sounding Passamaquoddy Bay, he ran *Examiner* past the Wolves on the 23rd and entered Saint John next day, remaining until the 29th. He then returned to Halifax, anchoring there on 5 November. On 24 August, the day after his critical appraisal of Lockwood's work, Griffith transmitted to the Admiralty a letter to him from Lockwood concerning two newly located shoals off Prince Edward Island, and on 21 November he forwarded Lockwood's survey of part of the Nova Scotia coast, but indicated that his earlier opinion of the survey's value was unchanged.[42]

However important might have been the connections Lockwood had established with Sherbrooke and his Council, they became moot when Sherbrooke was elevated to the governor generalship of Canada. Lockwood was in Saint John when Dalhousie was received at King's Wharf on 24 October by Major General George Stracey Smyth, the military president of the New Brunswick Council who was to play an important part in Lockwood's life. Smyth was at the time en route for Bermuda with his ailing wife.

During Dalhousie's first months in government, office-seekers such as Lockwood had an opportunity to gauge the man and ingratiate themselves. The new governor led a full social life, meeting the city residents and garrison. On 13 November he noted that 'Captain [the Honorable Philip] Wodehouse of the Navy now here Commissioner & Admiral Griffith, have both been extremely attentive', while on the 26th he 'patronised a set of players just arrived [who enjoyed] an overflowing house.'[43] He also made frequent public appearances – diplomatically attending both the Church of England and the Kirk – though he was scornful of the custom of the levée which he characterised as 'a most ridiculous ceremony'. Lady Dalhousie gave a ball on 15 November, 'to the better class of the society', attended by about two hundred people, described by her husband as 'not powerful in either beauty or good dancing, but on the whole . . . a good set of people, very much inclined to be pleased, at the same time extremely civil and attentive.'

Whether or not a naval surveyor ranked among the better class is questionable, but his surveying work and interest in lighthouses would certainly have recommended him to Dalhousie, who had a marked appetite for geographical information and a liking for practical men. Surely Lockwood made himself known. If so, did the question of his 'character' come up? His opportunity to put himself forward were all the greater because after 11 November the naval component of Halifax society thinned out. The fleet sailed that day for Bermuda, leaving only the *Niger* and *Opossum*, 'both of them in bad shape and unfit for sea.'[44]

It is consistent with his precarious professional position that Lockwood should at this time have moved to liquidate some of his family's assets, their slaves, but it was also a practical response to the changes taking place in Nova Scotia's society. By 1817 Lockwood knew that Able Seaman Bill Lee would fetch no buyers in Nova Scotia or New Brunswick. In both colonies a few remaining slaves in Loyalist families would live out their lives there, some being designated indentured servants, but the institution of slavery, though not formally abolished, had been rendered impractical by court cases which prevented the recapturing of runaways. Ward Chipman, who would play an important part in Lockwood's life in New Brunswick, had led a challenge to the legality of slavery in the New Brunswick supreme court in 1800, and although no judgement was reached by the divided court, and the passions aroused led to several lawyers challenging each other to duels, by 1822 there would be no more slaves in New Brunswick. Slavery was to be finally outlawed in 1833.[45] When Lockwood first landed in Nova Scotia both provinces, despite local resistance, had settlements of former slaves: at Loch Lomond, near Saint John, New Brunswick, and at Preston, near Dartmouth, Nova Scotia. All this made it financially sensible to ship Bill Lee back to Barbados, where demand for slaves that year was particularly strong. On 22 April Lockwood's land grant in Sydney County was finally assigned, but evidently he was not interested in employing his slave to clear it.

The first sale took place in Barbados on 16 June 1817 when a George Taylor of St Michael purchased a slave called George for £120 from Lockwood in his capacity as legal guardian of Sarah Lee and Marina Lockwood, then resident in Halifax. It was at this time, on 1 July, that the Sarah Lockwood sold 'the Negro Boy called Bill, alias Bill Lee, now at Barbados', to William Marcher for £82 'Halifax currency', while Anthony

Lockwood junior sold to the same buyer for £192 the negro boys William McKenzie and Toby Bynae, both tradesmen.[46]

These transactions were no more than the practical actions of a man familiar with local conditions. Nevertheless they were in striking contrast to humane claims Lockwood made on 29 May in a letter to John Wilson Croker, who had been appointed the Admiralty Secretary in October 1809. Lockwood explained that while he had been serving as master attendant at the Barbados Yard he had ordered that the released African slaves sent to the yard as apprentices by Admiral Cochrane be instructed 'in the trades most useful to His Majesty's Service agreeably to His Majesty's desire. Many of them were in six years our best workmen.'

> Having trained them from their native ignorance to the use of our language, and introduced among them the greatest order and comfort, they leaned on me as their guide, and the sole dispenser of the government's favours.
>
> On my departure Mr Parslow the late storekeeper's humane attention to their wants removed their apprehensions of neglect.
>
> The dissolution of the yard, the death of their Lordship's valuable servant Parslow, and my remote position, induce me to request you will be pleased to call their Lordships' attention to the interests of these men of colour in order that they may receive from their Lordship's their liberty or other equivalent for their faithfulness.

A note overleaf to his letter directs: 'copy to be sent A Cochrane to sound his opinion.' In reply, Cochrane recollected 'that several Refugees from the Enemy's Colonies were sent to Barbadoes to be trained as Artificers.' Nearly all were transferred to Jamaica, he wrote, while six remained at Antigua.[47]

Why did Lockwood take the time to write on this subject just then? The letter suggests an actively humanitarian conscience, but the sale of slaves who had worked with him, and could have become free residents of Nova Scotia, suggests otherwise. It rather seems that he was cynically seeking to impress upon the Admiralty a degree of importance that he did not justify; that the letter was part of his effort to secure his own future rather than a disinterested intervention on behalf of others. The whole subject of 'Negro' settlement in Nova Scotia was intensely debated during 1814–1817 and Dalhousie took a direct personal interest in the matter soon after his arrival. Lockwood's letter was addressed to the Admiralty, but this does not mean that he failed to talk about it in Halifax, or even to have shown a copy to those who were in Dalhousie's confidence.

Examiner was confined to Bedford Basin and Halifax Harbour for the first three months of 1817, sailed briefly out of Halifax for the first time that spring on 4 May to survey St Margaret's Bay and Hubbard's Cove, and on 31 May returned to St Mary River, Country Harbour, Indian Harbour, and Beaver Harbour on the 8th. On the 9th there was another accident: 'The Gig being prepared to go away and survey an inlet, accidentally swamped, whereby was lost, the Theodolite & Case, 2 Oars, 2 Boathooks, 2 Boatsails, 2 deepsea lines, 1 deepsea lead, 4 handlines, 1 line lead, 2 log lines, 1 grapnel 40 lbs, 2 shovels, 6 signal flags, 4 signal Pendants, 3 muskets, 2 Pistols, Powder Horn and Priming Wire, a handsaw, 4 gimlets and 3 chisels.' The frequency with which Lockwood's crew lost equipment may raise questions in suspicious minds. He was back in Halifax for replacements by 15 June, remaining there until 10 July, mainly because of bad weather and the need to replace crewmen. He then headed southward around the tip of Nova Scotia, joining a survey schooner *Research* at Shelburne. At 6.30 am on 5 August *Examiner* 'struck on a Rock with great violence' in sight of the bald Tuskets southward or southeast of Yarmouth. She entered Digby Gut next day for repairs to her bottom, parting company with *Research*, and remaining until the 10th, when she anchored off Granville opposite the old star fort at Annapolis Royal. Continuing the voyage to Saint John, and the Passamaquoddy light, Lockwood surveyed the passages between Duck and Cheney islands where he had previously gone aground, and between White Head and Green Island, as well as the Murre ledges east of Grand Manan. *Examiner* was rejoined by *Research* while at anchor at Grand Harbour in southeastern Grand Manan on the 18th. Lockwood then returned to the Saint John area before rounding back around Nova Scotia to enter Halifax on the 19th.

It was then that Lockwood received a letter from Admiral Milne, from his flagship *Leander* at Halifax, dated 1 October, directing him to return to Britain forthwith and report to the Admiralty.[48] From the 22nd the crew of *Examiner* were employed 'stripping the Sloop,' and returning stores and equipment, until 29 October. Turner made his final entry and *Examiner*'s service was ended: 'Crew sent to the Dock Yard to receive wages, then discharged.' It seems likely that Lockwood left immediately, sailing in a merchantman from Halifax.[49] He was in London by 19 January 1818.[50]

It was almost certainly close to this time that *Examiner*'s crew made an undated petition to Dalhousie asking him to confirm an earlier direction from Sherbrooke to the Surveyor General 'in consideration of the Service on which the *Examiner* has been employed ... to reserve for them 2500 Acres of Land in the County of Sydney.' By saving their wages, the petition claims, they had means to both clear the land and pay quit rent. Twenty-two men and four boys signed the petition, thirteen by mark. Leading in rank was William Forester, midshipman, and amongst their number was

Anthony Lockwood junior, clerk. Dalhousie noted: 'I see no objection to this being granted, and would be glad that a settlement were commenced on it, at the top of County [ie, Country] Harbour.'[51] Since these crew members were intending to settle close to their commander's own earlier grant in Sydney County, their relationship with him appears to have been at least amicable. There are no punishments noted in the *Examiner*'s logs.

That winter of 1817–1818 was critical for Lockwood. He was sailing towards a questionable reception in London, leaving his family in Nova Scotia, where he had five hundred uncleared acres in Cape Breton and no job. The survey was over, his naval income uncertain, and there was much unfinished business with the Admiralty, the Navy Board, and the hydrographer. He surely had little expectation of another warrant to survey. Yet his eligibility for half-pay was not secure, despite his long service, mainly because his status during the seven years as master attendant at Barbados was never confirmed and he remained as a master, third rate. He had to appear before the hydrographer and produce his charts.

5

To London

ALTHOUGH THE OCCASION for Lockwood's recall to London was the Admiralty's, and the hydrographer's, wish to bring him to account, he was to make this flying visit, and another the following year, the means of acquiring a permanent position to his liking. He arrived a master, third rate, with surveying experience, tried his hand at instrument maker, and eventually left as Surveyor General of New Brunswick. It was quite an achievement for a man with the humblest possible origins, and a distinctly spotty record.

When he arrived in London Lockwood was directed 'to wait on the Hydrographer and report your proceedings.'[1] On 24 January he informed Hurd that 'the Charts of Nova Scotia and Manan are in hand, receiving such additions as are necessary to their completion.'[2] For the next three months Lockwood's correspondence would be addressed from the Hydrographic Office, where he finished this work.

While engaged in that work, he also had to deal with administrative irregularities in the accounts for his survey work in Nova Scotia. Having examined the musters and pay-sheets of *Examiner*, Barrow wrote to Lockwood on 21 January questioning the promotion of James King to midshipman.[3] Lockwood replied next day that, 'Mr King was received on board *Examiner* in order to improve himself and without any expectation of pay, but in consequence of his Industry and attention while sounding the Bay of Fundy, I approved the Bills usually allowed in expectation Their Lordships would have in such service permitted them.'[4] Their Lordships reproved 'this very improper conduct of Mr Lockwood's' and disallowed King's pay. Lockwood also enclosed a note, signed by himself and dated 29 September 1817, certifying that William Forester had served as supernumerary midshipman on *Examiner* to that date from 1 May 1817 and 'assisted in the Survey with industry and attention. His knowledge of barometers and the use of Mathematical instruments will render him an acquisition to any of His Majesty's vessels.'[5] It appears that Lockwood's intention was to anticipate any further probing on the matter of the employment of supernumeraries.

There were other, lesser, squabbles. Lockwood submitted to the Admiralty bills for stationary, covering the past three years, for a sum of £18 5s 6d, and claimed £25 for his fare on board the merchantman from Halifax, in which he had been obliged to travel since no naval vessel was available. Croker advised the Lords Commissioners that some portion of the fare might be paid but noted that Lockwood received his thirty shillings per diem during the passage. As a consequence, they refused this claim, but allowed the stationary bills, which Hurd had found in order.[6]

As a first step towards securing his own interests, Lockwood wrote to Croker on the 27th requesting a copy of the orders 'under which I have [lately] acted', explaining that the originals 'were lost by shipwreck on Partridge Island, New Brunswick.'[7] This story seems typical of him; his was not a tidy life. Writing again to Croker three days later Lockwood clarified his story: 'A Merchant Brig having on board my books and papers, from Barbadoes bound to St John's [sic], New Brunswick, in November 1815, suffered wreck on Partridge Island.'[8] The only merchantman wrecked approaching Saint John during this period appears to be the brig *Mary Ann*, John Richards, captain, from Bermuda, lost on the Murre ledges off Grand Manan in early January 1815.[9] The letter of the 27th included an oddly casual and incomplete list of Lockwood's surveys, noting Guernsey, Bearhaven, Falmouth, and 'N America' but omitting those off the Spanish coast and in the West Indies. The very purpose of this letter baffled its recipients. 'What does he mean?' is written overleaf, with the further comment: 'Mr Lockwood will write you a fuller letter tomorrow.'[10]

With retirement in view, Lockwood made an attempt to improve his pensionable rank. He petitioned the Navy Board at the end of January, listing accurately the surveys he had submitted to the Lords Commissioners since 1801, and asking for a letter authorising Trinity House to examine him for First Rate.[11] This was followed up during the month of March, with a stream of correspondence to the Admiralty and Navy Board, attempting to obtain the best terms for his retirement. He requested the Admiralty Board on 18 March that he be awarded half-pay at the same rate as established masters attendant who were discontinued by the dissolution of foreign yards, and asked that they so direct the Navy Board.[12]

On the same day he also petitioned the Admiralty 'in consideration of his son's services as Assistant on the survey of Nova Scotia' that he be allowed five shillings per diem from his entry into *Examiner* on 9 October 1815 to the present day: 889 days in total. Overleaf may be found the following exchange: 'What authority did he have to employ his son? Not any sir. Cannot be complied with.'[13] This claim earned reproof from the Lords

Commissioners and Lockwood tried to justify himself. Writing to Croker on the 26th, he said that he was 'fully sensible of the irregularity of employing without authority Mr Anthony Lockwood Junr as an Assistant. But the circumstances of their Lordship's Surveyors Demayne and Holbrooke on the same station, each allowed an assistant at ten shillings a day, led me into the error.' He requested that 'as their Lordships Sir Joseph York and Sir Graham Moore have examined the young man's labor, and admitted that it was good', he would be recompensed.[14] This request was refused.

Nothing seems to have come of his request in January to be examined for First Rate, so on 31 March he wrote directly to the Navy Board asserting that the Lords Commissioners had 'been pleased to direct that I take my proper Rank as Master' and that 'since the nature of the Service on which I have been employed has prevented my passing for a First Rate; or serving Twelve months in any of the Large Ships,' he wished for 'the usual letter to the Elder Brethren of the Trinity House to pass for First Rate.' Their Lordships, he added, had 'expressed their approbation of my Labors' and Hurd had granted his certificate. The note overleaf is unusually full and explains Lockwood's special circumstances:

> After passing for a 3rd rate in 1804 Mr Lockwood was employed in the *Malta*, *Northumberland* and *Belleisle* for part of a year principally on the Surveying service – and was afterwards *Acting* Master Attendant at Barbadoes for Seven Years – since which time he has been two years surveying the North American coast.
>
> As the regulations of 1814 for serving one Year in a certain Rate before passing again was not in force for 10 years after Mr Lockwood passed for a 3rd Rate, I would submit whether his services do not entitle him to a letter to the Trinity House to be now examined for a first rate.

The records of Trinity House were destroyed by fire during the Second World War bombing, but it appears that Trinity House was not co-operative. Lockwood wrote to the Navy Board on 21 April 1819 that 'a difficulty occurring in my not having served in a 3rd Rate 12 months' he needed a special letter explaining his circumstances.[15] In another hand, the order was scrawled to 'Grant a letter to the Trinity House.' But Lockwood never took the examination and was never promoted.[16]

There would be additional correspondence with the Lords Commissioners and Navy Board for years to come, but by mid March 1818 he had done what he could do for the time being. His work at the Hydrographic Office was finished, Hurd having on 25 March formally accepted his 'North America' charts.[17] After 18 March Lockwood's correspondence was no longer addressed from the Hydrographic Office, some of it being from an address at 37 Commercial Road. On the 19th he wrote to the Lords Commissioners requesting leave of absence 'to visit His Majesty's colonies in North America' and was told to apply to the Navy Board, which granted him one year's leave on the 31st.[18]

To complete his hydrographic work, and clarify and improve his service record to ensure the best terms for a half-pay pension, was Lockwood's basic purpose in that spring of 1818. But he also had much grander designs, which proceeded simultaneously. During his time at the Hydrographic Office he invented a compass which he believed would be useful on the forthcoming Arctic expedition to explore the North-West Passage, which had excited great scientific and popular interest. Indeed, a paper by Captain John Ross, who would lead the expedition, 'on the Variation of the Compass and the Deviation of the magnetic Needle in the Arctic Regions', had been communicated by the Admiralty to the Board of Longitude as recently as 4 February.[19]

Writing to the Admiralty Board on 21 February, he reported that 'agreeable to direction' he had been to 'see the Compasses making at the Mathematical Instrument Makers.' He reported that Edward Troughton, an optician and mathematical instrument maker with premises in Fleet Street, had 'in hand a compass invented by Dr Woolaston, which can be used only on shore. Whereas the Model of the one invented by me, and submitted to their Lordships, possesses the properties of the Dipping Needle and of the Common compass: suited for the Binnacle, and it is presumed, will tend to facilitate the Discovery of the Magnetic Pole.'[20] On 2 March Lockwood wrote to Captain Hurd, in the latter's capacity as Secretary of the Board of Longitude, requesting that his 'Model of a Universal Compass, intended to facilitate the discovery of the Cause of the Magnetic influence' be placed before the Commissioners, enclosing 'a brief statement of its properties.'[21] This was read at the next meeting of the Board three days later, with the Prime Minister, Robert Jenkinson Lord Liverpool in the chair. A model Lockwood supplied was also inspected.

Lockwood's six-page pamphlet began with a characteristic claim of modest disinterest: 'Having many years served His Majesty's Navy, pursuing Nautical Astronomy as a pleasing duty; and being about to close my hydrographical labors, it will be a consoling gratification in my retirement, to leave a proof of my zeal for the service, should the following invention, though simple, prove in practice equal to the expectations formed of it.' He also related the circumstances which had inspired his 'zeal' – a word which, like 'labors', Lockwood freely applied to himself:

When perfecting the Charts of Nova Scotia, at the Admiralty, (agreeably to the scheme of Capt. Hurd, hydrographer,) a conversation took place on the doubts entertained of the common Compass traversing near the Pole. This generated the idea of contriving a compass, that would combine the properties of the Dipping Needle, and of the Common Compass by acting *vertically and horizontally*. On imparting the principle to Howells, an ingenious worker in the Chronometer line, he readily undertook to make a model, which was completed in the second week of February, 1818.

After describing the mechanical features and principles of his compass, and its superiority to Dr Woolaston's Dipping Needle, while avoiding 'all technical phrases . . . as unnecessary and superfluous to your enlightened conceptions', Lockwood cited the encouraging 'concurrent opinions of Captains Hurd, Owen and Ross, and many other officers of acknowledged abilities', which led him to have the model constructed. He continued:

> Should the members of your Honorable Board take it under their favorable consideration, it will doubtless facilitate the discovery of the place of the Earth's greatest Magnetic Powers; and I will most readily, on my return to Nova Scotia, or New Brunswick, undertake to make observations, relative to the Variation and Dip, on the coast of the continent of North America, and transmit the results of these experiments to the Royal Society, or the Board of Longitude.

The Board of Longitude was sufficiently interested to resolve 'that [the compass] be referred to the Lords Commissioners . . . to direct a Trial to be made of it at sea.'[22]

Lockwood's memorial is an expressive document, and the fact that he had it printed suggests his hopes for it were high. It states plainly his imminent retirement from hydrography yet opens the possibility of a commission to test the compass; it claims the professional approbation of Owen and Ross, both famous, even glamorous, figures at the time; it flatters Hurd, who was sitting with the Board while it considered the memorial; and overall, its purpose was plainly self-advancement. In his final paragraph Lockwood acknowledged vaguely the 'hope of reward . . . grounded on its simplicity, and probable very general public utility, as well as the comparatively trifling expence.' Obviously, a compass with the properties he described would quickly become the standard nautical instrument and the rewards were potentially immense.

Implicitly placing himself in the same category as Ross, Owen, and Hurd, men of 'acknowledged abilities', Lockwood displayed that self-assurance which had impressed distinguished admirals such as Seymour, Laforey, and Cochrane. During that spring of 1818, his 'zeal' was expended on vigorous self-promotion and he seemed to have succeeded initially in the matter of the compass. The Admiralty Board apparently ordered one for use on the polar expedition. Seeking recompense later for expenses incurred in making the model, Lockwood noted to the Board that they had ordered it 'for the use of the late Northern Expedition.'[23] Was the way to Lockwood's future to be bathed in bright northern light?

But the New Universal Compass was really only a piece of opportunism, however promising its prospects. Lockwood's main business, after the winding down of his naval career, was elsewhere. The day after he informed the Admiralty of his arrival in London, 20 January, Lockwood had addressed himself to Henry, Earl Bathurst, Secretary of State for War and the Colonies: 'The Admiralty having been pleased to employ me in making Surveys in North America, I have the honor to request your Lordship's acceptance of a Brief account of Nova Scotia, showing its properties. The sketch submitted to your Lordship, may afford you some information: permit me to add, that professing a local knowledge of the Province, should any question be agitated the ensuing Session, relative to Grand Manan, or other islands near the line of demarkation, I shall think myself proud, by your Lordship's command, to give any other information.'[24]

The 'Sketch' is almost certainly the book Lockwood had printed that spring which he entitled *A Brief Description of Nova Scotia, with Plates of THE PRINCIPAL HARBORS; including a Particular Account of the ISLAND OF GRAND MANAN.*[25] He had very little time for the *Description* to be set up in type, unless he had arrived somewhat earlier than indicated to the Admiralty or had sent the materials of the book on ahead. But it seems very unlikely that he would have sent a manuscript version to someone as elevated as Bathurst if his intention was soon to publish.

By boldly presenting himself thus to Bathurst, Lockwood was trying to parlay his brief acquaintance with the shoals and ledges of Grand Manan and his single day in Passamaquoddy Bay into a consultancy to the Colonial Office and Parliament on the boundary dispute with the United States which had simmered since the end of War of Independence. The British claimed the line of demarcation to be the St Croix River, the Americans the Magaguadavic. *Examiner*, according to her logs, had spent twenty days along the coasts of New Brunswick. Lockwood surveyed Saint John harbour over the four day period between 28 August and 1 September 1817, and was to publish while in London a map of the *Mouth of the River Saint John*.[26] He may have made some social contacts in the city at that time. There was also his letter concerning lighthouses to the New Brunswick Legislative Assembly in 1815. He may have made unrecorded winter visits to Saint John from Halifax, but his acquaintance with the province was certainly not extensive. At the time of his appointment as

Surveyor General, the Fredericton *Royal Gazette* would pointedly write of him as a stranger.

Grand Manan and other nearby islands figured in the boundary dispute. There was some interest in placing a military establishment on the island.[27] However, since the title page of *A Brief Description of Nova Scotia* implies that Grand Manan is part of Nova Scotia, rather than New Brunswick, Lockwood may have weakened his case as an adviser on boundaries. He does not appear to have found a way of meeting with Bathurst, and there is no evidence that the minister sought out his opinion.

But in truth Bathurst and the boundary dispute were long shots. Lockwood's best hopes of employment lay in Nova Scotia. The inflated claims expressed in his *A Brief Description of Nova Scotia* must be treated as conscious appeals to the political sensibilities of Governor Dalhousie and his council, but they were not made without peril. There was effrontery in describing himself on the title page as 'Professor of Hydrography, Assistant Surveyor-General of the Provinces of N S and C Breton'. This may not have sat well with every reader in Halifax. Lockwood was clearly angling for the job of Charles Morris, Surveyor General of Nova Scotia since the province's inception, and now old and infirm. Morris is specifically thanked in Lockwood's 'Introductory Remarks' for help in providing documents and for the 'free use' of his office, while he 'trebly enhanced the favor by his manner of conferring it.'

The *Brief Description of Nova Scotia* bears all the marks of hasty composition. It is a rambling, unfocussed series of jottings on coastal Nova Scotia and parts of New Brunswick, probably composed from notes taken during the Survey and written on the voyage to Britain. The illustrations seem to be adaptations of Lockwood naval charts, perhaps prepared by his son. There is no apparent organising principle; the chronology is erratic; the choice of locations described seems to follow no particular pattern, though some of the more carefully surveyed sites are included. The treatment throughout is impressionistic. Navigation, of course, is most important, but there are observations on social and political matters, on the management of resources such as timber and fish, problems of immigration and settlement, and the character of the Micmac, Nova Scotia's aboriginal people. As exposition, the whole book is amateurish and without structure.

Yet its intended purpose was to display Lockwood's grasp of colonial issues, his sound, practical opinions, and right-thinking politics. The Dedication identified the essential readership: 'To His Excellency The Right Hon EARL DALHOUSIE, Governor of Nova Scotia, etc etc etc, to the Hon Members Of His Majesty's Council, and to The Members Of The Assembly, This Work Is Dedicated; and as An Infant of Promise, Is Offered To Their Notice, Should it be received under a favourable consideration, no Industry or Care will be wanting, to mature its growth, and render it worthier of the Public, by THE AUTHOR.' Essentially an appeal for patronage, typical of the often coy supplicatory rhetoric of the period, the Dedication also implies that *A Brief Description of Nova Scotia* was only a preliminary sketch for a more 'mature' and 'worthy' account. Was Lockwood still seeking support for the much larger enterprise he had broached in his lighthouse report to Sir John Sherbrooke two years earlier, when he offered to provide 'returns . . . of the capacity and properties of every nook and inlet, the State of the Settlers, and such other particulars, as those in Authority might deem useful?' Such appears to be the case. In a transparent boost for his own surveys, and no doubt also a slap at Hurd, he asserted that 'all other charts' other than those of Desbarres, 'are miserably defective and contradictory,' while those of Desbarres were too expensive for general use (p. 15).

His commentary, he insisted, was practical, public-spirited, and hard won, being written only when 'a relaxation from my professional duties' allowed. Yet 'the Author's incessant servitude' allowed little time indeed: 'Traversing this terraqueous globe, and pursuing research as a pleasant duty, what exquisite delight should I have derived, had Providence permitted me to give to the world, in suitable language, a just description of the various scenes that have passed in review, during a period of twenty-five years' incessant peregrination.' This was both an appeal for sympathy, and a cry from the heart of a man of talent stifled by relentless 'professional duties.' For those with the means to release Lockwood's imaginative energies, it implied, he was ready and available.

Lockwood's observations about social conditions in colonial Nova Scotia are of great interest, and also opens his mind to the reader. His perspective is that of a man of humble origins, but also that of one with the racial expectations of his age. In his account of Sheet Harbour, the population of which he said was twenty-one men, twenty-two women, fifty-one boys, and sixty-two girls, he sketched the damaging effects of bad land-settlement policies:

> The extensive tracts of land in this harbour granted to individuals have much retarded its settlement. The parsimonious steps taken by the heirs, or agents of the grantees, teaze and harass the feeble attempts of the poor. They drudge on, loath to quit possessions held for many years, yet daily annoyed by the harsh measures of their weightier neighbours. On their first settlement, they erected a church. The frame having decayed, they blended their labors, and prepared a new one. On raising it, they were told the attempt would end in the destruction of the building. 'If they presumed to erect it, it would be burnt.' The possessor of 10,000 acres

could not spare two-thirds of one, for so laudable a purpose. In September, 1815, I saw the frame in a state of decay, lying on the point forming the fork of the harbour, and at the head is a saw-mill frame, under the same circumstances. Attempts have been made to dispossess these poor people of the sterile and barren spots they have reduced to order, by the labor of many years; and I am pained to add, they have partly succeeded. Neither the court, nor their attorney, was in possession of all the facts relating to the case. To remedy, or even represent the very many existing evils attending a newly settled country, would be useless and unavailing. The above instance of oppression was forced upon my notice (p. 32).

In contrast to the oppressive situation at Sheet Harbour, Lockwood provided an example of thriving honest industry at Mason's Point, where he had seen 'a good farm, well worked, and stocked by strong cattle. There are in this neighbourhood ten families, whose habitations are snug, warm, and crowded with healthy children' (p. 61). Commending the virtuous poor, championing the oppressed, addressing directly abuses stemming from outmoded land-grant policy, Lockwood raised issues close to Dalhousie's heart.

However, if deserving settlers were to be helped, he urged government not to be diverted, or its efforts dissipated, by misplaced humanitarianism directed towards the aboriginal people. Writing of the Micmac, Lockwood the former slave owner wrote out of firm racial beliefs.

The few that are left, say 350 families, 1500 persons, wander from place to place, in all the abjectness of deplorable stupidity. The attempts hitherto made to improve their condition, have not only been abortive, but even productive of evil, by lessening their little energy, and teaching them to expect by begging, what they ought to obtain by common industry ... Their ingenuity appears to be limited to the composition of trifling articles of bark and porcupines' quills, and to have long been at its zenith of improvement. Their honesty, which is exemplified in many instances, appears to arise from apathy; and if the remaining few possessed activity enough to follow their brethren, the Province would be altogether rid of a useless, idle, filthy race, whose disposition to ramble, and distaste for all social comforts and civilized life, will ever leave them in their present degraded state (pp. 7-8).

Lockwood believed that 'the most enterprising' of the Micmac had left Nova Scotia for Labrador, Newfoundland, Canada, and Cape Breton. He wrote of Micmac families on the Shubenacadie River whose 'uncivilized habits are unconquerable' despite governmental assistance, better applied in his view to 'the log cabins of poor settlers, immured with large families, in forests that conceal their wretchedness and rags.'

While declaring that 'whatever tends to improve the condition of men, is an object desirable to every feeling mind', he nevertheless cautioned that change was not necessarily improvement. Citing failed efforts by the government of Massachusetts and by 'the exemplary people called Quakers, in Pennsylvania' to instil the virtues of industry into native people, Lockwood concluded: 'an Indian never can be cured of the wandering habit that he has imbibed; all attempts to settle them have been found to establish this fact. Even the infants, taken from their tribe, cannot be civilized.' These were widely shared and commonplace opinions. His practical advice on public policy towards the Micmac was to put them to work:

> Should any further attempts be necessary to improve them, would they not be most usefully employed in improving the roads, or forming new ones? In felling and clearing new lands, preparatory to settling them? In thus giving them labor proportionable to their present habits, their wants might, without much loss, be supported by the Government, as a kind of compensation for its bounty, would accrue to the Province.

The man who wrote this had directed the labour of the black artisans of the Bridgetown yard. He had employed slaves and deserters on *Examiner*. He plainly thought he knew a thing or two about getting work out of the 'lesser breeds'. His plan for using the Micmac for road building and land clearance in Nova Scotia surely implied a certain amount of coercion, but the absence of any indication of punishments in Lockwood's captain's log suggests that he was able in the right circumstances to do without the more brutal forms.

In passages like this, Lockwood was trying to present himself as a framer of public policy. Elsewhere, he warned of the insistent Yankee threat. The enemy could be within, as at Beaver Harbour, where the inhabitants were 'strongly tinctured with American manners and principles', while 'a large portion of the best lands are the property of residents in the United States' (p. 33). At the same time, American fishing vessels lay offshore, plundering Nova Scotia's fish, its 'inexhaustible source of wealth'. 'Their Chebucto boats, from 25 to 70 tons, ride in the middle of the ocean, with buoyancy and ease; while our miserably constructed and ill furnished vessels, hover near the harbours, fearful of being caught by a gale' (p. 10). Lockwood had seized an American vessel himself while commanding *Examiner*; now he was warning his readers that the War of 1812 had settled little.

Lockwood advised conservation of the salmon fishery: 'Salmon are plentiful in their season, and, but for the improvident use of this valuable addition to their [the settlers'] means of subsistence, would continue for ages.' He noted the damage caused by mill dams and wood waste on the St Mary River and others. 'These abuses exist unknown to the Government, or means might be used to preserve to posterity this luxury' (p. 39).

But apart from these few items of social and political import, a disquisition on the correct way to arrive at the mean daily temperature and a single page essay on the moose, the 102 widely-spaced pages of *A Brief Description of Nova Scotia* are largely filled by short coastal descriptions of headlands, cliffs, bays and inlets, harbours, islands, rocks and shoals, lighthouses, and George's Bank, and by problems of navigation. And once more belying its title, *A Brief Description of Nova Scotia* also contains a brief account of the harbour and town of Saint John, New Brunswick, and the merits of the Partridge Island light, before concluding with a tribute to Annapolis as a shimmering gem of Acadia:

> In entering Annapolis Basin the scenery is inexpressibly beautiful, and if our wandering countrymen in affluence would cross the Atlantic instead of the Channel, the bold and imposing scenery of Canada, Cape Breton, Acadia, or New Brunswick, would rivet their astonishment. The features of nature are here presented on a grand scale. Lakes oceanic, rivers whose branches or arms would pygmatize the largest in Europe, if divested of their commercial importance.

Despite 'FINIS' being printed emphatically on page 102, *A Brief Description of Nova Scotia* was still a work in progress. Later that same spring of 1818 Lockwood added an Appendix (pp. 103–134) for a second edition, in an attempt to exploit the current interest in the polar expedition. After a two page introduction, the Appendix consists simply of extracts from the *Quarterly Review*, no 35. There are sections on the physical characteristics of the polar regions, magnetism, and the exploration of the North-West Passage. In addition, it includes a new map by Lockwood dated 1 May 1818: 'The Lands Round the North Pole Shewing the Intended Tracks of H M Ships, To Discover a N W Passage to the Pacific Ocean.'[28]

This augmented text for the second edition made most sense if designed for Nova Scotia readers, since Londoners had been bombarded with polar materials, including Mary Shelley's *Frankenstein*, published that same year, with its dramatic evocation of the frozen wastes, while the *Quarterly Review* would be readily available in London anyway.[29] Lockwood justified his seemingly odd decision to include polar information in a book on Nova Scotia by a piece of airy illogicality: 'there can be no sound reason for not rendering an account of the projected scheme of the voyage to our friends, who favor the publication of this work. The ships have sailed, are perfectly equipped, provided with every instrument and implement that a mature consideration of the difficult circumstances likely to present themselves, could suggest' (p. 103). 'No sound reason' indeed! However, if Lockwood believed his New Universal Compass was one of those instruments with which the Ross expedition was 'perfectly equipped', might not that fact also be made public in Nova Scotia when his book reached there? Was he trying to bathe himself in the glamour of the great adventure?

Taken together, all this busyness suggests that in the early weeks of 1818 Lockwood saw Nova Scotia, and the aged Charles Morris, as his best chance for a job. But another possibility had presented itself before he left for London. George Sproule, Surveyor General of New Brunswick, had died on 30 November 1817. He had held the position since 1785, one of the Loyalist founding elite. Lockwood acted quickly. On 17 February 1818 Vice Admiral Sir Edward Buller wrote to Bathurst commending Lockwood as a long-serving and gallant officer, to which Bathurst replied that since the position of Surveyor General, New Brunswick, was in the 'gift' of the Lords Commissioners of the Treasury, he had forwarded Buller's letter to them.[30] There it would sit for another year. This was typical of what Lord Dalhousie described later in 1818 as 'the total neglect and apathy of the Colonial department under Lord Bathurst towards these provinces.'[31] No copy of Buller's letter, referred to in Bathurst's reply, has been found, but his connection to the Prince Regent's court through his brother may have made it a weighty one for the Treasury with patronage to dispense. If Lockwood was to be the beneficiary of royal patronage, however, there is no record whatsoever of why that should be.

On the available evidence Lockwood's connections with New Brunswick were tenuous indeed. He had visited Saint John for only a few days on his coastal survey, and written his letter to the New Brunswick House of Assembly concerning the Brier Island lighthouse. It is possible he had travelled to New Brunswick, especially Saint John, during the winter periods when *Examiner* was in dock, and indirectly his connections with New Brunswick might have gone back as far as his time in Barbados. There it is quite possible that he met Saint John merchant seamen, and may well have met Michael Ryan who had been publisher of both the *New Brunswick Chronicle* of 1804 and the *Fredericton Telegraph* of 1806, and had moved to Barbados and founded the Bridgetown *Globe* in 1809, two years after Lockwood's own arrival there as master attendant. Michael's brother John was publisher of the Saint John *Gazette*. Those possibilities notwithstanding, Lockwood's application for the Surveyor General's job seems like a long-shot rattled off into the blue, but his ammunition, whether it was Buller's royal connections or not, would turn out to be highly effective.

As a devoted family man, Lockwood's application for leave to return to Nova Scotia needs no further explanation. But his pursuit of a civil appointment in Nova Scotia, or New Brunswick, also required that he remained in Dalhousie's thoughts. He needed to be on both sides of the Atlantic at once, which in 1818 required repeated ocean passages, each of which may have cost him the £25 he had claimed for the first. As his Navy pay had come to an end, he was playing for high stakes. But once back in Halifax, fortune was with him; he found employment in his own line, and strengthened his claims in the process.

Lockwood presumably distributed copies of *A Brief Description of Nova Scotia*, but he also advertised in the *Acadian Recorder* as 'Lockwood & Son Land Surveyors and Draughtsmen with instruments essential to accuracy ... Plans of properties will be executed either plain or highly finished.' He also did some work for Charles Morris.[32] A survey of land owned by Lieutenant John Fawson at St Mary's River, Guysborough Co, was signed 'Anthony Lockwood, Dept Surveyor General.' The bold assumption of this title, marginally more presumptuous than the 'Assistant' he had claimed to be in the *Brief Description*, was evidently not without some basis. Morris paid Lockwood and son £180 for assisting him in 'compiling and connecting the several detached Surveys of the Province, into one general map, on an enlarged Scale.' This was to be based, on Morris's own work, and 'the accurate Surveys of the Coast, by that able and celebrated Surveyor, T F W Desbarres, Esq, which, so far as respects Navigable Harbours, Bays and Indents of the Coast, have stood the test of minute examination, and excited the admiration of all experienced mariners who have visited these shores.'[33] The 'test of minute examination' was probably a reference to Lockwood's own work, and the map seems to have used at least some of Lockwood's own survey measurements.[34] When offered for sale at Belcher's Bookstore, Halifax, in 1827 'at the reduced price of 5s plain and 6s 3d coloured' it was described as 'the most accurate that have yet been published and of a neat and convenient size.'[35]

Lockwood made plans to settle in the Halifax region, on the evidence of some land transactions in 1818. On 26 August he bought two tracts of land of 210 and 230 acres, with houses, barns, etc, adjoining the site of his cabin on the west side of the Bedford Basin for £100 and £350 respectively.[36] This gave him a substantial estate on the water. Six weeks later he sold his granted land in Country Harbour to a Richard Thoms for £50.[37] This certainly looks like consolidation. By enlarging his Bedford Basin estate and working on the provincial map for Morris during the summer and early fall of 1818 Lockwood was evidently preparing for a professional career in Nova Scotia. On 7 September that year, furthermore, he would sign a deed in his capacity as legal guardian of Sarah and Marina Lockwood agreeing with the George Taylor of Bridgetown, who had purchased from Lockwood the previous year the slave 'George', to the sale of their property in the West Indies and the transfer of £240 in Barbados currency.[38]

It was no secret that Charles Morris was now incompetent. But Lockwood's natural ambition to succeed him was confronted by Dalhousie's humanity. The latter confided to his journal on 15 June 1819, after examining some land near Shubenacadie Lake: 'the Surveyor General is either ignorant of it, or more probably unwilling to inform the King's Government of these tracts at their disposal', so that it was 'only by accident that I pick up my information. I am sensible that my duty calls me to report this state of things, but yet to ruin this old man Morris & his family is what I cannot do. The present state of the Surveyor General's office calls out for a partial reform.'[39]

At some time during his residence in Nova Scotia, Lockwood made the acquaintance of the lawyer William Young and his brother John, a merchant. *A Brief Description of Nova Scotia* was sold at the latter's store in 1819 and in the following year, after Lockwood became Surveyor General of New Brunswick, power of attorney would be given to him in the sale of any remaining Lockwood land in Nova Scotia.[40] William then acted as witness for the sale of Lockwood's land on the Bedford Basin.[41] Born in Glasgow, Scotland, the brothers were sons of the manse who turned to business in the New World. Under the pseudonym 'Agricola', John Young published a series of weighty letters on agriculture in Nova Scotia, persuasive sermons on 'Improvement and Husbandry', which earned the warm approval of Dalhousie and a broad range of thoughtful citizens.[42] He was elected to an enthusiastic House of Assembly which voted loans of ten thousand dollars to the farmers of Kings and Annapolis counties and under Young's leadership encouraged agricultural societies throughout the province. Association with 'Agricola' placed Lockwood in the progressive, activist political camp, well positioned to seek office under a liberal minded and ambitious governor. Perhaps that account in *A Brief Description of Nova Scotia* of diligent and contented farmers in their 'snug' homes at Mason's Point was a nod to 'Agricola'. John's brother William was to become a barrister in 1826, and was to go on to the highest offices in the judiciary and government of the colony.

But in late 1818 there was still, of course, unfinished business in London. The fates of his New Universal Compass and of his application for the position of Surveyor General of New Brunswick were still undecided. There was also another squabble with the Navy Board. It claimed that between the time he left *Examiner* and the official completion of his charts at the Hydrographic Office on 25 March, Lockwood was eligible for only half the thirty shillings per diem he had received while on active, sea-borne duty,

and had overdrawn his account by £68 17s 6d. He protested to the
Admiralty Board, again attempting to use the Admiralty against the Navy
Board, in a letter from Halifax of 26 August 1818.[43]

This dispute, though irritating, hardly justified a wintry voyage to
London. But Lockwood sailed for Britain once again early in the new year.
He may have been spurred by the news reaching Halifax that George
Parker Kemball, Lieutenant Governor Smyth's preferred candidate for
Surveyor General, who had been dispatched on leave to Britain for his
health's sake, was at death's door. Smyth was sure to press the issue of the
appointment again. Indeed Smyth put forward the name of his current
aide-de-camp, George Shore, writing to Bathurst on 4 January 1819, com-
mending Shore's satisfactory performance as acting Surveyor General, his
'liberal education', and his gallant service as a captain with the 104th
Regiment in Upper Canada during the War of 1812.[44] Both the Fredericton
Royal Gazette for 19 January 1819 and the *Halifax Chronicle* of 8
February prematurely, and incorrectly, proclaimed Shore's appointment.

Those familiar with colonial affairs knew that in matters of patronage
London could rarely be trusted. Shore's brother in law John Saunders, who
was pursuing legal studies in Britain, wrote to his father, the Chief Justice
of New Brunswick, on 16 January 1819: 'I don't know when I have felt
more gratified than at the news of Shore's being appointed Surveyor
General, by the commissions being made out I suppose it is confirmed at
home.'[45] The tentative note was in order. 'Home' was capricious. Lockwood
urgently needed to be in London to make his case, if he had any reason for
hope. At worst it was better than waiting for Charles Morris to die. He set
sail during the first days of 1819.

PART TWO

The Honourable
Anthony Lockwood

6

King's Councillor

LIEUTENANT GOVERNOR SMYTH'S letter of 4 January 1819 to the Secretary of State, Lord Bathurst, nominating George Shore as Surveyor General of New Brunswick, may never have been forwarded to the Treasury. At any rate, it had not been answered. Accordingly, Smyth wrote again to Bathurst on 15 March asking whether the appointment could be confirmed. But by that time it was too late. On receipt of this second letter, Bathurst directed that it be forwarded to the Treasury, but a secretarial hand responded: 'Unnecessary as the Treasury have appointed a Mr Lockwood.'[1]

Lockwood had for once succeeded in creating a position for himself, and had stolen a march on General Smyth. Arriving in London early in 1819, he had written to Bathurst on 25 February from 12 Upper Thames Street, reminding him of his application.[2] On 9 March he was informed, as Sir Edward Buller had been, that the position was in the gift of the Treasury, and with remarkable despatch it was agreed at the next Treasury Board meeting, on 23 March, to appoint him to the office.[3] George Sproule's original instructions of 1785 were sent to Bathurst on 30 March for amendment if necessary.[4] Lockwood then received his instructions and commission, unamended, from the Receiver of Fees, Joseph Vernon, at the Treasury on 28 April.[5] The job was his. Unfortunately, nothing is known about who on the board may have promoted his claim, because the minutes record only the decision.[6]

Evidently he did not reckon his good fortune as being so great that he did not also pursue his existing claims on the Admiralty, and hopes from the Board of Longitude. This business began badly when, true to form, he again irritated their Lordships. A demonstration was being made at the Admiralty of a new sounding machine invented by Mr Massey, and Lockwood was invited. Apparently unimpressed with the working of the 'Buoy and Nipper', he wrote to the Lords Commissioners giving his 'opinion in writing without the least idea or intention of interfering with their Lordships regulations which I have at all times endeavoured to observe.'

This caused offence, and on 18 March he wrote to express his 'sincere regret' to their Lordships at having incurred their displeasure.[7] Evidently, however, he was not greatly disturbed, for he wrote to inform the Navy Board on the same day as his apology to the Admiralty concerning his attendance at Massey's 'experiments ... on the merits of his Sounding Machine.'[8] Their Lordships conceded in the turnover note on his letter that they were 'satisfied with his explanation.'

So far from being intimidated by the Lords Commissioners of the Admiralty, Lockwood characteristically returned to an earlier grievance, complaining about the Board's refusal to cover the cost of his passage from Halifax upon his recall the previous year, and the cost to himself of paying his son for 'the printing and lettering of the Charts' he had completed, and which had been 'inspected, and personally approved of by a part of your honorable board, in the presence of your Lordships' Hydrographer.' He therefore asked to be relieved of the imprest for £68 17s 6d said to be overdrawn on his last quarterly bill. This was the result, he claimed, of 'being considered as under the same regulations as the surveyors who are employed on the home station, and are laid up in the winter.'[9]

He also took up again the matter of his rank, and the consequential rate of his half-pay, writing to the Navy Board on 21 April. He reminded them that in March 1818 they had written to the Elder Brethren of Trinity House asking them to examine him on his qualifications to take charge of a First Rate, and that when they objected he had not served the regulation minimum of twelve months in a Third Rate, he had on 21 April 1818 requested a 'special letter' waiving the requirement. This had evidently been provided. A memo overleaf dated 22 April reads: 'Under the circumstances of Mr Lockwood's Case write as proposed.'[10] But Lockwood, apparently, had not followed through at the time. All the standard records of service in the Royal Navy give his rank as master, third rate.

And he still had hopes for the New Universal Compass that worked 'Horizontally and vertically'. On 22 April Lockwood addressed himself to John Barrow at the Admiralty requesting payment of the £5 he had paid the workman who made his demonstration model, and 'such additional sum as their Lordships may consider a just Compensation for the Time and Trouble the invention took me to perfect.' He asserted that 'the Lords Commissioners of the Admiralty were pleased to order one for the use of the Polar ships.'[11] Barrow had been the guiding force behind the current series of Arctic exploration, and of other expeditions to follow. Indeed, even as Lockwood wrote this letter, the *Hecla* and *Griper*, commanded by Captain William Parry, awaited a wind to set out on a second polar expedition. They would leave on 4 May, carrying, in Parry's own words, 'a number of valuable instruments' to further 'the improvement of geography and navigation, as well as the general interests of science.'[12] But Lockwood's New Universal Compass was not one of them. Barrow authorised no payment and his memo overleaf was dismissive: 'Not worth a farthing and he was told so. Compasses were delivered to Captain Hurd.'

Did he mean that Lockwood had been told not to expect anything prior to the 1818 Ross expedition, or that he had been so informed early in 1819, when any instruments carried by Ross might have been assessed? If the Universal Compass was indeed tested on the expedition, it seems likely that Lockwood was told of its failure only after returning to London in February 1819. He wrote again on 5 May to the Lords Commissioners repeating his request for compensation for the costs of constructing the compass, claiming that 'Captain Ross thought it just to speak favourably of its merits.' But he was again refused recompense.[13] So much for *that* path to glory.

Much more important to his present position than these naval skirmishes was the twelve-page memorandum Lockwood sent to Bathurst on 27 April, with suggestions for a complete survey of New Brunswick, its mapping into sections on the American model, in addition to proposals concerning emigration and the fishery. This Bathurst forwarded to Smyth for an opinion. Taken with Lockwood's earlier offer of advice to Bathurst and Parliament concerning the New Brunswick boundary dispute with the United States, and the wide-ranging, if incoherent, commentary contained in the *Brief Description of Nova Scotia* – to say nothing of his freely offered opinion concerning the Buoy and Nipper – this latest document was plain evidence of his assertive self-confidence. He presented himself as a man of ideas and resolute action, not some cautious place-man eager to conform.

Lockwood departed London about 20 May 1819 in the merchantman *Thornley*, accompanied by his eleven-year-old daughter Marina and a Miss Desbarres. Presumably Marina had been with him during his stay in London, perhaps her first adventure with her father. It is evident that Lockwood and Desbarres were on good terms, perhaps united by a dislike of Captain Hurd. *Thornley* reached Halifax by 30 June, and a week later the Fredericton *Royal Gazette* archly observed: 'We have no official communication as yet, of the appointment which report says has lately been made in England, of a Surveyor-General of Lands; but we copy the following from the [Saint John] City Gazette of the 30th ultimo – "We are enabled to announce that the office of Surveyor General of this Province is at length filled by the appointment of ANTHONY LOCKWOOD, Esq to that situation." We find a *Mr Lockwood* named in the list of Passengers lately arrived in the *Thornley*, at Halifax, and we suppose that gentleman to be the person above alluded to.'[14] It may well be supposed that in Fredericton, on King and Queen Streets, in Officer's

Square, and in the drawing rooms of the 'better people' in Saint John, a sense of outrage was palpable.

Hitherto, Lockwood had lived distant from government in most senses, carrying on a struggle for accreditation, rank, pay and expenses from the far reaches of the naval service. The Navy had begrudged him status, at times doubting his whereabouts, even his existence. Yet isolation of that sort had its compensations. From day to day he had been free from interference, with his immediate commanding officers far away. For months and years, if the Navy did not acclaim him, neither did it harass him. From the time that he took charge of the Bridgetown yard in 1807 he had known great freedom. Life on *Examiner* had been but loosely tied to naval authority, until the long string began to tug him home towards the end of 1817, when he had re-entered the world of pensions, preferment, and influence-peddling. The system had rewarded him at last, with erratic generosity, dramatically transforming this obscure master, third rate, into His Majesty's Surveyor General of New Brunswick and an 'Honourable' to boot. All those years of resentment at his 'acting' rank in Bridgetown dissolved; he would enter the colonial capital of Fredericton in July 1819 as a personage, a man of substance. Yet in other senses he was more isolated than ever – and more at risk. A prominent public figure now, part of government, he must learn anew how to govern himself. Freed from the spectre of insecurity, he must accommodate himself to the restraints of office and of a very different social order. No longer ignored, he would be only too closely scrutinised. New Brunswick in 1819 would not hide him as the bays and inlets of Cape Breton or Fundy had done.

The politics of interest and ambition in colonial New Brunswick was a dangerous web ready to entrap and destroy the newcomer. And inexperienced as Lockwood was, his energy, and his creativity, greatly increased the dangers. As a sailor ashore, he was neither part of the military caste, nor part of Loyalist civil society. These very qualities may have led the Treasury to appoint him, but they also put him at risk. The year spent in some proximity to Governor Dalhousie may have given him expectations about the value of vigorous administration, but Dalhousie was a general and an earl. Where rank and honour would be welcomed, a bumped-up master, third class, would be resented.

On the face of it, an appointment to the office of Surveyor General of a small colony was not something to require protracted discussion. From the standpoint of the Treasury, the job was unimportant and unappealing – just about right perhaps for a worthy master, third rate. The population of New Brunswick was small; its climate unappealing; emigration barely encouraged by London. The Treasury Board would have considered the office of Surveyor General as only worth about £450 a year in 1819.[15]

During the post-war demobilisation of the armed forces there was a real a sense of obligation to long-serving and meritorious naval officers. Lockwood had a reasonably strong claim on the basis of his service. He had been gazetted for gallantry; he had long service in the notorious West Indies station; and he had completed a series of maritime surveys, including his recent major one in North America. There was also recent precedent for his appointment: George Holbrook, another master, had become Surveyor General of Newfoundland in 1817.

In reality, however, colonial New Brunswick politics ensured that the decision who should be appointed Surveyor General was a matter of far more importance than it may have seemed to the London elite. While the Treasury Board may have considered the appointment a minor decision, in New Brunswick itself the whole process of replacing George Sproule as Surveyor General went to the very heart of the political culture of the province. There was a long-standing sense of grievance among the Loyalists who had settled in New Brunswick. They felt themselves to be neglected and unappreciated. The separation of the province in 1784 from the original colony of Nova Scotia, was intended to provide a means of rewarding Loyalists with offices in government, as well as substantial grants of land. But the first appointees lived long and never retired, however decrepit, leaving the second generation of Loyalists gloomily awaiting their turn, believing that government office was theirs by right of inheritance, as a continuing expression of gratitude by the British Crown. With patronage positions in short supply, competition for them ensured that fissures would open in New Brunswick society.

Smyth's announcement of George Parker Kemball's appointment as acting Surveyor General had caused very particular Loyalist outrage. From his house at Annapolis, Nova Scotia, on 20 January 1818, John Delancy wrote indignantly to Bathurst, enclosing a letter of support from the Duke of Kent, who had been commander-in-chief of land forces in Canada. Delancy's father had raised Delancy's Brigade which had fought with distinction against the rebels in the American Revolution and was honoured in Loyalist memories. Delancy complained that 'this Gentleman', Kemball, 'has been but a short time in this Country and the most of the time on General Smythe's staff as Aid de Camp.' And he stated his own claim as 'one of the colonists whose expectations stood the highest.'[16] Kimball protested that he 'had not the most distant idea of taking upon myself of the Surveyor General's Office (until the other day) than the man in the moon', but once offered the position he readily accepted, since his army prospects were not good.[17]

After Kemball's departure, Smyth's decision to appoint George Shore as acting Surveyor General, and then to recommend him to the

permanent office, was less blatantly offensive. Although a soldier, and
not therefore part of the Loyalist elite, Shore had married the daughter
of Justice John Saunders. Lockwood's appointment, in consequence,
disappointed not only Delancy and Shore but also the Saunders family.
And there were two other contenders.

Smyth's recommendation of Shore as Sproule's permanent replacement
had made him one of several candidates put forward to Lord Bathurst.
General Martin Hunter, himself a former military president of New
Brunswick, wrote from Edinburgh to Henry Goulbourn, Parliamentary
Under Secretary at the Colonial Office, on 22 July 1817, with the
information that Colonel William Harris Hailes had recommended S G
Carmichael, late paymaster of the 104th Regiment in Fredericton. If
Goulbourn's brother, an officer in the 104th himself, were at home, Hunter
wrote, 'he would most readily commend my recommendation.'[18] There was
at least one other declared Loyalist candidate for Sproule's position, Wills
Frederick Knox, whose father was the late William Knox, Esq, formerly
Under Secretary of State, and agent for New Brunswick and Prince Edward
Island. In his son's words, he had been 'a firm Loyalist and a great sufferer
by the American rebels.' Frederick Knox wrote from Norton, Kings County,
New Brunswick, on 26 June 1818, to Lord Castlereagh, who redirected to
Bathurst with a brief letter of support.[19]

For Lockwood, who would also receive half-pay from the Navy, the
appointment was a significant improvement on the £365 sterling he
received as master attendant, Barbados, and more than made up for the
loss of full Navy pay as captain of *Examiner* at thirty shillings a day.[20] But
the emoluments of the office had been disappointing to the previous office
holder. On 1 June 1816 George Sproule had petitioned Lord Bathurst
jointly with Jonathan Odell who had held the post of Provincial Secretary
until succeeded by his son William Franklin Odell in 1812, describing the
steady impoverishment of their positions.[21] The changing fee structure on
timber licences and grants had diminished receipts, so that 'the whole
amount received [since 1802] is about £930 Sterling, which sum remains
here to be disposed of by order of His Majesty's Government.' Sproule and
Odell respectfully proposed that the money be divided between them as a
more fitting reward 'for upwards of thirty years service.'[22] It would take
the Colonial Office more than four years, until Boxing Day 1820, and after
Sproule and Odell had both died, to turn this request down.[23]

From the beginning Sproule had faced a special problem due to the poor
demarcation between his duties and those of the now even more ancient Sir
John Wentworth in Nova Scotia, who had held the post of Surveyor
General of the King's Woods for British North America since 1766 prior to
the American Revolution. He had continued ever since to hold the office,

with an interval of one year when the post was temporarily abolished, and renewed in 1783 one year before the separation of New Brunswick from Nova Scotia. The ownership of land granted by the Crown did not extend to any pine growing on it, a fact the landowners who were expected to develop their holdings resented. Wentworth had recommended setting aside Crown Reserves to provide pine and black spruce timber for the Royal Navy, and he still retained nominal authority for their management. The strategic importance of New Brunswick's stands of white pine during the great age of British sea power can hardly be exaggerated. Masts for the biggest ships of the line ran from 100 to over 150 feet, and supplies of such 'sticks', as they were called, were dwindling. A mast of 100 feet, 30 inches in diameter at the small end, came from a tree measuring probably 150 feet and of exceptional straightness.[24] Suitable trees for masts were identified and blazed with the mark of a broad arrow to prevent poaching.

Wentworth supervised through deputies reporting to him in Halifax rather than to Sproule in Fredericton. They were appointed through the Colonial Office in London, and were not sensitive to local issues. That, of course, was intended to ensure they represented the Navy's interests, but in practice they went their own ways and made their own private deals with lumbermen, without much reference to Wentworth, or to anyone else.[25] Smyth wrote to Wentworth requesting a copy of their instructions, but in his reply of 22 June 1819, Wentworth complaining of 'indisposition', speculated that the instructions had been 'moved to another building.' They were 'being searched for', and meanwhile he had written to London for a new copy.[26] On 26 September 1819, after Lockwood was installed in office, Smyth suggested to Bathurst that it might be a good thing if the provincial government were provided with the names of Wentworth's deputies so that they could be given 'some Instruction of a local nature.'[27] He later complained that Wentworth's 'deputies are acting without their Powers being understood by the Government.' When the New Brunswick Council proposed a tax of one shilling per ton on felled timber to encourage the deputies to range the woods, Smyth observed sardonically that this was not more than he believed landowners and lumbermen had been 'in the habit of paying to the Officers in the Surveyor General's Department by private agreement.'[28] Some of those making cosy deals with Wentworth's deputies were members of the House of Assembly or their friends and relatives.

Despite the difficulties, however, to those close to the development of the New Brunswick forest industry it must have been apparent by 1818 that Sproule's declaration of his income substantially understated the true value of the office. The demand for timber for housing and shipbuilding in Britain had created a post-war boom in New Brunswick. By 1819 timber exports exceeded 240,000 tons.[29] Between 17 January and 4 November

1819, 327 square-rigged vessels and 295 sloops and schooners, in addition to coasters, were entered at the port of Saint John.[30] Lying at anchor or tied up along the wharfs they presented a vibrant spectacle of maritime enterprise. Cutting licences, and thus chargeable fees, increased proportionately. Over the next six years the office of Surveyor General became a rich prize in the colonial patronage system. By the time Lockwood went mad, only four years later, he had also become rich, his property and income being estimated at £2,467.[31] In May 1819 news of the downturn of business in Britain due to crop failures began to reach New Brunswick, and as a result timber dealers found that they were left with large stocks they could only sell at a discount. But the timber export slump proved to be but a brief aberration. By 1825, timber exports reached 450,000 tons, virtually doubling in five years.[32] One of Lockwood's immediate successor's earnings became so scandalously high that even the Colonial Office was forced into action. It was a long chalk indeed from the stagnant last years of old George Sproule.

Not only had the emoluments of office experienced mushroom growth, so had its responsibilities. The crisis that occurred in Britain in 1816, 'The Year without a Summer', when crops failed on both sides of the Atlantic, led to a wave of immigration. This was the worst of what were known as the Cold Years. Unemployed workers, with thousands of discharged soldiers and sailors, tramped the British Isles seeking any kind of work. The poor ate nettles. Parishes were overwhelmed by able-bodied paupers. This suffering in Britain created a boom of sorts in the colonies. Only two years later the flow of emigrants carried by outward-bound timber ships to the Canadian provinces, and to the United States as well, rapidly gathered strength. During the next five years New Brunswick received its first great post-Loyalist wave of emigrants, many applying for land-grants or needing surveys.[33] Lockwood would arrive in Saint John that summer of 1819 to find the city overflowing with immigrants, and the province in crisis from the slump in timber sales. His response was to show his metal. It may be considered to have been his finest hour.

While Shore, Carmichael, and Knox might have valued the office of Surveyor General chiefly for the potential emoluments, it was also of political importance. New Brunswick was very much a Crown Colony, founded by an Act of the British Privy Council, unlike the Canadas which had been established by Act of Parliament. Like the other North American colonies, New Brunswick was governed by a Lieutenant Governor and a twelve-man council consisting of the officers of state such as the Surveyor General and Provincial Secretary, and the Supreme Court justices, appointed directly by the Crown and in the gift of the Colonial Office, or

Treasury. The council sat both as an executive body, when it was presided over by the Lieutenant Governor, and as a legislative one presided over by the Chief Justice of New Brunswick – Jonathan Bliss until October 1822 when he died and was succeeded by John Saunders, who had in fact been deputising for him in council for several years. Otherwise membership in the Executive and Legislative Councils was identical. Both councils sat within closed doors. The Lieutenant Governor and Executive Council were advised by a popularly elected House of Assembly of twenty-six members representing the eight counties, with Saint John County having six seats. The first franchise established in the 1784 New Brunswick charter was surprisingly wide, extending to 'all male persons of full age who had been resident in the province for three months.'[34] All acts had to be passed in the Legislative Council as well as the House of Assembly, and were then subjected to the scrutiny of the Colonial Office, which could disallow the legislation, or direct the Lieutenant Governor to deny ascent. It was not until 1831 that the journals recording decisions of the Legislative Council were printed.[35]

The New Brunswick economy was dependent upon British preferential tariffs that in the 1820s favoured the New Brunswick timber trade, and the British Navigation Act that required imports into Britain to be carried by ships owned and largely manned by British subjects, or by those of the exporting nation. And the Crown paid from London the salaries of its appointed officials. At the same time, the Crown retained ownership of New Brunswick's lands, and claimed fees for the felling of timber, or quit rents for land grants to immigrants. In an age that believed fervently in the nearly sacred status of private property, which the political philosopher John Locke regarded as an essential limitation on the power of the Crown, it was inevitable that there should be conflict over the Crown's control of New Brunswick forests, and also over the effect on local politics of London's control of Crown revenues.

These were issues with which any Surveyor General of New Brunswick was necessarily closely involved. It had been the practice to make large land grants to individuals 'and associates', some of the latter being fictions. On 13 May 1817, Bathurst had written to Hailes, as acting President of Council, that this must stop, since it led to the selling off of land at low prices with no improvements. The Provincial Secretary, meanwhile, promulgated an order-in-council on 8 January 1818, that no timber was to be cut on land for which grants had not been confirmed and that all applicants for timber licences should be freeholders.[36] The House of Assembly, the members of which largely represented timber interests, responded with a 'Humble Address' to the Lieutenant Governor, less than a month later, on 2 February 1818, requesting that the Royal Instructions concerning land grants be made public, as well as 'copies of the Regulations under which the fees upon Grants of Land have been taken at the different Public Offices.' This was plainly a hit at Smyth and his Council, with a suggestion of fee-stuffing by Crown officials.[37]

Meanwhile, from the beginning of January 1818, the *Royal Gazette* carried lists of hundreds of early land grants in all the New Brunswick counties which were declared forfeited. They had been granted with the requirement that they be 'improved', and a warning of possible forfeiture had been issued in 1815. Some of the colony's most prominent names were among the forfeiters, including William Franklin Odell who was the Provincial Secretary, Ward Chipman who was one of the founding fathers of New Brunswick and the Solicitor General, Ward Chipman junior, Dr Adino Paddock and Adino Paddock junior, of Saint John, William Botsford, Jonathan Bliss the Chief Justice, Munson Jarvis, Thomas Wetmore the Attorney General, and members of the Hazen and Jarvis families. After Sproule's death, with George Shore acting as Surveyor General, there was briefly a real attempt to sort out land issues in general, now urgent as emigrants flocked to the province.

When forfeited grants reverted to the Crown any pine timber they contained became taxable under Smyth's new edict. On 8 March 1819, four months prior to Lockwood's arrival, the House of Assembly presented an address to Smyth complaining that the proposed timber tax would be 'ruinous to the trade of the province'. Writing to Bathurst, Smyth considered this issue 'of very great importance as involving Questions relating to the Rights of the Crown in this Country' – as earlier he had written of its 'great national importance'. The members making the complaint were 'all, more or less, engaged in the Timber Trade, and are desirous to prevent any Restraint whatsoever from being put on the Trespasses that are daily, and with impunity, committed upon the Crown Lands and Reserves.' The assembly's 'reprobation', he claimed, was an attempted encroachment upon the Royal Prerogative, as well as an attempt to win popularity, while creating 'discontent . . . in the minds of the People at large.' He urged the appointment of inspectors of Navy timber 'to restore that order and regularity in the different Departments of the Province, which has been too much lost sight of in the Indulgences that were considered necessary in the first Establishment of a new colony.' On 23 March Council unanimously approved his reprimand to the assembly for opposing the Executive Government of the province – that is, the Lieutenant Governor and his council. But the assembly nonetheless voted down a motion to rescind the offensive resolution.

The right of the executive to employ the revenues of the Crown was fundamental to the constitution, and Smyth had need of the revenue for the establishment of schools and the maintenance of churches. In reaction to the attempted invasion of the royal prerogative, he angrily prorogued the house.[38] But with the advantage of a later perspective it can also be seen that the assemblymen had a legitimate complaint, beyond the immediate one of the possibly negative effects the tax might have on New Brunswick trade, not to mention their own personal incomes. The struggle to restrict the use of the Crown's prerogative is ongoing. The Crown continues to claim to this day the prerogative right to make war without reference to the House of Commons. But in the twenty-first century the Commons has a strong influence on Crown prerogative by virtue of its control of the government's budget. The existence of parallel financing in 1819, where part of the money available for official purposes was not controlled by the assembly, was a brake on constitutional development. The pressure for more democratic or 'responsible' government was to increase with the growing influence of the mercantile class, especially in Saint John, but progress was to be slow. When in 1825 the Colonial Office suggested that the salaries of Crown officers should be paid by the assembly out of taxes there was to be stiff resistance from the Governor and Council.[39]

In the circumstances, from Smyth's viewpoint, it was imperative that Sproule's successor be free of tainted local connections with the timber interests. The policing of a vast wilderness forest by local deputies, tempted to turn a blind eye on the transgressions of men they knew well, sometimes members of their own families, was difficult at best. Such considerations, in his own mind, could justify Smyth's original selection of Kemball to succeed Sproule and that of George Shore to replace Kemball. The unknown Lockwood's appointment cannot initially have pleased Smyth. Yet on reflection the prospect of a vigorous naval surveyor in his forties with no Loyalist ties might have had some appeal.

Lockwood's naval rank might have been an issue, both because he was not a commissioned officer, and because he was a military man, but at the same time, not a soldier. As a navy man he was, for better or for worse, not directly affected by local concern about the role played by the army in New Brunswick affairs. Part of the justification for the creation of a new colony of New Brunswick had been to strengthen the St John River valley against American invasion, but the army had come to take a role in New Brunswick that was resented by the Loyalist settlers and their children. Military officers were viewed as 'transients' by the civil population, with no real stake in the country, or right to enjoy the fruits of civil office.

When the Lieutenant Governor was away on leave, the senior military officer in the province had hitherto been appointed temporary President of the Council. From 1808, when Lieutenant Governor Sir Thomas Carleton left New Brunswick, until his death in 1817, the province was administered during nine separate periods by military presidents – leading one Loyalist wag to observe: 'Presidents are relieved with as little ceremony as an officer's guard.'[40] One of these military governors, in 1814, was Sir Thomas Saumarez, brother of the admiral Lockwood defied in the Channel Islands. General Smyth had been accepted as president in 1812 because of the war with the United States, but the House of Assembly petitioned in March 1817 that the practice of military succession be abandoned. In the original Royal Instructions there was provision to appoint the senior member of Council as temporary president, and the assembly considered this expedient preferable in peacetime. They wished to ensure that someone truly familiar with New Brunswick, one 'known' to His Majesty by virtue of an existing civil appointment, be entrusted with the presidency. When General Smyth was elevated later that year to the civil position of Lieutenant Governor, it appeared to many that military rule was being extended by sleight of royal hand.

Smyth, continuing to be known as the General, made matters worse by his constant wish to get away from New Brunswick, making his own transitory status obvious. For him, New Brunswick was a grudgingly endured posting. Notice of leave to visit England during the winter of 1818 had arrived too late for him to travel that year, because of his 'delicate state of health.'[41] When he was again given leave to travel to Britain for medical advice the following year, Bathurst, with typical indifference to local feelings, authorised by letter the commandant of the 74th regiment, Sir Robert Le Poer Trench who had only been in Fredericton since July 1818, to act as temporary President of Council. He later rescinded his order, but the fact that he sent it at all plainly illustrates the Colonial Office's comfort with military governance.

Lockwood's naval, as opposed to army, credentials and his energy was to make him almost overnight one of the most valuable members of the increasingly elderly New Brunswick Council. When Smyth assumed office in June 1817 the eldest members of the Council were Christopher Billopp, Jonathan Odell and Andrew Rainsford, all aged eighty, followed by Jonathan Bliss, George Leonard and George Sproule, aged seventy-five. John Coffin, who had fought for the Crown in the American revolution and in 1812 raised a regiment for defence against the American invaders, had at the end of the war been promoted to General and was in 1817 aged sixty-six.[42] The relative youngsters were Ward Chipman, age sixty-four, John Saunders, age sixty-three, and John Murray Bliss, who was forty-five. There were also two vacancies caused by recent deaths. Odell, Rainsford, and Sproule would soon die. Billopp and Leonard were too frail to travel to Fredericton from their homes in Saint John and Sussex Vale respectively.

Coffin was frequently out of the country. The quorum for the council was five, and that number was achieved with the greatest difficulty.

Dying or decrepit, the aged men held on to their seats tenaciously, still clasping at the ghostly sleeve of power. This was a society which hoarded social honours and political position. Every member of His Majesty's Council was termed Honourable, a gentleman confirmed by royal favour, and the assumption of class extended to their families. How could men such as Billopp, Leonard, and Coffin be turfed off a council to which their very names, in the imagination of the Loyalist elite, gave lustre?

As military president, Smyth had certainly tried to do just that. He wrote to Bathurst on 25 March 1816 concerning the 'age and infirmity' of Leonard and Billopp, and the difficulty of gathering a quorum. On 18 May that year he wrote again, noting that he was departing the province on leave of absence, and that the council was nominally reduced to eight, though 'at the Seat of Government to only four.' He appointed John Murray Bliss as temporary replacement for the absent Beverley Robinson. When on 19 November Hailes, who had temporarily replaced Smyth as military president, informed Bathurst of Robinson's death, he repeated the point that government was extremely difficult without a quorum. He recommended that replacements should be residents of Fredericton so it would not be difficult to assemble them for business.[43] These pleas were ignored.

Not that Smyth was consistent. On his return, while again complaining about Leonard and Billopp, he proposed to Bathurst on 30 July 1817 two other members for Council from prominent Loyalist families, Thomas Wetmore and William Pagan. The latter would be a replacement, presumably temporary, for General Coffin, who had left for a stay in Europe. The Council was again down to eight members. Yet while Wetmore was an able, energetic, fifty-year-old lawyer, already Attorney General, Pagan, aged seventy-four, was another old man. Smyth wanted him because he was a founding member of the St Andrew's Kirk in Saint John and thus gave the Council a Presbyterian member.

When Smyth informed Bathurst on 1 December 1818 that Jonathan Odell, most senior member of Council, had died, he again noted that George Leonard, next in seniority 'would be totally incapable of Administering the Government' should he, Smyth, go on leave, as he had planned for his health's sake. Two months later, he reminded Bathurst of his earlier letters concerning Leonard, Billopp, and the difficulty in obtaining a quorum. Meanwhile he apologised, in the extenuating circumstances, for 'deviating' from his Instructions and appointing Hailes, who was 'now on Half-Pay, a very respectable inhabitant of Fredericton' to Council. The appointment of Hailes, of course, also added to the military presence on Council. Smyth also recommended the lawyer Samuel Denny Street and the

acting Surveyor General George Shore to fill further vacancies. When
another month brought the death of William Pagan on 12 March 1819,
himself a 'deviating' appointment, Smyth again pressed George Shore's
claim on Bathurst for membership of Council.[44]

The old men would go down fighting. George Leonard wrote to Bathurst
from his sanctuary in Sussex Vale on 27 February 1819. Noting that Smyth
had applied for leave to go to Britain, he declared: 'I am now most senior
in Council . . . but by some mistake in the order of transmitting a late list
(which cannot be presumed to be intentional) Mr Saunders' name has been
placed before mine . . . but the Lieutenant Governor feels himself obliged
to take this late list as his guide.' He trusted Bathurst to right this wrong,
since he, Leonard, was 'much recovered and hope I shall be able to do the
duties required of me.'[45] No, George Leonard's day was not done, nor that
of Christopher Billopp. Four years later these two and their supporters were
still clamouring for what they believed to be their dues.

Lockwood's professional naval experience, as a hydrographer and surveyor
working for months at a time far away from naval higher command,
apparently made him as much valued in the bustling commercial port city
of Saint John as in the colonial capital at Fredericton. As with the tensions
between Loyalists and the army, there was discontent in Saint John with the
selection of a site for the capital eighty miles inland, where it could not
easily be surprised by an invading force, and along the river route to
Quebec. As the only centre of trade and industry, with about six thousand
inhabitants when Lockwood arrived in 1819, Saint John had never
accepted Fredericton as capital of the province. To the Saint John merchants
it was an isolated outpost, at best a temporary military necessity. The Saint
John *Gazette* would describe Fredericton in May 1819 as 'the Sequestered
Village', punning on Oliver Goldsmith's poem 'The Deserted Village', while
Saint John was termed 'the patriotic city'.[46] Built at the mouth of the St
John River on rocky hills, and centred on Fort Howe overlooking the
harbour, the city consisted of a number of villages, each governed by its
alderman-magistrate who was elected annually.[47] This civic structure
reinforced the tendency of Saint John to welcome 'American' democratic
values, and commercial concerns inevitably ensured that Saint John would
be influenced by world events. Circumstanced as he was, Lockwood would
find his natural allies in Saint John.

The tiny population of New Brunswick made aristocratic pretensions on
the part of the Loyalist landed gentry misplaced and politically enfeebling.
About 1800 Edward Winslow, a founder-father and one of the first
members of the Council, bemoaned the consequences of these social
tendencies: 'Activity is unfashionable, and a spirit of enterprise is either

called by the name of enthusiasm or blasted in the bud by being imputed
to a romantic disposition. Our gentlemen have all become potato planters,
and our shoemakers are preparing to legislate.'[48] In contemporary usage,
'Romantics' were wild, emotional, drawn to radical political views, while
'enthusiasts' were carried away by powerful religious feelings. Both
threatened the stable structure of a hierarchic social order. It was romantic
to seek and even welcome change; it was romantic to allow the possibility
that wisdom and truth might exist even among the 'lower' orders.
Politically, romantics sought Reform, new structures. They preached
democracy – that abhorred and monstrous offspring of the American and
French revolutions. Enthusiasm, applied to religion, was the enemy of that
reasonable view of worship, embodied by the Church of England, as a
confirmation of traditional values of King and Country. Enthusiasts were
naturally dissenters, and dissenters were also likely to be democrats, or so
the Tory line of reasoning went. In Winslow's dark vision of a reversal of
hierarchy – the shoemakers legislating for the gentlemen – the fear was
expressed of radical change occurring by default, by inertia, the gentle-
manly class failing in that necessary 'activity' needed to maintain itself. He
saw the danger of a fastidious shrinking away from action – the notion that
'our servants will do our living for us' – and asserted the obligations of
those born, as they saw it, to rule.

An account written thirteen years later by a young officer on leave,
Edward Thomas Coke, catches the prickly consciousness of status which
ran through colonial society. The levelling effect was paradoxically achieved
by means of the aggressive assumption of rank:

> As in the Canadas [Upper and Lower], the same blunt manner and
> independent spirit which an Englishman is so apt to censure in the United
> States is here very perceptible, and the lower classes of people assume
> similar airs. A shopkeeper is mightily indignant if so addressed: forsooth
> he is a storekeeper; a blacksmith is a lieutenant of militia grenadiers, and
> sports his full-dress uniform, with gold wings, as proudly as a nobleman;
> a maid-servant, who has emigrated from England only three years before
> with scarcely a shoe to her foot, walks in to be hired, and, in the presence
> of the lady of the house, seats herself in the best chair in the parlour, and
> then enters upon business with the ease of one who is reciprocating a
> favour: in short, no one confesses a superior. They certainly possess the
> leveling system in full vigour, inhaled, I should imagine, from the opposite
> side of the frontier.[49]

In truth, the dream of a stable, decorous society, in which everyone knew
his place, was just as idealised, just as romantic, as the vision of a New

Jerusalem. Winslow and the more thoughtful of the old Loyalists were far too shrewd and pragmatic to maintain it with absurd rigidity. The lines between the classes blurred in the face of common problems and dangers. Survival meant compromise, expediency, accepting the force of circumstance. The universal adult male suffrage established in the New Brunswick charter was not to be even approached in Britain for another fifty-eight years, after forty years of agitation and riot in Britain overcame resistance to the Reform Act of 1832. Even then the British franchise was more limited than that in New Brunswick. Life in the North American colonies, for all the anti-democratic posturing, had a levelling tendency. While many of the same Loyalist families provided members of the House, it was in the House of Assembly that Winslow's shoemakers made their mark. Lockwood was to be employed frequently as liaison between the Council and the Assembly.

7

Surveyor General

THE SLUMP IN timber exports would not have been apparent as Lockwood came ashore early in July 1819 at Market Square Wharf, but he could not miss the landless poor gathered along the waterfront or the steep streets leading down to the landing place, many recent immigrants from Britain. The immigrant crisis was to be the first test of Lockwood's qualities.

In the immediate post-war period New Brunswick actively sought emigrants, even financing an early scheme to boost the population. On 8 March 1816 the House of Assembly had voted £1000 to assist the passage of emigrants, and this sum was then paid to James Taylor, of Fredericton, who contracted to bring 134 settlers from Scotland by 1 December that year.[1] The terms were specific. All the emigrants were to be under forty; a hundred were to be adults over fifteen; two children between two and ten would be considered as one adult; infants would not be counted. All were required to be healthy and possessed of certificates of good character signed by a minister. There was a bias in favour of young single men and women. Taylor chartered the *Favorite*, a new brig of Saint John, and she was in the Clyde by October, where Taylor advertised for emigrants. The *Favorite* turned round very quickly, carrying 136 passengers back to Saint John, where they disembarked on 22 November. But on their arrival, many were destitute. The shipboard health examination was cursory and there was no adequate plan in place to receive this flood of driven and desperate people. Arriving in winter, many were lodged in the almshouse or taken in by families in the city, assisted by the parish. Despite their arrival as a group they did not form a distinctive settlement in the following spring. The single men and women were expected to find work and fend for themselves; a few others could afford to buy land; some girls were probably taken into service in Saint John and Fredericton. Others in the party moved on to the United States as soon as they could put together the fare.[2] Some *Favorite* passengers settled towards the mouth of the Magaguadavic River in Charlotte County – the present-day St George district. 'I was shocked at the dismal and wretched appearance of the country,' wrote one of them, eighteen-year-old John Mann in an account of his *Travels,* published in Glasgow in 1824. 'From the severity of the winter, and the gloomy aspect which the woods and water presented, one would certainly conclude this to be a most excellent place of banishment.'[3]

The *Favorite* venture was a badly planned, and fairly expensive, failure. The time of arrival was disastrous; there was no land settlement scheme; the emigrants had obviously not been prepared for what to expect. The House of Assembly took pause. But emigrants continued to ship out. Fares to British North America were initially kept low by government decree. Parishes in Britain offered assisted passage to paupers so as to remove their expense from the Poor Law rolls. By 1818, assisted or not, as many as twenty thousand emigrants flocked to the 'America' ships and more than twenty-five thousand in the following year, often with the vaguest sense of geography, sometimes failing to distinguish between the British colonies and the United States. Many were conned by shipmasters into believing that the ports of Canadian colonies were only a short hop to New York, Boston or Philadelphia. Even the better organised emigrants frequently lacked 'means of cultivation' and few were prepared for the severe winters. John Mann, the young *Favorite* emigrant, met two Irishmen along a trail, with their wives and two tiny children, walking from Quebec to New Brunswick. Many others took off along the boggy, black-fly infested forest tracks bound in ignorance and hope for 'America'.

On 16 June 1818 the *Royal Gazette* in Fredericton was reporting news carried upriver by the steamboat, 'which arrived here early this morning.' 'We learn that there were five arrivals [ie, ships] at the City from Europe, on Sunday last, some of which brought *eight hundred emigrants* from the North of Ireland, and that another vessel was hourly expected there with three hundred more.' With little or no advance warning, there was no way of knowing how many would come, or how many might stay.

Loyalists felt anxiety as well about the strength of the Mother Country's ties to her colonies during the immediate post-war period, when domestic economic and political stresses absorbed her attention. This anxiety was well expressed by a long article entitled 'British North America' from the *Colonial Journal* of October 1816 republished by the *Royal Gazette* in Fredericton on 16 January 1818. The whole article is a sustained argument for active encouragement of the British North America colonies, since 'there are persons who hold forth the doctrine, that the North American Colonies are insecure. They pretend that those possessions must soon be overrun by the United States; and they infer that Great Britain would be wise in giving a preference to establishments elsewhere. . . . Yet the North American colonies are placed in countries so highly adapted to be valuable to the parent state, that it would be a matter of serious regret if we were forced to believe that there are any circumstances which should induce us to relax in promoting their advancements.' A sophisticated analysis follows of social and political developments in the United States and Europe, leading to the conclusion that the Canadian colonies 'are secure, we may safely labor for their growth.' By reprinting this article, the *Royal Gazette* – the voice of Smyth's administration – was admitting the need for reassurance on this point.

When the House of Assembly had encouraged emigration in 1816, it seemed indeed to labour for growth. But lack of planning meant that emigrants fell on the parishes for Poor Law relief, mainly in the vicinities of Saint John and Fredericton. The Overseers of the Poor at Fredericton petitioned the House of Assembly for aid on 16 February 1817. Those of Saint John reported to the Assembly on 23 February 1818 on the costs incurred over the past year relieving distressed soldiers and sailors. Meanwhile, three surgeons, William Home Smith, John Head, and Robert Leslie, petitioned the Assembly on 2 February 1818 to be paid for tending 'the foreign poor' at Saint John and County from 1816. Then on 2 February 1819 a petition was presented to the Assembly from the Justices of the Peace for the City and County of Saint John 'praying aid for the support of disbanded soldiers, distressed sailors and emigrants.' The Fredericton Overseers followed on 3 March petitioning for aid in supporting 'the transient poor.' Bills were presented on 5 and 6 February 1819 to provide almshouses in Saint John and York County. Another bill, authorising the citizens of Saint John to build a poorhouse, followed on the 11th. The old City Windmill, which had served as poorhouse since 1800, burned down four days later, on the 15th, as a result of dry oakum being left near a stove-pipe.[4]

On 6 April 1819 the Canadian colonies were informed that His Majesty's Government would no longer 'give encouragement to Persons proceeding as Settlers to His Majesty's possessions in North America' other than a land grant 'proportionate to [their] means of cultivation . . . on arrival.'[5] Nevertheless, petitions concerning poor relief continued over the next two years, such as that by the Justices of the Peace in Saint John on 5 February 1820 for funds to relieve 'the transient poor sailors, disbanded soldiers, and emigrants'.[6] Yet despite the crumbling Poor Law system, the Assembly introduced another bill to 'encourage the settlement of Emigrants from England in this Province' on 1 March.[7] The need for a coherent overall plan was plain to see.

What of the Executive Council? On 27 May 1818, they had taken 'into consideration the situation of Emigrants from Great Britain and Ireland arriving in this Province and desirous of obtaining Locations of Waste

Lands' and resolved that it was 'expedient' to survey one hundred acre lots for such emigrants 'recommended as settlers by any of His Majesty's Council.' Three such tracts were laid out and on 6 June applications for land were directed to ad hoc committees of any three Council members.[8] But this response simply ignored the problem of feeding and equipping destitute emigrants, while presuming an orderly selective process administered by that dysfunctional group of men.

The settlement of discharged soldiers in New Brunswick where they would support the authority of the royal government had begun with the peace concluded at the end of the American Revolution, and it was continued in the aftermath of war of 1812. Smyth warned Council on 23 April 1819 that Bathurst had 'intimated' that the West India Rangers would be discharged in New Brunswick.[9] The unit had been formed from European soldiers drafted in from the Royal Africa Corps in 1806, later augmented with recruits from British prisons and French prisoners of war. Lots near Saint John and Saint Andrews were assigned to them, although in fact most settled in the upper St John River valley. Three transports, the *Abeona, Buerdon*, and *Star* discharged 530 Rangers at Saint John on 12 June. Disbanded by the 16th, they were offered grants of land and farming utensils in New Brunswick or 'an equivalent of ten pounds per person' should they wish to settle elsewhere. At first, only 'about 40' chose to stay, preferring to take the money, and to spend it. The *Royal Gazette* was 'sorry . . . to see so many intoxicated and bidding fair to squander away the little pittance of which they are possessed, leaving them in a few days objects of compassion, if not a charge to the parish.'[10] This last phrase was almost decorative, a mere formula. No New Brunswick parish could meet such charges. Anyway, 'compassion' was not the predominant emotion experienced by the inhabitants of Saint John observing this liberated soldiery.[11]

The Rangers were only the most obnoxious and threatening problem. 'Upwards of *Two Thousand*' emigrants arrived in Saint John in ten days from 6 June.[12] By year's end the figure exceeded seven thousand, the majority Irish, three thousand as late as October – more than the resident population of the city.[13] The scale of this incoming wave threatened to swamp them all. Though the *Royal Gazette* observed on 16 June that 'our City is, comparatively speaking, remarkably quiet', a detachment from the Fredericton garrison was dispatched as a precaution.[14]

With a slowly dying Lieutenant Governor and few able-bodied members, New Brunswick's Council was simply not equipped to deal with the emigrant crisis of 1819. On 22 and 28 May Council had authorised four more tracts to be surveyed but the pressure kept rising. Bathurst had written on 8 May directing that 'half pay officers and common settlers' be given 'every facility' in taking up grants. On 29 June, just before Lockwood's arrival, Council tried to digest this and the enclosed scale of such grants. Lieutenant Colonels, they were told, merited twelve hundred acres, majors one thousand, captains eight hundred, and subalterns five hundred. As for 'common settlers' – their grants were to be 'proportionate to the means of cultivation.'[15] This was fiddling while Rome burnt!

Lockwood had a good deal of what his contemporaries called a 'projector' in his make-up. At different times on his long journey to New Brunswick he had brought forward ideas for improved windmills, surveys and maps, a nautical compass, salmon fisheries, the encouragement of emigration, settlement and agriculture, a scheme for employing the Micmac on road work, and the growing of flax and hemp. Above all, he had confidently projected himself – most recently by dedicating his *Description* of Nova Scotia to Lord Dalhousie; earlier by offering to advise Lord Bathurst on the border issue between New Brunswick and the United States; claiming the fictitious office of 'Assistant Surveyor General' in Nova Scotia. But his long naval career had been defined by practical abilities expressed in opportunistic action. As a naval master, he had fitted up and navigated ships of war, administered an important shipyard, and conducted lengthy surveys, commanding his own small vessels, gathering his own crews far from interfering admirals and the obtuse Navy Board, or those bothersome and uncomprehending Lords Commissioners of the Admiralty. His whole experience and instinct led him to take charge, to act with dispatch.

Faced by an immediate and tangible problem Lockwood came ashore at the double and by assuming responsibility for one particular group of emigrants he proclaimed himself assertively at Saint John and Fredericton. As a matter of political tactics, it was bold and impressive.

Lockwood took up the cause of 180 Welsh, who had sailed by the brig *Albion* from Cardigan in Wales and come ashore on 12 June. Many of these people spoke only the Welsh language and some of the women, in their tall hats and red shawls, had an 'ethnic' distinctiveness in the streets which caught the eye. But Lockwood had less romantic reasons to choose these people. Only a year or so earlier, while he and his son put up their shingle in Halifax for work in the surveying line, the brig *Fanny* had entered Halifax on 15 May 1818 with 112 passengers from the Welsh port of Carmarthen. Dalhousie and his Council gave every encouragement to the settlement of about half of the *Fanny* party near Shelburne, seeing the Welsh, mainly farmers and artisans, as superior emigrants. The founding of New Cambria, as their settlement was named, widely publicised in Halifax at the time, offered a clear recent example of resolute and enlightened policy. The *Fanny*, furthermore, returned from Carmarthen again in the following year, bringing to Halifax on 29 May 1819 another 94 Welsh.[16]

It seems very likely that Lockwood encountered or learned about this new Welsh wave when he reached Halifax in the *Thornley*.

A few *Albion* passengers in 1819 had been ferried ashore in Nova Scotia to join the New Cambria settlement. Lockwood talked to those who reached Saint John and would have been told that more Welsh were planning to follow. The *Fair Cambrian* brought 81 more emigrants to Saint John from Cardigan on 11 August. The notion of a Welsh settlement in New Brunswick made good sense. It would follow an apparently successful precedent, while also competing with Nova Scotia in attracting this continuing stream of apparently superior emigrants, with a high proportion of farmers and artisans and but a few paupers.

Before he could act, Lockwood needed to visit Fredericton, to find a place to live. After only a few days in Saint John, he and his family, or some of it at any rate, sailed upriver on 9 July on the steamboat *General Smyth* commanded by Captain James Segee. There is no indication whether he was bold enough to take his mistress, Harriet Lee, with him at this time.[17]

The *General Smyth* had been launched from John Lawton's yard in April 1816 by a syndicate of Saint John merchants headed by John Ward. The St John River and its tributaries were the only means of inland transport available when the Loyalist settlers arrived. Working boats upstream by oar, or sail when the wind was fair, was a slow and uncertain business. The seventy nautical miles upriver from Saint John to Fredericton could take as much as six days in a sloop. Above Fredericton horses had to be used to tow boats through the rapids at Meductic and Betts Rapids. The syndicate had first applied to the New Brunswick legislature for an exclusive right to run a steamboat on the St John in 1812, only five years after Robert Fulton began the first commercial steamboat service on the Hudson, but the launch had been delayed by the outbreak of war with the United States. The schedule advertised in 1816 showed that, from early May until the river froze, the *General Smyth* left Saint John at 9am every Monday and Thursday weekly, arriving before midnight in favourable conditions, returning on Wednesdays and Saturdays, leaving Fredericton at 8am. The top price for passage was £1 2s 6d, in the after cabin with meals included, and there were ten-minute stops at riverside inns en route – Worden's at Long Reach, Scovil's opposite Gagetown, and Taylor's at Maugerville. The steward, according to the inaugural advertisement, kept 'a supply of the best of Liquors.' The schedule was soon changed when experience showed that passengers found other days of travel more convenient, or was flexible when the great and powerful wanted to travel on a particular day. It was all a huge advance in travelling comfort.

On 17 October 1817, a Friday, Lord Dalhousie had boarded her at Saint

John with Admiral Milne, their ladies, and party, accompanied by General Smyth himself. She made six miles an hour upriver against a stiff wind. Like many others, Dalhousie was bowled over by what he saw en route. The river, he wrote, was 'magnificent'. After the 'romantic', that is hilly, first few miles they entered the Long Reach where it branched 'off right & left into immense lakes deep and navigable, into the very interior parts of the province. Of these the Kennebecasis, & Washadamoac, the Grand Lake & the Oromocto river higher up (in which last more than 200 sail of square rig vessels have been built within a very few years), are the largest, & give most important advantages to the rising agriculture & improvement of New Brunswick, but there industry is yet as in Nova Scotia in its infancy.'[18] Was Dalhousie's continual irritation with Smyth's torpor partly rooted in this direct witness, his spontaneous recognition of the vast promise of the St John River valley? He passed along its immensely fertile flood-plain and saw the valleys and ridges beyond still clothed with stands of fine trees. This surely was a land fit for 'Agricola' and some imagined team of lean and dedicated Scots.

There were 'most comfortable births [sic]' and even 'an elegant apartment separate' on the *General Smyth*. Did Lockwood take the latter? However it was, his passage upriver in high summer was a seductive introduction to the land. He saw what Dalhousie saw, vivid now with the lush vegetation of July, and also must have glimpsed the vaunting possibilities of his new role as Anthony Lockwood, Esq, Gentleman. At Sagwa at the mouth of the Nerepis, on the larboard side as the *General Smyth* swung right up the main river, standing on the rich flood-plain, was General John Coffin's six thousand acre 'Alwington Manor', named after his ancestral home in Devon, England. Coffin, whom Lockwood would soon join on Council, had done himself well, as had another long-serving councillor, Judge John Saunders, whose own spacious estate of 5,326 acres, 'The Barony', lay seventy miles upriver.[19]

The steamboat reached Fredericton late at night. Smyth was in Halifax, where he spent most of that summer, and since council meetings well into the fall were held at Saint John, there were few obligatory calls to be made. Smyth did not inform Bathurst of Lockwood's arrival in the province until 10 August, when he asked that the superseded George Shore be given the post of Auditor General, formerly held by Sproule while the latter was also Surveyor General.[20]

Lockwood must have called at the Surveyor General's Office, on Queen's Street, next to Province House where the Legislative Assembly met. This, and the office of the Provincial Secretary, had recently been built according to a contract, under the signatures of William Franklin Odell and George Sproule, which called for 'two substantial Stone Buildings, in each of which there is to be an apartment completely *fire proof*; the whole to be of the best materials and workmanship.'²¹

In an undated note pencilled into the Surveyor General's Cash Book Lockwood later summarised his duties, along with an estimation of his income from various sources. They were 'to Execute His Excel[ency] the Lieut Gov[ernor']s Warrants of Survey, Draughting Grants and local plans, Settling Emigrants by Location Tickets, keeping records and annexing certificates to Petitions [for land grants] for Land or Timber, on both the Deputy Surveyors – the actual admeasurements of the allotments for which Duties are paid by the Applicants. The Surveyors do not receive salaries.'²² Having introduced himself, Lockwood would have discussed possible locations for the Welsh emigrants. When they applied for land grants less than two weeks later they specified a recently surveyed site, outside Fredericton, which they could not possibly have examined. This suggests that Lockwood, advised perhaps by the acting Surveyor General, George Shore, had by then returned to Saint John with the location for the Welsh ready for their application.

But he also had to take his bearings. This would be the principal theatre for his landlocked role, a little village, a military garrison, deep in a vast forest. Did any shadow cross his mind, this man who had praised 'happy, happy Arcadia', and called a son Arcade, a daughter Marina? Was he, like Smyth, entrapped from the beginning? A navy man in an army encampment, he would spiral like Icarus to catastrophe in this 'sequestered village'. Since 'infancy', his own word, Lockwood had lived the mariner's life, and in his times ashore had never dwelt more than a short walk from the sea or the sail-blessed estuary of the Thames.

Named for the royal 'Grand Old' Duke of York, King George III's second son and Commander-in-Chief of the Army, Fredericton was a living monument to the Loyalist cause. Erected on the broad interval at St Ann's Point, site of an ancient Maliseet camp, it looked across to where the French had built Fort Nashwaak in 1692. Apart from reasons of military security, Lieutenant Governor Carleton chose the site because 'it has the advantage of being nearly in the Centre of the Province', and was at the limit of navigation by sizeable boats.²³ The river valley was very fertile and the established pre-Loyalist farming settlement of Maugerville stretched down river.

After his arrival in Fredericton onboard the *General Smyth*, Dalhousie confided to his journal on 24 October that 'Fredericton can only yet be rated a village'. Nevertheless, he continued, 'it is laid out very well in large broad streets; the Assembly, the Legislature, the Courts of Justice, and the Head Quarters of the Military, have gathered here a very respectable community, and their dwellings neat and clean give to Fredericton an appearance of superiority and prosperity.' On the down side, he commented that Fredericton was, as it remains, 'insufferably hot in summer, and intensely cold in winter'. It was small but busy enough. There were public landings and small wharfs along the river bank, with merchants' stores and a clutter of stacked wood. The water front was so 'lumbered up' at times, according to the York County minutes, as 'to prevent carmen from following their lawful calling in hauling from the sloops as well as in hauling lumber from the shores.'[24] And there was the daily bustle of the garrison; the drilling in the parade square; the bugle calls; the redcoats off-duty in the streets.

Carleton had intended Fredericton as 'the Metropolis of New Brunswick' and ordered a survey by Dugald Campbell in 1785 which laid out spacious lots and those wide streets Dalhousie had praised, with provision for public buildings and squares. The barrack was built in 1791 to house the 54th regiment, at which time its sergeant major was the William Cobbett who was to play an important role in British political reform. Regiments were regularly moved about the empire, so that none would become too closely associated with the local issues, but Fredericton remained a garrison town until 1870, with about five hundred men in place much of the time. In was from Fredericton that the 104th regiment set out in February 1813 on its six-week march through the snow to Kingston in Upper Canada. One of their number, John Le Couteur, wrote that on setting off 'it was impossible not to feel, in a certain degree, low spirited as our bugles struck up the merry air, "The Girls we leave behind us", most of our gallant fellows being, as it proved, destined never to return to their sisters or sweethearts.'[25] The 104th was disbanded in 1818 and Fredericton barrack now held soldiers of the 74th or Assaye Regiment, which had distinguished itself at the battle of Assaye in 1803 under the Duke of Wellington. Detachments were maintained at Fort Howe at Saint John where there were perhaps forty soldiers, while a few others were stationed at Grand Falls up the St John River, on the road to Lower Canada, and at St Andrews on Passamaquoddy Bay. In addition to the garrison, a number of the original grantees in the district were half-pay officers. Local men were also important figures in the provincial militia. Furthermore, the military fact was entrenched by discharged soldiers of the New Brunswick Fencibles, and of the 8th, 98th, and the 104th regiments who had taken up land grants along the upper St John River above Fredericton. Some of the former West India Rangers would soon join them.[26]

Though General Smyth retreated wearily to Government House for much of the time, he was of course entirely familiar with army officers and garrison life. Fredericton, in this sense, existed as his own redoubt against colonial society with its crass lumbermen, blustering merchants, and the screech of country fiddlers. In 1819, thirty-four years after the streets had been laid out, Smyth assigned to them official names.[27] It was a pious and predictable exercise. Smyth expressed loyalty by confirming royal references: King, Queen, Brunswick, George, Charlotte, Regent, York and Carleton merited a street. Smyth also echoed the names of counties and towns in the province at large: Province [Row], Sunbury, St John, Northumberland, and Westmorland. He honoured the greatest British military hero of the day in Wellington Street and Waterloo Row. The Navy received token recognition in Camperdown Lane. While Front Row was a tired effort – no doubt bowing to existing usage – Church Street was inevitable. His own name was to be attached to the last street to the east of the town.

As Anthony Lockwood first walked about Fredericton seeking a house, those streets made every step a stamp of political truth in what their names expressed: Crown, Army, Executive Government, stretching out to wilderness lands beyond, which though carrying the comforting names of English counties, were barely peopled, unsurveyed.

The stately spaciousness of Fredericton's layout was somewhat deceptive. Its elegance was skin-deep. By the summer of 1816 the presence of active and retired soldiery had helped to swell the number of taverns in both the village and the county 'far greater than is necessary for public convenience' in the view of the Court of General Sessions. Licensing laws were changed, requiring 'two good beds, four suitable stands for horses, two separate rooms', and 'such other accommodations for travelers' as the court deemed necessary. This was obviously an attempt to cut down on primitive drink shops which had no doubt proliferated during the war years. There were also occasional complaints about noise and petty vandalism on the streets. A York County grand jury on 13 June 1821, with George Lugrin, King's Printer, as foreman, considered the case of a house in King's Street, owned by one John Mitchell of Lincoln, which was 'now so old and out of repair as to endanger the buildings adjacent thereto.' But worse, it had 'of late become a resort for the most abandoned characters, that riots frequently occur there, to the great annoyance of persons residing in the neighbourhood.' Some problems with the soldiery were perhaps inevitable. A grand jury on 17 June 1820 found 'the Northwest Side of the Soldiers Barrack Yard' was 'a nuisance to the Public from the filth emitting therefrom into the Street.' A few months later, on 6 March 1821, a petition by 'sundry inhabitants' of Fredericton 'that soldiers may not be permitted to occupy stalls in the Market Square' was rejected on 13 June by another jury.[28] About the same time there were also complaints from the inhabitants of Carleton Street who 'would feel grateful if they could in any way be freed from the impertinence of two Military Sparks, who are constantly in the habit of patrolling that quarter, and from whose scrutinising gaze neither curtains nor blinds are sufficient to conceal the most private transactions of their families.' There were some attempts to give such men something other to do than peep or drink, including a move to 'have the Theatre at this place refitted' with a subscription opened at McLeod's inn. The proposers, C Ackerman and J Stevens, were eager to have members of the garrison join in and indeed take over the running of this venture.[29] But in general Fredericton had little to offer the garrison in the way of diversions.

'Finding great difficulty in procuring Lodgings, and an utter impossibility of obtaining a dwelling house', Lockwood concluded that he was 'necessitated to build a residence.' On his reconnoitre of the town, he noticed, at the corner of Queen and Smyth streets, 'an old defaced useless mill, standing on a vacant or ungranted Lot within the town Plot', and petitioned Council at their 21 July meeting in Saint John for a grant of the lot, offering to pay 'the value' of the mill. Though this was immediately granted, the lot was later deemed to have been previously granted, and Lockwood was required to pay an annual rent of twenty shillings to the College of New Brunswick.[30] However, he must have bought a house quickly, since his family was in residence within a year and the house would be offered for sale early in 1822.

He did not present his petition in person. His official status was still ambiguous and no formal appointment to Council had reached Smyth from Bathurst. In fact, the confirmatory letter was only penned in London on 25 July, to be read to Council by Smyth at the 23 September meeting, in Saint John.[31] Receiving Lockwood's petition on 19 July were Chipman, John Robinson whom Smyth had made the Provincial Secretary and Mayor of Saint John, Black, Billopp, and Wetmore. All were from Saint John, but Wetmore had recently moved his residence to Fredericton where Council usually met, often in a committee of three, to transact routine business.

At the same meeting a petition and supplementary petition was read from twenty-five Welsh men 'praying allotments of land to be made for them back of the Nashwaksis Stream at a distance of about 17 miles' from Fredericton towards Tay creek. This too was complied with. Grants were made of two hundred acres for married men and one hundred for single. Only four days later, in Fredericton, Lockwood signed a location ticket for one of these single men, the widower Jonathan George, evidently the first Welshman to make his way to the new settlement.[32]

The two petitions, Lockwood's and that of the Welsh, were linked. Before he had a roof over his head, before his appointment was even formally confirmed, in a new country where he was not known and plainly resented, Lockwood used the Welsh to help clear his path.

The settlement at Cardigan, as it became known, required immediate charitable help and an effective organisation to engage local people. Lockwood was back in Fredericton when the Welsh arrived en masse. On 5 August a meeting was held at the Jerusalem Coffee House (the name was adopted from a London original; there was also a Waterloo Coffee House in Fredericton) to 'form a Society for the purpose of assisting the Welsh families who are about forming a settlement between the Madame Keswick and the Nashwack [rivers].'[33] The merchants Samuel Grosvenor and Peter Fisher made a committee to collect subscriptions at the Coffee House, Avery's Tavern, their own premises, and those of Stephen Cameron and Jarvis Ring (also merchants). In Saint John the Cardigan Settlement was taken as evidence of the existence of a brazen policy to augment the population of Fredericton. The Saint John *Star* of 27 July sneered that 'such settlements in the vicinity of the *Seat* of Government will add weight and strength to a part which has hitherto received too *little* of either', at which the Fredericton *Royal Gazette*, the governmental news-sheet, huffed about the *Star's* ignorance: 'Our readers may judge in what way and to what degree those gentlemen [the *Star's* editors] stand *affected*.'

The Cardigan Society, as it became known, raised £76 10s 0d at that first meeting and issued a lengthy statement of intent in the *Royal Gazette* for the 14th. This responded to some criticism: 'There have also been objections to confining the purposes of the society to the Welch and not emigrants in general', but essentially it was first come first served. 'They had been sometime in town'; their land was surveyed; many of them were 'very destitute'; and they appeared 'particularly in want of some assistance'; 'Their families were straggling through the Streets or crowded in Barns; the season for peeling bark to cover the huts was nearly, if not already expired.' There was also more general criticism of the sort which always surfaced when the Poor Laws were under strain. Emigrants, after all, were only a special category within the broader mass of unemployed or indigent people, and critics argued that the Welsh were receiving exceptional favour. In its defence, the Society insisted that it could not 'at once take up a subject [ie, immigration] of such general importance to the Province', though 'it was the intention of the meeting to apply the over-plus to the assistance of emigrant settlers in general.'

Lockwood's identification with the immigration issue took another turn at the New Brunswick Council meeting on 23 September. Smyth then read Bathurst's letter of 25 July appointing Lockwood, Harris William Hailes and Samuel Denny Street to Council, and another letter from Bathurst containing an extract from Lockwood's lengthy memorandum of April 27 to the Colonial Office.[34] Lockwood had then claimed to be 'well-acquainted with the local circumstances which have hitherto obstructed the Settling of His Majesty's Provinces in North America', and recommended the

'Surveying Planning and Dividing into Sections all Crown Lands in New Brunswick and Nova Scotia, after the manner adopted by the United States, which method has proved to them of great advantage.' Slight indeed was his acquaintance with New Brunswick, a fact better known in Fredericton than in London, but Lockwood had plunged on, addressing the problem of emigrants choosing the United States over the British colonies. Writing of 'the multitude of Persons from Kent & Suffolk, as well as from this City [ie, London] and its environs who are desirous of going to America, and who would, most probably, continue excellent subjects to His Majesty, if they were transferred to the British provinces, instead of to the States', he asserted that it was not enough to leave the matter in the hands of shipmasters. He proposed direct governmental action:

> the hiring of a certain Tonnage annually – say from the Port of London 400 Tons, – Liverpool 400 Tons, – for the purpose of taking out emigrants . . . The consideration of this measure has pressed in upon my mind from the general, though very mistaken, belief that the participation of the Americans in the fishery has injured the interests of Nova Scotia and New Brunswick. On this subject I can confidently speak having visited the harbours and shores of both provinces unremittedly for the last four successive years. In neither province have the inhabitants pursued the fishery with either perseverance, spirit, or industry; and to grant to others what these people would not use themselves cannot with justice be complained of as an evil. An impulse has been lately given to agriculture, which the scheme of surveying the whole of the Vacant Lands of the Provinces would materially assist, and at once stifle the unfounded complaints of the people.[35]

This is a characteristic Lockwood document, made up of dubious, self-serving claims and confident assertions. Had it been made public, it would not have pleased colonial readers in general – though there is a nod to the 'Agricola' party – stating, as it does, that the current inhabitants of Nova Scotia and New Brunswick were whining losers who needed to be shown by new British settlers how to fish and use the land. The right of American fishermen to fish Canadian coastal waters, furthermore, was an especially touchy topic.[36] Lockwood actually praised the Yankees. Some Council members must surely have recoiled. The man had barely found his land-legs before laying about him. But his words about losing skilled emigrants to the United States did fall on fertile ground. The issue would be taken up a little later by Colonel Le Poer Trench, on behalf of the Emigrant Society. While writing to John Robinson in his capacity as mayor of Saint John, on 20 December, Le Poer Trench solicited support in encouraging emigrants from the Mother Country to stay in New Brunswick rather than move on 'as they have hitherto done.'[37] Since Bathurst's letter to Smyth contained only an extract from Lockwood's lengthy memorandum, the Council sensibly decided to leave the whole matter until he turned up and explained himself.

Even as those Welsh settlers hewed against the winter, Lockwood was at work on other fronts. Is it just coincidence that on 1 August 1819, only a month after Lockwood reached Halifax on his return from London in *Thornley*, the Nova Scotia government woke up to the fact that the money voted by the New Brunswick government to contribute to the maintenance of the Brier Island lighthouse had never been paid?[38] At the Council meeting on 23 September when Smyth had announced that Lockwood, Street and Hailes would be joining its number, Street took the oath and his seat immediately, while Hailes joined Council on 2 October, its next meeting. But Lockwood was absent at both meetings, as his fellow councillors knew, because he was too busy for oath-taking formalities. With his compulsive energy, he had at once taken up a commission from Smyth of 3 September and ridden off into the bush.[39]

Few tasks could have appealed to him more. He left Fredericton and the slowly progressing Cardigan project, the daily grind of organising basic supplies and meeting petty obstructions, to recapture the liberating life of strenuous action. His task was a surveyor's dream: to make a preliminary survey for a proposed canal across the Chignecto isthmus. On the face of it, this was a project which should have transformed New Brunswick's business community. Running from the head of the Bay of Fundy to the Northumberland Strait, and hence to the Gulf of St Lawrence, the proposed grade level waterway would marry those seas which Nature had set asunder, thus opening a more direct, less icy route from the Atlantic coastal American states to Quebec City, and beyond, to Upper Canada and upper New York State.

If the canal could be built, Saint John might become the first port of call, bypassing Halifax, for Atlantic vessels bound for Canada. Mercantile interests in Saint John had pushed the idea in the spring of 1819 and on 3 March the House of Assembly authorised £150 to be spent by Smyth 'in procuring a fit and suitable person' to explore a possible route.[40] Lockwood was a natural fit for the job. He took with him a team of axemen and chain bearers who cut and measured a fourteen and a half mile survey path while Lockwood assessed the surface terrain and geology, calculating inclines and descents where locks would be needed. According to W F Ganong, Lockwood became at this time the first surveyor to use a spirit level in New Brunswick.[41] His report would be completed two days after Christmas and printed early in the new year.[42]

Lockwood had reason to feel buoyant on the canal survey. His mood was evidently good enough to make new friends. At some time during that autumn he must have met Philip and Sarah Ayer Palmer of Sackville, the small settlement on the edge of the Tantramar Marsh at the sharp point of the Bay of Fundy. In their thirties, born in New Brunswick and Nova Scotia respectively, the Palmers came from early founding families of the area. The immediate cause of their meeting appears likely to have been Phillip Palmer's position as a deputy surveyor in Lockwood's department. Palmer was a good person to guide him through Chignecto. However, Lockwood must have charmed or dazzled the couple, judging by the name they gave their son, born 28 August 1820 and thus, if the baby was full term, conceived in December 1819 while, or soon after, Lockwood was in the vicinity. The infant, Acalus Lockwood Palmer, would go on to a distinguished career as Member of Parliament for Saint John (1872-78) and as a judge of the New Brunswick Supreme Court.

It is the combination of Acalus with Lockwood which provides evidence that the Palmers named their little boy after Anthony Lockwood. Among Acalus's fateful inventions were the saw and the compass. It is the latter, though of the geometrical type, which makes the link with Anthony Lockwood, inventor of a 'Universal Compass'. Did one of the Palmers playfully suggest the name? It seems much more likely that it came from Lockwood himself. He chose symbolic names for two of his children and had a distinct extravagance in his use of words, as well as a self-dramatising tendency. But whoever fixed on Acalus for Anthony, the name stuck. Three years later it was the name he used for himself, when he was mad.

Acalus had expressed his hubris by excelling in his inventions, thereby making his masters look bad, for which he paid a mortal price. Acalus and Icarus, cousins, both fell to their destruction from having flown too high. Lockwood's story indeed had classical dimensions.

8

A New Broom

LOCKWOOD RETURNED TO Saint John from the Canal survey in time for the 13 October meeting of Council, where he subscribed his oath and took his seat. As requested, he set to work providing clarification of the General Survey scheme proposed to Bathurst in the form of a personal statement of twelve folio pages, dated 29 October. Though addressed to Smyth, it was referred to Council at their next meeting. He claimed to have ranged England 'from end to end' during the approximately five months he spent there early in 1819 and to have found New Brunswick described in 'Catchpenny pamphlets for Emigrants' only as 'a wretched rocky fishing Country, a chilly cheerless waste, unfit for improvement.' He mourned that he had seen potential immigrants 'asking in vain for information, or allowed to seek it in the Rum shops, those execrable Sinks of impurity that are crowded in every back alley-corner in Halifax and the city of Saint John.' And he asserted that 'some hundreds of the surplus inhabitants were desirous of accompanying me, in my last voyage to this country. I knew from experience and observations the province was not prepared to receive suddenly any number of Emigrants – hence the suggestion. The local information in my possession and being chosen to fill an active and responsible position in this province, it became my duty to point out to His Majesty.' He suggested that £2,500 would suffice to cover the costs of the first year.

How much of this was bluff, or designed to draw in the pious Smyth, can only be surmised. The writing overall is unsophisticated grammatically, erratically punctuated, and politically naïve. Lockwood was dealing with some of the shrewdest and most powerful men in New Brunswick, mostly lawyers. They were not easily impressed, especially by a rank outsider throwing his weight around. His suggestion that New Brunswick could learn something from the Americans was hardly tactful for that audience – even if some councillors might agree with him. The General Survey proposal, rather like his *Description of Nova Scotia*, exposed Lockwood's brashness, hastiness, lack of caution, and insensitivity to the close-knit personal politics of the province. But the document is fuller and much more specific than the earlier memorandum to Bathurst and clearly draws on local information Lockwood had recently acquired – concerning the Isthmus, for instance – and the various figures, distances, and specific locations are all new.

Lockwood was disappointed that the councillors took the easiest way out, deferring the matter to the next meeting. He was plainly irritated by the delay and tried to circumvent Council by appealing directly to Smyth, forwarding a copy of his proposal on 15 November, 'as the consideration of it, here, is delayed from week to week, creating a probability of the intentions being defeated which is to open an avenue that may retain to His Majesty good subjects; and gain for the province an accession of Wealth and strength.' Again his language is urgent, emphatic, moralistic: 'Your Excellency is aware that we receive and keep the mere rubbish, (if I may use the expression) of the Emigrants, miserable, needy beings, incapacitated by poverty, to benefit from your liberal and encouraging mode of locating them and there can be no reason why the thrifty Emigrants should go to the United States, and leave the Idle and Indolent a burden to the province; but [for] the total ignorance of *all* England as to the soil, the climate, and advantages of this country.' A grant of £10,000 would be 'but the fourth of the amount of a sum voted by the British parliament for the Erecting of Fortifications in one of the counties under your Excellency's Government.' The sale of lands would cover all costs, he wrote, while 'the operation might be so conducted as to open the country' by employing emigrants to build roads to their settlements and teaching them 'the lessons necessary to their experiences in these provinces: ie, the axe, the quantities of [one illegible word] growth, the mode of Camping, procuring Fire, Building Log Huts, the mode of Felling Timber.'[1]

Apart from the idea of a General Survey, Lockwood, with the same sense of urgency to get himself gainfully employed that he had shown in London, added a suggestion that he be commissioned to make a 'Census' of New Brunswick, by which he apparently meant write an account similar to his Nova Scotia book. He requested £1,000 of public money. 'If I had money, it should be expended in the projected Task; but I am poor, tho not needy.' He went on, however, to dampen expectations, 'to guard Your Excellency against the expectations of extraordinary performance . . . my intention extends no further than a mere geographical sketch that will answer the double purpose of affording information, and of prompting an abler hand to give a perfect Historical Account of this portion of the New World, destined at no remote period to be rightly valued.'

Perhaps the slow progress of the Welsh at Cardigan, who lacked those basic pioneering skills, lay behind it. Since they were identified with him, as his personal project, he may also have felt politically exposed and let down. Lockwood's impatience is palpable, but he was also concerned that his initiative might be considered presumptuous: 'As I am not happy in conveying my sentiments,' he wrote, 'your Excellency may find a difficulty in receiving them.' Smyth responded by forming a committee of Wetmore, Hailes, and Street, the three most recent additions to Council, other than Lockwood himself, to assess the proposal for a General Survey and its likely expense. Though it looks as though Smyth opted for new blood, the committee was probably selected on the pragmatic grounds of availability at that time of year. They all lived in or near Fredericton.

Over the next seven months frequent reports on Cardigan appeared in the *Royal Gazette* accompanied by continued direct appeals for public charity, rooted in the biblical Epistle from St James: 'If a brother or sister,' says St James, 'be naked and destitute of daily food, and one of you say unto them depart in peace, be ye warmed and filled, notwithstanding ye give them not those things which are needful to the body, what doth it profit them?'[2] The reports are anonymous, but they have Lockwood's direct and emphatic tone, and the day-to-day operation of the Cardigan Society was conducted from his office. The biblical reference, however, failed to do the trick: 'The Overseers of Poor have their hands full already, the present rates are paid with extreme reluctance, and no friend to the country can wish to have the number of unproductive persons augmented.' It was more expensive to maintain immigrants in town than in the woods, where they had plenty of fuel and by felling trees could clear potato patches for next spring. Self-interest, it implied, was married to moral good. Life in town was fraught with temptation. It might 'lead them into idleness and knavery, or what is worse, drunkenness.'[3]

This public debate prompted a meeting in Saint John on 6 October to consider 'ways of assisting needy emigrants during the ensuing winter', and a Book of Registry and subscription list was established at the office of Charles Peake in Water Street. A plan to hut emigrants outside town was agreed upon, with landowners allowing squatters who might do some clearing work.[4] Meanwhile, outside Fredericton, the building of Cardigan settlement became a very public work-in-progress as, by trial and error, direct methods of assistance to emigrants were tested on the Welsh. As late as 19 October, though 'upwards of twenty men' had been working for two months, there were still no habitable cabins among huge stands of rock maple, beech, and mighty pines. These men lacked tree-cutting skills and only broad axes were in use at the time. Winter came early, too, as it did throughout those years, and the season began to bite. Jonathan George, first Welshman off the mark to his grant, lost his son to that implacable forest, 'through fatigue and the inclemency of the weather', according to the

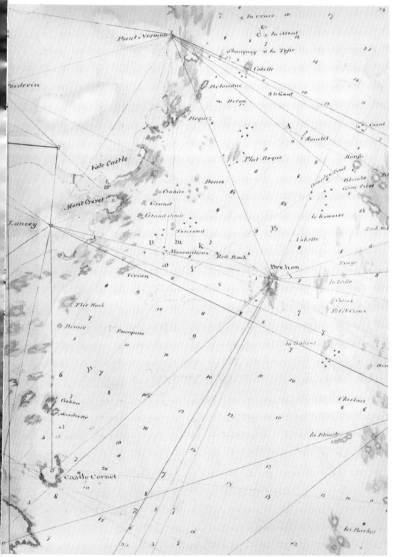

1. (ABOVE) *Platform Bay, Cape Nicholas Mole, St Domingo.*

2. (LEFT) *Detail from 'A Series of Triangles formed on Island of Guernsey in Year 1805.*

18. (ABOVE) *Sleighing Party, Fredericto[n]*

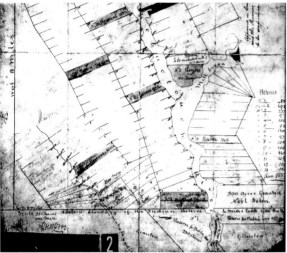

19. (LEFT) *Survey of Richibucto Reserv[e] Lands.*

20. (BELOW) *Sketch of Robert C[.] Minette's proposed route for Chignecto Canal.*

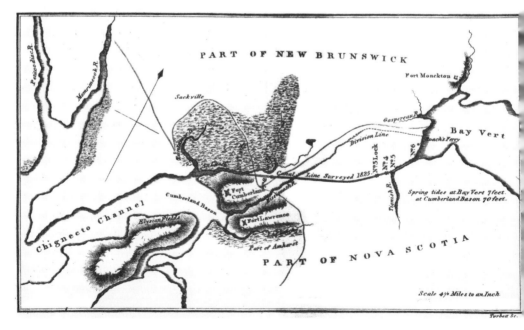

permitting schools and 'places of Public Worship' – two subjects dear to Smyth's heart – to be built. To date, they maintained, too much settlement had been in a 'straggling manner' by isolated individuals, meaning no schools or churches 'for a Century to come.' They believed that at least ten thousand lots of a hundred acres could be laid out, though it is not clear whether this referred to the trial period of one year, or the four Lockwood believed necessary to complete the scheme.

As to cost, 'the Surveyor General is of opinion' that it would take four years and £10,000. They fully endorsed a one-year trial, costing £2,500, and employing two deputy surveyors, with eight men each, for nine months in the woods. They would be supplied with canoes, instruments, etc, as required. The Surveyor General would be compensated for super-intending the whole, correcting his deputy's work, finishing maps, and compiling a report.

A more detailed costing followed, first of labour (per annum per man): deputy surveyors, £320; qualified chainmen, £90; 'other chainmen', £80; flag bearers and axemen, £75; two Indians 'to carry Baggage and make Camp', £65 each. In addition six canoes were needed at £20; 'Instruments' at £175; horses 'and other Contingencies' at £100. The total of £2,155 left £345 to pay Lockwood and his draughtsman.

The committee's report ended by proclaiming the value of settling 'a class of men, born and nurtured in the British Empire.' Furthermore, the scheme would cut the costs to individual settlers of surveying lots to 'not much exceed the twentieth part' of those currently incurred. Finally, they expressed cautiously worded optimism, being 'not disposed to think it may not be accomplished' in four years for £10,000.[8]

This clear endorsement by three new members of Council must certainly have enhanced Lockwood's political status. It came within days of his completing the *Report* on the Chignecto canal route and while the daily business of the Emigrant Society was being conducted from his office.

Lockwood's request to Smyth for money to finance a census was consistent with his interest in compiling accurate statistics.[9] He began to gather meteorological data about the province and a 'Meteorological Report for Fredericton. For the Seventh Month, 1819' appeared in the *Royal Gazette* for 25 July 1820. Subsequent reports were printed regularly thereafter. His claim that basic information about New Brunswick was lacking in the Mother Country was entirely accurate and newcomers to the province echoed this view throughout the nineteenth century.[10]

Lockwood seemed tireless. On 16 December, at another meeting in Saint John, Council read a letter from him proposing to run a line between the counties of Westmorland, Kings, and Queens 'agreeable to a Resolution of the House of Assembly.' The letter had been addressed on 23 November to

Wetmore at his home at Kingsclear, presumably as a member of the Survey committee. Lockwood had tracked down a resolution listed in the Assembly Journal for 1816 asking for such a line to be drawn. 'I am informed it is good land. If so it possesses capacity to receive 380 Emigrants. This Line of say fifty Miles might be admeasured and laid out for one hundred and forty seven pounds sterling. I have taken some pains to make the Estimate say it is advisable.'[11] The final phrase is ambiguous, even implying that he had massaged the figures to make them appealing. A quorum of the Saint John area Council members composed of Billopp, Chipman, Coffin, William Black and John Robinson simply referred the matter to the next session of the Assembly.

This new proposal, advanced while the scheme for a general survey was still in committee and before Lockwood had completed his Chignecto Canal report, again suggests a driving compulsion to be at work or to draw attention to his merits. But winter had already settled in. There was a huge blizzard and wind storm at the turn of the year which lashed the coast. On the morning of New Year's Day, Partridge Island, in the approaches to Saint John harbour, 'could not be perceived from the shore', and guns were heard indicating a ship in distress. Then, 'about 9 o'clock we had a lucid interval' and the brig *Mary*, owned by the local merchants Crookshank and Johnston, was identified. Inhabitants of the city crowded the shoreline and 'the public was now entirely engrossed in the fate of the Master and Crew.' It was not until noon the following day that it could be confirmed that all thirteen had perished, including their popular local master, George Bell. No large-scale surveying could be started before spring. Had Lockwood, after seven years in Barbados and four in the relatively mild climate of Halifax, really appreciated the difficulties presented by New Brunswick's winters – especially when, at this time, they were exceptionally cold and long?

Lockwood completed his canal report two days after Christmas. The pamphlet, printed by George Lugrin, the King's Printer, early in the new year, includes a prefatory letter of 27 December to Smyth as well as an extract from the *Journal* of the House of Assembly of 3 March 1819 authorising £150 to Smyth to finance such a survey. Another note states that the House of Assembly 'expressed a desire, to have Printed a few Copies for their immediate use.'[12] Lockwood's punctiliousness here, taken with his resurrection of that 1816 resolution to run that line between the counties, suggests that he had already begun to position himself politically by taking up initiatives originated by the Assembly.

The *Report* contains twenty-two pages of main text, for the most part factual description of terrain, with precise locations, distances, dimensions, soils, rocks, timber, and with commentary on the practicability of cutting a channel. There are occasional observations of his working party. Hacking

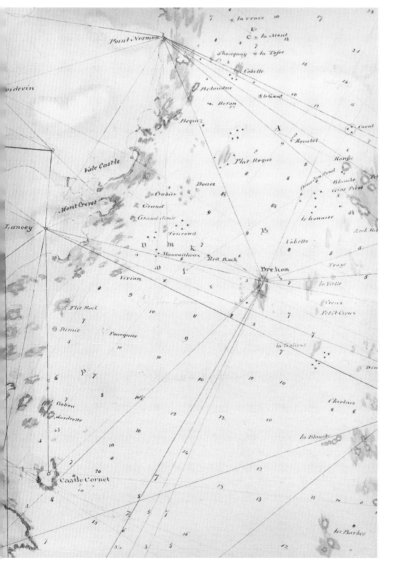

1. (ABOVE) *Platform Bay, Cape Nicholas Mole, St Domingo.*

2. (LEFT) *Detail from 'A Series of Triangles formed on Island of Guernsey in Year 1805.*

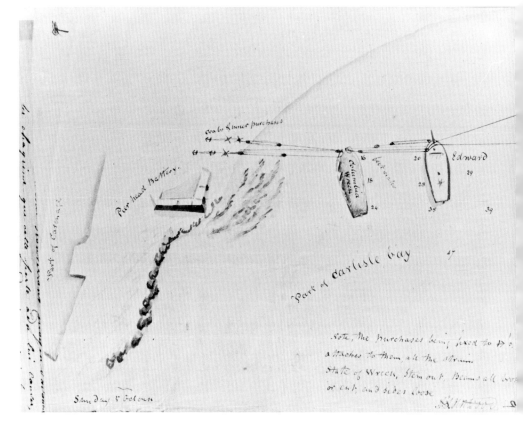

3. (ABOVE) *Clearing wrecks in Carlisle Bay.*

4. (RIGHT) *Detail from Îles des Saintes.*

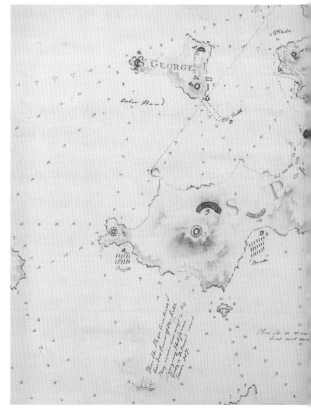

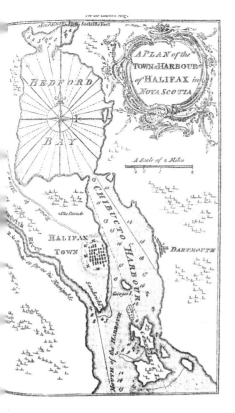

5. (LEFT) *Plan of the Town and Harbour of Halifax.*

6. (ABOVE) *The Commissioner's House in the Naval Yard, Halifax, 1803.*

. (BELOW) *Sketch of Gannet Rock off Grand Manan Island.*

. (RIGHT) *Sketch of Seal Island.*

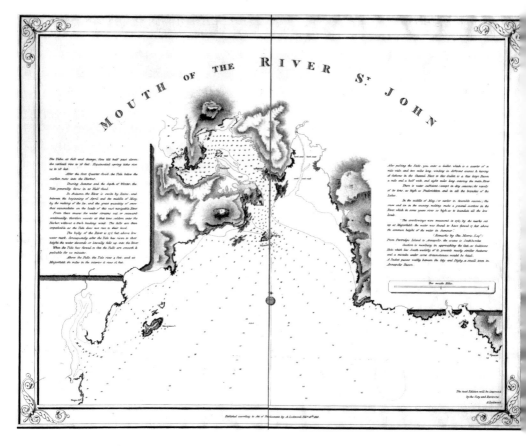

9. (ABOVE) *Mouth of the River St John.*

10. (BELOW) *A View of the City and Harbour of St John.*

1. (ABOVE) *A View of Saint John.*

2. (BELOW) *On the Kenibeckasis near St John.*

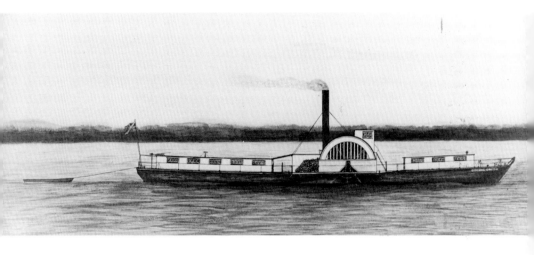

13. (ABOVE) *General Smyth, 1816.*

14. (RIGHT) *View of Province Hall and Public Offices, Fredericton.*

15. (BELOW) *Governor's Residence, Fredericton.*

6. (ABOVE) *Barracks and Market House, Fredericton.*

7. (BELOW) *Officers' Barracks, Fredericton.*

18. (ABOVE) *Sleighing Party, Fredericto[n]*

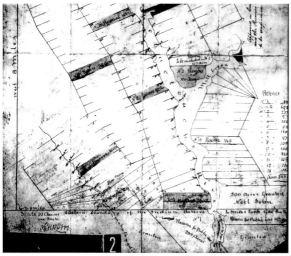

19. (LEFT) *Survey of Richibucto Reserv[e] Lands.*

20. (BELOW) *Sketch of Robert C[.] Minette's proposed route for Chignecto Canal.*

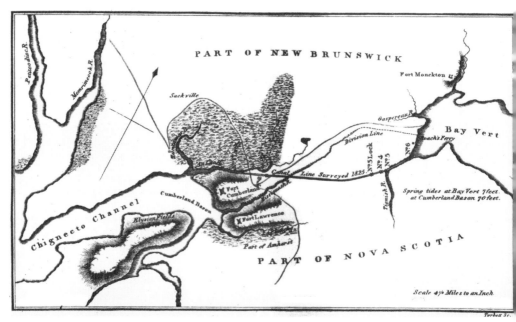

Inquest, but from 'want of sufficient nourishment' in the words of Lockwood, secretary of the Cardigan Society. Most of the Welsh were 'half starved', and even some whose cabins were built were too weak to move out of town. By 13 November eighteen families had been assisted, ninety-eight persons in all. 'They appear to be,' declared the *Royal Gazette*, 'without one exception, a quiet, inoffensive, moral people.' Lockwood would soon repudiate that judgement. As for now, the families who did move out were 'also in much want of bedding, a few muskets, powder, etc.' But the Society had reached the limit of private charity and complained of those who had failed to fulfil their pledges.[5]

It was time to replace these partial arrangements. On 16 November a meeting chaired by Judge John Saunders at the Court House agreed to form an Emigrant Society to assist 'Emigrants from our Mother Country', absorbing the Cardigan Society. A committee was composed of Judge Bliss, George Street, and the prominent Fredericton merchant Jedediah Slason, together with the Overseers of the Poor. A handbill was distributed calling the inhabitants of Fredericton to a full public meeting on the 29th. The merger was complete on 13 December.[6]

From the beginning it was a quasi-governmental organisation, marking a distinct shift in policy, with Smyth as patron; Colonel Sir Robert le Poer Trench as president; the young lawyer, George Frederick Street, son of Samuel Denny Street, as treasurer; and Anthony Lockwood as secretary. Lockwood also administered what was left of the Cardigan Society and both organisations were run from his office, with attendance between 10 and 12am each day. 'A building was procured and repaired for the sick in a remote part of the town, distinct from any other building.'

Lockwood engaged himself in this work at the most basic level, and kept the minutes and account book of the Cardigan and Fredericton Emigrant societies, as well as the subscription lists published in the *Royal Gazette*. These reveal the extent of public charity. An undated note in his hand to Slason, scribbled inside the cover of the Society's minute book, asks 'Can this poor man receive Ten Shillings to assist him to Travel up the Country?' The 'principal persons' of outlying York County were approached for contributions and farmers advised that labour was available. Yet 'persons having the means of giving employment' were slow to do so, threatening 'the intentions of the Institution' to 'fall flat to the ground.' Alas, some emigrants fell by themselves. 'Pat Kennedy obtained an axe, and aided by cash from Doctor Emerson, made off: axe pawned for 6/- & recovered.'[7] A sadly familiar figure reappeared on 18 January, when the Visitors 'exposed an imposition of the Welshman' George. But there was no doubt about the suffering. A month later the Visitors 'reported on Welsh family frozen: a man injured by the fall of a tree, relieved and dismissed.'

In day-to-day operations, individuals, especially those who served as Visitors, often simply advanced money or goods, billing the societies later. George Shore was repaid £7 10s 0d for potatoes on 5 May while Jarvis Ring received £5 16s 0d for carriage of potatoes and supplies on the 16th. On 13 August 1820, for instance, David Pickard, George Shore, Jarvis Ring, D Street, Jedediah Slason, and Peter Fisher were recompensed sums ranging from £1 17s 6d to £48 5s 4d for a total of £147 1s 4d. By working at the centre of this genuinely communal effort by a number of Fredericton's leading merchants and Crown officers, Lockwood must have quickly made himself part of that tight little society.

While the Council committee deliberated over his Survey proposal, Lockwood was present at a Council meeting in Saint John on 4 December 1819 at which George Shore was awarded £50 for preparing a map of the province during the time he had been acting Surveyor General. The attendance that winter day is worth noting: Smyth, Saunders, Bliss, Wetmore, Lockwood, Street, Chipman, Coffin, Robinson, William Black – as well as a Colonel Phillips. On an occasion like this, particularly since the Council had held all its meetings in Saint John for several months, it might reasonably be questioned whether the city had effectively become the seat of government. It was a question which would long smoulder, to erupt in flame at the time of Lockwood's personal catastrophe.

The Survey committee's report, dated 13 December, firmly endorsed Lockwood's scheme. They had 'been attended by the Surveyor General' during their deliberations. Conscious perhaps of his tactlessly over-enthusiastic approval of American practices, they began by stating that since 'the circumstances of that Country are so different from this Province' there was little advantage in learning more about what they did in the United States. All the same, 'it would be very advantageous to have a General Survey made of the Crown Lands' and, if directed by the Surveyor General, those advantages would far outweigh the costs. They agreed that 'hundreds and indeed thousands' of potential settlers 'have had their attention diverted from this Province, for want of preparation for their reception here', as well as by 'incorrect statements' concerning its soils and climate. Many had 'scant means to penetrate the Wilderness' to seek out settlement sites. And despite the earlier dismissal, the committee approved the American practice of offering surveyed tracts of land at auction and thus encouraging individual proprietors to sell off subdivided lots. At the least, a general survey would allow Smyth's initiative in setting aside Crown land for new emigrants to be greatly expanded.

This flattering reference to the Lieutenant Governor was implicitly reinforced when the committee argued the need to explore and survey the interior of the province so that 'compact settlements' might be established, through 'a thicket of thorny, scrubby, deformed spruce trees', 'the ax men were fatigued in advancing one mile in six hours.' 'It was with difficulty any place could be found sufficiently solid to place the instrument. The chainbearers and ax men were wading to their middles.' In assessing the merits of different routes he drew upon his experience as a mariner. Rejecting Cumberland Creek as an outlet, he pointed to the 'large rocks, and hard bottom [that] form the bed of the Bay, opposite the creek, and the Missiguash. On these, a vessel drawing eight or nine feet, would ground, and bulge, at low water spring tides. Ships ascending the Bay with south-eastern winds, would be compelled to anchor; they could not fetch.' He proposed 'a set of dry docks' to be cut on the Bay of Fundy side as well as a dock basin to a depth of fourteen feet with another at the Tignish end near Smelt Brook. 'It might be worthy the deliberate attention of the Legislature, how far it would be serviceable or otherways, turning the course of the Tignish. I merely glance at the expediency of such a step, feeling the necessity of a minute examination of the neighbourhood. Lockwood offered 'two directions for the Canal, both favourable to its execution', and concluded with an estimate of £63,500 over four years as the 'probable expense of cutting the proposed Canal.'

But he went beyond merely technical considerations. The advantage of using Allen's Creek as an outlet would be 'the large quantity of the choicest lands that would by draining be recovered for this Province . . . the sale of these would refund most of the expense. I therefore venture to advise the Government's retaining the lands in the direction of the contemplated Canal, as a measure of good policy and of general benefit.' Furthermore, 'two hundred laborers may be employed to advantage. The labor of the first year would be chiefly draining. Two-thirds of the men employed may be Emigrants, for whom I suggest a prospect of a grant in the neighboring vacant land . . . may be a great stimulus, as they will in the course of the labor, grow familiar with that part of the country.'

Lockwood's understanding that canal building could serve as a stimulus to the local economy, as a means to employ and settle emigrants, quite apart from the benefits to trade, would be borne out elsewhere in North America during the next decade or so. In Nova Scotia, work on the Schubenacadie Canal began in 1826, while in Upper Canada the Welland canal, work on which began in 1824, and the Rideau canal two years later, were massive public works drawing upon the pool of new labour provided by emigrants. The construction of the Erie Canal in upstate New York, commencing in 1817, gave a mighty impetus to the entire region, absorbing thousands of European emigrants in a transforming enterprise. The idea of a Chignecto Canal must be seen in this wider context, as potentially part of the so called transportation revolution spurred by new technology and massive engineering projects. For the next two years reports appeared in the *Royal Gazette* on advancing canal projects, beginning on 7 March 1820 with an item on the vast acreage surveyed for the 'New-York Grand Canals', extending up to Canada. The Saint John merchants would not let the matter drop and for the time being Lockwood was their man.

The 'few Copies' of Lockwood's *Report* printed for the members of the Assembly received wide distribution, according to a tantalising account in the *Acadian Recorder* many years later:

> The Saint John newspapers of the period were in ecstasies over the report of Mr Lockwood on the contemplated Canal 'through the Isthmus of Acadie.' A variety of opinions are afloat, said they, as to the means, the expense, and the practicability of making an inland navigation, but no very serious objections to the scheme have been heard. With one voice they declared it a pleasing duty to hold a prospect to the public of having *a shorter line of communication* from the Atlantic to the Polar seas by a short gateway through the isthmus of Acadia: 'the many advantages of such an undertaking do not immediately present themselves; the view is held to us in a moment of hurried business. Yet this hasty glance presents to our temperate fancy the enlivening picture of a Canal bearing upon its bosom the oil, the fish, and the furs of Labrador, the fruit and luxuries of the Tropic, with the grain and herbage of our own and neighbouring province.'[13]

'Ecstasies' or not, Lockwood had clearly earned approval in Saint John with the *Report*, and at the very least had pushed his name forward within the province's mercantile leaders. January 1820 may have been the high point of Lockwood's reputation in New Brunswick. After barely six months in the province he had forced attention. But, inevitably, he raised questions. How much of that bustle was really bluster? On the Council, furthermore, there were strong-minded individuals with an elevated sense of themselves, who were not in the habit of conceding power to anyone, starting with each other. The rivalries between them will be considered later. How, meanwhile, did they regard this obscure naval warrant officer, imposed on them from London, who had taken centre stage since his arrival in their midst only a few months ago?

On 26 January Council approved payment to Lockwood of the £150 previously authorised by the Assembly for a survey of 'the Isthmus at the hind of the Bay of Fundy.'[14] The House of Assembly, which during these years held a single February-March session, convened in Fredericton on 3 February. Council meetings were held almost daily during the session to consider legislation proposed by the Assembly. Throughout Lockwood's term in office he would act as the liaison between Council and the House, carrying Council decisions, proclamations and the like, a formal role which nevertheless gave opportunity for informal relations with members – and for gauging personal responses to the Council. He seems to have been assigned this role as junior member of Council, and sometimes Samuel Denny Street, next in seniority, would join him. It could only encourage his sense of being at the centre of things.

There was no let-up. Lockwood presented a petition to the Legislative Council 'from certain Merchants, Ship-Owners, and Mariners of the County of Charlotte' on 8 February and another three days later from the Cardigan settlers requesting a grant towards building a road.[15] Both were tabled. Two days later he transmitted to Smyth a schedule of emigrant lots taken up by tickets of location. It showed, he stated, 'the consequent advantage of locating by Ticket and Your Excellency will be pleased to observe that these people have received their Tickets of Location free of any expense.' Lockwood was clearly an active proponent of this scheme, which required payment of a quit rent at a later date in order to obtain full title to the land. Smyth and the Council decided that ticket holders should have two years' grace, presumably to induce paupers on parish relief to become settlers.[16] Identified in this document were two hundred lots on the Shepody Road; seventy-four on the Quaco Road; thirty-four at Cardigan; forty-four at Nerepis settlement; and thirty-six at Lake George; a total acreage of forty-two thousand. All but fifty-five were taken and a number of the vacant lots were reserved for glebe or school use. In all 228 tickets had been issued and thirty-nine applicants awaited lots on Washademoak Lake. These sites were widely dispersed from the lower St John River valley almost to the coast. Whether Lockwood had visited them all is questionable, though his readiness to take to his horse is not, nor his intense involvement in the emigration issue. This schedule certainly gives some scale to recent emigrant settlement. Two hundred and forty-six of these lots had been assigned to married men. Even at a low average of four members to each family, the total number of emigrants settled at these locations must have been well over a thousand.

On the 14th Lockwood provided Smyth with 'a schedule of Military Locations, made agreeably to your order.'[17] These consisted of Nashwak Portage (113 lots; 11,300 acres); Prequ'ile Settlement (311 lots; 31,000 acres); and St Andrews Road (118 lots; 12,200 acres). Most of the 331 soldiers located by ticket were, not surprisingly, single, and about a third of the lots were still vacant. This report was presented to the House of Assembly on the following day.[18]

On the same day, Lockwood's report on the Cardigan Society, summarising its history and progress to date, appeared in the *Royal*

Gazette. He reported that 'as many as a 100 souls' had been assisted, and 'a populous village, added to the Province, and a foundation laid in the wilderness, for a chain of Settlements.' Smyth and Lockwood had donated sums sufficient for the Society to pay off its outstanding debts. The significance of Cardigan as a *demonstration* of emigrant policy is plain to see. On 26 October Council approved Lockwood's report on a plan for an emigrant settlement between the Nerepis and Oromocto, with a major upgrading of the roads between that site and Fredericton and Saint John.[19]

Lockwood now returned tenaciously to the canal issue, warning Smyth by a letter 16 February that the prospect of a canal might inspire speculators. 'As the contemplation of a Canal may induce persons to make application for Lands contiguous', he repeated his earlier advice to keep all Isthmus land in Crown hands until after a full survey had been made.[20] Speculation was undoubtedly in the air. When Lockwood's report was officially delivered to the Assembly, a motion by Colin Campbell of St Andrews was carried 'praying that His Excellency will be pleased to give such direction as he may think proper, for the printing and publication of the highly interesting report of the Hon A Lockwood of his Survey of the Isthmus – and that the House will make provision for defraying the expenses thereof.' Lockwood also gained the approval of Council on 24 February for an appraisal of the standing timber on the Isthmus.[21]

Lockwood's canal survey, and the proposal for a general survey, was consistent with Smyth's objectives for the development of New Brunswick. The province remained a restricted society – a sizeable port, smaller ones at Miramichi and St Andrews, a small garrison capital, a few village outposts, the scattered cabins of poor settlers. Most villages were no more than collections of partially cleared wooded lots with simple log cabins. The only exceptions were the pre-Loyalist Maugerville region, the lower St John River valley, and the Sackville area with its farms worked since before the late eighteenth century Acadian expulsion. For the rest, neighbours were out of sight. In most such homes candlelight was a luxury. The inhabitants of isolated cabins were often squatters. Social manners fitted the case.

In the larger centres, however, there were hints by 1819–20 of greater sophistication and some demand for more genteel 'amenities'. Gradually, the mores of middle-class society in Britain and the larger cities of the United States began to penetrate. For instance, a letter to General Coffin's daughter Carline Boyd, written on Christmas Day 1819 by John Barclay, observed that 'the arrival of a Lady to teach dancing and a professed organist in St John's [*sic*] I think will be of great advantage to that famous city, the one teaching the young folks good manners and the other in improving the Voices of the Ladies.'[22] This 'Lady' may have been the Miss

Powell, who in August 1820 advertised a Dancing Academy at Miss Dennison's Seminary for young ladies in Fredericton, having received 'great encouragement' in Saint John.[23] Miss Powell was holding a 'Public evening' in Fredericton by early 1821. Dancing started promptly at 6pm, ending 'about 9.'[24] Later in the year, on 8 October, the Reverend William Howden opened an Academy for the Instruction of Youth at John West's house, Queen Street, Fredericton, 'in the Classical, Mathematical, and Mercantile branches of education.' He claimed to have taught for 'several years' in North Britain and Ireland, and offered stenography as an option.[25]

For readers, there was limited opportunity to keep up with contemporary writing. A subscription library in Fredericton was advertising shares in the *Royal Gazette,* the government news-sheet, from 1816. For general news, residents of the province had to rely upon newspapers from Saint John or the *Royal Gazette,* published in Fredericton. These were purchased by subscription, or consulted at the coffee houses, which also subscribed to British and American newspapers as well as those from other Canadian colonies. For those with philosophic interests, the Society for the Propagation for Christian Knowledge (SPCK), with its collections of 'improving' materials, became active under the leadership of Jedediah Slason from early 1819.[26]

A centre for business, gossip, political intrigue in Saint John was the Exchange Coffee House, familiarly known as Cody's after the owner, which provided 'entertainment, liquors, good board and good stabling for horses.' There was a Subscription Room for private members paying twenty shillings annually for access to *Lloyd's List,* a tri-weekly London paper, a New York daily and Boston daily, and a Halifax weekly and Saint John weekly paper. The proprietor provided fuel, candlelight, and a blank book for insertion of news, and pen, ink, and paper. The members included many of the male Loyalist and mercantile elite. Subscriptions for charitable causes and various petitions could be left for signature. According to John Russell Armstrong, Cody's was a little 'hub of creation'. The Court House, City Hall and Market were close at hand on the Market Square, and for some years the Post Office was only a little further south on Prince William Street, while a printing office (Henry Chubb's) was just alongside. It was the meeting place of the citizens for a great variety of purposes, social, political, and otherwise. Here were held many of the annual anniversaries of the national societies of Saint George and Saint Andrew. Civic, political, and military dinners were given under its roof. Even balls were held at Cody's, notably that in honour of Nelson's victory at Trafalgar. The Freemasons of Saint John met at Cody's for ten years.[27]

The huge increase in post-war ship traffic brought with it a far greater inflow of news. Private correspondence was also a widely shared primary news source. By the time Lockwood arrived in New Brunswick the province was decidedly opening to the wider world.

But the most powerful engine of cultural exchange at this time was public education. Smyth's administration was most notable for establishing schools. Though Lord Dalhousie dismissively called them 'low', the charge was unfair, even ridiculous. It is true that those aided by the government came under a Church of England dispensation and might be seen as underpinning that aspect of ultra-conservative orthodoxy. But Smyth's care for education was more broadly based. The *Royal Gazette* had published a letter on 14 July 1818 asserting that education, 'the original principles of instruction', was the key to 'the bravery, the magnanimity, the national, the moral, character, of kingdoms.' The improvements in this sphere, and the show of political will, were rapid and impressive. In that same month of July, Madras schools for boys and girls were established in Saint John by contributions from Trinity Church, the city Corporation, and public subscription. 'Madras schools' used older students as monitors to instruct the younger. A Council resolution on 11 February 1820 then called for the establishment in Fredericton of a Madras school, and at the same meeting, Council also voted aid for a grammar school at St Andrews.[28] The memorial tablet to General Smyth in Fredericton Cathedral mentions particularly his support for schools for the black community. Lockwood presented the Legislative Council with a petition from the inhabitants of Sussex 'for aid to establish a School on the Madras system' on 15 March, and the Madras School for girls opened in the capital in April 1820, with a Miss Baird as schoolmistress.[29] On 26 January the Executive Council responded positively to a request by Colonel Le Poer Trench to assign two lots in Fredericton's town plat to support the Regimental School at the Fredericton garrison, which opened its doors to the children of the poor.[30]

On 29 February that year a pamphlet was published 'out of the Receiver General's Office' by the King's Printer, listing the existing schools in New Brunswick, the acts and regulations governing them, and qualifications for prospective teachers.[31] Some of their number were private academies, such as Mrs Dennison's which provided girls with 'the requisites of an useful and genteel education.'[32] Under the heading, 'Female Education at Miramichi' an advertisement by a Mrs D M'Donald in the *Royal Gazette* of 2 April 1820 offered board and education for 'a few more young ladies'; her offerings included 'Figures and Velvet Painting.' The girls were to 'provide their own washing, bedding and Linen.' The basic rate was £10 per quarter (£8 under ten years), with extras at £1 each for French, music, drawing, and 2s 6d for the 'use of Piano Fortes.'

The New Brunswick College at Fredericton supposedly provided an education based on the classics for the families of the Council and 'Family Compact' while, in the words of Esther Clark Wright, 'their sons made life miserable for students from outside the circle.'[33] Public examinations of the students were held on 26 February 1820, which 'friends to the Progress of

Literature' were invited to attend. When the Regimental School held its public examinations on 4 March the sights were set lower. Attendees were invited simply to 'witness the progress' of the children.

Apart from the direct action of Smyth and Council, this flurry of interest in education signified a rapid maturing of this small society. Literacy, numeracy, some of the genteel graces, were part of the generally expansive spirit of the times. Despite the sheer chaos of the emigrant issue, with its strains on the whole social system, there was also a sense of release and progressive purpose in New Brunswick after the long incarcerating wars with France and the United States.

For those who *could* read, the columns of the weekly *Royal Gazette* reflected political issues in New Brunswick from the perspective of Smyth and his Council. No other news-sheet was published from 'the seat of government', and the *Gazette* tried to steer provincial thinking. Its governmental bias was obvious but it was required reading; Saint John newspapers of the time necessarily played off against it.

Though printed and edited by George Lugrin, the King's Printer, the *Gazette* was administered and in effect censored by William Franklin Odell, the Provincial Secretary. Since his esteemed father's recent death, Odell had assumed his status as senior member of one of the province's founding families.[34] The *Gazette* was not a forum for controversy but expressed the views and sentiments of the 'safer' members of government, including the Legislative Assembly, as well as printing governmental notices and proclamations. For instance, the regulations for cutting pine timber, and warnings against illegal encroachments, appeared regularly. But its content was also eccentrically miscellaneous. There were items culled from other newspapers, especially news from Britain and foreign places, including comic anecdotes, signed or anonymous articles on local topics, legal notices, information concerning societies and other organisations, advertisements of various sorts, mainly from Fredericton and York County, and notices concerning lost dogs, cows, straying hogs, dissolving partnerships, repudiation of wives' debts, the sale of oxen, and public apologies. The *Gazette* undertook lengthy campaigns on the subjects of education, emigration, and agriculture. Even dissidents had to take the *Gazette* into account.

Lugrin and Odell permitted differences of opinion on public matters to appear but not without the *Gazette* weighing in on one side. Saint John newspapers would often be quoted, while shipping news from the New Brunswick ports appeared regularly. What was printed in the *Gazette* was what was considered fit from the standpoint of executive government – Smyth and his Council – and the *Gazette* supported staunchly the political status quo. On 4 January 1820, for instance, the Prince Regent's speech of

28 November in London, attacking 'Reformers', was quoted with complete approval as 'vigorous and convincing.' 'All reverence for ancient Institutions – all respect for Church and State – for Ministers and for magistrates, thrown off and despised, prove that the Constitution demands additional laws for its protection.'

Yet despite growing fears that this social and political unrest might spread to the colonies, the *Gazette* defended the most vulnerable target and actively combated anti-emigrant feeling. It was not simply that reports from the Emigrant Society or other informative items about emigration appeared constantly.[35] The *Gazette* attempted to win hearts and minds, beginning with a simple appeal to finer feelings about the poor or victimised, in keeping with enlightened, paternal government. A poem such as 'The Female Convict's Address to her Infant' (25 Jan 1820) called for compassion: 'Deserted and helpless – to whom can I leave thee? / Oh! God of the fatherless – pity my child!' Even an announcement of the death of Robert Burns' friend 'Soutar Johnny' in the same issue was a reminder of the liberal sentiments of the poet himself and his hymns to the common folk. With the extracted passage from 'The Huts of the Poor' in the next issue (1 February 1820), undersigned 'O', readers were admonished to break out of their comforting shells of security: 'Too long do the mazes of ignorance hide, / The hovels where Poverty's children reside.' Was this Odell himself? His father was a notable poet. Meanwhile, reports, and lists of new subscribers to the Emigrant Society and Cardigan Society, were listed on 8 and 15 February; more general items on Emigrants appeared on the 22nd and 29th, as well as 28 March and 4, 18, and 25 April.[36]

The *Gazette*'s campaign in behalf of the dispossessed and unpossessed ran in parallel to a series of announcements on agriculture. These matters were closely related, since the *kind* of settlements emigrants formed should preferably be self-sustaining and diversify the provincial economy. Significantly, Lockwood's emigration proposals had emphasised soils, climate, growing conditions. They did not mention lumbering. In the earliest years of the province, agriculture meant subsistence farming or sales to small local markets, and during most of the long war years the internal economy of New Brunswick stagnated. When the timber trade began to expand rapidly after 1809 there was a huge incentive for landholders to cut trees for export as lumber, rather than expend their labour on increasing crops or improving grazing. Indeed, during these years a staggering eighty-five per cent of the male population was involved in the export of wood.[37] The early issues of the *Royal Gazette* are virtually free of significant reference to agriculture, other than merchants' advertisements for seed and the like, before 1818 and the first large influx of emigrants. On 7 April that year, however, a curious item appeared extolling 'Agriculture in China' which declared: 'By reason of the universal industry of the Chinese, together with their superior skill in husbandry, and their simple mode of living, almost every man is able to support a family – accordingly they marry young and multiply and cover the earth like grasshoppers.' This last was an odd simile for agriculturalists.

The familiar Canadian image of the lumberman as folk hero is of later vintage and did not fit the conservative political ideal of stable, hierarchical order. Lumbermen operated in the dead of winter, unsupervised by authority. Out of direct control, they invaded Crown Reserves and by cutting Navy timber weakened the first defence of the Mother Country. Lumbering, according to this view, was unpatriotic if not traitorous. Consuming the capital of the province, it did little to ensure a prosperous future for immigrants. In his 1828 *Historical and descriptive sketches of the maritime colonies of British America*, John McGregor conceded the commercial and economic importance of the lumber trade in New Brunswick, and gave an excellent detailed account of lumbering parties, their preparations for winter logging, their life and work in the camps, and the logs-runs downstream with the spring freshet. But McGregor warned about the lumbermen's 'habits of drunkenness', and characterised 'their moral character, with few exceptions', as 'dishonest', 'worthless', and improvident. 'Should he even save a little money, which is very seldom the case, and be enabled for the last few years of life to exist without incessant labor, he becomes the victim of rheumatisms and all the miseries of a broken constitution.'[38]

Support in the Assembly for the logging interests challenged Smyth's hope to establish a prosperous British community in New Brunswick, and it was seen as a challenge to the Council's place in the cherished 'British Constitution'. In the sense that Smyth understood it, lumbering in New Brunswick *subverted* social order. Anonymous letters had been published concerning the propriety of the dissolution in the previous year, and raising again the discontent in Saint John about being governed from Fredericton. A letter to the Saint John *Star* of 11 May 1819, signed by 'A Freeholder', pointedly expressed pride in the charter of the city of Saint John and the relatively democratic tradition of elections for city council. He acknowledged that previous commentary had inflamed the dissolution issue, creating a 'fever'. All the same, 'the event happened, and cannot be undone.' Instead, he wrote, citizens should concentrate upon electing representatives – that is, members of the Assembly – of disinterested probity, whose sole concern would be the public good. The first tangible benefit might be '*to remove the Seat of Government from the* SEQUESTERED *Village where it has heretofore been held,* to the *Metropolis* of this Province, this populous, flourishing and *Patriotic* City: a City at once the residence of enterprising and wealthy Merchants, of *professional* men of *great* talents, of ingenious and industrious mechanics, the constant resort of our own neighbouring country Gent'n, farmers, etc, for the purpose of that Trade, which has been, is, and will be, the true source of the prosperity, riches and ultimate establishment of every part of the Province.' This would also mean removing, he pointed out, the Supreme Court from Fredericton, which location greatly inconvenienced lawyers, their clients – who mainly had to travel from Saint John or elsewhere – and thus even justice itself.

The exchange that developed in the *Royal Gazette* between 'Freeholder', 'Farmer' and 'Villager' expressed basic and conflicting views of provincial society. More than anything, as manipulated by the *Gazette*, the articles gave a socially conservative, and 'country' colouring to emigration policy. 'Farmer' and 'Villager' put the case for a province modelled on the broad acres of the English shires, where honest husbandry kept farmers contentedly following the season's round and doffing their caps to the parson and the squire.

Lockwood, in Council and as Surveyor General, as well as by the levelling reality of his appointment to a station well above his birth, was unavoidably a part of the drama. By 1820, the agrarian movement had acquired force and clarity. The year began with an article entitled simply 'Agricultural' which appeared in the *Gazette*'s 5 January issue followed by an extract from the *Halifax Journal* stressing the value of a Central Agricultural Board. In the background lay John Young's *Agricola* letters that had caused such a stir in Nova Scotia, and led to the formation of agricultural societies with Dalhousie's support. The Nova Scotia journalist and politician, Joseph Howe, records that 'his Lordship's example set all the Councillors and officials and fashionables mad about farming and political economy. They went to ploughing matches, got up Fairs, made composts and bought cattle and pigs. Every fellow who wanted office or wished to get an invitation to Government House read Sir John Sinclair [a Scottish proponent of advanced farming methods], bought a South Down [sheep] or hired an acre of land and planted mangel wurzels.'[39] By the end of the year *Agricola's Letters* were on sale in Fredericton for $2.50 to 'Gentlemen disposed to aid the cause of Agriculture in these Provinces', their names to be listed at the Receiver General's Office.[40] An 'Agricultural and Emigrant Society' held an organisational meeting in St Andrews on 16 January over which the Reverend Jerome Alley, the Rector, presided. Lockwood's support for 'the Farming Interest' could be relied upon, though the immediate demands of the emigrant crisis and the canal survey commanded his attentions during the second half of 1819.

When the General Assembly of 1820 gathered in Fredericton the ground was thus well prepared. The Assembly first addressed its perennial issues: the maintenance and improvement of the 'Great Roads' of the province, timber cutting licences, emigration. But agriculture had become a pressing topic, and on 12 February a meeting was held at Province Hall in Fredericton under the chairmanship of William Botsford, Speaker of the House, where it was resolved that a Central Agricultural Society be formed to serve the province. Some measure of its serious intent can be gauged from the number, nineteen, and composition of its steering committee, a mixture of Council including Lockwood, members of the Assembly, garrison officers, and others.[41] When they met on the 19th the *Royal Gazette* noted that 'many Gentlemen were present, whose pursuits are entirely commercial, that appeared to take a sincere interest in the object of the meeting' as well as 'residents of the Remote Districts.' After 'a few Rules' were read out subscription lists were made up. The *Gazette* waxed eloquent: 'should these Patriotic measures be followed up, as they doubtless will be, the issue cannot be uncertain. The soil, the situation, the local resources of New Brunswick, will remove from the face of nature the rugged features of barreness and want. The hand of Industry will no longer solicit charity.'[42]

This commentary, signed 'Stranger', is rhetorically very similar to Lockwood's pitch for the development of wilderness land in his General Survey proposal, and the pseudonym is certainly appropriate for him. 'Stranger' went on to praise the Nova Scotia Assembly for advancing £1,500 for agriculture during the previous year. 'If the present House of Assembly were to set aside half that sum it would be returned with compound interest. . . . Commercial and Agricultural interests combined, will make this hitherto neglected nook of the world, the abode of plenty; and subdue, in great degree, the frigidity of the climate.' He claimed hay yields of five tons per acre at 'the sequestered Village' and Newtown Pippin apples as good as any in England.

This item was followed up in the 29 February issue of the *Gazette* by a lengthy piece by the same author headed 'Emigration' that made explicit the link with settlement and agricultural policy. Pointing out the impossibility of employing emigrants in the existing economy, he continued: 'It is from Husbandry alone that sufficient and effectual employment can be expected . . . Agriculture wants encouragement – no other employment has so good an effect on the morals of a people. Innocence, health, and happiness are its natural attendants – vice and poverty are seldomer found in its pursuits than in most other occupations. No country can be independent without it.' There is in 'Stranger's' polemic a strong whiff of both *Agricola* and the *Rural Rides* of William Cobbett who had left the army and was now in England, actively campaigning for political change. Stranger, however, learnedly directs the reader to the example of Syracuse during the second Punic war, as described in Charles Rollin's *Ancient History*. Whatever his sources, whoever he was, Stranger plainly spoke for an emerging consensus that New Brunswick needed to broaden its economy and make settlement easier by improving agriculture.

On 4 March, with Botsford again in the chair, the New Brunswick Central Society for Promoting the Rural Economy of the Province was founded.[43] The name, dropping the original reference to agriculture, suggests an accommodation with those well-disposed 'commercial' gentlemen at the second meeting – it allowed for a more generalised idea of 'improvement' – but no one could doubt that the promotion of agriculture was its first aim. Indeed, subsequent correspondence restored the 'Agriculture' to the name. By 18 March the new Society could hold its inaugural annual general meeting, addressed by Smyth, who had 'condescended' to act as president. Among the resolutions were the expenditure of £200 on seed grain; the import and purchase for the coming season of one ram, one boar, and one sow for every county, as well as a 'Drill Plow'.[44] To give a sense of scale, the next column of the same issue of the Gazette, that for 21 March, included a brief report of the Annual General Meeting of the Nova Scotia Provincial Agricultural Society with its expenditures of £1,500 in the current year. Nevertheless, it was a good start, as even Stranger might agree. The momentum continued when a meeting at the Burton courthouse on 2 May founded the Sunbury County Auxiliary Agricultural Society. Porridge supplies were secured by 'seed oats from Scotland', along with seed wheat, timothy, and clover advertised in the Gazette for 16 May.

Lockwood was deeply implicated in this whole agricultural enterprise from the beginning. Indeed, the Surveyor General's office became an administrative centre for subsequent initiatives, as it continued to be for the Emigrant Society. The Royal Gazette reported on 11 July 1820 that Smyth had agreed to let ungranted meadows to the Central Society for a year, with Lockwood's office in charge of the scheme. Throughout the spring and summer months of 1820, items concerning the practice of agriculture, including extracts from various treatises, appeared in the Royal Gazette. The Sunbury Agricultural Society published its annual report in the Gazette for 3 October. The spadework had been done; husbandry was on the up.

It was while the Central Society was forming, however, that Lockwood received his first hard check, three days after receiving the praise of the House for his canal report. He was absent from the Council meeting of 25 February which discussed his proposal for a general survey. The support of the original committee of Hailes, Wetmore and Street had been eroded by the death of Hailes on 30 December. While acknowledging Lockwood's scheme to be 'desirable', Council rejected it.[45] Lockwood had, after all, two expensive proposals before Council, the general survey and the canal report. Since the estimates were his own, hard heads may have doubted his figures, while cautious Council members may simply have baulked at the *scale* of Lockwood's ideas, while also resenting the way he was pushing himself forward. Smyth was disinclined to embark upon adventurous governance and his own scheme to lay out settlement areas piecemeal was apparently working for the short term. Lockwood had himself – perhaps tactically – reported favourably upon it. Now, faced by the sheer immediate pressure of the emigrant tide, it might have seemed better to put off this ambitious 'desirable' plan for the time being.

The Surveyor General's office itself was now under great pressure from the volume of business.[46] Lockwood had petitioned the Assembly successfully for the expenses of a clerk on 15 February.[47] This meant he could employ his son, who soon afterwards joined the secretary, Edward M Miller, in the office. Council awarded Lockwood office expenses of £86 11s 6½d on 22 March but required that 'no new charges be in future admitted for Posting at the Secretary's and Surveyor-General's offices but for such Letters [as] are on Public Service only, and not for the convenience of individuals.' He would also be granted payment by Council on 26 May of £50 for office rent and a further £50 for his canal survey.[48] These changes improved Lockwood's ability to cope with the quickening demands on his energies, beginning with proposals laid out in a new Act to Encourage the Settlement of Emigrants, under consideration by April 1820. These included administrative committees to be set up in the counties; expansion of the Cardigan Settlement area to accommodate further emigrants; further land to be laid out on the Shepody Road; land to be surveyed between the Oromocto and the Nerepis with a view to settlement and improving the Great Road up the St John valley.[49] On 4 May, Council recommended that the Surveyor General have surveyed 'as many good lots as may be', not exceeding one hundred, on the road from Cape Tormentine to the Gaspereau River.[50]

During this first quarter of 1820, there is an inescapable sense of Lockwood's accumulating responsibilities, and a consequent reversal of his roles. For a few months he had seemed to impose his will, to be the agent of change. Now the sheer weight of accumulated tasks began to transform him into its servant. His hand writing, still neat, began to broaden out on widely spaced lines, at least on the quick notes and receipts he wrote to Smyth.[51] From 1819 to 1824, essentially his term of office, the number of timber cutting licences issued increased threefold.[52] Demand for land grants and for the surveying of emigrant settlements demanded lengthy journeys on horse and foot. And though these were usually conducted by Lockwood's deputies, he would personally be directed to the far corners of the province in the coming season. For instance, he had inherited a position as one of two commissioners – the other coming from Lower Canada –

formed to inspect certain islands in the Restigouche River on the border
between the two provinces. It meant that he would have to attend at 'the
Indian [Micmac] village on the River Restigouche' between 10 and 20 June
1820.[53] This was at the northerly limit of New Brunswick, a region which
few prominent provincial figures had ever visited.

Throughout the Assembly Lockwood had continued his role of liaison
between Council and the legislature, but he did not neglect his other
responsibilities. Lockwood was still pressing the theme of industry in a
report from the Emigrant Society. Now, however, he was talking tougher.
'The Secretary reported that in various instances the applications of idle
persons were easily dismissed by offering them labor.' At the same time, the
Society's work meant that 'the Inhabitants of Fredericton have been freed of
Rates to a considerable amount.' Yet 'the want of a House of Industry has
been clearly proved. The Society has unavoidably encouraged idleness, from
the little employ that could be found, and the absolute necessity of providing
subsistence.'[54] This was obviously written defensively, against implied
criticism. In his advocacy of a workhouse Lockwood followed the House of
Assembly, which on 3 March had introduced a bill to levy a tax on the
various parishes of York County to pay for the erection of a county
poorhouse.[55] He again tried to enlist Smyth to rapid action on the general
survey, with its projection of lots for thousands of emigrants and their
families. But after experiencing the two-month term of the General Assembly
during which he talked with members of the House and measured opinion,
his impatience bogged down in the soft clay of political reality.

Lockwood's frustration with the Welsh at Cardigan continued to sour
his mood. His entry in the Emigrant Society minutes for the first week of
March was contemptuously dismissive.

> All the Welshmen came to town, asking for work, and saying, that unless
> relieved, they must starve. They were immediately employed to cut seven
> cords of wood: however, they proved sluggish, avaricious and petulant.
> The funds of the Cardigan Society are exhausted, and these people, now
> permanently fixed amongst us, must be relieved. It is suggested to the
> Society, furnishing a few bushels of potatoes, and a quantity of salt fish
> [sic]. They will have one resource in the road work, and it may be
> expected they will be enabled after to shift for themselves. The Irish
> families for the most part have been furnished with labor, and proved
> themselves industrious.'

Ten pounds was advanced on 6 March to provision the Welsh and bills
'for aiding the Welsh settlers' totalling £147 1s 4d were submitted by
individual members of the committee later in the summer.[56] Lockwood

then delivered a further thudding judgement: 'The Welsh, who were the first cause of the Institution, prove a beggarly, helpless, inert set; and have abused the Charity.' He declared that 'no further aid is intended to be given.' Given his impatience and outrage, the attraction of a workhouse for the placement of such sluggish, avaricious, petulant, beggarly, helpless, inert emigrants was compelling. On 20 March the Assembly nonetheless voted £100 for the Fredericton Emigrant society in recognition of the good work it was doing.[57]

There was a broader political motive in seeming to take a harder line with emigrants. By the fall of 1820 the increase in court cases in Saint John was being attributed to emigrant lawlessness.[58] But Lockwood had good personal reasons for impatience. 'Applicants came in from every quarter of the Province: the door of the Office was constantly surrounded.'[59] Again, the contrast with George Sproule's last years as Surveyor General is dramatic. Meanwhile, Lockwood gave thanks to 'the Ladies' for providing children's clothing; 'and as several Emigrant Females with young Families are yet in want, they are requested to continue and extend their good office.' He also floated a money-raising scheme. 'The sum of £24 was this winter distributed in Halifax to the poor, being the net proceeds of sundry hogs which were caught at large in the streets of the town, and sold according to law. How long the poor in Fredericton might be fed by such means!'[60] This was clearly a practical proposal, since early in the following year Lockwood found two hogs in his wood cellar and advertised them in the *Royal Gazette*: 'If not claimed by Wednesday noon, they will be sold to pay expenses, and the residue given to the Poor.'[61] High office in New Brunswick was not always conducted at the level of vaunting dreams or shadowed by the fate of a distant king.

Lockwood's workload certainly increased after a notice appeared in the *Royal Gazette* for 18 April, following the dissolution of the Assembly, setting out new regulations for the cutting of pine timber. They required petitions for new cutting rights to be confined to British subjects, and freeholders, with no connection with 'Aliens'. Applications were to be lodged at the Provincial Secretary's office, prior to submission to the Lieutenant Governor, and licences, if granted, would be distributed through the Surveyor General or by deputies of the absentee Nova Scotian Charles Wentworth, Surveyor General of Woods. Meanwhile, and contentiously, a bond of one shilling per ton for the timber to be cut was also to be entered at the Secretary's office. Smyth was tightening the screw. Even Wentworth's deputies would route these transactions through Lockwood (via Odell). But if the workload was growing rapidly, so would the emoluments. A pot for gold was set in place; it would soon chink merrily.

9

A Man of Respectable Appearance

IT WAS NOW that Anthony Lockwood struck a blow for private order and chose to marry his mistress, Harriet Lee, widow of the Bridgetown tailor. On 23 May 1820 the following notice appeared in the *Royal Gazette*: 'Married by the Rev Dr Willis, in the City [Saint John], at half past 4 am on Thursday last, the Honorable Anthony Lockwood, Surveyor-general of this Province, to Mrs Harriet Lee, Widow. Present, – the Rev George Burns, the Rev James Milne, Hugh Johnston, Esq, Zalmon Wheeler, Esq, Captain Anderson of the *Willington* [*Wellington*].' Harriet was entered in the marriage register as a resident of Saint John.[1]

The three most prominent leaders of the New Brunswick religious establishment were in attendance. The Reverend Dr Robert Willis was Rector of Trinity Church where the marriage took place; James Milne was Rector of Christ Church in Fredericton; Dr George Burns was Minister to St Andrew's Presbyterian Kirk in Saint John. At this time the latter two were engaged in a public debate, exchanging published pamphlets, on the vexed question of whether the Presbyterian Church should have the same right to conduct legally binding weddings as the Church of England. Burns' attendance that morning, whatever the personal relationship he may have had with Lockwood, had some political symbolism. The Kirk was registering its presence at the marriage of one of the principal officers of the Crown.

Hugh Johnston and Zalmon Wheeler were leading Saint John merchants, both members of the House of Assembly, and both timber merchants with business reasons to cement relations with the Surveyor General. Johnston was one of the leaders of the Scots in New Brunswick, a prominent elder of the Kirk, and one of the signatories to a petition to Lord Bathurst on the marriage issue.[2] His attendance at Lockwood's wedding, like that of Wheeler, was surely more than politeness. Lockwood had worked daily with such men in Bridgetown. Furthermore, his canal report had been received very favourably by the Saint John merchants only four months earlier. For Johnston and the other Scots, with no Presbyterian member of Council, Lockwood might also be seen as an ally, if not a proxy agent.

Captain Anderson was a naval officer whose ship was briefly in port at Saint John. Perhaps Lockwood had known him earlier. It would have been fitting if a Royal Navy man gave away the bride.

Seemingly absent were any members of Council or officers of government at any level. Why was this? It could simply be that Lockwood wanted a quiet wedding. He was marrying a widow; neither of them was young. But Milne, Burns, Johnston and Wheeler were all substantial public figures, and a wedding at the Saint John parish church was hardly secret. Though the time for the ceremony, 4.30 in the morning, may suggest a wish for privacy, dawn weddings were customary, followed by Communion and a breakfast for the guests.

The modest wedding may reflect upon Harriet's status. She had been Lockwood's mistress for at least thirteen years, having followed him from Bridgetown to Halifax and then to Saint John. Harriet was at least in her mid thirties when she married Lockwood. She had given birth to Sarah, her illegitimate child by Joseph Lee, in 1802. Even assuming she was then very young, say fifteen, she would be in her early thirties by 1820. Apart from her age, she was obviously not a gentlewoman, and some knowledge of her may have percolated from Bridgetown through trading connections with Saint John or Halifax. Gossip about prominent figures, in this case a controversial outsider, was wine to colonial communities. Then there was the question of whether Harriet was mulatto. At the very best, she was not the sort of woman of whom the acutely class-conscious New Brunswick 'aristocracy', especially the women, would readily approve. When Lockwood took Harriet and the girls to live with him in Fredericton, their social position could not have been comfortable.

This wedding was thus attractively defiant. It proclaimed Lockwood's sense of responsibility, despite his sexual forays, to Harriet and their daughters, who clearly needed protection. It also showed his readiness to face down the snobs. In making Harriet an 'honest woman' he acted more like the old salt come ashore than the Honourable Anthony Lockwood, gentleman.

So he may not have invited Council members or other elevated personages to avoid embarrassment, especially to Harriet herself. This also, perhaps, says something for Johnston and Wheeler – that they were both worldly and friendly enough to be trusted. The clergymen, meanwhile, could rejoice at the regulation of sin.

The fact that the marriage ceremony was performed in Saint John begs a question about the Lockwood family home. It is evident that the

Lockwoods had some sort of accommodation in Saint John, from which Lockwood travelled to make his surveys, and which he used when Council met at Saint John. But what of the new house in Fredericton on the corner of Queen and Smyth? Was it not yet ready for its family, or was Saint John a more comfortable home for a sailor and his compound family? If the latter, was the growing alliance forming between Lockwood and General Smyth, one based both on Lockwood's utility and possibly also on a shared appreciation of music, to make a difference? Indeed, Smyth's religious perspectives might have been stimulus for Lockwood embracing the sacrament of marriage.

Could there have been any connection between Lockwood's marriage and his next preferment? Only three days after Lockwood's wedding, Andrew Rainsford, Receiver General of the King's Casual Revenues since the inception of the province, died at the age of eighty-six.[3] The original Instructions stated that the Receiver General was to gather for the Crown in New Brunswick 'all our Quit rents, Rents Revenues, Fines Forfeitures, Escheats, Casualties or other Incomes whatsoever (our revenue of Customs only excepted).' But much greater efficiency was needed, both to ensure that the King got his cut, and that Smyth and the Crown officials others got theirs. Smyth had informed Bathurst on 18 May 1818 that Rainsford was too old and unwell to conduct business, and that he had appointed his son, L B Rainsford, as his acting deputy.[4] The Receiver General did not even have an office of his own, as, just before his father's death, Rainsford's son had moved it into that of Thomas Wetmore's son, George Ludlow Wetmore, on Queen Street, opposite Market Square.[5] Smyth had written to Bathurst on 12 October 1819 complaining of the state of affairs in the Receiver General's office, and the following May, on Rainsford's death, he wrote once more to press the issue, without making a specific recommendation.[6] Then, before a reply from Bathurst could be received, Smyth dismissed the younger Rainsford from his acting position, and appointed Lockwood acting Receiver General.[7] This appointment entitled him to appropriate ten per cent of Crown revenues – and set him fair to becoming a very rich man.

In their joint petition to Bathurst in 1816, Sproule and Jonathan Odell had claimed that the accumulated sum in the Receiver General's account, collected over many years, amounted to only £930. Clearly, these 'casual' Crown revenues were considered trivial. However, the surge in economic and settlement activity in the province after 1815 changed this. The post-war increase in the number of timber licence fees, as well as land sales and grants, brought more revenues. By 13 October 1819, Smyth was writing to Bathurst asking that £400 of the 'nearly sixteen hundred pounds' in the Receiver General's account be allotted to Jonathan Odell's widow, the remainder to be expended within the province by himself.[8] In a scrawled note dated 21 March 1821 Lockwood indicated that the licence fees charged to three people for cutting on a total of 375 acres came to a total of £20 7s 3½d, of which £4 came to him.[9] Lockwood's successor Thomas Baillie noted in September 1824 that the 'average fees' of the Surveyor General were £800 per annum, and those of the Receiver General, £150.[10] That may have been an exaggeration. The valuation of Lockwood's estate submitted to Chancery on 10 June 1823 after the writ of lunacy had been drawn up indicated that his income as Surveyor General consisted of his allowance from the British Government of £150, and fees amounting to £500.[11]

Lockwood's appointment certainly made sense on grounds of efficiency. Fees passing through the Surveyor General's office could now be entered in the Receiver General's accounts at the same time. The Surveyor General's office, which was next door to the Assembly building, seems to have functioned as a sort of clearing house. A notice in the *Royal Gazette* for 5 February 1821, for instance, notes that a promissory note for £9 5s 0d had been 'dropt' at the office and might be picked up by the owner. Patronage, however, rarely functioned in the service of efficiency. The Loyalist elite certainly saw the Receiver General's office as desirable and would want it to go to one of their own. With few allies in Council or the House of Assembly, Smyth might have bought a little support by awarding the Receiver General's position to some sycophant, though the office held little direct political power as there was no presumed seat on Council for the Receiver General. Smyth chose instead to consolidate the support on which he could already count.

Indeed, the evidence suggests that early in 1820 Smyth felt briefly more secure. When on 10 March he informed Bathurst of Hailes' death, he observed that it was unnecessary to replace him as there were still twelve members on Council, including General Coffin who was 'at present in England with Leave.'[12] Smyth clearly felt he commanded a majority, though the effective membership of Council was at most nine because of the absence of Billopp and Leonard by reason of decrepitude, and Coffin's visit to England. The Council quorum was five. Lockwood's importance, in this context, is self-evident. Smyth needed his reliability not only on matters of policy but also in attending meetings regularly. In fact, Lockwood was exemplary in this latter respect. He was a workhorse, attending more Council meetings than any other councillor during his time in office. By combining the offices of Surveyor General and Receiver General, Smyth had strengthened the only true outsider on Council, the only member without firm New Brunswick connections and loyalties, and a military officer who might conceivably be tamed by deference to rank.

There may also have been a private relationship which disposed Smyth

towards Lockwood, although the evidence for this is entirely circumstantial. Smyth would certainly have appreciated the regularising of
Lockwood's family, and a common interest and pleasure in music may have
drawn them together. In the spring of 1820 Smyth was a lonely, sickly,
angry man, still seeking leave to travel to England. Yet behind his austere
and formal exterior, his love of music remained intense and passionate. The
absence of good music, he considered, was one of the direst curses imposed
by living in 'this Country', and Smyth's feelings for music were entangled
with his feelings for his dead wife, whose memory remained a source of
active bitterness against those who had failed to appreciate her.

When Lockwood's house and its contents were put up for sale in 1823,
three keyboard instruments were listed, with their valuations: a pianoforte
(£100), an organ (£40), and a harpsichord (£40).[13] This argues for a
distinctly musical household. In later years, Anthony junior gave piano
lessons and played the organ for the Methodist Church in Fredericton.
However, it seems doubtful that all three instruments belonged to
Lockwood's son, on grounds of cost alone, or that Harriet, the Bridgetown
tailor's widow, was a skilled instrumentalist. It is much more likely that the
son followed the father and that musical talent, allied as so often with
mathematical abilities, ran in the family.

If Smyth had found out that his new Surveyor General and his son were
musicians, as he certainly would in a tiny community like Fredericton, it
suggests a possible personal bond between the two men, both essentially
strangers, confined during those long winter nights to houses only a few
steps apart. Simply on the grounds of courtesy alone it seems likely that they
shared some music. The Receiver General's position was certainly a mark of
favour. Might it have been also an overture of something like friendship?

On 22 May Lockwood 'presented the names of Hugh Johnston and
Thomas Milledge Esquires as his securities for the faithful performance of
the Duties of Receiver General', signing jointly a bond in the substantial
amount of £2,000. Johnston had, of course, been present at Lockwood's
wedding, and the trust put in Lockwood by these two prominent Saint John
merchants provided symbolic confirmation of his status in the province
and, particularly, seemed to confirm his standing in the port city.[14]
Lockwood received his commission on 29 May 1820 and wrote to Bathurst
on 19 July enclosing Rainsford's Instructions for confirmation.[15] This,
however, never came because Lockwood's appointment as Receiver General
was only a small move in a much larger financial reorganisation.

Lockwood's new appointment was to make him a man of real substance
in New Brunswick commerce. Until 1820 there was no central bank in New
Brunswick. The ad hoc credit facilities managed by the Saint John
merchants and their suppliers in England and Scotland restricted their

potential for growth, and also meant there was no bank available to the government for the deposit of its revenues. To supply the government's need, and to ensure the mercantile community a regular source of credit, at a meeting in the Exchange Coffee House on 12 June 1820 it was agreed to establish the Bank of New Brunswick (BNB), with thirteen elected directors.[16] There was an cosy quality to its early administration, with the President carving the roast for the staff at the midday meal. Each member of the Board had a veto over loans, arriving at decisions by voting anonymously with white or black beans. A director might occasionally threaten to veto loans needed by other directors if they did not support his own requirements.[17]

The government found it necessary to print calming statements in the *Royal Gazette* throughout January 1821, but the public's concern was most particularly directed at the other local currencies in use, and the bank proved to be sound. Shares in the BNB were advertised for sale at Peter Fraser's in Fredericton by late June 1820, and within a year it had acquired £30,000 capital, of which Lockwood supplied at least five shares at £50 apiece.[18]

Within this larger financial structuring Lockwood's new appointment was a vote of confidence in his soundness and competence. It suggests that soon after he married Harriet and took her to Fredericton he may have achieved that 'respectability of appearance' he would later deem essential to his position as a member of Council.

Marriage certainly did not interrupt Lockwood's work in Council, nor slow down his activities as Surveyor General. Council considered the petition of the Richibucto Micmac for a grant of land on the Richibucto River on 2 June, and it was agreed that a 'licence of occupation' of five hundred acres would be made to 'each of the chiefs' and three hundred acres for other married men, with two hundred acres for single men. 'Grants to be made when cultivated in turn ... provided each cultivation be made within five years.'[19] Lockwood had been dismissive of the Micmac in his *Description* of Nova Scotia. Here in New Brunswick he was instrumental in a decision which typified New Brunswick governmental attitudes towards the aboriginal peoples for most of the nineteenth century. The 'grant' came as a 'licence of occupation', rather than the 'tickets of location' awarded to emigrants. The latter were only required to pay a quit rent to obtain title to their land, while title to 'Indian land' remained vested in the Crown. The Micmac were expected to transform themselves from hunter-gatherers into tillers of the soil. By offering these licences to individuals, the government went against the aboriginal tradition of collective territorial occupation, although they also recognised their special status. Lockwood was obliged to meet his Lower Canadian counterpart, as boundary commissioner, at

the Restigouche Micmac village in mid-June and must have left for the
north shortly after the Council meeting. If he took in Richibucto en route
he might have hired a local boat to carry him up Chaleur Bay. Having
inspected the Richibucto land, he reported on it to Council on 22 July,
when his recommendation that the lots be laid out 'in the usual manner'
was approved.[20]

Lockwood appears to have spent the summer surveying in the region of
Saint John, and along the coast towards the head of the Bay of Fundy. This
led to the completion of a map of 'Part of Saint John County showing
existing and proposed roads Loch Lomond-Hammond River', and a survey
of 'Lots in the vicinity of Otter Hole Saint John County', including a two
hundred acre lot for one Stephen James, 'next to St Andrews Church land.'
He also 'endorsed' a 'Return of Survey on grant of Shag Rock to the
Governor and Trustees of Madras School, NB.'[21] He was party to the
proposal by Council and the Assembly that portions of reserve land in
Charlotte County be granted for settlement, and when later, at their 27
September meeting, the commissioners for emigrant settlement in Charlotte
County complained that the tracts chosen were too remote, Council
recommended that the commissioners choose better sites.[22]

Much of his work was the routine of his official duties, but he carried
these out with unparalleled energy. At its meeting on 5 October, Council
agreed to Lockwood's recommendation by letter of 30 September that 'the
space between the Eastern and Western Districts of Lots laid out for
Emigrants on the Shipody Road be laid out in Lots also for the accommodation of Emigrants.'[23] He then reported to Council on 26 October
concerning the contentious lot No 5 in Maugerville/Sheffield, proposed as
a Burial Ground in 1794 but not properly surveyed. Council allotted five
acres for the Dissenters' meeting house.[24] At the same meeting one of his
deputies provided Council with a sketch of the route for a road from the
Nerepis to the Oromocto rivers which Lockwood had traced out during
the summer.[25] Since the land in question abutted his estate, General Coffin
offered his services as a commissioner to supervise the road construction
and the laying out of emigrant lots, to which Council agreed.

Perhaps the clearest evidence of Lockwood's continuing energy was his
personal survey of eighty-four lots for emigrants between Cape Tormentine
and the Gaspereau River on the Northumberland Strait nearly opposite
Prince Edward Island, through which he also marked a road.[26] On 13
December he wrote to Smyth forwarding an unidentified petition to cut
timber on an unidentified reserve, the applicant being prepared to pay 2s 6d
per ton. Lockwood tactfully suggested it be 'applied as you may think fit,
say to erecting a School House on the adjoining Lot.'[27] The quite literally
vital importance of his work was underlined when in its 19 December issue

the *Royal Gazette* reported that 'On Friday, an Inquest was held on the body of Ann Davis, (a Welch girl) who died on the road to Cardigan Settlement – Verdict: Died from excessive fatigue, want of nourishment, and the inclemency of the weather.' Certainly, the work of the Surveyor General to bring order and prosperity to the wilderness had the utmost importance to the struggling communities of immigrants.

The *Royal Gazette* published on 24 October 1820 a letter from 'A Member' to the Secretary of the Central Agricultural Society, declaring: 'The reign of agricultural ignorance is, I trust, on the wane, and reason about to resume her empire in the human mind. It is the earnest duty of every lover of his country – the duty of every one as *a citizen of the world*, to extirpate prejudice root and branch – to promote to the utmost of his abilities the objects for which this society has been established.' In a similarly positive vein, Lockwood reported on the Emigrant Society in the 14 November issue of the *Gazette,* offering a soothing and uplifting version of things, containing a proposal he had aired in the West Indies long before. 'The support given to it by the Legislature, enables the Society to keep from the doors of the inhabitants, the needy stranger, and in the course of a year or two, its views will doubtless be directed to the employment of the poor by some simple machinery, conducive to the good of the Province, in manufacturing some staple commodity, such as flax or Hemp, to both of which the soil in every part of the country is congenial.' The *citizen of the world* could take comfort, Lockwood implied; in 'a year or two', New Brunswick's needy would become self-sufficient by spinning thread from the products of local farms, at the same time sustaining reason's pre-eminence over 'the empire of the human mind'. This set a high purpose indeed for the province's homeless poor and the 'rubbish', as Lockwood had earlier termed them, who might arrive on its shores.

10

Noises Off – Loyal Dancing

WHAT MADE THE issues troubling New Brunswick particularly difficult was that they resonated with the news from 'Home' of political agitation, and a tottering throne. The talk about reshaping New Brunswick in the mould of an idealised agrarian rural England was pure fantasy. That wished-for Old England was breaking up, or so it appeared, with frightening speed. The news fell like cold rain in the streets of Fredericton and Saint John.

Britain remained 'Home' in the vocabulary of the Loyalists, some of whom traced colonial roots back through several generations. Peacetime made it possible for members of the New Brunswick elite, including members of Council, to visit their relatives in Britain periodically, and some sent their sons and daughters there to be educated culturally or professionally. General Coffin, for instance, could not attach his name to the Loyal Address of 1820 because he was living in Britain at the time. For years to come he frequently crossed the Atlantic, living in London or Bath, and rarely attended Council meetings. Reports on the widespread rioting in the United Kingdom published in the *Royal Gazette* in Fredericton, and in the non-governmental news sheets in Saint John, conjured up the nightmare of 'sedition' by rampant 'democrats' – the very outrage that had driven the Loyalist families from their homes a half century before. Despite the laws which had been passed between 1799 and 1802 against 'Combinations', the gathering of two or more people for such 'seditious' purposes as the raising of wages or lowering the price of bread, between 1811 and 1817 'Luddite' artisans had effectively organised covert action against the introduction of machinery that robbed them of their employment. The unemployment, and local starvation, which followed the end of the war in 1815 and which had driven so many in desperation to the immigrant ships, ensured that the problems of the Mother Country were a central concern in the colonies.

While Lockwood was preoccupied with the Welsh settlers of Cardigan, the famous Peterloo massacre had taken place on 16 August 1819, when a crowd of sixty thousand gathered in St Peter's Fields, Manchester, to hear the radical speaker 'Orator' Hunt on the subject of political reform. Though the people were unarmed, with many women and children present, the authorities panicked, caught up in anti-Jacobin hysteria. Magistrates first sent in yeomen to break up the meeting and then the cavalry charged with drawn swords. Eleven people were killed, including two women and a child. Four hundred were injured, of whom 113 were women. The event galvanised the country in anger and contempt when the government endorsed the magistrates' actions.

Symptomatic of the political tumult in Britain, and multipliers of the insecurity felt by the establishment in New Brunswick, was the mental illness of King George III, and the licentiousness of the Prince Regent. The article that had led to Leigh Hunt's imprisonment in 1812, 'The Prince on St Patrick's Day', had been written in response to eulogies of the Regent in the Tory press, where, among other absurdities, the fifty-year-old Prince, debauched and obese, was described as 'an Adonis in loveliness'. Hunt's version was much closer to general opinion and the truth: 'A violator of his word, a libertine over head and ears in debt and disgrace, a despiser of domestic ties, the companion of gamblers and demireps, a man who has just closed half a century without a single claim on the gratitude of his country or the respect of posterity.'[1]

With the advantage of hindsight, the future George IV can be seen as a victim of a royal status he would gladly have set aside. After years of sowing wild oats, and without his father's royal consent, in 1785 he had secretly married for love Maria Anne Smythe, Mrs Fitzherbert, twice a widow and a Catholic. This love-match violated the Royal Marriages Act which required the King's consent, and as a result could not produce a legitimate heir to the throne. In 1795 Prince George was at last persuaded to permit Parliament to annul his marriage, in return for payment of his huge debts. He had been found an acceptable wife, Caroline, daughter of the Duke of Brunswick. But he could not love her, and the marriage was not to produce a male heir. Caroline declared that on their wedding night the intoxicated prince 'lay under the grate, where he fell, and where I left him.'[2] Later the marriage was consummated, and in 1796 a princess had been born, Charlotte Augusta. But after her birth, the couple unofficially separated, to begin years of unseemly wrangling over money, the care of Charlotte – of whom George III tried to obtain custody in 1804 – and the constant insistence by Caroline that she be accorded full social precedence as Princess of Wales. In 1814 she had chosen to live abroad, and her relationship with her courtier Bartolemeo Pergami led to George III forming a Commission on 29 May 1816 that included the Lord Chancellor and Lord Chief Justice 'to enquire into the truth' of certain written statements alleging adulterous and outrageous behaviour by the Princess. The whole matter, serious already, darkened with the terrible news that on 6 November 1817 Princess Charlotte, who had married Prince Leopold of Saxe-Coburg-Saalfeld in 1814, had died after giving birth to a stillborn boy child. On New Year's Day 1818 the Regent presented papers to his ministers laying out a case for bringing divorce proceedings against the Princess of Wales, with the underlying purpose of freeing him to father a male heir to the throne.

These events were profoundly disturbing in New Brunswick where the monarchy was the heart of social and political order, more so even than it was of that in the homeland. New Brunswick's franchise was wider than was that of the United Kingdom, and Catholics had been given the vote in 1810, but the House of Assembly had fewer effective powers than did the British Parliament, where the restrictions on the monarchy were established by jealously guarded precedent.

The *Royal Gazette* had published on 16 January 1818 an excerpt from an unnamed London source, dated 17 November, headed 'Royal Succession to the Throne of Great Britain' which declared that Charlotte's death had 'disappointed the national hope of a lineal order of succession to the Crown through the Prince Regent.' There remained the prince's younger brother, William, who was indeed to succeed to the throne in 1830. But William had no legitimate son, and of his two legitimate daughters, Charlotte had died in March 1819, and Elizabeth was to die in 1821, bringing to an end the Hanoverian line. Five years later Sir Howard Douglas was to write to Sir Robert Wilmot-Horton, who had replaced Henry Goulbourn as Parliamentary Under Secretary at the Colonial Office, of his fears that the British inheritance in New Brunswick was in danger: 'In a Colony bordering upon a Republican government, and with which the intercourse is so frequent, it is of great importance to check, by all practicable means, the introduction of Republican Principles, and to sustain and strengthen the King's prerogative in every way in which it can be done without touching upon the privileges to which the popular Branch of the Legislature have firmly established their claim. This, in a Country where there is nothing like a hereditary Aristocracy, must always be attended with some difficulty.'[3]

The Anglican Church was not officially an 'established' religion in New Brunswick, but the Bishop of Nova Scotia was a member of the New Brunswick Council, and the church viewed its social role in a monarchical light. When the Right Reverend Charles Inglis had visited Fredericton in 1809 he had complained when he discovered that the pews of the church at Kingston were held in common; that is, that none were assigned to individuals. As a result, he wrote, 'men – perhaps of the worst character – might come and set themselves down by the most religious and respectable characters in the parish. This must ultimately tend to produce disorder and

confusion in the church and check the spirit of true devotion and piety.'
Anglican order, by this measure, was not democratic. Lord Dalhousie found
King's College in Windsor Nova Scotia too strictly Anglican for his taste
and laid the foundation stone of what became Dalhousie University, but
General Smyth's sentiments were quite different.

General Smyth's concern about the impact the royal scandal might have
on New Brunswick politics was not altogether wide of the mark. In reality,
colonial society was more commercial than genteel, and commerce was
alive to the changes taking place in the world. At the larger country estates
of General Coffin at Nerepis, Judge John Saunders above Kingsclear, and
old George Leonard at Sussex Vale, the squires played their game in the
country fashion. But little as they liked it, their lives were increasingly
peripheral to the growing commercial community, and their interests were
increasingly under pressure from demands for 'responsible' government.
Ward Chipman maintained some style at his house in Saint John, and in
that city the bigger merchant families such as Hazen, Symmonds, Millidge,
and Johnston, lived substantially. But they, and such merchants as Peter
Fraser, Jedediah Slason, or Mark Needham, were men of substance rather
than style, or *ton*, as fashionable contemporaries termed it. They were
engaged in the practical life of the community at almost every level, as
Justices of the Peace, members of the Legislative Assembly, fire wardens,
jurymen, trustees, and members of countless committees. Their names were
attached to subscription lists for charitable causes, such as the Society for
the Propagation of Christian Knowledge, and the Emigrant and Agricultural societies. Their commercial connections were trans-Atlantic, and
with the United States and the Caribbean countries.

It was in the context of political conflict, and a dissolute monarchy, that
Lockwood's work to settle immigrants must be seen. What spin Lockwood
put on his own experience at the heart of the 1897 Spithead mutiny is a matter
of conjecture. It is most probable that he distanced himself from the episode
long before he became one of the New Brunswick Council. Nevertheless, his
activity as Surveyor General suggests that he was not unsympathetic to
constitutional reform. And his violent reaction to the circumstances of 1823
suggests that in his heart he would have been glad to see the old order that he
had joined, but of which he was not a true part, replaced.

The scarcely manageable influx of immigrants in 1818–1819 threatened
disorder. The newcomers were an unscreened, undifferentiated, mass.
Lockwood had privately declared to Smyth, clearly anticipating agreement,
that 'we receive and keep the mere rubbish' – and while it was their 'miserable
neediness' he stressed, the news from Britain raised questions of political
reliability.[4] Was New Brunswick importing His Majesty's seditious and
'alienated' subjects? Was immigration, so ardently desired, a Trojan horse?

A particular concern was that of the three thousand Irish who had
arrived at Saint John in late 1819. Although many were Ulster Protestants,
the rest were Catholics and hence undesirable in the eyes of more than a few
firm Loyalists. When the Council committee approved Lockwood's General
Survey plan, which was later dismissed by the full Council, they also
proposed a model of settlement including provision for a school and a
church. The church they envisioned was not Roman Catholic.

Lockwood was deeply involved in the political process during February–
March 1820. It was the custom for the Council and House of Assembly to
issue a joint Loyal Address to the Sovereign at each annual session of the
House, which as a consequence of George III's madness had since 1811
been directed to the Regent. Smyth proposed his own formula on 4
February 1820, and four days later the Council had its draft ready,
deploring 'the continuance of His Majesty's lamented Indisposition' and
'the hostile spirit to our excellent Constitution . . . as displayed in various
parts of Great Britain.' They were heartened, they declared, by 'those
general sentiments of veneration for His Majesty' expressed by 'the more
respectable classes of Society' to the Prince Regent. 'The satisfaction derived
from those decided proofs of loyalty and steady attachment to His
Majesty's government, can be more truly gratifying to no description of
His Majesty's subjects, than to the loyal inhabitants of this Province.'[5] On
11 February members of the Assembly and Legislative Council agreed in
'deprecating the riotous and seditious practices of the disaffected in Great
Britain', and by the 15th Council agreed on the final wording of a joint
Address. It affirmed 'the most unalterable attachment to the inestimable
Constitution under which we have been bred, and for which we abandoned
the Country wherein we were born, and sought an Asylum in the wilderness. We view with astonishment and detestation, the attempts of seditious
and unprincipled men to alienate the minds of His Majesty's subjects
therefrom.' Those present and assenting were Smyth, Saunders, Wetmore,
Black, Street, Bliss, Robinson, and Lockwood, although he, the odd man
out, had obviously not shared the experience described in the first part of
the declaration.

His signature on the Loyal Address, however, was not the full measure
of Lockwood's political attitude. Some indication of his positioning in the
relations between the Legislative Council and the House of Assembly came
at the beginning of March, when the latter voted a twenty shillings per diem
allowance to members while the House was sitting. Council first passed a
resolution deploring this extravagance on 2 March and then, on the
following day, voted down a motion by Judge Bliss to reopen the issue.
Bliss, Wetmore, and Lockwood voted in favour of the motion – evidently

in sympathy with the House – while Saunders, Black, Chipman, Robinson, and Street voted against. A motion to rescind the earlier motion deploring the daily allowance was then presented on 14 March, and again defeated, with Lockwood once more among the yeas. The core of the matter seemed to be Council's need to 'deplore' rather than reject, since they turned round and approved the allowance by six to three, with Lockwood now joining the majority. Buried in this issue was suspicion of any perceived enlargement of the power of the House. Lockwood apparently thought the payment fair.

Perhaps even more revealing of Lockwood's 'democratic' tendencies, however, had been his support for a motion before Council on 10 February to permit any member of Council to admit up to six persons to listen to Assembly debates. This was a distinctly innovative notion, a move towards 'open government'. Lockwood, Wetmore, Street, and Judge Bliss were in favour; Chief Justice Bliss, Judge Saunders, Robinson, and Black voted against. The Chief Justice, as chair, had the casting vote.[6]

When news of the deaths of both George III and the Duke of Kent reached New Brunswick at the end of March, Smyth prorogued the Assembly on the 29th, after giving rapid assent to a number of bills, including a new one to encourage emigration. He 'expected' New Brunswickers to 'put themselves into deep mourning' from 9 April.[7] Official word of the King's death finally came by letter from Bathurst, read by Smyth to Council on 18 April.[8] Lockwood's signature was third of 110 prominent Fredericton residents who signed a 'Proclamation of Loyalty' to George IV on the following day.[9]

On the same date, Smyth demonstrated his stiffly legalistic mind and some inconsistency when he tried to suspend, as illegal, all acts passed while the King's death was unknown. He wished to deny Royal Assent for virtually the whole period of the 1820 Grand Assembly. Council, however, were 'of the opinion that the Lieutenant Governor cannot constitutionally suspend the operation of said Acts.' This settled that matter, but Smyth and Council took new oaths that day, just to be sure they were loyal to the right monarch.[10] While the direct political impact of the deaths may have been symbolic, that symbolism was powerful. George III had been the King for whom the Loyalists had given so much, and his son, the Duke of Kent, had been commander-in-chief of British North America forces. For the older Loyalists the sense of changing times must have been acute. It surely was for Smyth, who had soldiered directly under the Duke's command, and later joined his household.

The change of a monarch necessitated a general election in Britain, and in London the opposition presented the Queen, despite all evidence, as a symbol of Reform, against the perceived tyranny of the King and the Tory government which in December 1819 had passed the notorious Six Acts to put down sedition. And sedition there was, although it was stimulated by agents provocateurs. A plan hatched on 22 February to kill the Cabinet may have been entrapment by the Home Office, but it led to five ringleaders of the Cato Street plot being hanged on 1 May.

The news from London was relayed to New Brunswickers six or so weeks late by the *Royal Gazette* and the Saint John newspapers. In consequence, what might in reality have been nothing more than a drunken brawl in Fredericton was taken very seriously. On 2 May the *Royal Gazette* reported on 'great disturbances' in Ireland two months before, where the Ribbonmen were taking revenge on landlords for injustices, and on Anglican clergymen who insisted upon their tithes in hard times, by hamstringing cattle, burning ricks, barns and houses, firing shots through windows, sending threatening letters. While the Irish were perennial scapegoats, and there was of course no necessary connection between Ribbonmen and distressed Irish immigrants in New Brunswick, it was easy to see smoke and fear fire. On 23 May the *Gazette* copied a report from London papers of rioting in Scotland: 'Men inimical to the order of society, taking advantage of this unhappy state of our manufactures, have diffused the poison of republicanism, of faction, of discord: with that promptness so desperate a case required, His Majesty's Ministers have dispersed these tumultuous assemblages by the regulars. Lives were lost, but private letters say, not to the extent stated in the public prints. These events although to be regretted, have materially strengthened the hand of our present Government. All good subjects, and many of the most violent Oppositionists, have avowed and shown their intention to support intire, the frame of our Constitution.' Playing down governmental repression, and claiming press exaggeration, the *Gazette* (William Franklin Odell?) tried to spin the whole dark event, on the authority of private letters, by claiming that it had resulted in 'general tranquility' and a consensus in the Mother Country to 'support intire the frame of our Constitution.' Like Smyth's praise for those who resisted 'all innovation' this was the authentic voice of ultra-conservative wishful thinking. Only two months after the Ribbonmen blazed in the columns of the *Royal Gazette*, however, there was an Irish 'riot' in Fredericton.

On 25 July, in the next issue after its report on the Fredericton brawl, the *Royal Gazette* announced that the King's coronation would take place on 11 August. Just below the coronation notice, however, dated London, 8 June, came the following: '*Arrival of the Queen of England*. This long surmised and till of late unlooked for event has at length took place, Her Majesty having landed at Dover on Monday last, and arrived in London on Tuesday evening.' The effect was explosive. Rumour now ran rampant. Caroline's progress to London was accompanied by cheering crowds who identified her with all other citizens denied their rights. In London no residence was provided for her, another deliberate slight, so she took refuge in the home of Alderman Wood, a Radical MP and former Lord Mayor of London. Perhaps misleadingly, this suggested an appeal to the common people, as opposed to the ruling aristocratic elite.

George persuaded the Cabinet to have Caroline's name omitted from the liturgy of the Church of England, of which the King was head as Defender of the Faith, and the coronation was postponed. He was advised not to seek a divorce because his own adulterous relationships would inevitably be brought up in the trial, and accordingly he demanded the introduction in parliament on 5 July of the Pains and Penalties Bill 1820, under which the marriage could be annulled and Caroline stripped of the title of Queen, without a trial in a court of law. By 8 August the *Gazette* was reporting 'on the authority of a Private Letter from Saint John by the Steam Boat' that '*Her Majesty the Queen had been arrested.* The improbability of such a step . . .', etc. The *Gazette* was sensation-mongering while affecting a high moral tone, but Queen Caroline had indeed been arrested and on 17 August brought before the House of Lords charged with adultery, an offence of high treason in a royal consort. The Bill against Caroline passed three times, with diminishing majorities, until the government tactically withdrew it for 'further consideration'. The outcome was considered an acquittal, though Caroline was technically found guilty. 'It is said,' the *Royal Gazette* reported on 24 October, 'that her Majesty's popularity increases daily.' As she left the Lords for the last time the streets were thronged with her joyous supporters.

It was not only the British throne that was tottering. The year 1820 was one of revolts in Europe, forcing the monarchs of Spain and the southern Italian kingdom of the Two Sicilies to grant liberal constitutions. Welcome as that might be, it was also worrying to the British elite, even those in the colonies. After all, it had been revolution that had spawned Napoleon, and the Bourbon monarchs of Sicily and Spain who had done what they could to stem the tide of revolt. No less interesting in New Brunswick than the drama of events in southern Europe was news of revolution in the Spanish empire. Its impact on life in New Brunswick was as a not very subtle commentary on the nightmare events surrounding the British monarchy, one that could excite the imagination without directly indicating any seditious thoughts.

Napoleon surfaced in the *Gazette* during December 1820, first with the comforting news that 'a gentleman who has recently arrived from St Helena' reported Napoleon had 'grown extremely corpulent, unwieldy and slovenly in his person', and utterly reclusive. But this was followed by a report that Bonaparte's eldest son, whom it was believed was to have gone into the church, had instead become a soldier in the Austrian service. 'I have seen in a letter from Vienna, an account of the promotion of the young Prince Reichstadt (this is his title) to the rank of a corporal in a regiment which forms part of the garrison of Vienna, and into which regiment he entered as a private soldier. He appears in the parades with the regiment in his uniform, goes thro' his military exercise with great precision, and is a very great favourite with the soldiers.'[11] Here we go again, it seemed to hint. Would hostile forces still loyal to the father rally around his son?

The Austrian government was in fact careful to keep Franz, the Duke of Reichstadt, a virtual prisoner, but Simon Bolivar was very much an active force, and in September 1821 he was to bring into existence the independent state of Grand Columbia, and became its first, and only, president. On 2 January 1821 the *Gazette* reported dramatic news from Haiti where President Henrie Christophe had shot himself, after which Jean-Pierre Boyer had been proclaimed president in his place. On the same page an item appeared headed Philadelphia, 29 November: '*Liberty! Equality! Independence!* REPUBLIC OF HAYTI. Address to the People and Army.' Signed by various magistrates and generals, this declared that the government was secure. It was followed by Boyer's assertion that 'this time of discord and division is passed.' 'We ought never to forget the names of those brave patriots who ceased not to contend against despotism to the very last. Those who gave the most solemn pledge to the people, to make an effort for the recovery of their liberty, are worthy of the national remembrance.'

It is hard to believe that Lockwood, who had sailed Caribbean waters for so many years, and knew them far better than he knew New Brunswick, could have read such reports with indifference. The news from Haiti, in particular, must have prompted memories of the events of 1795 when he personally witnessed the bloody British rout, ferrying the desperate survivors to Jamaica – itself so often on the brink or in revolt. Toussaint's bold strike for Liberty, and his betrayal in 1801 by Napoleon, had inspired the very distant William Wordsworth to write 'thou hast great allies; / Thy friends are exultations, agonies, / and love, and Man's unconquerable mind.'[12] Lockwood was now a landlocked functionary, dispensing land grants and mainly routine surveys in a distant land, to emigrants he had quickly come to despise, and administering an office silting up with paperwork. But he had spent years in the fighting school of such as Admiral Thomas Cochrane who had gone into exile after implication in a stock fraud in 1818, and become a hero of the revolts in Spanish America. The patronage of Thomas Cochrane's uncle, Admiral Alexander Cochrane, best known for burning Washington and the operations against New Orleans, had rescued Lockwood from his hubristic disaster in Guernsey, and given

him his chance in Barbados and Nova Scotia. Was he glad to be free of all
that, in a safe berth, or did he still yearn for action down there, skirmishing
among the Antilles or off Cartagena and the Trinidad shore?

In the circumstances, General Smyth's address on 23 January 1821 to the
new session of the General Assembly, if nervous, expressed an all too
pervasive concern. The facts were bleak enough: 'several kingdoms on the
Continent are apparently revolutionizing'; meanwhile, 'with respect to the
Mother Country we have to lament that the times are turbulent, and can
only unite in an earnest hope (not without the expectations of its being
realised) that the greatest trials are now past.' This struck a less confident
note than hitherto, surely reflecting the chaotic state of the monarchy.

Lockwood was deputed by the Legislative Council to draft with Samuel
Denny Street a reply to Smyth's address. They struck the customary note of
toadying hypocrisy by loyally describing the reign of George III as
'unparalleled for its length as for its glory' before praising Smyth's three
main initiatives: institutions for promoting agriculture, the 'diffusion of
Knowledge', and 'the Settlement of the Country.' Finally, they joined with
him in offering thanks 'to a gracious and Divine providence, for the
bounties of the past season and the general prosperity that has rewarded
rural industry throughout the Province.' This last statement was notably
false, since by 10 March the Assembly presented Council with a bill 'to
provide for the necessities of the Province, occasioned by the failure of the
late crop.' The timber trade was also distressed. On the theme of public
order Council acknowledged the need to revise the Militia Act and noted
with 'anxiety' Smyth's review of 'the state of Politics in the Old World',
particularly his concern that 'a revolutionizing spirit prevails on the
Continent of Europe.' They too lamented 'the disturbances in the Mother
Country.'[13]

Nor could they, ever, ignore the Americans. In its summary account of the
boundary dispute, the *Gazette* of 26 February 1821 noted suspiciously that
American surveyors were working 'at this inclement time of the year.'
Wherever they were working was bound to be disputed territory.

Council met virtually daily throughout February with Lockwood in
constant attendance. On the 26th he voted with a clear majority on a third
reading to approve payment to the Speaker and defray expenses of
members of the House – again putting himself on the side of mild reform.
Two days earlier Council had considered a letter from Smyth, with accompanying map, describing progress on the Nerepis emigrant settlement. Lots
had been laid out, a third of which to be available to residents of New
Brunswick, and a road laid through the settlement with the additional
purpose of improving the communication between Saint John and 'the seat

of Government.' This was the road which General Coffin had offered to supervise, approved by Council on 26 October 1820. In addition, Smyth recommended that Council make provision for the improvement of the Great Road up the Saint John valley.[14]

Some sense of Lockwood's close engagement in the daily business of government and his increasing workload can be gleaned from the number and diversity of petitions he presented to Council. He was the constant liaison for the Emigrant Society, presenting a petition for further aid to Council on 8 February 1821, while on 7 March 1821 he brought the petition of seven individuals for the refund of timber duties paid by them, followed by that of 'sundry inhabitants of the parish of Alnwick' for aid towards opening a road. On that same date 'sundry inhabitants of Newcastle' requested aid towards establishing a school. Finally, David Burpee, on behalf of himself and other Dissenters in Sheffield, prayed to be incorporated. All these petitions, presented by Lockwood, were tabled.

He continued to be deputed to inform the legislature of Council's decisions. On the 6th he conveyed approval of certain bills. Next day he returned to the House with news that the Militia Bill had been passed by Council. This Lockwood carried back to the House for concurrence on the 12th. The Assembly was dissolved on 20 March.

On the face of it, Lockwood was too busy participating in the King's government of New Brunswick to pay much attention to revolutionary news from Latin America, or to interest himself with the humiliation of the monarchy, and the agitation for political reform in England. But these issues were certainly the talk of the town, and probably amongst the councillors. General Smyth was soon to stir himself to address the threat, and Lockwood had become Smyth's man. It is not surprising that the image of the man on horseback sweeping away the accumulated baggage of the past should have lodged itself in his mind, where he found it when mental illness broke down his self control.

Smyth did what he could to reinforce the King's administration in New Brunswick, to stave off whatever threat of revolution there might be, whether on the streets or in Council. Thomas Wetmore's presence in the Council was divisive because there was bad blood between him and Smyth over a grant of five hundred acres to the Saint John Kirk, which Wetmore first attempted to block in Council, before delaying his signature. When their disagreement over the Fredericton Riot prosecutions led to Wetmore's resignation on 21 May 1821, ostensibly on grounds of the great increase in the Attorney General's work, Smyth ensured there was no going back. At the same time as he resigned as Attorney General, Wetmore offered himself to succeed the doddering Jonathan Bliss as Chief Justice, although his motive may only have been to be provocative. In forwarding Wetmore's letter to Bathurst, Smyth agreed that Bliss's extreme age and infirmity meant an appointment was imminent, but he would not recommend Wetmore. He offered three names from which a replacement for Council might be chosen: George Shore, the Reverend Robert Willis, Rector at Saint John, and Frederick Robinson. Pushing Shore's case, Smyth noted that he was 'connected with one of the principal families in the Colony.'[15] He may have meant his own, as in his will dated 19 June 1821 he referred in a codicil to Shore and Dr Alexander Boyd as 'my friends.'[16] Without waiting for Bathurst's answer, Smyth then appointed Shore *pro tem* to Council, and this stratagem worked. His appointment was quickly confirmed by the King in Council, and he took his place on 21 June.[17] Shore's, and Smyth's, influence had also been strengthened by appointing him in early March Adjutant General of Militia with rank of major.[18] He was also to became secretary of the Central Agricultural Society that year.

Wetmore's resignation removed an awkward customer and Smyth was now fairly secure of a quorum of supporters in Council. He could count on Shore and his father-in-law, Saunders, who would be soon appointed Chief Justice in place of Jonathan Bliss, Bliss himself while he survived, Lockwood, and Street. The Saint John councillors were less reliable, being strongly influenced by the mercantile agenda of the city.

Smyth also returned to that old bugbear: the position of Surveyor General of Woods, North America, that shadowy Lord of the Pines, now vacant on the death of Sir John Wentworth. On 28 March 1821 he asked Bathurst whether the rumour that Michael Wallace of Nova Scotia had been appointed was true.[19] The matter remained a major irritant. The House of Assembly's address to Smyth that session had raised the question of what was to become of reserve lands in Charlotte County and who indeed was to be appointed Surveyor General of Woods. In the continuing turmoil concerning timber cutting rights, the timber tax, and sites for emigrant settlement, this issue mattered. Smyth also had a good personal motive to bring it under control. Although the Council minutes of 19 May 1821 refer to 'the present embarrassed state of the Timber Trade', the volume of land and timber business passing through Lockwood's dual offices had clearly increased, as did the fees collected – of which Smyth took his cut. Recognising this greater administrative pressure, Smyth obtained Council's authorisation for an immediate sum of £14 4s od from the Pine Timber Fund for the Surveyor General for stationary relating to pine business and in future, clearly anticipating an increase, an annual sum of £35 14s 10d for same purpose.

These moves to reinforce Smyth's position, however, were only the least spectacular part of Smyth's efforts that year on behalf of the beleaguered monarchy. Considering his usual niggardly style, huddled in Government House with his personal physician, Smyth really outdid himself in the spring of 1821. Rousing himself from his depressed torpor, he sent out invitations to 'those Ladies and Gentlemen who have been introduced to him' to a celebration, followed by a ball, to mark the King's Birthday.

Everything about the *Gazette*'s 1 May report of this occasion was upbeat, painting the occasion as an unqualified expression of Loyalist joy. The language was heavy with regal metaphor. Even the sun's 'unobscured majesty, illuminating the whole face of nature by a general diffusion of his splendid rays, tempering the atmosphere to serenity and mildness' appeared to demonstrate the benefits of 'majesty' in achieving calm and order. It was also a show of military might. 'At 12 o'clock the whole of the Troops and Artillery in the Garrison, marched in full dress to the Church Square, when the Colonel Commandant, The Hon Robert Le Poer Trench, drew them up, placing His Majesty's 74th or Assaye regiment in the centre, covering his flanks with the Artillery.' George Stracey Smyth, representing the King, was publicly honoured. 'The approach of His EXCELLENCY the Major General being announced, the Regiment was ordered to take open order, and the music having advanced through the opening in the centre, to the front, the whole stood ready to receive Him, who, having arriving at a convenient distance in front of the Troops, He was received by them in military stile, the Band playing 'God Save the King.' 'The music having ceased, the firing in honor of the day commenced by seven discharges of Artillery and then a *feu de joie*, or running fire of the Infantry, which being twice repeated, the whole Corps formed in close order, wheeled backwards into divisions, and marching in that order, passed in review before HIS EXCELLENCY.'

There was horse racing in the afternoon although the writer felt the need to defend this 'ancient and Royal amusement'. 'Why the Royal Personages of modern times do not indulge themselves in this ancient custom is more owing perhaps to political motives than to want of inclination.' King George IV's girth might have been noted in this context, but instead a rhapsodic passage followed, noting the pleasure of 'a great number of all ranks of the inhabitants' in the display of speed, 'ardour', 'grace and harmony'.

That evening the ball was held at Government House, 'given by His EXCELLENCY upon a very extensive scale of invitation.' Though the 'state of the river' – presumably in full freshet or even still breaking-up – limited attendance by invitees from Saint John and the other communities along the St John, the 'Loyal Festivity' drew 'a numerous collection both of well dressed Ladies and Gentlemen', first to the 'great Audience Chamber, where the dances commenced.' At 1am they retired to the Supper Tables, 'covered with a profusion of delicacies,' after which 'the dancers feeling themselves reanimated . . . and allured by the bewitching charms of the music, repaired with jocund air and sprightly step to the Ballroom', where they danced on until nearly 3am. All this was testimony to 'the ardour of their Loyalty' and Smyth was said to be 'in high spirits, and to be much gratified by the general joy, and to interest himself greatly for the accommodation of his guests.' In conclusion, the *Gazette*'s writer gushingly anticipated, 'When glorious dreams stand ready to recall, / In pleasing visions the splendours of the Ball.'

This was all purposeful puffery. Over Smyth's well-earned reputation for niggardliness a bucket of syrup had been poured – 'spinning his image', in modern terms. It cannot be supposed that he enjoyed the event himself. Whether the boisterous dance music was to his taste or not, he would have been missing his wife. For him the event was a strictly political one, proclaiming the elite's loyalty to the new King. The guests surely enjoyed a good time at the end of that very long winter, but the degree of their joy in George IV's birthday cannot be taken for granted. The Caroline affair was still front and centre and she certainly had her allies at Smyth's ball. Perhaps for most the May festival was enjoyed in the older and less political sense. To cover that eventuality, in the next column of the newspaper, as an unconscious reminder of the real business of colonial government, the *Gazette* printed advice on the culture of apple and pear trees: 'To produce good Apples and Pears is as much within our powers as to produce potatoes.'[20]

Among the dancers, would Anthony and Mrs Lockwood have stood out as being not to the manor born? For both it might have been an ordeal, to be followed quickly by retreat into their home, and to business. But that too was to have its bitter ironies, at least with hindsight. Lockwood was given a job which, unknown to himself at the time, was to be particularly poignant. On 13 June 1821, shortly after the release from the Fredericton jail of the Irish rioters, a grand jury made up largely of parish officers for Fredericton examined it and found it 'to be wholly insufficient for the Safe Keeping of persons confined therein and that from the filthiness of the rooms designed as well for Debtors as Criminals, they are rendered very injurious to the health of those persons who now are or may happen to be confined therein . . . and it is in their [the grand jury's] opinion, considering the present distressed state of the County, that no unnecessary burden should be laid thereon, they therefore humbly suggest that the said Gaol be immediately cleansed, and the rooms repaired and strengthened, by proceeding with the Planking and Grating of the walls, until such time as the County should be considered capable of bearing the expense' of a new building.[21] A supreme irony, considering that later he was himself to be incarcerated in the jail following his abortive coup, was that Smyth directed Lockwood to draw up a plan of it and of the adjoining lots. This he completed by 18 June, but no improvements would be made before Lockwood found himself within its walls.[22]

Alas for the monarchical order, Smyth's celebrations for the King's birthday did not put an end to the period of turmoil. On 6 June Smyth informed Council that he had received sundry accounts of the disordered state of Northumberland County and advised that 'a Military Force be immediately sent to the River Miramichi to aid the Civil Power', and that a special commission be issued for holding a court at Newcastle on 18 July.[23] The expenses of moving the troops would be taken from general provincial revenues. Meanwhile, the *Royal Gazette* for 11 June reported: 'Ireland. Horrible Outrage', telling of the rape and mutilation of nine women, wives and daughters of British soldiers, by a mob of fifty 'insurgents' near Mitchellstown. On the Miramichi, despite the troops, and unlike the Fredericton Irish riot, this trouble didn't go away quickly. On 15 August in the following year the magistrates 'and other citizens' of the Miramichi would petition Ward Chipman, by then president of Council, for regular troops to be stationed there to subdue 'gangs of emigrants from Ireland.' New Brunswick was thus compelled to maintain some level of localised armed alert throughout this period and suspicion of Irish emigrants was sustained.

The coronation of George IV at Westminster Abbey would be described by the *Royal Gazette* in a lengthy account on 18 September as 'a splendid pageant'. However, it was impossible to avoid reference to Queen Caroline's attempt to gain entry to the ceremony. She had been turned away from the very doors of the Abbey. And the news that George was at last crowned was substantially upstaged by another item of news, Napoleon's death at St Helena. This had taken place on 5 May but the *Gazette* was not able to publish the official news until 4 September, when the Corsican Tyrant's better qualities inevitably suggested invidious comparison with the new King. Following a morbid account of his autopsy, the *Gazette* writer remarked on his charismatic harangue to his soldiers massed to engage the enemy in what became known as the battle of the Pyramids: 'Soldiers! Forwards! And bear in your minds that from the height of yonder monument forty centuries behold your conduct.' Let us ask here the simple question,' the *Gazette* continued, 'What other military man of the age would have thus addressed his army? Does any military name ever occur to any one of us, who would have thus conceived, thus felt, and thus spoken?' Certainly not the new King. Neither could such inspiration be looked for from General Smyth.

Napoleon was, in short, 'a great bad man'. Comparisons were inevitable between the heroic stature of the man who had died – the man of action beyond compare – and the man who had been crowned. And worse was to come.

Only days later, on 25 September 1821 (dated 8 August, London), the *Gazette* announced the 'DEATH OF THE QUEEN'. By suddenly dying she had once more stolen her spouse's burp of thunder. The natural sympathy her death inspired, coming so soon after her exclusion from the coronation, inevitably left the new King exposed to further contempt. Evidently the rumour that the Queen believed herself to have been poisoned did not reach Fredericton, but details of Caroline's will were published in the *Gazette*. Scandal nodded her head with grim satisfaction when it was disclosed that Caroline had left all her property in trust for the benefit of William Austin, the baby she had 'adopted', and which many believed to be her illegitimate child. The will also contained a last defiant proclamation: 'Her Majesty desires that her body may not be opened – that three days after her death it may be carried to Brunswick for internment, and that the inscription on the coffin may be – *'Here lies Caroline of Brunswick, the injured Queen of England'*. King George was en route to Ireland when she died.

Yet again Smyth attempted to rise above the distinctly lowering news from home. He represented the King in New Brunswick, and must do his sickly best. Impelled by duty to a show of heroic sociability, he caused new celebrations and a ball to be held – this time in Saint John, so that all those excluded from the birthday festivities could express joy in their new sovereign.

As before, the public prints rallied round the royal standard. The Saint John *Courier* of 7 October believed there could be no 'transactions more truly characteristic of the loyal feelings of our fellow-citizens than those demonstrated in this City during the present week in commemoration of the coronation of our Most Gracious Sovereign GEORGE THE FOURTH.'[24] A 'select battalion', from the county militia of Saint John, was reviewed by Smyth with the regular garrison 'on the sands in the neighbourhood of the city.' That evening 'A Ball was given by His Excellency the Commander in Chief, which in splendour and magnificence far surpassed everything of the kind we have witnessed on this side of the Atlantic.' The Madras School Room was appropriated by its Trustees. 'Starry lamps,' greenery, arms and trophies hung on the walls, with 'upwards of 200 ladies and gentlemen' assembled. 'The following day was also devoted to festivity; and being the anniversary of the landing of many of our forefathers for the first time on these shores 38 years ago, may be deemed an era in the history of this Province, justly consecrated in patriotism and loyalty.' 'That all ranks might participate,' three tables were laid out in King's Square, and at 1 o'clock a roasted ox conveyed to each.' 'Copious libations flowed in the mean time. And the whole terminated in peace, hilarity, and good humour.' The following night, in that same hall where 'New Brunswick's beauteous daughters' had shimmered, a dinner and 'entertainment' was laid out for men alone that did 'great credit' to the caterer, Mr Cody. 'The company was highly respectable.' Nearly two hundred sat to dinner at 6pm with Smyth in the chair supported by the mayor, John Robinson, and General Coffin. The King's health was drunk, followed by a salute by the 74th in King's Square and a display of rockets. 'Mr Chamberlain' sang the national anthem, accompanied by the band of the 74th. Nineteen toasts followed, each with appropriate musical accompaniment.[25]

On leaving, Smyth was toasted, as was the mayor, but it was the incorrigibly popular General Coffin 'who left the room amid the loud and reiterated plaudits of the company.' Coffin was *their own* general, after all, tempered by fire in the Revolutionary War, who had raised the New Brunswick Fencibles to fight the Yankees again in the war of 1812. He had fought two duels, wrestled a bear, and quarrelled, it seemed, with everyone at least once. Coffin was the heart-of-oak, beef-fed, true-blooded colonial Englishman, who gave them cause to cheer as he sat beside the pale and withdrawn Smyth, the man to whom they must loyally defer. How many cared that Coffin, the proverbial loose cannon, ignored his responsibility to serve the King on Council, where his attendance was rare and whimsical?

The evening ended well. Despite the 'vast concourse' gathered outside, 'neither riot nor intemperance were seen in our streets.' Smyth provided at his expense roast beef, plum pudding, and 'a goblet of good liquor' which Mr Nowlan, the jailer, distributed to prisoners. This was a powerful show of loyal unity in time of strain. Smyth's two royal celebrations in 1821 were perhaps formally required of him but he does seem to have put himself out, in full knowledge of the circumstances. It had been a dismal coronation, a stern test of faith in the hereditary principle. Now, surely, they could go forward.

Well, not quite yet. The symbolic purpose of that evening of conviviality in Saint John had been well served, but the room was abuzz with something else, more local, much more intense. There was perhaps some irony in those whoops for pugnacious old Coffin. He had set a high standard as the flash-tempered 'man of honour'. But a number of the first generation of Loyalists had been similarly quick to take offence – quick to 'call out' offenders according to a demanding martial code of honour and it carried over into the next generation.

Four days before the coronation dinner, early in the morning on Maryland Hill just outside Fredericton, a duel was fought between George

Street and George Wetmore, the sons of Samuel Denny Street and Thomas Wetmore respectively. George Wetmore died at 10.15am from a gunshot wound to the head. The immediate cause of the quarrel had been a court case in which the men were rival barristers, George Street appearing for the Sheriff of York County, Edward W Miller who was accused of false arrest, while George Wetmore acted for the plaintiff. After a scuffle outside the court, Wetmore issued the challenge. The duel, being illegal, had necessarily been arranged in secret.

Wetmore was twenty-six, with three children, and a pregnant wife who named the subsequent baby girl George, and never spoke to Street again. Street and his two seconds, Richard Davies of the 74th and John F W Winslow, fled to Maine. In New Brunswick a 'hue and cry' was raised for their capture – whereupon Samuel Denny Street roamed the streets of Fredericton tearing down notices offering a reward of £30 for their arrest.[26] The fugitives would return voluntarily to stand trial for murder in February 1822, when all were acquitted on the tacit understanding that Wetmore had more or less brought about his own death.

That trial would expose the corrupting nature of personal allegiances among leading Loyalists, and exposed the sheer virulence of feuds within the Executive Council. The fatal duel was steeped in the sins of the fathers. Samuel Denny Street had a long-standing grievance against elements of the Loyalist elite which controlled patronage within the province.[27] Though a successful lawyer, and twice elected as an MLA, the elder Street had received no government office, being twice turned down for the Supreme Court. When he was appointed to Council in 1819 it was something of a consolation prize late in the day. Inevitably, this was attributed to the web of family relationships in New Brunswick. The younger Wetmore and Street were both members of the same Freemasons' lodge in Maugerville, but that had not been a bond strong enough to overcome generations of anger.

Early in 1800 Samuel Denny Street had joined Ward Chipman in the landmark legal case, defending a runaway slave called Nancy against her master, Caleb Jones, represented by Jonathan Bliss, his nephew John Murray Bliss, Thomas Wetmore, William Botsford and Charles J Peters. When the younger Bliss accused him of lying in court, Street had challenged him to a duel. That evening, outside the Fredericton courthouse, both men fired a single shot at nine paces and missed. Street was ready to try again but Bliss, pressed by his seconds, offered an apology which was reluctantly accepted. Showing that this episode was not entirely out of the ordinary, a slave-owner, Stair Agnew, also challenged one of the judges to a duel. Perhaps partly inspired by Street's example, there had been a rash of duelling in New Brunswick and Nova Scotia around 1800, especially between lawyers. The presence of large garrisons in Halifax and

Fredericton, with young officers eager to establish their credit as 'bucks', probably made things worse. Over the years the *Royal Gazette* carried lengthy articles denouncing duelling, and by the time Richard Uniacke junior killed William Bowie in Nova Scotia in 1819, public patience was nearly exhausted. George Wetmore's funeral on 9 October 1821, on the same day Queen Caroline's burial was described by the *Gazette*, was thus an occasion for more general anger as well as regret – another death claimed by a vicious rite of manliness and its stale glamour.

Lockwood and Samuel Denny Street had been paired on Council as the liaison with the House of Assembly, and consistently voted the same way. They also served together on the many occasions when, lacking a quorum, Council was reduced to a committee. Street was second only to Lockwood in attendance at Council and together they were the workhorses of Council, quite simply essential to the running of its affairs by reviewing material and presenting proposals for a quorum to vote on later. Both were outsiders – though hardly to the same degree – both English-born, both pugnacious. Meanwhile, the son, George Frederick Street, was treasurer to Lockwood's secretary of the Emigrant Society. Father and son had their law office on Queen Street in Fredericton and would necessarily have often spent time with the Surveyor and Receiver General.

There is no need to assume a close bond between them, but the Streets and Lockwood were clearly in much closer contact than with other members of Council. In the circumstances, the explosive effects of the duel and its aftermath could hardly be avoided; some personal and political choices were inevitable. It was just not possible for Lockwood, the non-Loyalist, even if he was so inclined, to retreat into his house and play the harpsichord.

In truth, the atmosphere was acrid. This may have given some urgency to the list of texts available from 9 Oct 1821 at Jedediah Slason's store. As treasurer of the Society for the Propagation of Christian Knowledge, Slason offered a long list of moral stiffeners, including 'The Sin of SLANDERING and BACKBITING'; 'Exercises against LYING'; and 'An office for people troubled in mind'.[28]

How troubled Lockwood's mind was is an open question. But New Brunswick was not a settled state and the death of George Wetmore was framed by anxieties rooted in a more general unease – of rampant 'liberators' such as Bolivar, clamouring 'patriots', the strange emptiness which followed Boney's death, and the dismal spectacle of monarchy. The blood spilt on the grasses of Maryland Hill had served a violent ritual, a small version of the high style of heroic action playing out in the larger world.

PART THREE

The Fall

11

A House of Brick

ON THE FACE of it, Lockwood had established himself in New Brunswick and had every prospect of spending his days in high office, and in comfort. But that was not to be, and one of the reasons might have been the extent to which he had become the General's right-hand man. In the short term this gave him the influence in Council he needed, but it also tied him to an unpopular man, and to a soldier who was neither of a Loyalist family, nor a permanent immigrant. As a matter of principle, governors were never selected from the local community.

It is a matter of conjecture how socially isolated were the Lockwoods. From the time of his wedding to the onset of his madness there is little evidence available of Lockwood's personal life or his connections with general society in New Brunswick, such as church membership or ties with other communal organisations. After her marriage, Harriet disappears from sight, only to reappear as the distressed victim of an insane husband. The Lockwoods do not figure in the surviving papers of New Brunswick's leading families. This may be a significant absence: a collective cold shoulder presented to an upstart and his common wife. Fredericton society was very limited, compared even to Saint John, and Lockwood's surveying journeys kept him out of any potential social circle some of the time, while Harriet, with no apparent preparation for a life of polite conventions, may have kept to herself. She had been set down in a colonial garrison village on an unfamiliar continent, enclosed by vast forests, knowing no one, with an adolescent daughter and stepdaughter as her companions. Then there were the brutal winters, cold and entrapping, so very remote from Bridgetown and its year-round stalls laden with bright fruit.

One important family friendship can be traced to 1822, and was to play a part in the dramatic events surrounding Lockwood's madness a year later. Robert Carden Minette had emigrated with his wife from Ireland to Saint John in June 1818, a year earlier than Lockwood arrived, and set up as a civil engineer before being appointed City Surveyor, a post he held for fifty years. He became an assistant alderman of the city and a captain in the militia. It is not difficult to see what the Lockwoods had in common with Minette. They were all newly arrived, practical men engaged in the surveying line, with unpretentious social origins and with no local connections. Indeed, the Minette friendship, as well as that with William Reynolds, a bookseller of Saint John, may partially explain Lockwood's preference for surveys in the city region during 1821. In June 1823, in a deposition to the Grand Jury examining Lockwood's case, Minette described the latter unequivocally as 'my friend'.

Minette had become a Freemason in Ireland and joined the Saint John's Lodge on 15 June 1819. The Masons had flourished in New Brunswick from its beginnings, attracting prominent men, and were officially sanctioned. There were several lodges, in Saint John, Fredericton, St Andrews, and Maugerville. The *Royal Gazette* published lengthy articles extolling the virtues of Freemasonry, on 24 September 1816, for instance, reprinting an item from the Lancaster *Journal* by 'BONUS', providing a history and praising the tradition of tolerance and benevolence. This item may have been a nod to Lord Dalhousie's arrival in Nova Scotia as governor. Dalhousie was a former Grand Master of the Scottish Masons. Among early New Brunswick members were Council members George Leonard, George Spoule, Beverley Robinson, William Black, Samuel Denny Street, and Thomas Wetmore, as well as William Campbell, Christopher Sower, who was the King's Printer between 1784 and 1799, Henry Chubb, another printer, Gabriel Van Horne, who was an innkeeper, and three Scottish merchants, Alexander Crookshank, Hugh and Alexander Johnston.[1]

It might be asked why Lockwood did not himself join. In the very small world of colonial New Brunswick it would have been a logical step for a man seeking preferment, and society. Membership in a lodge might have helped Lockwood cement his social position. Minette and Hugh Johnston were Lockwood's friends, and could have introduced him. Perhaps his meteoric rise was too much resented amongst the Loyalist members, and perhaps Lockwood's naval rank of master was not considered acceptable by the military officers and Loyalist farmer members of the Masonic order in New Brunswick.

Even assuming he might have been able to join a lodge, however, the value of membership was limited. It would be a long stretch to find anything conspiratorial in the Masonic influence on New Brunswick life at this time. Lodge meetings were advertised in the newspapers, religious services were held in both Anglican churches and the Presbyterian Kirk, and convivial dinners were held at Cody's in Saint John. The Masonic tradition of enlightened rationalism, it is true, may have contributed to the American Revolution. Several of its leaders, including Washington, Franklin, Hancock, Madison, Paul Revere, John Paul Jones and La Fayette were Masons. But there were also prominent Loyalist members of the society, and the Prince Regent, two of his brothers, the Dukes of Sussex and Kent, served as Grand Masters of the English Grand Lodge. Hints of republicanism nevertheless attached themselves to the Masons from time to time, and there was undoubtedly an anti-Catholic bias in Freemasonry, but in the colonial context those tendencies implied little more than a certain modernity or openness to new ideas. The chief appeal of fraternal organisations was social, in communities where isolation could be deeply threatening.

Certainly Lockwood's remaining aloof from the Masons did not impede his continual advance as a career man in the secretive political world of Council, where timber regulations remained a central issue. He continued to get through mountains of detailed, respectable, and sometimes controversial business. With the authority of the Surveyor General of New Brunswick over Crown timber uncertain until the office of Surveyor General of the King's Forests was either filled or abolished, the Crown Reserves were still being poached and the regulations breached. In June the Council ordered a few lots to be laid out at Bartibog, near Miramichi, for emigrants – the expenses not to exceed £50. This belatedly responded to the steady influx of Irish at the port of Miramichi. Lockwood personally laid out lots on the Shepody Road; made a survey of Hopewell; surveyed a grant to Dennis, Francis, and Patrick McMannary at Hillsborough; drew a map of Fort Howe in Saint John; completed a survey of the Kingston Penninsula, and a 'Plan of Grants along Grand and Kenebaccis Bays.'[2] The map of Fort Howe is dated 5 October but that may signify its registration rather than completion. What is clear is that Lockwood spent weeks, if not months, away from Fredericton during the time of these surveys, another indication of his restless need to be up and doing – as well, perhaps, as a preference for Saint John and the coast. It seems probable that he extended his travels as far as Halifax, where his natural son, Henry Arcade, was baptised at St George's Church on 17 July 1821. But rank fixed manacles. At the end of the season he had to return to Fredericton. On 10 November he wrote to Smyth recommending 'the expediency of placing a period to receiving Petitions to cut Pine Timber for the present season, say [to] 25th December in order to avoid the subterfuge the Sunbery men had last year of covering them and [two words] by Licences a few days old.'[3] As a member of the College Board which met in Fredericton on 20 November to amend its regulations, sitting with Samuel Denny Street, William Franklin Odell, J M Bliss, Peter Fraser, F P Robinson and the Reverend James Milne, Lockwood was the very picture of sober responsibility.

At the end of 1821 Lockwood attempted to regularise his office as Acting Receiver General, writing to Bathurst asking for confirmation of the appointment. In doing so, he presented 'an Idea of the Casual revenues ... to shew that it is not sufficient to sustain a separate office.' 'The Receiver General's income for that year [1820: Lockwood's first in office] was £7/9/4½ and will the present year probably yield 15 or 17 pounds. These sums tho' small, are useful in assisting me to support a family in that respectability of appearance that every Member of His Majesty's Council is bound to observe and as the Receiver General's office is not incompatible with that of the Chief Surveyor's, having always heretofore had the Auditor's office attached to it which is now separate.' Hoping his request for confirmation was 'reasonable' he attached a certificate of 'Receipts at the Receiver General's Office': 'Purchase money for 64 grants £56/13/11¾. Fines imposed on trespassers £18/0/0.'[4]

The rewards were indeed insignificant and even allowing for Lockwood's possible economy with the truth the evidence does suggest that up to that date the Receiver General's revenues were very small. The contrast between high title and the facts of colonial life is almost farcical. Surely an office carrying an annual income of less than twenty pounds was hardly a matter for the Colonial Secretary's attention, even if the Crown officer's respectability of appearance was at stake? But perhaps Lockwood already understood that those slim pickings were grossly misleading and that it would be wise to lock in the Receiver General's job. A crock of gold lay very close at hand. His own time of trouble was close by too and money would be a big part of it.

On 4 January 1822 he repeated his petition to Smyth that applications for cutting pine should have an expiry date set. Smyth passed it on to Council, meeting in Saint John (with Lockwood absent), which agreed that none should be accepted after 1 March for the present season and that notices to that effect should be posted. Lockwood was clearly trying to bring some order to the process before a momentous change took place. Smyth had decreed that by the beginning of March 1822 all such licence fees would be routed through the Receiver General's office and Lockwood would in future be accountable.[5] On 18 March Council noted that bonds for licences had not been collected during 1820–21 and there was already a substantial amount of money to be gathered in.

Lockwood may have played a small role in the deliberations of the General Assembly, which was elected following a vigorous campaign in the winter of 1821–22. A freeholder of Queensbury complained in the *Royal Gazette* of 16 December 1821 that, notwithstanding it was the middle of the winter, he had 'never witnessed half so much canvassing, contention, and strife, prior to an election, as at present. In fact, sir, the whole County may be said to be in motion. The fag-rags ride up and down the river in legions, visit every house like a pestilence, and torture every man who has the misfortune to fall in their way, with long harangues on the issue of the approaching election.' At the beginning of February 1822 the newly elected Assemblymen gathered in Fredericton. Even General Coffin was there that spring.[6]

It is possible that a report in the *Royal Gazette* on the 12th purporting to be an address given by an anonymous President of the Fredericton Philomathean Society, 'formerly the Society of Small Talkers', was intended to be a parody of General Smyth's speech from the throne opening the session. It is pompous blather, full of mock humility, elaborate thanks for the honour bestowed, and virtually empty of content. The contemporary obsession with plots and subversion is revealed in a veiled reference to 'dangers and difficulties which have for a season, like a cloud over-shadowed us', and to some sort of 'attack' on the 'regulations' by 'a spirit among us.' It was printed immediately following the end-of-session 'Solemn Address' to Smyth by the House of Assembly, and his thanks to that body, and was published by the 'Secretary and Treasurer', Anthony Lockwood junior, 'at the unanimous request' of the members. If the Fredericton Philomathean Society really existed it sounds like a young men's club, devoted to conviviality while mocking high seriousness and solemn elders, but the piece must have appeared with the compliance of the *Gazette's* editor, George Lugrin, and perhaps even Odell, and the context suggests that Lockwood senior might have been trying to find a place for himself in New Brunswick popular politics.

Benjamin Franklin had founded the first Philomathean ('love of knowledge') Society in Philadelphia in 1793, although he preferred to give the credit to a fictional Richard Saunders. Branches were later established in New York and elsewhere in the United States. Among 'Poor Richard's' many sayings which passed into the common currency of the English language, at least in North America, was 'Great Talkers; little Doers'. The Fredericton Society of Small Talkers, then, by inversion, might have pretended to be Great Doers.

The 'Great Doers' on Council were certainly at work. Writing to Bathurst on 28 March 1822, Smyth noted that Council recommended that in future the timber duty of one shilling per ton be paid directly to the Receiver General rather than in the form of bonds. Smyth would write again to Bathurst on 21 June 1822 expressing satisfaction with the success of the duty. The practice had been followed, he claimed, 'for three or four years' and had 'been salutary in establishing the right on the part of the Crown to make such regulations.' As a gesture of conciliation, he had agreed with the Assembly that all bonds already taken for the duty would be cancelled.[7]

The move to pay such taxes directly into the Receiver General's office led to a steep rise in revenues through 1822. The gathering-in went briskly. By 2 April the *Royal Gazette* issued notice that bonds must be given for all timber licences issued since 1 January, otherwise such timber would be seized by 'the Seizing Officers in the several counties', by order of 11 March. The same notice also referred to an order of 22 March creating new regulations for granting licences on Crown land. 'Actual payment' of the tax of one shilling per ton was required on the 'quantity mentioned in the Licence'. The money was to be paid directly to the Receiver General, first deducting fees for the licence – in proportions as follow: Lieutenant Governor, 10s; Provincial Secretary, 10s; Surveyor General, 5s. So the chief beneficiaries were Smyth, Odell, and Lockwood. A limit of a thousand acres per year was set on any licence; all applicants had to be British subjects, freeholders, or inhabitants of New Brunswick. Later, on 17 May, Council decreed that no more than forty licences be issued for cutting less than a hundred tons, presumably an effort to contain the numbers of small operations, difficult to keep under scrutiny.

By this flurry of executive action the money flowed into Lockwood's office. It is evident that the books were never 'kept' in any coherent way. This would become abundantly clear in the aftermath of Lockwood's lunacy proceedings, and as late as 16 June 1827, W Hill of the Treasury wrote to the Lieutenant Governor, Sir Howard Douglas, noting that 'no account of this Revenue has been rendered to this Board for many years past, my Lords therefore desire you will call on Mr Bliss [the new Receiver General] to make out Annual Statements of Revenue.'[8] It is clear that by late March 1822 Lockwood's finances had very substantially improved, both by means of his portion of fees payable to the Surveyor General and Receiver General in addition to the ten per cent he collected from monies entered directly into the Receiver General's account as payable to the Crown. The general increase in transactions passing through the Surveyor General's office since his arrival in 1819 was already generating more than George Sproule's £450 a year.

Lockwood now chose to proclaim his new wealth by a very public symbolism. From 4 January 1822 the *Royal Gazette* carried 'For Sale' notices for Lockwood's house at the end of Queen Street on the corner of what became Smythe Street.[9] 'Its situation and out-houses are well adapted for carrying on business of any kind; or, being seated on the banks of the river, commanding and extensive and pleasant view, make it a delightful private residence.' The terms, as stated, were to be one third of the purchase money on delivery of the deed, the rest to follow in equal payments over three years with interest. The same advertisement continued: 'Any person willing to contract for Building a brick House in the Town of Fredericton, is requested to deliver in proposals to Mr Reynolds, at Saint John, at whose shop a plan of the intended building is left for inspection.' This advertisement was shortened in the 29 April issue, with a sketch of a three-storey house added, and repeated until 25 June.

In the same 4 January issue of the *Gazette* appeared a 'call for proposals' to be received by either Odell or Lockwood for 'an addition to Government House' and two additions to Province Hall, to be completed by 20 October, as well as 'a stone building, with slate roof, for an office for the Surveyor General – the Contractor to specify the time within it can be completed.' Lockwood's new house was intended to be built during the same time as these major extensions to his office and other government buildings.

In settler society there was a clear progression, defining affluence and rank, from the log cabin to the framed house and finally to that of stone or brick. Lockwood clearly judged it time, in the first days of 1822, to build a home fit for a gentleman of 'respectability of station'. With a house of brick the arriviste would truly arrive.

Giving substance to this demonstration was a flurry of financial dealing that spring. Dated 1 May at Saint John, a 'statement Sale of Hon Anthony Lockwood's Bank Stock at Auction' lists five £50 shares in the Bank of New Brunswick sold at a ten per cent premium: four to George Mathew, one to Zalmon Wheeler. The latter is noted as selling this stock for Lockwood. After expenses, £273 3s 8d was paid to a Joseph Gaynor, probably to cover a debt. Gaynor was the child of a Connecticut Loyalist who settled in Fredericton and was a relative of Zalmon Wheeler. He and his brother were prominent businessmen, and ascetic converts to Methodism.[10]

Lockwood also made up a statement of income over the past years (1819–21), which was also a kind of summary of his position: salary £150; fees (average) £430 4s 6d; stationary allowance £32 2s 5d; allowance for fuel, £23 10s 0d; allowance for office rent, £23 10s 0d. Deductions: for clerk hire, instruments, stationary, fuel, office rent, etc, etc, £326 0s 1d. Total income: £338 7s 10d. He noted that no house was allowed as a residence, but £25 currency for office rent was paid out of the provincial treasury. He then added 'Receiver General's Return: similar this, mutatis mutanda, as under. Amt. of percentage recd in 3 years – £58/9/8. Deduct incidental Exps. £12/15/0. £45/14/8. One year £22/17/4.' His pride in his accomplishment is manifest in a note: 'Receiver General's office held pro tempore, and late a Master in the Royal Navy on half-pay. Absent at no period. No other advantage.' Overleaf there is a reference to 'Mr Wheeler a/c of Bank Stock sold in 1822 for A Lockwood' as well as a page devoted to 'Bank and other drafts 1821' with dealings mainly with Z Wheeler. Zalmon Wheeler was a merchant of Saint John, who acted, it seems, as Lockwood's financial agent, banker, and perhaps adviser.[11]

Lockwood seemed to be taking stock before taking up his expanded duties as Receiver General, or possibly making notes for an undetermined disclosure of his situation. The figures stated are prior to the bounty of the timber tax.

It is probable that his decision to send his son on a trip to London, probably about mid-April, was part of Lockwood's efforts to better himself. Anthony junior wrote to Robert Wilmot, Under Secretary of State at the Colonial Office, on 30 May, having just arrived in London. In what must have been cold panic, the younger Anthony told of being 'furnished on my departure with certain papers for Government, in order to deliver them in London. These documents were by the Surveyor General of that Colony [NB], my father, rested in a [illegible word] case, in which, I suppose conceiving himself at Liberty as an officer of Government, he enclosed some private letters, and other open papers for my use, and directed the whole to the Rt. Honble Lord Bathurst. My object in thus troubling you, is to obtain the open papers, that were undirected, as they contain in part the business which brought me to London; the sealed letters I find have been safely delivered, according to their direction.' He solicited 'an early answer, as it is of extreme consequence, my obtaining those papers with as little delay as possible.'[12] Was it possible that one of those letters or papers contained the financial details of the 'Cash Book'? A strong likelihood is that Lockwood was again trying to convince Bathurst that he should be confirmed as Receiver General. A petition that the younger Lockwood evidently delivered to the Admiralty on his father's behalf requesting the loan of a 'timekeeper, one artificial Horizon of quicksilver, a Dipping Needle, a Barometer and a Thermometer' may have been intended to support the claim for preferment, as painting him as a man of action.[13] The Admiralty Secretary noted on the corner that such instruments were only loaned for naval purposes.

While his son was on his mission to London, Lockwood was again involved in the question of what should be done about the Fredericton jail. On 18 January 1822 a grand jury had reported to the Supreme Court that they had visited the Fredericton jail 'and in their opinion [it] is not worthy of any repairs, and ought to be condemned.' On 17 May 1822 Council responded to the grand jury report of the previous year condemning the Fredericton jail as unfit for human habitation. The original land grant for the site was rescinded and Lockwood made a sketch of a new lot with ninety-eight feet of frontage on King Street.[14] A 'Residence' was to be built there for sale, with the money used for a new jail. Sadly, the scheme would be too late for Lockwood's own case. He would reside for weeks in the stinking cells of the old building.

Ten days later Council confirmed the minutes of 8–9 February that lots for the Indian band at Buctouche should be so laid out as to leave intermediate vacant land for settlers. This was another measure designed to encourage integration of the Micmac, who would be obliged both to practise agriculture and to live alongside newcomers. A survey later that year, which Lockwood signed, showed the Buctouche Reserve to consist of 'about 30,000 acres.'[15] There is no evidence of any other activity by Lockwood that spring, although there was the usual work of his office.

Selling his house and building a grander one; selling stock; taking stock; sending his son as courier to London on 'business', with private letters and papers for Lord Bathurst's eyes, a matter of 'extreme consequence'. Lockwood's restless urgency seems at odds with that solid house of brick. Certainly, something seems to have disturbed his friends. On 11 June Lockwood's guarantors as Receiver General, Hugh Johnston and Thomas Millidge, wrote to Ward Chipman stating that they wished to withdraw as securities forthwith.[16] These were the two Saint John dignitaries who attended Lockwood's wedding. There was no explanation in the note. It can be assumed that the statement was for the record and that reasons were conveyed privately. Something had evidently troubled these two shrewd and well-informed men. Lockwood found two new sponsors, the Fredericton merchant and philanthropist Jedediah Slason, and his financial agent Zalmon Wheeler. Nevertheless, the withdrawal of two very prominent Saint John figures, both members of the Assembly, was more than a straw in the wind. The advertisement for the sale of Lockwood's house appeared again in the *Royal Gazette* a week after his guarantors backed off, but the house of brick would never be built.

Lockwood attended Council meetings with his usual regularity during that troubled June. But he also found time to write to Lord Bathurst on 2 July: 'A Meteorological Table herewith sent, will exhibit to your Lordship the state and changes in the atmosphere in this His Majesty's province – It was carefully kept and may be relied on. I have to request your Lordship's acceptance of it, and am your very humble and respectful servant.' This was sufficiently odd to merit a Colonial Office memo overleaf: 'What does this mean?'[17] On 20 November 1822 Lockwood wrote to the Admiralty, replying to theirs of 'May last', and enclosing 'a record of my civil employment' as Surveyor General at a salary of £338 7s 10d per annum.[18] It sounds as though Lockwood had some scheme for self-advancement in hand.

From the perspective of Saint John merchants, the proposed canal from the Bay of Fundy to the Bay de Chaleur was the most important of Lockwood's undertakings. The *Acadian Recorder* in July 1821 had commented on the rapid advance being made in the construction of the canal joining the Hudson River with Lake Ontario: 'Nothing will counteract the pernicious effects of this vast and spirited enterprise upon the exports of Canada, but a zealous improvement of the internal navigation of that country.'[19] In Canada there was progress in the construction of a canal around the La Chine rapids on the St Lawrence river, but if the port of Saint John were to prosper as an entrepôt for trade to the interior it needed easier access to the Gulf of St Lawrence.

This article, and another on 13 August, was followed within days by a public meeting at Saint John, at which 'A numerous and respectable' group of 'Merchants and other Gentlemen of the City' with Judge Chipman in the chair resolved that a committee be authorised 'to engage with some competent person in the United States' to survey a route 'without loss of time'. £250 was raised 'in a morning by 50 subscriptions of £5.'[20] A petition was prepared to Smyth dated 28 August 1822 at 'The City of Saint John' requesting governmental assistance for a more detailed survey of the possible canal sites, and a better estimate of the cost for the channel itself and the construction of locks enabling vessels of 120 tons burthen and 12 feet draught to pass. Lockwood's survey of 1819 was cited as establishing the practicability of such a scheme, and Smyth was asked to take note of Lockwood's observation that suitable Crown land for canal routes lay in both Nova Scotia and New Brunswick. It further requests he recommend to His Majesty's Government that such land be set aside for the canal project and that Smyth also seek the approval of the Lieutenant Governor of Nova Scotia for such a procedure.[21] The merchants of Saint John knew better than to wait for Smyth to act. On the 31st the *New Brunswick Courier* reported: 'We understand that Mr Johnston, Architect, and Mr [Robert] Minette, Surveyor of this City, have been appointed to make the survey of the intended Bay of Verte Canal. These gentlemen propose to set out on this business on Monday the 9th of September.'[22] Evidently it was no longer considered necessary to find an American expert.

Is there an implication that Lockwood's suitability to pursue the project, was coming into question? Thomas Millidge and Hugh Johnston senior, who had withdrawn in June as Lockwood's sureties for the office of Receiver General, were both members of the committee, but then, so too was Zalmon Wheeler who had stepped forward to replace one of them as a surety. Anthony Lockwood had been present at the Council discussions of a new canal survey. On the face of it, he was the obvious person to conduct, or at least supervise, this enterprise, especially since his first report had been so warmly received in Saint John. But the Saint John committee, pointedly, did not request that the Surveyor General take charge. Why was he excluded?

If Smyth succeeded in his wish to take leave in the Mother Country, Lockwood, like his fellows on the Council, had to be interested in the question of who would be his deputy. And the sad end of this man would affect Lockwood profoundly. It may, indeed, have triggered his descent into madness.

The question of who would be the deputy had in fact already been settled, although apparently nothing of that was known in New Brunswick. Heedless of the negative attitude in New Brunswick society to the use of serving soldiers, Bathurst had warranted Colonel Le Poer Trench of the Fredericton garrison as long ago as 1819 to take over as military president of Council should Smyth go on leave, and Smyth had so informed the Council on 22 June 1819.[23] On 5 May 1822 Le Poer Trench, himself on leave in Britain, wrote to Bathurst from Cheltenham. He had heard that Smyth had again applied for leave. If he took it, could Le Poer Trench take up the warrant? He was ready to leave with his family at the shortest notice. He wrote again only five days later enquiring whether the first letter had miscarried and making the same request. By 12 June he was thanking Bathurst for confirming the warrant. Since Smyth might return at any time, he would hold himself ready. 'I shall be in readiness to proceed to New Brunswick, for the purpose of acting upon the Warrant which, thro' your Lordship's kindness, I hold for administering the government there.[24]

But in truth Smyth was too sick to ever make the journey. And in his weakness he ached with private needs. Throughout the spring and summer of 1822 he wrote a series of personal letters to his brother in England, the Reverend John Gee Smyth, with whom his daughter Amelia was living. His emotional isolation is plain to see. The letters are highly repetitive, even to individual phrases, which may be explained by the letter of 6 June, where Smyth wrote of being 'mortified that none of my Winter letters had reached you of a later date than the 24th of January – they must have failed by more than one conveyance.'[25] Perhaps he simply repeated himself in the hope that at least one letter would get through. This correspondence had three main topics: Smyth's wish for his daughter Amelia to join him in New Brunswick; his proposal to import three professional musicians; and his directions to John Gee concerning an organ which he was to purchase and have shipped, along with a collection of sheet music. What he had in mind, as a counter to the buzz of colonial disaffection, the vulgarity of store-keepers, woodcutters, and poor Irish, was a small court over which he might preside and which would sustain his daughter by the gracious standards of her class.

There is a clear sense of agitation, of pressing time, well expressed by Smyth's birthday letter of 4 April: 'Reflecting on my age and that of my child I am determined not to delay the comfort of having her with me any longer.' He wrote of his irresolution about returning home 'from season to season'. 'Our meeting in this world, my dear Brother, grows daily more uncertain, and even this happiness might not warrant me in quitting the high station I fill. Amelia has time to live with me in this Country before she will be of a suitable age to form a matrimonial engagement after which I could expect but little of her company.' 'If I remain another Season, don't fail to let Amelia join me! If the opportunity be a direct one from London to Saint John, I have no objection to have her Pony sent, should you think the animal worth exporting.' Later letters express Smyth's need to justify himself to John Gee; his ingrained sense of social status and propriety; the pathos lying behind his fear of 'indulging' Amelia too much, which led to niggardliness, and a constant anxiety about whether she would indeed join him. 'I shall not repeat how sensibly I enter into your feelings my Dear Brother upon this occasion, not only at parting from the Child you have educated with so much affection and anxiety, but also from the possible prolongation of our separation – altho' free agents, these events are influenced by Providence, and a parent ought to be with his Child.'

In various letters Smyth advised on Amelia's outfitting. She should bring with her 'a genteel stock of cloths [sic] without finery'; 'plenty of shoes, and half boots' (for bad weather), 'coloured short gloves, plenty of fine flannel', a side-saddle, a bridle, and whips. Smyth was a loving puritan. 'Let her wardrobe be ample, but with as little ornament as possible.' She should also bring 'a new small Piano from Tomkinson', 'some good Sonatas' and 'her vocal Musick.' 'I have her mother's box of Colours in complete order, but let her bring some Drawings to copy.'

Finding a suitable chaperone for his daughter's passage was a difficulty, and Smyth was also concerned to acquire suitable servants – 'some respectable Widow would come to take the management of my house, without living at my table', and he was interested in his brother's mention of 'a lad in Suffolk about 16 – qualified for a Madras teacher and Servant, in the latter capacity I should be glad to have him, or others from a respectable stock (as we get nothing but Irish servants here) but they must engage in writing that passage money advanced to them may be deducted by degrees from their wages, which shall beat the highest rate of the Country.' He also asked that 'the four quarters of the Globe' be cut into pieces so that his son, Brunswick, 'may amuse himself in learning their relative situation.' 'Send the best Gazeteer and Geographical Treatise at present extant to elucidate the maps.'

On 8 August 1822 the *Blücher* took on board at London, with a shipment of 'Plate, clothes etc', seven cases of music for Lieutenant Governor Smyth, as well as two organs, apparently both the church and drawing-room instruments, although perhaps one of the two was a piano wrongly identified.[26] And Amelia also took passage. On 12 October Judge

John Saunders wrote Smyth congratulating him on her arrival, 'especially as I am informed that she possesses both in person and manner all those qualities and if I may say so those feminine amiabilities which cannot but endear her to a fond parent.'[27]

Another who arrived in Fredericton that year, and was to play a part in creating the monuments that transformed the colonial capital in the forest, was a soldier-artist, John Elliot Woolford. According to the Ordnance Department's 'Foreign Establishment' returns, Woolford was made Barrack Master at Fredericton on 23 November 1821. He had established himself as an artist while serving in the 2nd Queen's Regiment in the Mediterranean. There he had attracted the attention of Major Ramsey who was to succeed as the 9th Earl of Dalhousie, and he had accompanied Dalhousie to Halifax in 1816 as the Earl's draughtsman. When Dalhousie was promoted from Governor of Nova Scotia to Governor of Canada, Woolford had obtained the post in Fredericton.[28] Lockwood must have met Woolford in Halifax. His artistic abilities must have interested Smyth but he was to make more of a mark on New Brunswick following the arrival of General Sir Howard Douglas as governor in 1825, perhaps because he was a kinsman of Douglas's wife. He was to remain in Fredericton for forty-four years, and to become a welcome addition to the society of such as the Saunders family. In 1847 the small son of John Saunders junior, Henry Charles, was to write to his father that he 'breakfast[ed] with Mr W every Sunday morning and he enquires very much after you.'[29]

12

The Perfect Storm

WHETHER LOCKWOOD'S DOWNFALL is best characterised by the classical myth of Icarus who provided himself with wings but flew too near the sun, or by that of Acalus who embarrassed his mentor by his too great creativity, and was destroyed by him, 1823 was to be the year of reckoning. A Fredericton surgeon, Thomas Emerson, later stated that 'some time in the autumn of last year, he . . . attended the Hon Anthony Lockwood as a Physician [when the latter] was then decidedly in a state of mental derangement and in [my] opinion unfit to conduct his official Business.' Lockwood, he said, 'soon after went to Saint John for the purpose of putting himself under the charge and care of Dr [Thomas] Paddock . . . from which place [he] returned to Fredericton during the Winter, and then appeared to be recovered.' According to the later report by Ward Chipman, Lockwood had entered a depressive phase after 'aggravated symptoms' had led him to seek treatment by Dr Paddock. This had left him 'in a quiet but very dejected state of mind' for that winter.[1] Nevertheless, his attendance at the Executive Council and its committees continued to be exemplary; indeed, he was present at thirty of thirty-one meetings of the full Council or its committees between 4 January and 1 May. At the committee meeting on 4 January he absented himself during discussion of a grant application by his son for five hundred acres 'near Restook, in the parish of Kents, between Germaine Dubic and Raphael Lagasse', but the matter was referred until his return.[2] Nevertheless, all was not well, and when on February 5 Xenophon Jouett, Gentleman Usher of the Black Rod, required both houses to attend in the Council Chamber at Fredericton for the third session of the eighth General Assembly, Lockwood entered the last, intense phase of his political life.[3]

Smyth's address to the Assembly defined policy goals for his administration, with a clear emphasis upon communication and education. The members were urged to provide for improvement to river navigation, particularly on their upper reaches, by the removal of obstructions and the construction of towpaths; the system of building and maintaining the 'Great Roads' also needed to be improved; and schools and 'seminaries' must be provided. In particular, legislation was proposed to provide for improvement to the bridges and roads in Saint John, to change the procedure for levying and assessing parish charges, to address the plight of confined debtors, to regulate taverns and the sale of strong liquors, to encourage the fisheries, and to improve the provisions of the Poor Law. A nightly watch was proposed for Saint John; a grammar school for St Andrews; a bill for the establishment of schools was to be introduced; Justices of the Peace were to be given authority to establish ferries. It is evident that the scope and dimension of public business had grown, and the programme was substantial. The frequency of Executive Council meetings had increased sharply during 1822 and the first months of 1823 saw the trend continuing. Council committees were busy with a flood of land grant applications during this period and Lockwood, both as Surveyor General and Receiver General, was necessarily at the centre of this activity, 'dejected' or not.

Nothing in the official record suggests directly that he was avoided, shielded, or otherwise treated with circumspection. At the 6 February meeting of the Executive Council, Lockwood was selected, with George Shore, to draft a reply to Smyth's address. The draft was then brought to Council on 10 February, accepted, and presented to His Excellency at 1pm on the 12th. But when, two days later, the proposed detailed survey of the route of a Chignecto canal was brought forward, it appears that Lockwood's 'dejection' was already sufficiently advanced that he was kept from the central role he should have played.

On 18 February 1823 Lockwood wrote to Smyth in response to a question about appropriations of lands to churches and schools, and he indicated that he was 'ready and most willing to comply', and he was present when Smyth set before Council the report from Ward Chipman and others 'to adopt measures for procuring a more minute survey of the Ground through which it may be expedient to open a Canal between the Bay of Fundy and the Gulph of St Lawrence.' The petitioners who had already financed the 1822 Minette survey out of the privately subscribed £250 'prayed' that the Lieutenant Governor would recommend to the Assembly that the expenses should be reimbursed. Furthermore, 'the same petitioner having suggested to his Excellency the propriety of some provision being made for a complete Survey of the Route from the mouth of the Memramcook River to Chaldaic with a view to the same object – the Funds at the command of the petitioner being not only insufficient for that purpose but also inadequate for remuneration for the services already performed by the Persons employed', he asked that the 'requisite steps' be taken to have the survey done by 'Persons competent to such service.'[4] Smyth brought the matter to the legislature three days later, on 26 February, recommending in virtually identical words that the subscribers be reimbursed and costs covered, as well as 'the making of suitable provision, to enable the Lieutenant Governor to take the requisite steps for making the proposed survey and exploration by persons competent to such service.'[5] This clearly suggests that the Minette survey, like Lockwood's, had been preliminary to a 'more minute' one which required heavy financial backing. The House finally approved £150 for this purpose on 15 March, but this was a somewhat grudging acceptance of the scheme in principle since the sum allotted was significantly smaller that already expended. A proposal to vote £370 5s 3d was negatived.[6] It is arguable that the dream of the Chignecto Canal was lost here – not simply by a lukewarm legislature but as a consequence of peculiar personal circumstances.

Lockwood was not only identified with the scheme in principle; his survey had associated him with Saint John merchants interested in the scheme. But now, just when that earlier experience and his official position as Surveyor General made him the natural agent for the detailed survey – indeed, in the usual order of things the Surveyor General would select 'persons competent to such a service' – his 'dejection' sapped any immediate will to act.

Lockwood did manage to present plans of the rivers Chebuctouche and Richibucto, ('whereon is exhibited thirteen Reserves') to the approval of Council on 13 March. But the legislature was showing caution about larger scale plans. On 14 March, Peter Fraser reported to the House from a committee 'appointed to enquire and report what further sums are necessary for the Improvement of the Roads and Bridges, and for removing obstructions, and deepening the Channels of the Rivers throughout the province, and forming towing paths along the banks of the same . . . that in consequence of the sum of £10,000 granted in the years 1820 and 1822 for the above purposes remaining unexpended, and the present limited state of the Funds of the Province . . . no further appropriation [should] be made at this Session.' The caution was justified; the expansionary schemes had outrun will and resources – perhaps reflecting the decline of certain key figures, Lockwood among them. But it is also true that the political climate was sour, if not petty. The House also refused funding for a private secretary for Smyth, for the completion of two further wings to Province House, and for the furnishing of the public rooms at Government House.[7]

The Chignecto Canal was sunk by those formidable opponents: depression, madness, and death. Ten days after the legislature's allotment of funds to the proposed survey, Smyth died. In the political crisis which followed, Chipman was fully occupied – not least with the Lockwood situation. He died himself less than a year later, on 9 February 1824 – to be followed by the politically much weaker John Bliss as interim President.

On 25 February, Smyth had been forced 'by reason of illness' to require both houses of the legislature, Assembly and Council, to attend him at Government House, where he gave assent to those bills which were ready. It was Lockwood who acted as liaison between the Council and the House on the following day. On the 27th, 'in consequence of the extreme illness of His Excellency the Lieutenant Governor', the House met at 7am, when Lockwood and William Black delivered further messages from the Council. Meanwhile, 'a Commission under the Great Seal, signed by the Lieutenant Governor, having been issued ... authorizing and empowering John Saunders Esq, the Chief Justice, and Ward Chipman and John Murray Bliss, Esquires, two of the Justices of the Supreme Court, or any two of them, to give the Lieutenant Governor's Assent to such Bills as had passed the Council and the House of Assembly, two of the said Commissioners, to-wit, the Chief Justice and Mr Justice Chipman ... did ... require the attendance of the House of Assembly in the Council Chamber', where the session was closed.[8]

Smyth died that day, his death being officially confirmed at a Council meeting.[9] 'The King's Commission and Instructions to the Governor General being read – [it was] ordered that notice immediately be sent by Express to the Hon George Leonard, the Senior Member of the Council, apprising him of this Event and requesting him to repair immediately to the Seat of Government and assume the administration of the Government – and in case Mr Leonard be in any way prevented from repairing immediately to the Seat of Government that he be requested to signify the same in writing and that thereupon the like notice be sent forthwith to Mr Billopp the next Senior Member and that he in like manner be requested to repair immediately to Fredericton in order to assume the administration – or communicate his answer in writing.'[10] These letters, however, were nothing but formalities. In quickly jotted notes the Provincial Secretary, William Franklin Odell, recorded the discussion about how to meet the crisis. The councillors were acutely aware that both Leonard and Billopp 'were upwards of eighty years of age, neither of whom from age and infirmities had been able to give their attendance at the seat of Government for upwards of [blank] years.' Odell left blanks for the text of his letters, and of the answers when they arrived, and then continued with an account of the Council's reaction. 'Being of opinion' that the King's commission called for the 'business and affairs of the Government' to be conducted 'at Fredericton, where the public officers and records of the Province are kept and deposited, and that the public exigencies will admit of no further delay', it was decided that 'the next in seniority' should be sworn into office.[11]

Leonard had retired to his home in Sussex Vale for the past fifteen years and had long ceased to attend Council meetings. Chipman was to explain to Bathurst in a long letter of 9 September that Leonard was 'laboring under the effects of paralitic attack which had deprived him in a great degree of the intelligible exercise of the faculty of speech, and the signature of his name could only be obtained by his hand being held and guided by another.'[12] Billopp, it is true, had been present at Council in Saint John, where he lived, as recently as four years ago. Yet age and infirmity disqualified him from the supreme provincial office as plainly as they did Leonard. On 1 April the Council, meeting in Fredericton, received a letter from Billopp saying he could not make the trip to 'the seat of government'.

As Chipman wrote to Dalhousie on the 3rd, that difficulty, the fact that Billopp was 'upwards of four score years and very infirm', and had not attended Council in Fredericton for fifteen years, persuaded the Council to swear Chipman in as the interim President.[13] He told Dalhousie he would gladly relinquish the presidency to Billopp, but that it would be absurd to do so, suggesting that Billopp was senile as well as old. The Council minutes tidied up Odell's notes, and justified the decision on the grounds that it was necessary 'as appears by the King's Commission and Instructions that the Person to administer the Government should be sworn in at Fredericton', and that the 'exigencies of the Government' admitted of no delay.[14] Two days later, on the 5th, Chipman attended General Smyth's funeral in his new role as President and Commander-in-Chief, and Lockwood served as one of the pall-bearers.

Smyth was given full military honours, and the following day the Reverend James Somerville, president of the College of New Brunswick that later became King's College, and chaplain to the House of Assembly and to the garrison, preached at Christ Church about his old friend. Smyth had been supportive when Somerville was badly treated by the College Board, and he now tried to set the record straight about the general's virtues, while avoiding taking sides in the divisions of New Brunswick society. 'Panegyrick' was, he said, out of place when Smyth had gone 'to answer at the Bar of an unerring Judge'. 'Politics,' he asserted, 'have nothing to do with this Sacred House, and men of our order are the very last who ought to intermeddle with them: "Fear God, and honour the King, and meddle not with those that are given to change" are the only politics of the Christian Clergyman.' But clearly Somerville thought Smyth deserved to have his reputation cleared. 'His anxiety to procure Missionaries for the different and distant parts of the Province, and to make for them suitable provision; the readiness and zeal with which he entered into every plan for the erection of new Churches, and the efforts he made, as far as depended upon him, amply to endow them, will be long

and affectionately remembered, by those who had the best opportunities
of knowing them. To the Ministers of that Church, whilst they acted in a
manner suitable to their profession, he was ever ready to extend his
countenance, patronage, and support. The unwearied exertions which he
made for the education of the Youth of the Country, particularly those of
the lower orders, are universally known through the whole extent of this
Province.' The humility with which he faced death, 'when power could no
longer protect, when pomp could no longer dazzle, and when human pride
was soon to be laid in its kindred dust, a prey to corruption and to worms',
was consistent with the humility of his life, and a model for the soldiers.[15]
Among Smyth's bequests was an organ given to Christ Church Cathedral.
A monument was ordered, which now is in the south transept, and in
March 1828 George Shore wrote to John Gee Smyth to tell him that it had
arrived at Saint John in December and moved up river 'as soon as the ice
was sufficiently safe.' He also expressed pleasure that Amelia Smyth was
well established. The memorial particularly mentioned Smyth's efforts to
provide schools for the blacks who had come to New Brunswick as slaves,
and were now freed into abject poverty.[16]

What had Lockwood felt about Smyth's piety and good works? Was an
appreciation of his qualities a factor in the loyal service Lockwood had
given, and in his extravagant behaviour in the following months when New
Brunswick was to experience an unprecedented crisis? How important had
been their shared passion for music?

Chipman's succession to the government was not to be uncontested. It was
out of the question that Leonard or Billopp should travel at the end of
March, on New Brunswick's 'Great Roads' to the seat of government. The
whole province was still locked in winter, the forests dense and impassable.
Though the rivers and lakes were still iced and sledable, the break-up was
imminent, making a journey even from Fredericton to Saint John by horse
a tough slog at best, and not to be thought of by octogenarians. It was a
dreadfully inconvenient time of year for Smyth to die. Death had come
while the Winter King still ruled. But was it really necessary to be in such
haste to swear in a president?

Fredericton was the established capital – but some Council meetings were
regularly held in Saint John, and the Assembly was no longer in session. If
the old men could not go to the seat of government, could not the
government be conducted from Sussex Vale, or Saint John? Was the
establishment of the seat of government in Fredericton in the King's commission of more importance than its provision that government should be
assumed by the most senior councillor? Leonard sent a letter to Chipman
on 2 May that, while he refused to make the journey to Fredericton to be

sworn in, it was only the journey that prevented him, and he asked why he could not be sworn in where he was.[17]

Any just resolution of that question had to deal with the persistent rivalry of Saint John and Fredericton. Although the Council did sometimes meet at Saint John, and a house was kept in Saint John for the Lieutenant Governor, in no sense was Saint John a co-capital. When making an address to citizens of Saint John during a tour of the province the previous July, Smyth had referred to his 'annual visits to the City of Saint John.'[18] But Saint John partisans quickly saw an opportunity to shake the security of a 'Seat' they never failed to resent. If they were able to take advantage of the crisis, and become the capital while one of their citizens was the president, they might establish a claim for a more enduring transfer of government.

On Tuesday, 8 April, according to the editor of the *City Gazette*, some Saint John citizens called a meeting at Cody's Coffee House under the chairmanship of Charles Simonds to press Billopp's claims. A 'Loyal Address' was brought to the meeting, addressed to him, stating that 'We the undersigned Inhabitants of the City of Saint John, conceiving that the administration of the Government, on the demise of our late Lieutenant-Governor, ought to have devolved on' the Honourable Christopher Billopp, 'as Senior Member of His Majesty's Council residing in the Province, next in succession to the Honourable George Leonard, who has resigned, and that agreeable to the Royal Instructions, no other person can exercise the functions of Executive Government.' And, it continued with more than a whiff of humbug, 'we beg leave further to express our alarm at the introduction into this Province, of any proceedings or principles, which have a Democratic or Republican tendency, and we disclaim the idea of Elective Rulers, satisfied that under our present happy constitution, we enjoy as much freedom as is consistent with public security, and the good of society.' A motion that the chairman should sign was negatived, but 'five or six of the most violent and democratic characters' put their signatures to it.

It is possible that Christopher Billopp was himself behind these posturings; in any event he promptly replied, begging 'leave to assure you of my readiness and determination on this as on every other occasion, to do my utmost to comply with His Majesty's Instructions and to assert by every Constitutional means, the right that has devolved upon me.' He had already, on 8 April, written a long and coherent letter to the Earl of Bathurst asserting his claim. In it he mentioned that two councillors, William Black and Edward James Jarvis, had been en route to Fredericton at the time Chipman had been sworn in before a mere quorum of councillors, and they appended their own protests to Billopp's.[19] In the same issue of the *City Gazette* was also published an address to Ward Chipman, signed by 'upwards of 60 of the inhabitants' of Saint John, dated

15 April, congratulating him 'in succeeding, by the determination of His Majesty's Council, to the high and dignified situation you now hold, and they trust that the late unlawful and unjustifiable attempt, originating in a few malicious and designing Individuals, to excite a commotion in our peaceable and loyal City, by [?disputing] the constitutional mode of that appointment, may meet with the fate it so justly merits.'[20] But Billopp, once roused, was not to be discouraged so easily, and on 17 April published a proclamation asserting his claim to the administration of the colony. He also wrote to the Secretary to the Council commanding him to summon Council to Saint John on 6 May. This was followed on 21 April by another proclamation in which he, Billopp, asserted that 'all Proclamations, Civil Appointments, and Public Acts whatsoever, done and issuing in the name and by the authority of the said Honorable Ward Chipman, as President, or Administrator of the Government, are absolutely illegal and of no effect.'[21]

The fat was now in the fire with a vengeance. On the 30th the Council considered Billopp's letters and his proclamation, and on 1 May were shown a proclamation Chipman had prepared, and which was published the next day, forbidding anyone to publish any apparently official document until it had first been published in the *Royal Gazette*.[22] It was also ordered that a special messenger be dispatched to the Governor of Quebec requesting a copy of the Commission and Instructions.

In September, Chipman was to give a long account to Bathurst of Billopp's participation in New Brunswick government:

in the course of twenty seven years since the date of his appointment [in 1796], it does not appear that he has attended the Privy Council at the seat of Government more than six times, and he has attended the Legislative Council during one Session of the General Assembly only, namely in the year 1797, being at the time he attended to be sworn in as a member; and in fact he never has since his last attendance at Fredericton appeared to take any part or interest at all in the conduct of the affairs of the Government of the Province; with regard to his representation, that he has frequently been in the habit of attending Councils, not held in Fredericton, I beg leave to submit the following statement to your Lordship. . . . These Councils were generally held at . . . [the Lieutenant Governor's] house in Saint John, when the attendance of five members, which was requisite to form a Council, could be procured exclusively of Mr Billopp, who by reason of his age and infirmities was confined to his own house, and never did attend these Councils thus held at the house of the Governor, though at a short distance in an adjoining street. When it happened that the attendance of four members only could be procured exclusively of Mr

Billopp, inquiry was made by his Excellency's direction, whether the state of Mr Billopp's health was such that he could permit his Excellency and these members to meet at his house, to transact such business as was previously prepared, (a task which generally devolved upon me) for the consideration of the Council. Mr Billopp was frequently under the necessity of refusing such permission, and even when his health admitted of compliance, complaint was made by the members of his family, that he did not for some time recover from the agitation of mind occasioned by his fixed and retired habits of life being thus intruded upon . . .[23]

By the time this was written, the crisis was over, and Chipman was only writing to justify himself. When the first letters from Chipman and Billopp, written between 5 June and 12 July, reached Bathurst in London they were both reproached, but also partly vindicated. Bathurst speedily demolished the idea that Billopp could not have been sworn in at Saint John, and acknowledged his claim, but deprecated the means he had used to try and assert his authority, and in view of his age advised him to waive his right to the interim presidency. Chipman, although reproached, was confirmed in his temporary office.[24] By then, however, a veritable torrent of water had flowed under the metaphorical bridge, sweeping away Anthony Lockwood from his prominence in the small pond of New Brunswick. At the end of April the Winter King was losing his grip, and travel becoming possible, but the succession crisis of April was to be followed by madness in the month of May.

Smyth's death had cast Lockwood adrift politically, an outsider in a 'Loyalist' province, and a sailor in a province dominated by soldiers. He may well have regarded himself as compromised as a man who had become too closely associated with the general, but without any reason to hope that other military men would welcome his driving energy. It is a big step from being an active junior councillor to being a revolutionary, but in the last years the stability of his world had been openly challenged by the rotten core of the monarchy, and by the triumphs of Simon Bolivar, president of Gran Columbia. The struggle for power between Ward Chipman and Christopher Billopp, with both on shaky constitutional ground, may have seemed to create an opportunity for Lockwood, always on the lookout for ways of bettering himself, to become the dominant figure in New Brunswick. He might have been right about that, had he kept a firm grasp on realities. But the dejection he had been suffering from through the winter was transformed into a mania, which proved his downfall. And when he fell, in the words that Shakespeare put into the mouth of the disgraced Cardinal Wolsey, 'he fell like Lucifer, never to hope again.'

Sir Howard Douglas, after he succeeded General Smyth as Governor, reported to Bathurst that Lockwood

> held offices in the Province (Surveyor General and Receiver General of the King's Casual Revenues) which yielded him at least £2,000 per annum. He only enjoyed these offices a few years; but until the dreadful calamity (insanity) came upon him, appears to have acted so providently as to have realized about £2,000 of property in the Province. The first indications of insanity which attracted notice consisted in squandering the money at his disposal, in a way which, ere he could be laid under legal disabilities by Statute of Lunacy, involved his property so that upon the adjustment of his Accounts by the Commissioners, his estate was insufficient to do more than provide for balance due to the King.[25]

What this extravagance was Douglas did not particularise.[26] However he embarrassed his finances, it was to be disastrous for his family because of the ruling by the Commission of Lunacy, signed by Anthony junior and Harriet Lockwood, that 'the said Lunatic had not alienated any lands or Feuemeuts [sic] during his Lunacy.'[27]

Lockwood had been present at the Council meeting on 1 May when Billopp's proclamation was discussed. He was absent at the meetings on 2 and 3 May, but he likely heard about Leonard's letter of the 2nd indicating that he was not disinclined to assume the government if only he did not have to travel to Fredericton for the purpose. This must have occasioned talk in Fredericton, at least among the councillors who had to deal with Billopp's claim to an authority he was clearly unfit to wield. This anxiety can only have weighed on Lockwood's unstable mind. The preamble of the commission of lunacy that was completed on 5 June indicated that his derangement had begun on 19 May.[28] It may well have been then that Lockwood, the man of action, mounted his horse and plunged off along miry roads on his way to Sussex Vale to persuade Leonard to withdraw his resignation from the presidency of the government.

The evidence is that Leonard found him an alarming guest, but the upshot was that he issued a proclamation dated the 24th, which may be assumed was dictated by Lockwood: 'To prevent all future contest & confusion among the good & Loyal people of this Province,' Leonard wrote, 'I now therefore assume my right to the administration of the Government, and direct the members of His Majesty's Council and the Secretary of the Province to assemble at my residence in Sussex Vale on the sixth day of June next at mid-day, for the purpose of administering the oaths of office, necessary to qualify me for the discharge of the duties which must now devolve upon me as President of the Province.' Lockwood added his own signature to the proclamation as 'Acting Secretary.' A covering letter was also written by Leonard to Odell as Provincial Secretary, again dated the 24th, which was a Saturday.[29]

When Lockwood left Leonard's residence on the 25th he headed to Saint John. In an affidavit that was taken on oath at the meeting of Council on the 31st, his friend Robert Minette declared that 'Lockwood came to the House of . . . this deponent on Sunday the twenty-fifth of May Instant – that the said Anthony Lockwood although often absent considered the Deponent's House as his home – that [this] deponent has seen the said Anthony Lockwood daily since the said twenty-fifth of May', and he was clearly deranged and unfit for office. Lockwood was visited at Minette's house by Dr Paddock and 'took the Medicines prescribed . . . but altogether disregarded his directions in other respects as well as the advice and admonition given, with a view to his safety and person . . . [he] frequently used violent expressions threatening the Lives of several Persons in the City of Saint John, who had either offended him or expressed displeasure at his disorderly behaviour.' Perhaps in expectation of the glittering hours he foresaw ahead when he would want to make a good impression, on the 27th Lockwood scribbled an order for twelve pairs of shoes and three pairs of silk stockings from a merchant by the name of T B Milledge.[30]

On the 26th, still unaware of Leonard's proclamation and letters that might have been en route to Fredericton by a messenger, Chipman forwarded to Leonard a copy of Dalhousie's reply to Chipman's report of Smyth's death, Leonard's declining the responsibility, and Chipman's own swearing in. It was only a brief note because, as he said, the hour was late and he had to rise early the next morning to catch the steamboat to Saint John which sailed at 7am.[31] Was he off to meet with Billopp, or to track down Lockwood? Probably both. His home was in Saint John, but that was probably only an additional reason for the journey. He sent a note to Dalhousie before catching the steamboat saying 'There is good reason to believe that the interested advisors of Mr Billop are alone responsible for the disgraceful measures which they have made use of his name to justify.'[32]

Meet with Lockwood he certainly did, probably on the morning of the 28th. It is even possible that Lockwood had himself carried Leonard's proclamation and letters, and now delivered them in person. Chipman's immediate reaction was to communicate his concerns about Lockwood's condition in writing to Dr Paddock. He was told in replies of the same and next date that 'from witnessing and attentively watching his conduct and behaviour I feel satisfied he labors under such a degree of mental derangement as should exclude him for the present at least' from his offices. 'I regret it is not in my power to make a more favourable report . . . regardless of my advice and persuasion he has conducted himself in such a manner as affords unequivocal proofs of his laboring under a state of mental derangement, committing outrages such as would arraign him in a court of Justice, dissipating his property and by his singular appearance and behaviour collecting mobs and engaging in quarrels in the streets, threatening the lives of certain individuals. As these are but a repetition of occurrences that happened when he fell under my care last Fall it is to be feared there exists in his System a predisposition to Insanity.'[33]

For his part, Lockwood found Chipman's conduct to be 'mild and liberal' and this, for the moment, deflected him from his purpose. Following his meeting with Chipman, he dictated to Minette a letter in which he assured Chipman that 'the object of my visit to Sussex Vale was to prevail upon my aged and respected friend The Hon George Leonard to assume the Administration of the Government of the Province, and which assumption if I recollect right every Councillor agreed in when the question was agitated at that Honourable board, on the demise of our late lamented Lieutenant Governor.' He claimed that he had 'removed all objections on his Mr Leonard's part' and that 'the other branches of the family were very desirous of the benefits which might arise' from his assuming the office. But he then rambled on making it evident that his intentions had been nothing less than a *coup de main*.

Having obtained Leonard's agreement to figurehead the administration, Lockwood wrote that he 'immediately determined to relinquish the high and important situations held by me and prepared myself to act in the double capacity of civil Aid-de-camp & Inspecting Field officer for a purpose and to an end that your mild and liberal conduct has rendered totally unnecessary. I now in confidence suggest that you continue in the Administration of a duty to which you are entitled by your abilities.' He may have persuaded Leonard that his assumption of the presidency would reduce political strife, but it appears that for his own part he had been tempted to ride the wave of that strife, taking charge as 'Inspecting Field officer.' His 'purpose' and 'end' can only have been to enforce Leonard's authority, and perhaps ultimately to supplant it.

His concluding notes for Chipman, in which he laid out the manner in which he believed New Brunswick should be governed in the days ahead, confirm that his grasp on realities was tenuous at best: 'Secondly, that the income be divided into three equal parts. Thirdly, that the patronage if there be any shall be yours with the consent of the junior Councillor whose recommendations are to be respected. I will not proceed further with this outline until I receive your opinion and my Ideas are now given with the utmost confidence in you. At the same time I beg leave to say that I would be flattered by the appointment of your Civil aid-de-camp in which capacity I am desirous of embarking to England on the first of July.' The idea of applying to the Colonial Office for an appointment as Chipman's civil aide-de-camp was in startling contrast to the plan to depose Chipman by force, but it can be dismissed as a familiar straw grasped at by a desperately troubled man.[34]

The Mayor of Saint John and a member of the Council, John Robinson, filled in the blanks about Lockwood's activity while he was living at Minette's house: as the 'Mayor of the City of St John and a Commissioner for providing a Residence for the Lieutenant Governor in the said City,' he reported, he was

> informed by a Person employed to take care of the House provided for the said purpose, that the Hon Anthony Lockwood had taken possession of the said House and was bringing furniture into it, and that he had acted with great violence towards him ... This deponent wrote to the said Anthony Lockwood a very civil letter desiring him to leave the House as he the Deponent was responsible for the safety and care of it and could not suffer it to be used for any other purpose than that for which it was hired. The next morning [I] was informed that [he] remained in the house and had been breaking down some of the fence around [it]. [I] went there immediately and found him in the enclosure in front of the house talking very loudly to a number of persons collected round the same enclosure, and threatening them violently. Upon [my] going up to him and speaking coolly to him, he after a little time promised upon his honor he would leave the house at ten o'clock and not return to it without [my] consent. Upon this [I] left him, but [he] did not leave the house as he had promised ... On Thursday morning the 29th Instant [I] received a Note from [him] stating that he was then in the Watch House. [I] went immediately to the Watch House, where [I] found [him] eating his breakfast through a grated window with a number of idle Persons collected around it, to whom he was talking with great warmth. The Watch House door was open and he had been desired to go out, but he would not. [I] asked him why he did not come out, upon which he answered that he would if [I] would first come inside it, which [I] did, and he came quietly out with [me]. [He] appeared to have been in a scuffle, having one severe bruise on his face, and one hand bloody. He walked some distance very quietly with [me], and then left [me] to go to his lodgings, and make himself clean as he said, but had not gone twenty yards before he met Alderman Disbrow, and began an altercation with him, threatening to horsewhip him, and shoot him.'[35]

Clearly something had to be done about the man. Chipman took charge, and, as he described to Bathurst, 'with great difficulty' he bundled

Lockwood on board the steamboat for Fredericton.[36] Chipman gave the date to Bathurst as the 30th, a Friday.

The scene on board must have been remarkable. When the new Lieutenant Governor, General Sir Howard Douglas, arrived in October of the following year he was to be much more critical than had been Dalhousie on the same river voyage. Douglas complained of the 'great inconvenience to which, in moving between this City [ie, Saint John] and Fredericton, I am exposed personally, and the serious embarrassment which attaches to me officially, by being obliged to embark in a wretched Steam Boat (to the Proprietors of which an exclusive privilege has been most improperly granted, by letters Patent, for a time not within years of expiration) having one common Cabin, Table & Society.'[37] Douglas did not care to rub elbows with lesser folk, although he was to make a good impression on New Brunswick. Be that as it may, Chipman was no doubt glad to let Lockwood occupy himself writing letters at the common table, if indeed the private cabin Dalhousie had mentioned had been removed. He wrote a letter to 'the President' in a hand so shaky it is hard to read. His mental illness, or the medication he had been given, whatever that was, did continue to affect his handwriting for many months, but it is to be supposed that the tremor was exaggerated by the vibration of the engine. A second letter addressed from Fredericton was in a much clearer hand. Both are dated the 30th.

The first note was a plea for help: 'Sir, I respectfully beg your Honor to relieve me from the weighty and responsible duty in Council my present ailment being subject to increase by confinement. I have the honor to be Sir your devoted Servant. A Locwood [sic] Rec & Sur Gen.' The second, written after he arrived in Fredericton, begins: 'I beg to inform you that the Government House is prepared sufficiently for your reception and Dinner will be on the Table at half past five O'clock – with five covers for such guests as you may be pleased to countenance. Beds are also prepared for yourself and servants. I am Your Honors Humble Servant A Lockwood – In the Council Committee Room, One of the Commissioners of Government House.' The first was probably written to Chipman, and both are certainly preserved among his papers, but the content of the second suggests that it may have been meant for Leonard. The reference to Government House being prepared for him suggests that Leonard was in Lockwood's mind, and the reference to 'five covers' could be a reference to the quorum of five councillors that would be required to swear him into office.[38]

When the Council assembled at Fredericton on the 31st the affidavits were read, but no mention was made in the minutes of Lockwood's letters of the 28th and 30th. To the affidavits from Saint John was added one from Dr Emerson in Fredericton dated that morning in which he reported that Lockwood 'has lately been again to Saint John . . . from which place he returned last night.' Having seen him since his return he was 'of opinion that he is again in a state of decided mental derangement, and to a greater degree than before.'[39]

The next day, 1 June, was to witness the dramatic end of Lockwood's attempt to take control of the government, if that is how his actions should be characterised. If he found that confinement added to his difficulties, that problem was to be increased immeasurably. Robert Minette had also made the journey to Fredericton, and in sworn testimony he said that he 'met the Honorable Anthony Lockwood this morning, being the first day of June, near his the said Anthony's dwelling.' He 'appeared to be in a state of great irritation.' He had ordered 'a table and chairs to be placed in the public square, where he drank coffee, and ordered the deponent to sit there and copy a proclamation: that the said Anthony said he had assumed the government of the province, and that he had been forced so to do: that the President had deceived him, and that he would cause him the President to be arrested and made a prisoner, and also made use of violent language towards the President, threatening to be the end of him.'

Lockwood was apparently quite even-handed in his threats, which he also made to the gardener at Government House, and 'all the rest that had offended him.' Minette said that he understood Lockwood to be threatening to 'kill the said gardener, or do him some bodily harm.' To give point to his language, he 'had about him a pair of pocket pistols, but the ends of the barrels were taken off.' Minette concluded that 'the said Anthony appeared to the deponent to be in a state of phrenzy, and not fit to be trusted to go at large.'[40]

Lockwood had included the High Sheriff of York County, Edward W Miller, Esq, in his threats, saying that he would 'displace the Sheriff, and appoint another.' It was Miller, however, who had the last word. In the morning, he reported to Council, he had found 'the Honorable Anthony Lockwood the Surveyor General riding about the streets of Fredericton armed with Pistols and threatening the lives of Sundry Persons.' Miller was also 'informed of divers acts of outrage and violence, committed by the said Anthony Lockwood.' He decided it was his duty to arrest Lockwood, 'which he accordingly did, and confined him in the Gaol of the said County and that the said Anthony is now in confinement in the said Gaol.' 'His Conduct,' Miller declared, 'is such as to leave no doubt in the mind of the Deponent that the said Anthony Lockwood is in a state of great mental derangement and totally unfit to go at large.'[41]

High noon in Fredericton was played out without shots exchanged. As Surveyor General Lockwood had been tasked with designing a replacement for the jail, because the old one was condemned it as unfit for human habitation. Now he was locked up there, where his crazed mind turned again to the myth of Acalus, flung from the top of the Acropolis.

As though he were determined to substantiate Miller's account, Lockwood now wrote from the jail to Jedediah Slason, one of his sureties, accusing him of having 'stolen from the Receiver General's deposit, a sum to me unknown. I have to request before Justice overtakes you, that you place the same again whence you took it. Given under my hand at the Head Quarters of Acalus in the centre of the village of Fredericton, where the enemies of the King are assembled. A. Lockwood.' The inevitable result was that Slason immediately wrote to Chipman on his own behalf and that of Lockwood's other surety Zalmon Wheeler begging 'the favor of your Honor to allow us to withdraw from being any further accountable for him as we conceive that we would not be Safe in so doing.'[42] 'Whereupon the Council being fully satisfied of the mental derangement of the said Anthony Lockwood, and of his unfitness to execute his official duties, and of his incapacity to make any rational answer to the Representation and Proofs above set forth, advise that the said Anthony Lockwood be suspended from his several Offices of a Member of the Council, Surveyor General of Lands and Receiver General of His Majesty's Casual Revenues conformably to the Royal Instructions in that behalf.'[43]

Leonard had received Chipman's letter early on the 27th, 'by an express who appeared in great haste for an answer; I immediately desired my daughter to acknowledge receipt of it.' With Lockwood now far away, Leonard was glad to wiggle off the hook, and 'requested Mr Odell not to proceed further in the matter of Paper to be laid before the Council . . . My motive in that Paper was the hope that it would produce tranquility in the province.'[44] Leonard's letter was dated the 28th, and the express rider thundered off back to Fredericton.

13

Never to Hope Again

HUBRIS, THE FATAL mistake of seeking to meet the gods on equal ground, is the stuff of tragedy. When Anthony Lockwood stumbled in the forests of New Brunswick he had friends who stood by him. The grip of insanity was not to be always tight. But there was to be no way out of the crisis of May 1823 other than flight and poverty.

For Harriet Lockwood the month must have been a nightmare. The day after her husband's arrest she sent Chipman a letter requesting that a commission be set up to protect his, and her, affairs: 'I have the honor to acquaint you that Mr Lockwood's understanding is so much deranged, that he is at present incapable of transacting any business either public or private; and I have therefore to request the favour of Your Honor, to appoint some trusty person, in conjunction with myself, to superintend the arrangement of his private affairs; begging only to recommend Mr William Reynolds of Saint John as exceedingly fit, from his long knowledge of Mr Lockwood, and having for a considerable length of time managed his many transactions. In Your Honors disposition for temporarily filling up his place in the public departments, I wish to recommend to your consideration that his son, Mr A Lockwood, has actually arrived at Halifax, and is every moment expected here, and I need not acquaint Your Honor, that the long practice he has had in the office duties will render him fully competent to undertake the duties required.'[1] What a homecoming it must have been for Anthony junior!

Already Chipman had drawn up a commission of lunacy empowering Denny Street, George L Street, George P Bliss, Henry Smith and Peter Fraser, or any three of them, 'to inquire of the lunacy of the said Anthony Lockwood.' He explained to the Earl of Bathurst that he had authorised the writ on his own authority as Chancellor of New Brunswick because Harriet Lockwood feared 'future violence' if she should herself put a request in writing.[2] He had also acted on the advice of Sheriff Miller 'that the family of the said Anthony Lockwood, are for various important reasons prevented from applying in their own behalf to your honor.'³ On the 7th Harriet asked that Anthony's Fredericton physician Thomas Emerson and his friend Jedediah Slason should be added to the commission looking after his affairs, and the three sureties were duly sworn, signing a bond of £1,350 of 'lawful money' enabling them to form 'a committee to have the custody, care, and management of the person and estate of Anthony Lockwood, Esquire, a Lunatic.'⁴ On the 10th the commission was in possession of an inventory of Lockwood's 'Real and Personal Estate and Income', when it was found that his total net worth, in the phrase used by bankers, was £2,467.⁵

The requirement to ensure the continued functioning of the Surveyor General and Receiver General's offices was quite clearly urgent, and on the 5th George Shore was commissioned by the 'President and Commander in Chief' of New Brunswick, Ward Chipman, to act in the place of Lockwood as Surveyor General. Is it just coincidence that on 19 May, the supposed date in which Lockwood's sanity came into question, George Shore had drawn up a memorial outlining his career?⁶ Shore, supported by Judge John Saunders and William Franklin Odell, also signed a bond committing them all to act on Lockwood's behalf, each bonded to the value of £2,000 of lawful money, and Shore undertook to pay Lockwood or his executors half of the profit ('one full moity') of the Surveyor General's office.

Shore found Lockwood's office in a state of disarray. A week after receiving the commission, he reported that he had

carefully examined the publick documents in the Office of the Surveyor General, and find that, the system established by the first Surveyor General, the Honorable George Sproule, and which has been acted upon by those who have succeeded him, of Recording the Grants as they pass through the Office, and of invariably entering in a Book kept for that express purpose, a particular Description of each and filing the copies of the Grant Plans, has, since the appointment of Mr Lockwood been generally neglected; and in some instances, the Plans, a very great number of which are not to be found, and of those that are in the Office, some have been much abused by improper handling, and others so cut and mutilated as to destroy their authenticity.

He suggested that 'some fit person should be immediately employed for the purpose of Recording the Grants that have passed since Mr Lockwood has been Surveyor General, and also to renew such Grant plans as have been destroyed, or neglected to be made out and filed.'⁷

It was even more important to appoint someone to undertake the office of Receiver General, and while Chipman was considering who to appoint,

Anthony Lockwood junior arrived home from England. On the basis of his previous work as Lockwood's assistant he requested the temporary position, and, as Chipman later informed Bathurst, 'being disposed to alleviate the effects of his father's unfortunate situation as respected his Family to the utmost of my powers, and being satisfied of the capacity and qualification of his Son for this temporary trust, I consented to make the appointment if he could find the requisite sureties in such a Sum as should be deemed necessary by His Majesty's Council.' Until Anthony Lockwood junior could find such guarantors, Shore also undertook to discharge the duties of Receiver General for him, and to reserve three quarters of the 'fees and emoluments' for Lockwood. But Shore naturally wanted the position for himself.[8]

While the wheels were turning, Lockwood was languishing in jail. On 15 July he wrote Odell a long and incoherent letter beginning sadly, 'pent in a fetid Jail I shall assuredly lose my health – let me pray you therefore to move the president for leave of absence to change the scene. . . . He is aware of the persecution executed by the Ignorant petty Tyrants who have charge of my person & property.' He then rambled on vaguely charging that the funds in the Receiver General's office were being plundered.[9] He did have reason to be worried. On 8 August Samuel Denny Street was ordered to take an account of Lockwood's financial affairs. When on the 16th Emerson and Slesson, acting at Harriet's request for her husband, made a report about his assets and debts, Chipman minuted on it 'Let it be referred to the Honorable Samuel Denny Street.'[10] Perhaps it was inevitable that Harriet's friends should be shuffled aside. So much of Lockwood's finances were official, or derived from official sources. In October Lockwood was still complaining his estate was 'in hands the most ignorant and improvident', but on the 11th Chipman reviewed the proceedings in a letter to Bathurst with an account showing that there was some £1,582 10s 2½d missing from the audit of the Receiver General's office.[11]

As the summer progressed, Lockwood's mental state did begin to improve, as is evident from his taking an interest in the problems of a fellow prisoner, John Armstrong, who was incarcerated for debts to a Richard Magee. On 9 August Lockwood in his capacity as Justice of the Peace, which went with the office of Receiver General, took Armstrong's oath in a petition for Chipman to hear his case.[12] Another month, and he was able to obtain his own release from jail, although he continued to be closely supervised in his home. On 10 September Thomas Wetmore wrote to congratulate him on his restoration to his home and family, 'Your communication this morning has given me great pleasure.' Lockwood had sent him the draft of a letter and Wetmore replied that it met his 'approbation – I could not amend it. When you are permitted to come out

I shall be happy to see you.'[13] Twelve days later, 'restored to my House and family and feeling in sound Mind and bodily Health', Lockwood sent a letter to Chipman 'to request you will be pleased to direct that the legal steps may be taken to restore my liberty and property.'[14]

But it was not to be that easy. Five days later he wrote again to Wetmore, sending him a statement, and complaining that his 'full expectation' of a reply to the request for 'legal steps' had not been met. Evidently Chipman was in Saint John, and Lockwood said he had waited for the steamboat, but there was nothing. 'I think it my duty both to His Majesty my Royal Master – and to my own responsibility as His Receiver General,' he wrote somewhat incoherently, 'stating briefly my Case to you as His Majesty's Attorney General requesting your advice desirous of avoiding any and every offence I do not, and intend not to complain or remonstrate at, or against the Indignities that are heaped upon my Person, not even allowed a servant – or the use of my Horses. Anxious only to preserve my name unsullied and the Kings purse (which by diligence I have made a respectable weight for so small and poor a province) from the peculation [sic] of those knavish and designing men.' The letter then rambled off with vague accusations against Reynolds and Slason, and complaint about Dr Emerson's passivity.[15] Not surprisingly, Wetmore only replied that his 'publick situation' as Attorney General rendered it impossible for him 'to afford you any professional advice as to the Legal measures.'[16]

Lockwood was understandably impatient. On 18 October he wrote to Bathurst himself, complaining: 'On my release from the Common Jail, I discovered that all my communication to the Captain General the Rt Hon Earl Dalhousie, and those to your Lordship had been intercepted by Ward Chipman Esq and his servant, under a plea of my Insanity. I have to beg your Lordship will be pleased to suspend your Judgement of my Acts, and of my Situation as to Mental Health until the matter be fully investigated by the Lieutenant Governor on his arrival.'[17] Intercepted or not, these letters have not been traced.

At the end of November Chipman wrote to Robert Wilmot (who had adopted the name Wilmot-Horton) warning him that Lockwood intended to petition for the restoration of his offices. 'He undoubtedly has for some weeks past been restored to, and still enjoys an interval of apparent sanity of mind', but he remarked that the apparent return to sanity echoed the pattern of the depression Lockwood had suffered in 1822: 'as was the case after a derangement attended with aggravated symptoms when in this place during the Autumn of the last year, remaining afterwards during the winter in a quiet but very dejected state of mind, and in the wonted discharge of his duties of his several offices until his mind became again alienated in the month of May last.' Investigation of his office showed 'great mutilation and disorder and in some cases remediless; and since that time instances of error and irregularity in his proceedings have been discovered, which it will be attended to with great difficulty to rectify, nor can the extent of the mischiefs of this nature be foreseen till the occasions of their discovery from time to time arise in making further Grants of Crown Lands.'[18]

On 19 January 1824 Lockwood was still writing to Chipman 'that your Petitioner prays to be relieved from the Commission of Lunacy being now in sound mental & bodily Health.' His handwriting, however, was still scrawling, and a few hours later he wrote in another scrawl, from 'My Room of confinement – Fredericton', to petition Chipman to restore him to his former position: 'If I have in any instance failed in my Duty to my Royal Master or His Representative here I am amenable to law and its just decision am ready to bow to. If I have broken any local rule – or violated any sacred duty there are modes of punishment to which I am ready to submit. If I am as reputed a Lunatic I am willing to be confined. But if none of the above are charges against me I respectfully pray to know why I am denied the common privile[g]es of my nature.' He continued, undermining his plea by repeating his charges against those in trust, Reynolds, Slason, Emerson and apparently even his wife, although he does not explicitly name her. 'I am not uneasy, although I feel the want of air – being confined to a small dirty room and constrained to sit in company with a constable who is allowed to dine at the table of a member of His Majesty's Council.' The next day he was at it again, writing to Chipman with charges and pleas, and mentioning the medical attention of a Dr McCartney.[19] But Chipman was to die in Fredericton on 9 February, and with his passing Lockwood's situation passed from bad to worse. In March, Anthony junior was to characterise his father a lunatic 'but enjoying lucid intervals.'[20]

It would be interesting to know whether Lockwood heard about the replay of the succession crisis of the previous spring that took place after Chipman's death. On 11 February George Leonard wrote to the Provincial Secretary, William Franklin Odell, instructing him to summon the Council to come to his house in Sussex Vale to administer 'the oaths of office, preparatory to taking on me the administration of the government.' This the Council refused to do, basing their objection on 'the Legislature being in Session at Fredericton.' It instructed Odell to advise Leonard that he would have to 'repair to Fredericton' to assume the government – and Odell thought it best to ride himself to Sussex to minimise the confusion. In this he succeeded, and he reported that Leonard asserted he had only summoned the Council 'to prevent a repetition of the confusion and very improper conduct which, as he considered, had taken place on a former occasion', but that his health prevented him travelling to Fredericton, and in the circumstances he 'perfectly acquiesced in the decisions of the Council and in every arrangement respecting the administration that may appear to them proper.' Odell had been instructed, if Leonard could not make the trip, to sound Billopp, and the latter also waived his claim, without 'abandonment of the principles' which had moved him to action the previous year.[21] Chipman was succeeded as acting President by the Honourable John Murray Bliss. So this time the tempest remained in the teapot. What might have happened had Lockwood been free of restraints, however, is anyone's guess. It was already known that General Sir Howard Douglas was to be appointed the next Lieutenant Governor of New Brunswick.

Bliss, as President pro tem, appointed his own son, George P Bliss, to fill the office of Receiver General pending an appointment from London. In making this temporary appointment, Bliss did not renew the order made by Chipman that three-quarters of the income from that office should be reserved for Lockwood's support. If Shore were to be confirmed in the office of Surveyor General it was to be anticipated that the Lockwood family would also lose their share of its income, and be left nearly destitute. In a letter to Bathurst on 17 March 1824 petitioning for the recovery of the income, Anthony Lockwood junior wrote that 'it appears from the Report of the Committee appointed to manage the estate of your petitioner's father, that after the payment of the monies due to the Crown, from the Receiver General's Office, and of the private debts of the estate, a very small provision will remain for the support of him and his family', which would be 'reduced to great distress, particularly as his mental malady, much encreases [sic] the expenses of the estate.'[22]

On 20 March Douglas, while still in London, wrote to Bathurst recommending Shore for the office of Receiver General.[23] The day prior to Anthony junior's appeal, he had written on his behalf to Bathurst – but not to support the idea that Lockwood should retain a share of the revenues of the Receiver General. Instead, he urged that Anthony junior be made a naval officer, by which he probably meant a customs officer. Failing that, it appears that he was willing to see Anthony junior succeed to the office of Surveyor General. 'Under all the circumstances, I earnestly recommend Mr Lockwood Junior for the situation of Naval Officer; and should the situation not be in Your Lordship's gift, I venture to engage your supporting influence in favour of a succession [of the Surveyor General's office] which will endow the son of an old officer with the means to provide for the wants of an afflicted and distressed family.'[24] But to Judge Saunders's indignation, Thomas Baillie, the younger brother of the First Secretary of the Colonial Office, was to be appointed Surveyor General.

Saunders complained to his son that 'so young a man without so far as

we hear any great connexions or eminent services should have offices upon
him, the income of which greatly exceeds that of the Civil income of the
Lt Governor – his income is said to be more than £4,000 a year.'[25] Baillie
himself believed the combined fees of the Surveyor General and of the
newly created office of Commissioner of Crown Lands to which he was
also appointed amounted to £1,800, but even that exceed the income of
the Lieutenant Governor by £262. He was highly indignant at the proposal
to replace his fees with a salary of £1,390, of which he believed £1,200
would be absorbed by his costs.[26]

Having settled into the Surveyor General's Office, Baillie wrote to
Douglas complaining that there was no record kept of 'four hundred grants
of land issued during my predecessors time. . . . I am now in the actual
payment of £500 a year to draftsmen who are repairing the damage which
has been done and I appeal to your Excellency's justice for an allowance of
£300 per annum for two years to assist me in the expenses which I must
incur on the Public Account.'[27]

On 16 January Street had submitted an account of Lockwood's estate,
and on 6 April the Lockwood family obtained a ruling from Chancery that
they could sell some of his effects to pay their debts.[28] On the 20th it was
published in the *Royal Gazette* that, 'Pursuant to an order issued out of
the Court of Chancery the 6th instant', would be auctioned 'all the personal
and real estate of the Hon Anthony Lockwood' on 5 May.[29] An additional
blow may have been a house fire, although it need not have been a major
one, and may in fact have been a convenient fiction later used by Lockwood
to justify to the Navy Board his inability to submit all the documents he
needed to support his claim for half-pay.[30]

By that date, May 1824, Lockwood was apparently clear-headed
enough that he was able to petition for his release from the commission.
His signature on the document is as it had been during the years of his
good fortune.[31] This did not lead to any immediate change in his situation,
but it did create a problem for Sir Howard Douglas who finally arrived
in August. He explained to Bathurst his concern that 'the Statute of
Lunacy taken out against the Late Surveyor General the Honourable
Anthony Lockwood only suspends him from exercising the functions of
a Member of HM Council. But Mr Lockwood is moving the Court of
Chancery for a hearing to supersede the legal disabilities under which he
is laid, and it is possible that humane consideration towards this
Unfortunate Gentleman may induce a Jury to pronounce him in such a
mental condition as to remove the disabilities and restraints under which
he is laid. Were this to be the case, Mr Lockwood would immediately
claim his seat on Council . . . I beg to recommend that Mr A Lockwood
be definitely removed from His Majesty's Council, and I hope soon to

receive advice to that effect.'[32] Bathurst's reply arrived from Dalhousie on 6 November, indicating that it was 'His Majesty's Pleasure that you erase Mr Lockwood's name from the List' of members of Council.[33] That only left the problem of sorting out the accounts at the Receiver General's office, including an undisclosed sum 'supposed to be contained in an iron chest deposited in the custody of the Bank the key held by his trustees', and the chaos in the office of Surveyor General.[34]

Despite the substantial grounds for irritation, Douglas clearly wished to provide for Lockwood and his family. He wrote to Bathurst in November 1824 that it had never fallen to his lot 'to deal with a case of more accumulated misery than that in which Mr Lockwood and his family are involved. . . . Mr Lockwood enjoys Half Pay as a Master in the Royal Navy, for Services which are well-known to have been important. I mention this resource because it is right that all the case be stated; but I hope reward for past services anterior to his employment here, will not interfere with any disposition there may be, upon this urgent recommendation, to make some charitable provision for the better support of the unfortunate Lunatic, and at all events for that of his utterly dependent Wife and two daughters.'[35]

On 2 March 1825 Lockwood again petitioned Douglas for release from the commission of lunacy, and Douglas ordered that he have a hearing. But Douglas had also ordered that accounts drawn up by Lockwood's agents, and indicating that his debts exceeded his assets, be submitted to Chancery. When this was reviewed on 11 April it appeared that the auction sale of Lockwood's property had not produced enough to cover his debt to the Crown, and it was ordered that 'no further allowance be made by the said Committee to the said Lunatic and his Family out of the said Estate until the said Debts are all paid.' How the Lockwood family was to survive was certainly not clear, and on 22 October Emerson and Slason, reporting that Lockwood 'remained at home quietly with his family', petitioned Douglas for advice as to 'what sum they are to pay weekly to Mr Lockwood and Family for their subsistence.'[36]

On 12 November Chancery finally dissolved the Commission of Lunacy, putting Lockwood back in charge of his own affairs. Two days later he discharged his agents with a certificate that they had 'satisfactorily accounted' to him for their proceedings. But without either office or property Lockwood's ability to support his family was reduced to his Navy half-pay.[37] The loss of his home had put an end to his last tie to New Brunswick, and he evidently left on the first available boat, despite the late time in the year, returning across the Atlantic to live in London. On 25 January 1826 he wrote the Colonial Office that 'your petitioner has returned to England restored to his perfect mental health', and explained that he had moved because, with 'his small income [he] can support his family in much greater comfort in England, than he can in North America.' His story, however, does not have a happy ending.

Sir Howard Douglas's appeal had its effect, and Lockwood was granted a pension of £150 a year 'from the casual revenue of New Brunswick.'[38] Lockwood's income from his half-pay and from the New Brunswick pension was adequate, apparently, to support him in London. On 6 February 1826 he wrote from 14 Villiers Street to the Lords Commissioners of the Admiralty pressing his claim for 'the highest rate of half pay' in view of his long naval service, 'since when I have surveyed the North American Colonies' – a distorted claim, of course. This letter was signed but not otherwise penned by him. A note overleaf states that he would not be allowed the top rate but would be sent to Trinity House. Possibly the implication was that he should again be examined for First Rate.[39] Possibly as a result of such a meeting, and the medical examination which followed, the Lords Commissioners then informed the Navy Board, that Lockwood was 'of insane mind and incapable of managing his affairs', directing them to 'dispense with his Half Pay Affadavit so long as he shall continue in that State' and enclosing a certificate signed by G M Burrows, MD, Member of the Royal College of Physicians.[40]

Harriet, Anthony junior, Sarah, and Marina evidently did not immediately accompany Lockwood to London. On 28 April 1826, however, there was a sale of the Lockwood household and kitchen furniture 'in the residence of Mrs Lockwood.'[41] The three women then apparently crossed the Atlantic, and made a home for Anthony senior, or lived nearby. Anthony junior remained in New Brunswick.[42] Alas the move from the forest of New Brunswick to the filth of London was one Lockwood's daughters did not long survive. Marina died, aged twenty-two, on 13 November 1830, in Camberwell, while Sarah died in Stepney during the following month.[43]

Harriet, bereft of her daughters, wrote to the Admiralty Secretary on 14 April 1831 from 6 Upper St George's Place, Albany Road, Camberwell: 'As my husband Mr Anthony Lockwood Master of the Royal Navy is now unhappily confined as a Lunatic in Peckham house (a copy of the Certificate being annexed hereto). I humbly request you will be pleased to grant me an order to receive his half Pay during his Illness that I may be enabled to defray the expenses of his Maintenance.' The handwriting appears to be her own. A note from a James Middleton, Surgeon, Peckham house, Surrey, declares Anthony to be of 'unsound mind and confined to this institution at the charge of Mrs Harriet Lockwood.'[44] How often, during the further twenty-four years he survived, did Anthony emerge from madness? Harriet's fate in those years is not known; she died or fled.

By 12 March 1849 Lockwood was confined in Bethnal House, Bethnal

Green, one of the most famous madhouses of the time, where the poet Christopher Smart had been incarcerated – as had been the father of Ellen Ternan, Charles Dickens' mistress.[45] Surprisingly, he remarried on 6 October 1849 to another Harriet, widow, who it seems likely had been the wife of a Henry Lockwood who might have been Anthony's cousin or brother.[46] Harriet was thirty-two at the time of her marriage to Anthony, and he seventy-one. She probably took care of him in return for the protection of his naval pension and the pension on the New Brunswick establishment. For a widow of her lowly status, illiterate, daughter of a labourer, an annual income amounting to more than £200 would certainly be great affluence. They lived at Henry's address, 15 Whitehorse Terrace, Stepney, a respectable working-class area.[47] This has all the appearance of a marriage of convenience, a poor widow taking on the nursing and care of an ageing lunatic for the sake of his pension.[48]

Anthony's true condition at the time of his marriage can only be guessed at. He was sane enough to attempt an answer to a query from the hydrographer, Sir Francis Beaufort, on 12 November 1849, concerning 'my labors between 1801 and 1849.' Writing in his own hand – the letters clearly formed with difficulty – he provided a sprawling, partial, confused list of his surveying activities and those who ordered them. Lockwood claimed that Lord Dalhousie had authorised a 'Brief History or rather Book of Directions'. A history of what or where, or directions to or for, are unstated. The covering note starts rationally enough, in formal manner, before the mysterious statement: 'If you will be pleased to allow me a Copy of Bantry Bay in addition I shall feel obliged.'[49] There appears to be a leap of logic here but the passage may refer to an earlier letter from the Hydrographical Office.

When he died on 25 January 1852, according to his death certificate he had suffered from 'ulcerated legs 2 years' – the official cause of death. His age on the death certificate was given as seventy-seven years. The second Harriet signed with her mark.[50] He was buried on 3 February at St Dunstan's, on the same day as was Harriet's youngest child, Alfred, from her earlier marriage.

Reflections:
The Theatre of Life

LOCKWOOD'S LIFE OF struggle, his amazing rise to prominence in the province of New Brunswick, and his precipitous fall to obscurity, is the matter of Shakespearian tragedy. The heroic determination of the man to raise himself from a birth in such humble circumstances that they remain almost unknown, through application to the technical requirements of hydrographic surveying, and through self-promotion, expressed the spirit of democracy struggling into existence in an age in which connections by birth remained the accepted basis for office. His refusal to be cowed by aristocratic pretensions gave him strength, but also tripped him up when he confronted those who assumed a greater right to authority. Such conflict continues to exist in a world that gives lip service to the achievements of the talented, but closes ranks against outsiders. The ancient myth of Acalus, which Lockwood regarded as mirroring his own experience, continues to portray the fate of those whose creativity exposes the establishment in a poor light. The steps of the dance that the aspiring must lead, treading a path between originality and conformity, requires a steady heart and mind. Their absence at a critical time proved to be Lockwood's fatal flaw.

The nature of the insanity that destroyed him can only be guessed at. Posthumous diagnosis is notoriously uncertain. If it was the delayed effect of syphilis, as it might have been, the seed of his destruction was probably sown in a seaman's brothel in the West Indies, or in his native East London, where the portionless victim of the brutalities of the late eighteenth century Royal Navy had gone to find some solace with a woman who was herself a victim of stratified society. The insanity of tertiary syphilis can take thirty years to mature. But the energy Lockwood had shown in the years of his struggle and rise, which had as often laid him by the heels as it had given wings to them, suggests that the roots of his madness were close to the surface at a much earlier time.

His spectacular grasp at the reins of power in the days before his imprisonment was consistent with the drive of a self-made man bayed round by privilege. It is not fanciful to see his actions in the light of the decay in the monarchy at the heart of Britain's empire, and the triumph of revolution in South America. Should Lockwood be regarded as a potential Bolivar of New Brunswick, chancing his hard earned offices for that of personal aide-de-camp to the elderly George Leonard, and inspecting field commander? Would the next step have been to declare New Brunswick a republic, with the backing of the more radical elements in Saint John? But what of the regiment quartered in Fredericton? There is no evidence that he had courted their support. Revolutionaries need a political base, and spend years developing one. Lockwood to all appearances had not. For a brief hour, riding armed in the streets of Fredericton and threatening his foes with death, he evidently imagined himself as a revolutionary. But Sheriff Miller pulled him off his horse, and put him in jail. There his ambitions were confined by four walls and a commission of lunacy.

There are fashions in madness, just as there are in all walks of life. Lockwood was not a serious revolutionary, but his madness took that form because of the prevailing winds of change blowing through the political world. Fredericton may have been the conservative heart of a Loyalist colony, but Saint John was a commercial centre with connections into the United States republic, and the tumultuous cities of Spanish America. Try as he would, General Smyth could not on his own dispel the concern created by the succession to the British Crown of an ageing, corpulent, and dissolute prince and by the rebellion inherent in his wife's independence and hostility. The riots in Britain connected with the movement for political reform, dispelled violently and with loss of life, were mirrored by disturbances in New Brunswick when immigrants found themselves far from home and without the means to support their families. Lockwood's fortunes had become connected with Smyth's, and when the latter died, Lockwood came adrift. Disease unbalanced Lockwood's mind, but circumstances tipped it in the direction taken by Napoleon and Bolivar.

It does not appear that Lockwood valued his hydrographic work for more than a means of escaping the drudgery and humiliation of service as master on board a warship, under the direct eye of commissioned officers. As a surveyor he worked away from the hubs of naval activity, and was in direct command of his vessel and crew. But his surveys are nonetheless monuments to his life, and for years his sailing directory of the coast of Nova Scotia was the main Admiralty publication available for shipping in the area. His conflict with Desbarres over the Nova Scotia survey, and the evidence that his own survey work in Nova Scotian and New Brunswick waters was a perfunctory recheck and correction of work undertaken by others, may be held to be typical of a public servant who has already done his time and is in a hurry to move up the ladder.[1]

His role in promoting the isthmian canal between the Bay of Fundy and the Northumberland Strait may equally be regarded as a means for his advancement as it was promoted as a means for the economic development of the region. It could have been his greatest monument, but it came to nothing. When Sir Howard Douglas succeeded as governor he would take a vigorous interest in the isthmian canal project, to the extent of writing in 1825 to Thomas Telford, as 'an Engineer of the highest ability', for advice. The matter 'would have political tendencies of the most important character', and he had 'procured a liberal vote from the Legislature.' He wanted Telford to suggest 'a highly competent person' to come over early in 1826 and spend the summer assessing the project, as well as another at Grand Falls, to ease passage of timber.[2] In the meantime he instructed a Mr Hall, surveyor, of Pictou Nova Scotia, by letter of 11 July 1825 to proceed 'with as little delay as possible' to Judge Botsford's at Cumberland, where 'you will have access to the several surveys, Reports and Estimates, which have been made of the projected Canal.' He personally visited the site, met with the engineer, and by year's end had received a new Estimate and Report.[3] He regarded the canal as 'a matter of some importance . . . so that when the Schubenacadie Canal shall be finished, the ports of Halifax, Saint John and St Andrews, may become entrepots' for Canadian grains and milled by water power before shipping to West Indies.'[4] Proposals for a Chignecto Canal surfaced periodically throughout the nineteenth century and were advanced seriously into the second half of the twentieth. Soon after Confederation a Dominion government commission investigated the matter. Lockwood's first report, however, was ignored by reviews of the subject. All start with Minette's survey of 1822.[5] Lockwood's final descent into madness tainted the work he had earlier done with credit.

What then should be the last words on Lockwood's life? He has fallen through the cracks of history because of his pathetic demise, and his protracted plunge into obscurity. Perhaps if Sheriff Miller had shot him off his horse that day on Queen Street he would now be remembered in Fredericton. But it is not necessary to wish Anthony Lockwood on a monument, or in school textbooks as one of the founders of modern New Brunswick. It is enough to remember him as part of suffering humanity, part of the theatre of life. A passionate man, a family man, a victim of his humble birth but determined to pull himself and his family out of its poverty, who experienced one remarkable stroke of luck, worked exceedingly hard to make a good thing of his new fortune, and then in his prime was struck down by disease. He was not an 'American' but his story is that of the 'American Dream', and his fall is consistent with the flaw in that vision – hard work and dedication, passion and commitment, are not guarantees of good fortune. Inadequate as were the social and political concepts of colonial New Brunswick, and empty as was the vision its leaders sustained of a bucolic Eden governed by a natural aristocracy, it was based on the idea of community and charity. Those values were expressed, imperfectly but according to the abilities of a struggling economy, in the efforts to provide for immigrants into the province, and were also expressed in the concern felt by Howard Douglas to provide for Lockwood and his family after his fall. Lockwood's story is important as much because it is that of 'Everyman' as because of the heights he scaled, and the wreck to which he fell.

References

Abbreviations used in references to public archives are as follows:
BA   Barbados Archives
NAC   National Archives of Canada
NAS   National Archives of Scotland
NA UK   National Archives, UK, Public Record Office
NLS   National Library of Scotland
NBM   New Brunswick Museum
PANB   Public Archives of New Brunswick
PANS   Public Archives of Nova Scotia
SNA   Scottish National Archives
UKHO   United Kingdom Hydrographic Office
UNB   University of New Brunswick Archives

References to document series within each archive are provided in the bibliography.

Illustrations
1 Letter to the author from Peter Larocque, New Brunswick Museum, 5 May 2011.
2 The painting was reviewed and attributed to John Elliott Woolford by Rosemarie Tovell (formerly curator of Prints and Drawings at the National Gallery) and Rene Villeneuve, Curator of Pre-Confederation Art at the National Gallery of Canada, who used it in their major travelling exhibition on Lord Dalhousie. The attribution is supported by Peter Larocque of the New Brunswick Museum in a letter to the author, 5 May 2011.

Introduction
1 ADM 1/4849, Lockwood to Croker, 30 January 1818.
2 NA UK, ADM 11/2, Memorandum of Services: Anthony Lockwood, c.1833.

1 Dead Man's Cloaths
1 NA UK, ADM 36/11522 and ADM 36/12344, Admiralty: Muster books for *Iphigenia*, September 1795 to September 1796, and *Duke*, September 1796 to September 1797; Guildhall Library, Parish Records, Middlesex baptismal records, R & J Lockwood; NA UK, WO10/73-78 and 102, Artillery muster books and pay lists, 1759–1762. When providing a 'Statement of Civil Employment' for the Navy Board in May 1822, Lockwood was to give his age as 47, implying that he was born in 1775 – ADM 11/2, Memorandum of Services: Anthony Lockwood, c.1833. His death certificate dated 31 January 1855 gives his age as 77, indicating that his date of birth was 1777 or 1778.
2 Nicholas Rodger, *The Command of the Ocean*, p. 443.
3 Dudley Pope, *Life in Nelson's Navy*, p. 202.
4 Bryan Edwards, *The History, Civil and Commercial, of the British West Indies*, III p. 67; Robert Debs Heinl, *Written in blood: the story of the Haitian people, 1492–1971*, p. 46.
5 Heinl, p. 67.
6 Edwards, III, p. 409.

7 Edwards, III, 411.
8 NA UK, ADM 51/1138, Captain's Log, *Iphigenia*, 1794 June 2–1796 Sept 10; Edwards III p. 411.
9 NA UK, ADM 51/1138.
10 Admiral John Holloway: born 25 January 1747, Post-Captain 17 January 1780; died 26 June 1826.
11 NA UK, ADM 36/12344.
12 NA UK, ADM 51/1197, Captain's Log, *Duke*, 1796 Aug 22–1797 Aug 31.
13 NA UK, ADM 51/1197.
14 Michael Lewis, *Spithead: An Informal History*, p.126.
15 NA UK, ADM 51/1197.
16 NA UK, ADM 1/5125, Admiralty: Petitions and a related instruction from George III to Admiral Howe, 1797.
17 Laffin, *op cit*, Lewis, *op cit*; George Ernest Manwaring and Bonamy Dobrée, *The Floating Republic*; and James Dugan, *The Great Mutiny*. Only direct quotations from these sources are identified individually.
18 NA UK, ADM 1/5125.
19 Peter Turner Bover, Lt: 3 January 1794 (1), Cmdr: 14 February 1798; Post-Capt: 11 August 1800 (5), died: 14 December 1802.
20 NA UK, ADM 51/1197.
21 Manwaring and Dobree, *op cit* p. 89.
22 Dugan, *op cit* pp. 166–167.
23 Admiral Sir Ross Donnelly, KCB, Post-Captain on 24 June 1795.
24 NA UK, ADM 51/1197.
25 NA UK, ADM 6/153, Masters' Passing Certificates, statements of service, &c, L, c.1800–1850, Elder Brethren, Trinity House, to Navy Board, 20 April 1797, 'pursuant to your order of the 13th.'
26 NA UK, ADM 6/153; Bridport to Lockwood, 27 May 1797.
27 W P Gosset, *The Lost Ships of the Royal Navy*, n.p. Vice-Admiral Charles Sterling or Stirling, born 28 April 1760, and commissioned Post-Captain on 15 January 1783 (1).
28 NA UK, ADM 36/13155, Muster Book, *Jason*, September 1797–September 1798.
29 NA UK, ADM 51/1203, Captain's Log, *Jason*, 1 January 1797–31 December 1797.
30 On 21 November she captured *La Marie*, a 14-gun privateer, off Bellisle; on 23 February 1798 in the Channel she took *Le Coureur*, another privateer, of 24 guns; and assisted by the *Russell*, she then took *La Bonne Citoyenne*, yet

another privateer, of 12 guns, on 20 March.
31 Admiral Sir William M James, *The naval history of Great Britain*, II, pp. 320–321.
32 NA UK, ADM 1/110, Sterling to Lord Bridport, 2 July 1798.
33 NA UK, ADM 1/2498, Sterling to Nepean, 15 September 1798.
34 NA UK, ADM 1/3737, Transport Office to Nepean. See 'French Officers Taken at Ballinamuck', *Annual Register*, 1798, 114.
35 NA UK, ADM 103/476, Register of Prisoners of War, Britons released from France,1798. Anthony was incorrectly listed as Arthur Lockwood.
36 NA UK, ADM 1/5348, Stirling to Nepean, 20 January 1799; Court Martial *Jason*, 25 February 1799.
37 Post-Captain 1 September 1795. NA UK, ADM 6/153, Lobb to Nepean. Memo overleaf, 23 April 1799: 'Sir Andrew having read an application from Capt Lobb desiring Mr Lockwood might be appointed to the *Crescent* ordered his warr[ant]. to be made out.'
38 NA UK, ADM 52/2893, Master's Log *Crescent*, 1799 Apr 22–1802 March 31.
39 NA UK, ADM 52/2893, Master's Log *Crescent*, 1799 Apr 22–1801 July 26. All subsequent information concerning the *Crescent*'s daily regime is taken from this source or from the Captain's Log, ADM 51/1429.
40 ADM 12, Pro L, Lockwood to Lords Commissioners, 28 May 1799.
41 NA UK, ADM 1/2498, Seymour to Nepean, 10 November 1800. NA UK, ADM 160/42, Naval Ordnance Departments in letters, 1798 June 20–1799 Dec 31; ADM 12, Digest.

2 A Saucy Young Puppy
1 Parish Registers, Cumberland, Cumbria Rec Off, Carlisle.
2 Hugh Owen, *The Lowther Family*, p. 249 and *passim*.
3 NA UK, ADM 36/5973, *Lenox* muster book, 1762 Sep–1763 Feb.
4 BA, RB1/255/12.
5 John Frederic Gibson, *Brocklebanks*, p. 12.
6 *Ibid*, p. 15.
7 Trinity Churchyard Register; *The Monumental Inscriptions of the Church & Churchyard of St James, Whitehaven*, Town Library Whitehaven.
8 NA UK, ADM 6/153. Lockwood to

Navy Board, 16 March, 2 June and 12 July 1804.

9 Dudley Pope, *op cit*, p. 138.

10 Quoted in Dudley Pope, *op cit*, p. 247.

11 Cumbria Record Office, Carlisle, St Nicholas Parish Records.

12 NA UK, ADM 1/4822, Cochrane to Lockwood, 19 August 1804.

13 James Ralfe, *The naval biography of Great Britain*, II, p. 437. Nicholas Tracy, *Who's Who in Nelson's Navy*, pp. 75-6.

14 NA UK, ADM 344, Chart of West Coast of Europe.

15 NA UK, ADM 1/4822, Lockwood to Admiralty Secretary, 6 November 1804.

16 NA UK, ADM 6/153, Trinity House to Navy Board, 15 November 1805.

17 NA UK, ADM 1/4822, Lockwood to Admiralty Secretary, 15 November 1804.

18 NA UK, ADM 1/4822.

19 NA UK, ADM 1/4849. Writing from the Hydographic Office to John Wilson Croker, the Admiralty Secretary, 27 January 1818, Lockwood listed the Bearhaven survey in a memorandum of completed service.

20 NA UK, ADM 1/4824, Lockwood to Marsden, 19 January and 10 April 1805; PRO, ADM 12, Pro 'L', 7 February 1806.

21 NA UK, ADM 12, Pro 'L'. Lockwood to Lords Commissioners, 31 May 1805.

22 Murdoch Mackenzie Jr, *Treatise of Maritime Surveying ...* London: Edward & Charles Dilly, 1774.

23 Sir Archibald Day, *The Admiralty Hydrographic Service 1795–1919*, HMSO, 1967, pp. 98–102, 99.

24 NA UK, ADM 1/4824, Lockwood to Marsden, 31 May, 10 and 29 June, 19 August, 7 September, 6 and 26 October, and 4 December 1805, 3 and 13 February and 28 May 1806; NA UK, ADM 12 (1805), Saumarez to Navy Board, 10 September 1805; NA UK, ADM 106/1560, Lockwood to Navy Board, 1 December 1805.

25 UK HO, 1 Shelf Od*, United Kingdom: England, S Coast: Cornwall: Falmouth. English MS tracing, unassigned, of a combination of three superimposed surveys of Falmouth, attributed to Lieutenant McKenzie [*sic*] (black), Lieutenant Manderson (red) and Mr Lockwood (yellow), showing coastline and detailed hydrography. Scales: 6 and 7 inches to 1 mile. NA UK, ADM

1/3520, Dalrymple to Marsden, 15 June 1804.

26 Lieutenant Commander Andrew David to Peter Thomas, 12 May 1983. Captain Thomas Hannaford Hurd's *Plan du Port de Falmouth, de la Rivière d'Helford, et de la Côte jusqu'à Manacle Rock. Levé en 1806 par la Capitaine T Hurd* was published in Paris in 1825.

27 NA UK, ADM 106/3517, author unknown.

28 NA UK, ADM 1/4824, Lockwood to Marsden, 31 May, 10 and 29 June, 19 August, 7 September, 6 and 26 October, and 4 December 1805, 3 and 13 February and 28 May 1806; NA UK, ADM 12 (1805), Saumarez to Navy Board, 10 September 1805; NA UK, ADM 106/1560, Lockwood to Navy Board, 1 December 1805.

29 NA UK, ADM 1/223, Kelly to Dickson, 19 June, in Saumarez to Marsden, 23 June 1806.

30 Alfred Thayer Mahan, *Types of Naval Officers Drawn from the History of the Royal Navy*, 1901, pp. 421, 383. For Saumarez's career as a whole see Otto von Pivka, *Navies of the Napoleonic Era*; David A Thomas, *A Companion to the Royal Navy*, pp. 225–226. After seeing off Lockwood, Saumarez gave further distinguished service in the Baltic (1808–1812) as commander of the British fleet there (see Anthony Ryan, 'An Ambassador Afloat: Vice-Admiral Sir James Saumarez and the Swedish Court'.)

31 His younger brother, Sir Thomas Saumarez (1760–1845), was the army commander and Lieutenant Governor of New Brunswick in 1813, six years before Lockwood's arrival in that province.

32 NA UK, ADM 1/4826. Included with Lockwood's letter to Marsden were Lockwood to Grey, 22 June 1806; Grey to Lockwood, 23 June 1806. A memo overleaf directs that a copy of this correspondence be sent to Saumarez.

33 NA UK, ADM 1/223, Saumarez to Marsden, 23 June 1806.

34 NA UK, ADM 1/223, Saumarez to Marsden, 30 June 1806.

35 NA UK, ADM 1/4826.

36 NA UK, ADM 1/223, Saumarez to Marsden, 9 July 1806.

37 NA UK, ADM 1/4826, Lockwood to Benjamin Tucker, 31 July 1806; Doyle to Lockwood, 21 July 1806.

38 NA UK, ADM 1/223, Saumarez to Marsden, 4 August 1806. NA UK, ADM 1/4826, Overleaf memo, Lockwood to Tucker, 31 July 1806.

39 NA UK, ADM 1/223, Saumarez to Marsden, 4 August 1806.

40 NA UK, ADM 1/4826, Lockwood to Marsden, 16 and 18 August; and see NA UK, ADM 1/223, Saumarez to Marsden, 24 August 1806.

41 NA UK, ADM 1/223, Saumarez to Marsden, 24 August 1806.

42 NA UK, ADM 1/4824, Lockwood to Marsden, 18 August, 4 September 1806.

43 NA UK, ADM 1/223, Lockwood's 'apology' of 6 September is included with Saumarez's reply to Lockwood, 15 September 1806.

44 NA UK, ADM 1/4826, Lockwood to Marsden, 20 September 1806.

45 NA UK, ADM 1/4826, Lockwood to Marsden, 11 October 1806.

46 NA UK, ADM 1/223, Saumarez to Marsden, 19 October 1806.

47 NA UK, ADM 1/4826, Marsden to Lockwood, 22 October 1806; Lockwood to Marsden, 25 October 1806; Lockwood to Marsden, 27 October 1806.

48 NA UK, ADM 1/4826, Lockwood to Marsden, 28 October 1806.

49 When Thomas Hurd succeeded Dalrymple as hydrographer in 1808 he persuaded the Admiralty to appoint George Thomas as Head Maritime Surveyor, a post 'which had lapsed since Graeme Spence retired from active surveying in 1804.' A H W Robinson, Marine Cartography in Britain, p. 127. Perhaps the position had not quite lapsed, with Lockwood serving as Spence's active complement on the Channel Islands survey – though not officially confirmed as Spence's full time replacement.

50 NA UK, ADM 1/4826, Lockwood to Marsden, 28 October 1806.

51 Llewellyn Styles Dawson, Memoirs of Hydrography, p. 67.

52 Brutus, Julius Caesar, IV.iii, 218–224.

53 NA UK, ADM106/3517 warrant to Belleisle, 1807.

3 Equal to the Task

1 NA UK, ADM 1/4828, Lockwood to Marsden, 12 July 1807.

2 NA UK, ADM 1/4841, Cochrane to Lockwood, Belleisle, Carlisle Bay, 19 and 21 July 1807, enclosure in Lockwood to Admiralty, 1814.

3 See P F Campbell, 'St Ann's Fort and the Garrison', passim.

4 P F Campbell, op cit, p. 13.

5 NLS, Cochrane Papers, 2322, Cochrane to W Marsden, Northumberland, at sea, 13 June 1807.

6 NLS, Cochrane Papers, 2322, Cochrane to W Marsden, 7 August and 27 December 1807; Cochrane to W Pole, 10 July and 2 November 1808.

7 John Poyer, History of Barbados, p. 639.

8 Bridgetown Mercury, passim.

9 Anthony Lockwood, A brief description of Nova Scotia with plates of the principal harbors: including a particular account of the Island of Grand Manan, 1818, p. 2.

10 BA, PR St Michael, RL 1/66.

11 BA, PR St Michael, vol 6, p. 268.

12 BA, RB 2/235, Index.

13 BA, RB 4 (1807), Index.

14 BA, PR St Michael, 6, p. 323.

15 BA, RB 1/255/12. Sealed and witnessed by Lynch Thomas and Thos Hoddle, 2 July 1796, this deed was not formally entered until 1 May 1813.

16 Ibid.

17 BA, PR St Michael, 6, p. 355.

18 BA, PR St Michael, RL 1/70, p. 378.

19 BA, RB 1/251/164. See p. [32] above.

20 BA, RB 1/254/264, and RB 2/2.

21 BA, RB 1/264/84-85.

22 NLS, Cochrane Papers, 2399, Cochrane to Lord Melville, 6 February 1808.

23 NA UK, ADM 37/8608, Yard Muster Book, Barbados.

24 NA UK, ADM 42/2118, Barbados pay lists, 1813.

25 NA UK, ADM 1/4841, Lockwood to Lord Melville, 19 January 1814.

26 NA UK, ADM 1/4833, Lockwood to Pole, 1 December 1809.

27 NA UK, ADM 37/8608, Yard Muster Book, Barbados.

28 NA UK, ADM 42/2121, Yard Pay Books, Barbados lists of persons entered dead or discharged, 1809 to 1816.

29 Paul Webb, 'Construction, repair and maintenance in the battle fleet of the Royal Navy, 1793–1815', p. 207.

30 Roger Morriss, The Royal Dockyards During the Revolutionary and Napoleonic Wars, p. 6.

31 Dudley Pope, op cit, p. 256. Melville had been impeached by the House of Commons on 11 June 1805 over the loss of £20,000 of naval funds and dismissed as First Lord. For an account

of frauds perpetrated at British naval yards, home and abroad, see Morriss, *op cit, passim.*

32 NLS, Cochrane Papers, 2322. Cochrane to William Pole, 23 February 1808. See also 2296, Cochrane to Lord Moira, 12 April 1806.

33 NA UK, ADM 1/329, Cochrane to W Pole, 11 June 1808, enclosing both Lockwood's report and Kingston's letter to Cochrane of 5 May 1808.

34 UKHO, HD 274 Ag1, 1808 survey by A Lockwood of an 'Anchorage at Barbados'.

35 NA UK, ADM 1/330, Cochrane to Admiralty, 2 June 1809.

36 NA UK, ADM 1/331, Tracy to Cochrane, 11 May 1809.

37 NA UK, ADM 106/1987, Admiralty to White, 6 July 1809.

38 *Ibid.*

39 NA UK, ADM 106/1987, White to Barrow, 15 August 1809.

40 NA UK, ADM 12 (1809), digest.

41 NLS, Cochrane Papers 2296, Cochrane to Melville, 10 February 1806.

42 UKHO, 314, Ag 2. 'A PLAN of the SAINTS By Order of the Honble Rear Admiral Sir Alexdr Cochrane KB', on a scale of three nautical miles to the inch, signed by Lockwood, Barbados, 1810.

43 NA UK, ADM 1/333, Laforey to Barrow, 13 April 1812.

44 NA UK, ADM 1/333, Lockwood, 7 December, in Laforey to Croker, 31 December 1811 and 14 March 1812. The division of dollars into fifty-sixths was unusual.

45 NA UK, ADM 1/335, Laforey to Barrow, 18 November 1813.

46 NA UK, ADM 1/4842, Lockwood to Barrow, 23 September 1814.

47 NA UK, ADM 1/3523, First Report of Sea-Officers . . ., 27 November 1807.

48 NA UK, ADM 1/505, Cochrane to J W Croker, 2 January 1814.

49 NA UK, ADM 1/4839, Hurd, 4 January 1813; UKHO, 274 Ag1. An 'Anchorage at Barbados', 1808.

50 NA UK, ADM 1/505, Cochrane to Croker, 2 January 1814, and memo 11 January.

51 NA UK, ADM 1/4841, Lockwood to Lord Melville, 19 January 1814.

52 NA UK, ADM 12 (1814), digest, Navy Board 19 April 1914.

53 NA UK, ADM 106/1698, Navy Board to Lockwood, 14 January 1814.

54 Admiral Sir Philip Charles Henderson Calderwood Durham, GCB.

55 NLS, Cochrane Papers, 2349, Cochrane to Durham, 1 April 1814.

56 NA UK, ADM 1/4842, Lockwood to Barrow, 23 September 1814.

4 An Emissary of Light

1 Geraint Nantglyn Davies Evans, *Uncommon Obdurate: The Several Public Careers of J J W Desbarres*, pp. 18–19.

2 Evans, *passim.*

3 LAC, MG23-F1 Desbarres Papers, Series 5, 4681 (Film A-2083 cited by Evans, *op cit*, 96n), Henry Chesner to James Desbarres, 7 March 1814; also Evans, *passim.*

4 *Ibid*, 4767.

5 NA UK, ADM 36/5973, Muster Book for *Lenox*, 1762 September–February 1763; and see NA UK, ADM 12, Digest, Lockwood to Navy Board, 27 and 29 October, reply 18 November 1814.

6 Judith Fingard, 'Sir John Wentworth', *Dictionary of Canadian Biography*, vol 5.

7 Quoted by Thomas Raddall, *Halifax: Warden of the North*, p. 152.

8 *Ibid*, p. 158.

9 *Ibid*, p. 159.

10 NA UK, ADM 1/4842, Lockwood to John Barrow, 23 September 1814.

11 NA UK, ADM 12, digest, Admiralty to Navy Board, 14 October, and In-Letter from Navy Board, 18 November 1814.

12 Anonymous, *Acadian Recorder* (Supplement), 12 December 1896; and 'Surveys of the Roads from Halifax to Windsor and from Halifax to Truro', John Elliott Woolford ('copy Mr Wallace 1855'); and PANS, F209, WM 1819, *Plan of a Survey of a Proposed new road from West Branch to St. Mary's River to the middle settlement of Musquadobut.* Sherbrooke's country house is also shown on a sketch map of the road from Hammond's Plain to Salmon River; PANS, Vertical Map Case III, 209.

13 PANS, RG 20 Series A, Land Papers – Anthony Lockwood, 1817.

14 PANS, MG 20, Collections of the Nova Scotia Historical Society, volume 679, 1: Reverend K B Wainwright, 'Admiral Sir Alexander Cochrane GCB and the Landed Proprietors of Shubenacadie', and Marjory Whitelaw, *The Dalhousie Journals*, vol 1, pp. 60–61.

15 PANS, Churches: Saint George's – Halifax.

16 NA UK, ADM 51/2067, Admiralty: Captains' Logs: *Examiner*, 1815 July 1–816 July 31; and ADM 52/4484, Masters' Log: *Examiner*, 1815 Mar 20–1815 Oct 5.

17 NA UK, ADM 37/5973, Admiralty: Ships' Musters (Series II), *Examiner*, 1814 Oct–1817 Sept. Anthony Lockwood, master & commander; John Harris and Will Priddle, 2nd masters; Peter Donaldson, clerk; John Anderson, Boatswain; John Windsor, Able Seaman; Will Adams, Pierre Cashin, Jas Johnson, and William Lee, all Ordinary Seaman; William Campbell, Midshipman; and Will Langley and William Bartlett as supernumerary boys.

18 The muster for 1 July to 31 August 1815 lists each pilot with his place and dates of entry and discharge: Jos Thomas (at sea, 10 July; Fort Amherst, 15 July); John King (Fort Amherst, 11 July; Barrington, 16 July), Isaac Kenny (Barrington, 13 July; Barrington, 16 July), Elisha Pike (Point Lepreau, 18 July; Saint John, 18 July), Thomas Read (at sea, 18 July; Saint John, 18 July), Jas Read (Saint John, 21 July; at sea, 21 July), Alex Lockhart (Saint John, 21 July; Halifax, 16 August), Isaac Small (Grand Manan, 21 July; Grand Manan, 24 July), William Franklin (Grand Manan, 25 July; at sea, 26 July), Sol Hains (Boryman's Island, 31 July; at sea, 31 July), Abner Nickerson (off Cape Negro, 1 August; at sea, 1 August).

19 NA UK, ADM 1/4846, Hurd to Admiralty, 2 and 11 July 1816.

20 From 31 May to 7 June 1815 *Examiner* worked southward along the shore to Chester and Dover Harbour before returning to Halifax. Lockwood turned northeastward, again, and by the 10th *Examiner* was back at Sheet Harbour ('at daylight Mr Lockwood away surveying'), then by Bridge Cove, Island Harbour, to Cranberry Island east of Canso, which Lockwood surveyed on the 15th. 'Working up the Cape Canso', Lockwood surveyed Glasgow Head next day. Entering the Bras d'Ore lakes, on the 18th they were at Plaster Cove near Iona where Lockwood and a crew took measurements on Porcupine Head. Reversing course, on the 21st they were engaged in 'sounding across the Gut of Canso'. There was trouble at the mouth of the St Mary River when they smashed the bowsprit and had to put back to

Glasgow harbour on the 26th for repairs. By 1 July, however, they were back at Sheet Harbour for more soundings, then to Halifax again on the 5th.

21 For this cruise we have the benefit of Lockwood's own log. Three days after leaving Halifax, on the 7th, *Examiner* anchored at Cape Negro south of Shelbourne. By the 12th Lockwood had entered Barrington Bay and was sounding off Cape Sable on the 14th and 15th. The following day *Examiner* 'rounded Cape Sable & bore up to run into the Bay of Fundy', continuing 'running up the Bay' through fog on the 17th, still sounding, and at 10.45am on the 18th Lockwood 'shortened sail and came to . . . in St John's New Brunswick in 14 fthms water.'

22 NA UK, ADM 36/5973; *Examiner*'s muster 30 July 1815. George Hobbins, Isaac Holbrook, John Alexander, and Isaac Dyer. Detained on 30 July.

23 They set sail on 26 August, moving out to McNab's Cove, then up the coast, reaching the breaker on the Roaring Bull by the 29th, working further up the coast to Pictou by the 31st, and on 1 September, at daylight, they 'stood over to Prince Edward Island.' They rounded Hillsborough Head to Charlotte Head and sailed again on the 2nd, anchoring off Pictou, entering the harbour briefly, then running out to sea once more. Between the 4th and 9th they surveyed in the vicinity of St Peter's Head. On the 9th they were in the Gut of Canso, returning to Pictou next day, and on the 11th they 'fired several Guns to ascertain the distance across the Harbour by the Sound.' Until the 14th they remained surveying Pictou Harbour, but by the 16th they were off Cape George and reached the Gut of Canso and Cape Porcupine again on the 19th. They made Arachat Town and Canso on the 21st, surveying between there and Country Harbour until the 26th. At Canso, Lockwood purchased '672 lbs of Bread and 50 Gallons of Rum.' By the 30th they were back at Sheet Harbour and on 2 October anchored at Halifax.

24 During the last weeks of 1815 Lockwood's own log is the sole record. William Grant was discharged to the *Centurion* on 5 September. From 1 January 1816 the master's log was kept

by J Turner, the new second master.

25 NA UK, ADM 1/509, Griffith to Croker, 23 April 1815. See John Marshall, *Royal Navy Biography*, vol ii, p 548. Ralfe, vol iii, p 164.

26 PANS, RG1 /141, *Provincial Secretary's letter Book*, 1814–1818, J Cogswell to Lockwood, 28 March 1815.

27 PANS, RG 31, Treasury Papers, Series 106, Lighthouse Papers, volume IV, 1815, number 10, Lockwood to M Wallace, 26 June 1815, 'Report of Cranberry Island as a Site for a Light House'.

28 Nova Scotia, House of Assembly, *Journals and proceedings of the House of Assembly of the Province of Nova Scotia*, 1816, PANS RG1, volume 305, number 51, Lockwood to Griffith, 30 July 1815 (Copy in PANB RS 541, Brier Island 1815–1830), and Griffith to Sherbrooke, 22 September 1815; Margaret Ells, *Calendar of the Official Correspondence of the Legislative Papers of Nova Scotia, 1812–1815*, p. 305 (51); PANS RG1/305, *Letters of the House of Assembly 1815–1818*, number 42. Copies are in PANB, RS 541, *Provincial Secretary – Lighthouse Administration, Brier Island 1815–1830*, and RS 8, *Executive Council, Lighthouses, 1812–1833* (F7899).

29 PANB, RS 541, *Provincial Secretary, Reports of the State of Lighthouses, 1815*, Lockwood to New Brunswick House of Assembly, 6 November 1815, with a copy in RS 8, *Executive Council, Lighthouses* (F7899). The copy in Sessional Papers is missing: RS 24 S24-Z2, Letter to the House from Anthony Lockwood, 18 January 1816 – p. 9 [missing].

30 PANB, RS 1, *New Brunswick House of Assembly*, Journal, 26 February 1818, 3 March 1819, 13 March 1821, 18 February 1830 (Report by the Committee on Light Houses); RS 21 C4/2, *Provincial Secretary: Treasury Administrative Records, Requests for Warrants, 1819–20*, f. 5906, Wallace to NB Provincial Secretary, 2 August 1819; RS 541, *Provincial Secretary, Lighthouse Administration, Brier Island, 1815–1830*, NS Board of Revenue, Richard M Uniacke, Michael Wallace, J B Robie to Lieutenant Governor Sir James Kempt, 14 February 1821; copy in RS 8, *Executive Council, Lighthouses*; Committee to William Hill, 16 February, and Wallace to William Black, President, 24 February 1830.

31 PANS, RG1/ 305, *Letters of the House of Assembly, 1815–1818*, number 42, Lockwood to Sherbrooke, 22 January 1816, and *s.v.* 'Brier Island Light'; and RG1/193, *Executive Council Minutes*, 1816, p. 193.

32 Nova Scotia, House of Assembly, *Journals and proceedings of the House of Assembly of the Province of Nova Scotia*, p. 305, 41.

33 PANS, RG1/2141/2A. Griffith wrote to Dalhousie on 20 August 1819 concerning the number of deserters from British vessels who were fleeing to the northern and western parts of the province 'with a view to ship on board vessels bound for England.'

34 PANS, RG1/193, *Executive Council Minutes*, 1816, p. 193.

35 *Nova Scotia Royal Gazette*, 22 May 1816.

36 NA UK, ADM 12 (1822), 13, 16, 25 February.

37 NA UK, ADM 1/4846, Hurd to Admiralty, 2 and 11 July 1816 .

38 NA UK, ADM 1/4846, Griffith to Admiralty, 23 August 1816; Admiralty to Milne, 12 October 1816.

39 NA UK, ADM 1/4846, Lockwood to Admiralty, 3 August 1816.

40 Rounding Cape Canso next day, anchoring at Pilot's Harbour, Lockwood moved on to Plaster Cove on the 26th, before spending a day surveying the 'Rock in Balhack's Cove.' At 3.30pm on the 28th *Examiner* 'saw the Magdalen Islands from NW to NNE 10 or 11 leag[ue]s' and on the following day they anchored in the vicinity of Deadman's Island and Sea Cow Rock. After a day in Amherst Harbour, at the southwest end of the Magdalen Islands, the boats were 'surveying the Magdalen Islands' from 31 July to 3 August. They sailed back past Prince Edward Island to Pictou Island on the 4th and 'bore up for Bay Verte.' Reaching Cape Tormentine next day, they spent the following three days in Bay Verte itself, leaving to survey Badec Harbour on the 9th, and arriving at Cape West, Prince Edward Island, that evening. Between 11 and 13 August they were at Amherst Harbour again, and, passing through the Gut of Canso on the 14th and spending the next five days at Country

Harbour, they returned to Halifax on the 22nd.

41 A day was spent at Mahone Bay and another at Chester before they rounded Gorham's Point on the 8th and anchored off Lunenburg. An examination was made of the Sculpin Rock next day. Passing Shelburne on the 12th, they reached the Tusket islands by the 17th, before doubling back to spend the next two days anchored at Barrington and in Cape Negro Harbour. They then put in to Shelburne on the 21st, where they remained for three days before proceeding to Liverpool. Remaining there at anchor from the 26th to 3 October, they returned to Halifax on the 4th.

42 NA UK, ADM 1/4846, Griffith to Admiralty 24 August and 21 November 1816.

43 Vice Admiral Wodehouse was Resident Commissioner at Halifax from September 1811 till 12 August 1819.

44 Marjory Whitelaw, *The Dalhousie Journals*, vol 1, pp. 21–22.

45 NA UK, CO 193/5, New Brunswick Blue Book, 1822, p. 37; William A Spray, *The Blacks in New Brunswick*, Fredericton: Brunswick Press, 1972.

46 BA, RB1/264/84-85, 244.

47 NA UK, ADM 1/4848, Lockwood to Croker, 29 May 1817,

48 NA UK, ADM 1/4846, Lockwood to Milne, 12 October 1817.

49 NA UK, ADM 1/4849, Lockwood to Croker, 24 January 1818: 'No opportunity offered to obtain passage in a vessel of war.'

50 NA UK, ADM 1/4849. Lockwood wrote to John Barrow at the Admiralty, 19 January 1818, informing him that he had arrived in England.

51 PANS, RG 20, Series A, Land Papers – Anthony Lockwood, 1817.

5 To London

1 NA UK, ADM 1/4849; Lockwood to Barrow, 19, 20 January 1818.

2 NA UK, ADM 1/4849; Lockwood to Hurd, 28 January 1818.

3 NA UK, ADM 1/4849; Lockwood to Hurd, 28 January 1818.

4 NA UK, ADM 1/4849; Lockwood to Barrow, 2 January 1818.

5 NA UK, ADM 1/4849; Lockwood to John Barrow, 22 January 1818.

6 NA UK, ADM 1/4849, Lockwood to Croker, 24 January 1818.

7 NA UK, ADM 1/4849; Lockwood to Admiralty, 27 January 1818.

8 NA UK, ADM 1/4849; Lockwood to Croker, 30 January 1818.

9 *New Brunswick Royal Gazette*, 26 January 1815.

10 NA UK, ADM 1/4849, Lockwood to Croker, 27 January 1818.

11 NA UK, ADM 106/1693, Lockwood to Navy Board, 31 January 1818.

12 NA UK, ADM 106/1693, Lockwood to Navy Board, 18 March 1818.

13 NA UK, ADM 1/4849, Lockwood to Barrow, 18 March 1818.

14 NA UK, ADM 1/4849, Lockwood to Croker, 26 March 1818; York and Moore had probably been shown Anthony junior's work on the drafting of the charts.

15 NA UK, ADM 106/1693, Lockwood to Admiralty, 21 April 1819.

16 NA UK, ADM 106/1696, Lockwood to Navy Board, 31 March 1818.

17 NA UK, ADM 1/4850, Hurd to Lockwood, 25 March 1818.

18 NA UK, ADM 1/4849, Lockwood to Croker, 19 March 1818; NA UK, ADM 106/1693.

19 RGO 14/3, Board of Longitude records.

20 NA UK, ADM 1/4849, Lockwood to John Barrow, 21 February 1818.

21 RGO 14/29, Board of Longitude Papers, 'Inventions of and improvements to various astronomical and nautical instruments, including … Lockwood's universal compass'. See Eva Germaine Rimington Taylor, *Mathematical Practitioners of Hanoverian England, 1714–1840*, p. 398.

22 RGO 14/4, Minutes of the Board of Longitude, 5 March 1818.

23 NA UK, ADM 1/4851, Lockwood to Admiralty, 5 May 1819.

24 NA UK, CO 217/101, Lockwood to Bathurst, 20 January 1819, addressed from Cotton Place, near the East India Docks, in London's East End.

25 Printed by G Hayden, Brydges St, Covent Garden, and sold by Cadell and Davies, Strand, 1818. All subsequent page references in the text are to this edition.

26 H Series Maps: H2-203.29-1818, A Lockwood, Mouth *of the River Saint John*, J Walker sculpt, 1818.

27 NA UK, T 28/48, G Harrison to Goulbourn, 9 January 1819.

28 This second edition of the *Description* is identical with the first to p. 104.

Presumably, Lockwood printed the Appendix later and added it to unbound sheets of the first edition. The map's publication date ('published as the Act directs by A Lockwood 1 May 1818') is probably also the date of publication for the second edition.

29 Reports on the Parry expedition appeared in the *Halifax Journal* from 23 January 1819.

30 NA UK, CO 43/56, June 12; Bathurst to Buller, 21 February 1818.

31 SNA, GD45/3/540-611 (NAC A536), Dalhousie Journals, 10 September 1818.

32 *Acadian Recorder*, 23 April 1818, p.3.

33 PANS, *Journal of the House of Assembly*, 1820, pp. 157–8. Morris had to defend to a committee of the Assembly his payment of £180 to Lockwood for the map, since no provision had been made for this in the budget.

34 W K Morrison, letter to Peter Thomas, 9 November 1988. I am also indebted to Mr Morrison for locating a copy of Lockwood's map of Nova Scotia in the Bibliothèque Nationale du Quebec: #0851, *Documents Cartographiques depuis la découverte de l'Amérique jusquà 1820*, Montreal, 1985.

35 *Acadian Recorder*, 1 April 1819, p. 3, 25 January 1826 and 14 June 1827, p. 201.

36 PANS Index of Deeds, Halifax Co, 1749–1836, Reel 17811, 44, 213 & 44, 214; Anthony junior acted for his father in purchasing from Robert Grover a tract 'beginning at Ebenezer Crowls land to north to Mr George Wasuls land in south' including houses, outhouses, barns, etc, and from Darius Pace the lot originally granted to Robert Branham. In these documents Lockwood senior is described as 'gentleman' and 'mariner'.

37 PANS, Index of Deeds, Halifax Co, 1749–1836. Reel 17811. Again Anthony junior acted for his father.

38 BA, RB 1/264/244.

39 SNA, GD45/3/540-611 (NAC A536), Dalhousie Journals, 15 June 1819.

40 *Acadian Recorder*, 14 June 1827, p. 201; PANS, Index of Deeds, Halifax Co, 1749–1836, 44, 647.

41 PANS, Index of Deeds, Halifax Co, 1749–1836, 46, 6 & 54, 72. The first, in 1820, was the sale of 350 acres to Frederick Haverstock for £300. The second sale occurred in 1831, long after Lockwood's disgrace, and after he had returned to Britain, being the sale of 187 acres to Wm Mathews for £30.

42 John Young, *The letters of Agricola on the principles of vegetation and tillage: written for Nova Scotia and published first in the Acadian recorder*, Halifax, NS?: s.n., 1822.

43 NA UK, ADM 1/4850, Lockwood to Croker, 26 August 1818, referring to a Navy Board letter of 18 May. His defence was that nothing had been said about the matter during the three months he was in Britain, his final bill had been paid in full, and the Lords Commissioners had written to him on 2 May without comment.

44 NA UK, CO 188/25 f.3, Smyth to Bathurst, 4 January 1819. Smyth began by stating that Kemball 'does not return'.

45 UNBA, Saunders Papers, John Saunders to Judge John Saunders, 16 January 1819.

6 King's Councillor

1 NA UK, CO 188/25 f. 17, Smyth to Bathurst, 15 March 1819. The Registry of In-letters to the Treasury (T2) has no record of Smyth's letter to Bathurst of 4 January being received. However, communications from other departments, especially if accompanied by private memoranda from officials, might not be recorded in the Registry.

2 NA UK, CO 188/25 f. 125, Lockwood to Bathurst on 25 February 1819.

3 NA UK, CO 43/58, Goulbourn to Lockwood, 9 March 1819; T 29/171, Minutes, 23 March 1819.

4 NA UK, CO 188/25 f. 75, and T 28/15, Lushington to Goulbourn, 30 March 1819.

5 NA UK, CO 188/25, Layton to Goulbourn, 30 March 1819. T 28/3 (421) pp. 423–24, Instructions for Anthony Lockwood.

6 The Treasury board in 1819 consisted of the Earl of Liverpool, Viscount Lowther, N Vansittart, John Maxwell Berry, B Paget, and Wm W Odell, with C Arbuthnot and S R Lushington, as joint secretaries, in addition to the private secretaries of the commissioners. The only name obviously, though tenuously, connected to Lockwood was that of Lowther, his landlord in Whitehaven.

7 NA UK, ADM 1/4851, Lockwood to Admiralty, 18 March 1819. I have not

traced the whereabouts of Lockwood's written opinion.

8 NA UK, ADM 106/1698, Lockwood to Navy Board, 18 March 1819.

9 NA UK, ADM 1/4851, Lockwood to Admiralty, 20 March 1819.

10 NA UK, ADM 106/1693, Lockwood to Navy Board, 21 April 1819.

11 NA UK, ADM 1/4851, Lockwood to Barrow, 22 April 1819.

12 William Edward Parry, *Journal of a Voyage for the Discovery of a North-West Passage from the Atlantic to the Pacific*, p. vii; *Royal Gazette*, 13 November 1821.

13 NA UK, ADM 1/4851, Lockwood to Admiralty, 5 May 1819.

14 Nova Scotia *Royal Gazette*, 19 May 1819; 30 June 1819.

15 NA UK, CO 188/23 f. 28, Hailes to Bathurst, 22 May 1817, letter reporting on Sproule's services and remuneration.

16 NA UK, CO 188/24, 20 January 1818. 'I appeal to your Lordship at the appointing of a Gentleman as one of the transient Military in preference to those of us who conceived we have a much stronger claim in every respect. . . . My Father was one of the American Loyalists and settled in this Country after the American Revolution and was proud of having served his King even at the sacrifice of much private interest in the State of New York heading the Loyalists, having His Majesty's Commission as Colonel in that War, and as he has been dead now thirteen years and left behind him a large family of ten children of which I am one of the oldest, I deem it well to mention the same to your Lordship. I lately embarked in the Army in the late New Brunswick Fencibles and held His Majesty's Commission as Captain with temporary rank which has been the means of leaving me rather destitute as I expended the most of my little patrimony in recruiting men for that Regiment and am now unprovided for.'

17 NA UK, CO 188/24, Kemball to Delancy, 8 December 1818, and Delancy to Bathurst, 6 July 1818.

18 NA UK, CO 188/23, General Martin Hunter to Henry Goulbourn, 22 July 1817.

19 NA UK, CO 188/24, Wills Frederick Knox to Lord Castlereagh, 26 June 1818. Knox was also prepared to accept the position of Naval Officer to New

Brunswick.

20 NA UK, ADM 42/2118, Barbados pay list, 1813.

21 W F Odell did not formally receive his commission as secretary, registrar, and clerk of the Council until 31 March 1815.

22 NA UK, CO 188/22 ff. 52–55, George Sproule and Jonathan Odell to Lord Bathurst, 1 June 1816. Copy at PANB F1388: They had, they claimed, incurred very substantial expenses during 'the first seven years after the erection of this Province', when 'the emoluments of their Offices fell very far short of the amount actually paid . . . for the assistance that was required to Expedite the Settlement of the Loyalists and disbanded Troops; and afterwards during a period of twelve years were reduced to a very trifling amount by the restriction on passing Grants.' No allowance had been given for clerk's wages 'or other necessary assistance', and the cost of living in New Brunswick had doubled since 1784. Only three months after the first letter, on 3 September 1816, CO 188/23 f.74, Sproule again wrote to Bathurst, reviewing a career of fifty-six years in public service, of which twenty-four were spent in the Army, including nine surveying the coasts of North America. An engineer during the Revolutionary War, he had laid out the lots of Saint John, then called Parr Town, and received his Instructions as Surveyor General on 22 March 1785. Now he was an old man. His Memorial relates that 'in the last year [I] lost [my] wife, having brought up a Family of 2 sons and 3 daughters, the former both died in the military service of their country, and two of the latter married officers in the Army. From the expences which [I have] been obliged to incur, not only on account of [my] Family, but from the Public situation in which [I have] been placed [I have been unable] to lay by any Fortune.' His unmarried daughter was 'wholly unprovided for', and he was 'nearly worn out in [my] Country's Service.' Sproule therefore asked permission to retire with provision for himself and his daughter. Underlining his debility, the letter was transcribed by Elizabeth Sproule 'for my father'. He was not actually destitute. An 'Inventory of the Real and Personal Property' of

George Sproule dated 14 March 1818 amounted to £2,438. But apart from his annual salary of £150, unchanged since 1784, Sproule averaged only £300 annually from his share of licence and grant fees during the last three complete years of his life, 1814 to 1816. At Sproule's death Smyth wrote to Bathurst reminding him of the earlier Odell/Sproule petition, 15 December 1817.

23 NA UK, CO 188/25 f. 51, Smyth to Bathurst, 13 October 1819; NA UK, CO 189/12, p. 29, 26 December 1820. Copy at PANB F1561.

24 Wynn, *Timber Colony*, pp. 21–22.

25 NA UK, CO 188/22, Smyth to Bathurst, 31 January 1816. Copy at PANB F1388. Smyth, then acting as military president of the New Brunswick Executive Council, informed Bathurst of 'a matter of great national importance': 'The Deputies of the Surveyor General of the Woods are in the daily practices of granting Licences to cut Pine Timber for private use not only on the Tracts particularly reserved for the King's use, but generally on the unlocated Lands throughout the Province; for these Licences fees are paid to these Deputies according to the quantities of Timber permitted to be cut, so that, instead of preserving the Timber [it results in] the cutting of very large quantities.' 'It has been reported to me,' Smyth continued, that Crown Lands had been leased to individuals. 'But how far these licences may be conformable to the powers vested in the Surveyor General of the Woods I am unable to judge, as the Commission and Instructions to that officer have never been communicated to His Majesty's Government in this Province.'

26 PANB RS 336/A/2, 1819/2, Wentworth to Smyth, 22 June 1819.

27 PANB, RS 336/A/1, Smyth to Bathurst, 26 September 1819.

28 CO 188/23, on 30 October 1816, Bathurst directed that in future all licences to cut pine on Crown Reserve land be given only for specific locations, and that they should be examined before deputies were allowed to sign permission. On 6 April 1818 Smyth reported back that a committee of Council now scrutinised all such applications 'but notwithstanding these Precautions, it is found that great abuses

still exist.' There was no money to pay inspectors 'to range the woods.' He repeated his request for a copy of the full Surveyor General's Commission and Instructions.

29 Wynn, *Timber Colony*, p. 33.

30 *Royal Gazette*, 16 November 1819.

31 PANB, RS55, and RS8, Legal Papers, Identification Case 1/3, Lockwood, Request for Care and Custody of Anthony Lockwood, 7 June 1823; Minute signed by Harriet Lockwood, 7 June, and Inventory of the Real and Personal Estate and Income of Anthony Lockwood Esq. Copy at PANB F7897.

32 'By the winter of 1824–25, a threefold increase in the number of timber licences authorised the cutting of twice as much timber as in 1818–1819.' Wynn, *Timber Colony*, pp. 33–36.

33 Wynn, p. 45.

34 William Odber Raymond, 'New Brunswick: General History, 1758–1867', p. 159.

35 Raymond, *op cit*, 167.

36 *Royal Gazette*, 13 January 1818, no 45, p. 1.

37 PANB, RS 1, *Journal of the House of Assembly* (1818), p. 9, Humble Address, 2 February 1818.

38 NA UK, CO 188/25 f. 33, Smyth to Bathurst, 31 March 1819.

39 See *Dictionary of Canadian Biography*, *s.v.* Saunders.

40 Quoted by Raymond, *op cit*, p. 184.

41 NA UK, CO 188/24, 17 December 1818.

42 See Cleadie Barnett, *Beginnings*: Coffin, John.

43 NA UK, CO 188/22 f. 74, Smyth to Bathurst, 19 November 1816.

44 NA UK, CO 188/23 f. 58, /24 f. 88, and /25 ff. 7–9, Smyth to Bathurst, 30 July 1817, 17 December 1818, and 15 February 1819.

45 NA UK, CO 188/25 f. 121, George Leonard to Bathurst, 27 Feb 1819.

46 Quoted by the New Brunswick *Royal Gazette*, 25 May 1819.

47 William Acheson, *Saint John*, p. 8.

48 William Odber Raymond, *Winslow Papers*, p. 399.

49 Edward Thomas Coke, *A subaltern's furlough: descriptive of scenes in various parts of the United States, Upper and Lower Canada, New Brunswick, and Nova Scotia, during the summer and autumn of 1832*, London, Saunders and Otley, 1833, p. 377.

7 Surveyor General

1 PANB, RS1, *Journal of the House of Assembly*, 8 March 1816.
2 See William Spray, 'Preface' to John Mann, *Travels in North America*.
3 Mann, p. 5.
4 New Brunswick Historical Society, p. 289. The Almshouse in Halifax also burned down in January 1819. The fire was blamed on 'a deranged individual' who slept in the attic. *Halifax Journal*, 23 January 1819.
5 NA UK, CO 384/4, 6 April 1819.
6 PANB, RS24 *Legislative Assembly, Sessional Records*, S28-P7, p. 185. Copy at PANB F17107.
7 PANB, RS 1, *Journal of the House of Assembly*, (1822 p. 225), 1 March 1820. Copy at F5 p. 225; and RS24, *Legislative Assembly, Sessional Records*, S28-B17, F17107.
8 PANB, RS 6a, *Executive Council Minutes*, vol 2, pp. 239 and 242, 27 May and 6 June 1819.
9 PANB, RS 6a, *Executive Council Minutes*, vol 2, p. 210, 23 April 1819.
10 *Royal Gazette*, 22 June 1819 (St John 16 June).
11 John Mann was again a witness. Mann, *op cit*, p. 11.
12 *Royal Gazette*, 22 June 1819 (St John 16 June).
13 Cowan, *op cit*, p. 53; The Census of 1824 counted 11,531 inhabitants of Saint John; McNutt puts the figure at 12,000, perhaps allowing for error. Stewart McNutt, *The Atlantic Provinces: the emergence of colonial society*, p. 164.
14 Raymond, *loc cit*, p. 192.
15 PANB, *RS 6a, Executive Council Minutes*, vol 2, pp. 318, 320 and 330, 22, 28 May and 29 June 1819.
16 *Acadian Recorder*, 29 May 1819. These Welsh did not settle at New Cambria, however, and probably passed on to the United States.
17 *Royal Gazette*, 13 July 1819.
18 Dr George MacBeath and Captain Donald F Taylor, *Steamboat Days: An Illustrated History of the Steamboat Era on the St John River*, based on the notes of Captain C C Taylor (1868-1941), St Stephen, New Brunswick: Print'N Press Ltd, 1982, pp. 3–16; Marjory Whitelaw (editor), *The Dalhousie Journals*, 24 October 1817.
19 General Coffin's grave is at Woodsman Point, above the St John River at Westfield, New Brunswick.
20 NA UK, CO 188/25, Smyth to Bathurst, 10 August 1819.
21 *Royal Gazette*, Fredericton, 19 March 1816.
22 PANB, RS 107 RNA/C 13/4/1, *Surveyor General's Cash Book*, 1819–24.
23 Austin Squires, *History of Fredericton : the last 200 years*, pp. 18–22.
24 PANB, RS 160 A/1/b f. 388, *York County Minutes*, 13 June 1821.
25 Donald E Graves, *Merry Hearts Make Light Days: The War of 1812 Journal of Lieutenant John Le Couteur, 104th Foot*.
26 Raymond, p. 191; Squires, *passim*.
27 Squires, p. 21.
28 PANB, RS 160, A/1/b ff. 371 and 378v, *York County Minutes*. Copy at F836.
29 *Royal Gazette*, 12 August 1816. The proposers, C Ackerman and J Stevens, were eager to have members of the Garrison join in and indeed take over the running of this venture.
30 PANB, RS 6a, *Executive Council Minutes*, vol 2, p. 334, 21 July 1819. Copy at F1688.
31 *Ibid*, p. 349, 23 September 1819.
32 PANB, RS 8 Location Ticket, 26 July 1819, p. 121 (F7918).
33 *Royal Gazette*, 9 August 1819.
34 PANB, RS 6a, *Executive Council Minutes*, pp. 349 and 353, 23 September and 2 October 1819.
35 NA UK, CO 188/25 f. 122v, Lockwood to Bathurst, 27 April 1819.
36 See Hugh Gray, *Letters from Canada*, p. 355. As late as 1847, however, Abraham Gesner would follow Lockwood in asserting that 'the Americans are far more successful in fishing than the inhabitants of the British Provinces.' Abraham Gesner, *New Brunswick: with notes for emigrants*, p. 280.
37 PANB, MG H28, *Minutes of the Fredericton Emigrant Society*
38 PANB, RS 21 C4/2, *Provincial Secretary: Treasury Administrative Records, Requests for Warrants*, 1819–20, f. 5906, Wallace to NB Provincial Secretary, 2 August 1819.
39 PANB, RS24 (1820) S28-R4, Chignecto Canal Report, 11.2.1820 – p. 195 (missing).
40 PANB, RS 1, *Journal of the House of Assembly*, (1822 p. 137), 3 March 1819.
41 NBM, Ganong Collection, Box 12 #3, 'Cartography'.

42 Lockwood, *Report*, np, i.

8 A New Broom

1 PANB, RS 637 2C/2, and RS 8, Executive Council Records – Surveyor General, Lockwood to Smyth, 15 November 1819. Copy at F7918.
2 St. James, 2/15-16.
3 *Royal Gazette*, 28 September 1819, p. 3.
4 *Royal Gazette*, 12 October 1819, p. 3.
5 See Peter Thomas, *Strangers from a secret land*, pp. 162–4 and *passim*.
6 UNBA, MG H28, *Minutes of the Fredericton Emigrant Society.*
7 *Ibid*, 16 November, 12 December 1819, and p. 17 nd, Dr Emerson died 14 October 1843.
8 NA UK, CO 188/26 ff. 9–15, Thomas Wetmore, H W Hailes, and S D Street, to George S Smyth, 'Your Excellency having referred to us as a Committee of His Majesty's Council . . . '13 December 1819, in Smyth to Bathurst, 25 February 1820. See PANB, RS 7, Draft *Executive Council Minutes*, vol 5, p. 2617, 16 December 1819.
9 The first New Brunswick census was taken in 1824.
10 In 1832 Thomas Baillie, Lockwood's successor, was 'surprised to find, on my arrival in England, how much ignorance still existed on the subject' of 'our American colonies'. *An Account of the Province of New Brunswick*, p. 2.
11 PANB RS 6a, *Executive Council Minutes*, vol 2, p. 368, 16 December 1819; and RS 637 2C/1 p. 8316, Lockwood to Wetmore, 23 March 1819. Copy at F1695.
12 Anthony Lockwood, *Report on the Projected Canal*, 1820.
13 *Acadian Recorder*, 12 December 1896, Supplement. It is tantalising because very few copies of Saint John newspapers of this period survived the city's many fires in the nineteenth century.
14 PANB, RS 6a, *Executive Council Minutes*, vol 2, p. 373, 26 January 1820.
15 PANB, RS1, *Journal of the House of Assembly* (1818), pp. 187 and 194, 8 and 11 February 1820; and New Brunswick, *Journal of the Legislative Council*, vol 2, pp. 604 and 607, 8 and 11 February 1820.
16 PANB, RS 6a, *Executive Council Minutes*, vol 2, p. 379, 23 February 1820.
17 PANB, RS 637 2C/2, Lockwood to Smyth, 14 February 1820.
18 PANB, RS1, *Journal of the House of Assembly* (1818), p. 201, 15 February 1820.
19 PANB, RS 6a, *Executive Council Minutes*, vol 2, pp. 398, 441–42, 15 April, 26 October and 2 November 1820.
20 PANB, RS7/16 Executive Council Records, Crown Lands and Forests, file 2 pp. 144–45, Lockwood, 16 February 1820; RS336/A/3a f. 144, Lockwood to Smyth, 16 February 1820.
21 PANB, RS 6a, *Executive Council Minutes*, vol 2, p. 380, 24 February 1820.
22 NBM, MC1804, Jarvis Collection, Box 1 File 4/6.
23 *Royal Gazette*, 29 August 1820. Her fee was 1gn or 2gns per quarter. No gentlemen under 16 were to be admitted.
24 *Ibid*, 9 Jan 1821.
25 *Ibid*, 16 Oct 1821.
26 See *Royal Gazette*, February 1819 *passim*. At the founding meeting Slason was made Treasurer and keeper of the Depository of Books.
27 John Russell Armstrong, *The Exchange Coffee House*, p. 7.
28 Madras Schools had been developed by Reverend Dr Andrew Bell for the East India Company in Madras. After his return from India, Dr Bell promoted 'the Madras system', and by the time of his death in 1832, over ten thousand schools were using his methods.
29 New Brunswick, *Journal of the Legislative Council*, vol 2, p. 630, 15 March 1820. Ward Chipman and Edward Jarvis were among the Trustees.
30 PANB, RS 6a, *Executive Council Minutes*, vol 2, p. 373, 26 January 1820; RS 7, Draft *Executive Council Minutes* f. 194v, 11 February 1820.
31 *Royal Gazette*, 29 February 1820 (advertisement).
32 *Ibid*, 21 March 1820.
33 Wright, Esther Clark (b.1895), *The loyalists of New Brunswick*, p. 235.
34 His father, the Reverend Jonathan Odell died on 27 November 1818, whereupon the *Royal Gazette* observed that 'Mr Odell's exit has closed the Scene with the Governor and twelve Councillors first appointed in the organisation of this Province at its erection in 1784.'

William Franklin Odell was also a commissioner, with Ward Chipman, negotiating the border issue with the United States which stemmed from the confusing terms of the treaty of Ghent. He had led a survey of disputed border territory in the Mars Hill region north of Fredericton during the summer of 1819 and Thomas Mann, the Scottish emigrant quoted earlier, was employed on this work.

35 There was a definite attempt by the *Gazette* to 'raise consciousness' concerning the Welsh. On 7 Sept 1819, an article appeared on the legend of the Welsh Indians, supposed descendants of Prince Madoc. On 16 May 1820 'A Specimen of Welsh Preaching' appeared; a week later 'Anecdote' told the improving tale of a morally upright Welsh sea-captain captured by a Yankee privateer whose honesty was rewarded by his honourable captor.

36 The 8 February 1820 column on the Cardigan Society was essentially a winding-up report. It noted the receipt of unspecified sums from Lockwood and Smyth to pay off outstanding debts.

37 Acheson, *Saint John*, p. 22.

38 John Macgregor, *Historical and descriptive sketches of the maritime colonies of British America*, p. 167.

39 Quoted by Marjory Whitelaw, Introduction, *The Dalhousie Journals*, p. 9.

40 *Royal Gazette*, (28 December) 4 January 1820.

41 Judge Bliss, Judge Saunders, Samuel Denny Street, Thomas Wetmore, and Anthony Lockwood; Colonal Le Poer Trench, Majors Allen and Robinson; and Stair Agnew, William Botsford, Colin Campbell, Peter Fraser, S Humbert, Hugh Johnston, William Franklin Odell, John Saunders, James Taylor, D B Wetmore, R Yeamans.

42 *Royal Gazette*, 22 February 1820.

43 *Ibid*, 4 March 1820.

44 A notice 'to the Respectable Inhabitants of Fredericton' appeared in the *Royal Gazette* for 2 May advertising 'the New Suffolk Patent No 3 Plow' to be seen 'in the neighbourhood of Mr Odell's.'

45 PANB RS336 A/3 1820/4, Smyth to Bathurst, 25 February 1820; Bathurst directed, by memo on Smyth's letter, that the Survey committee's Report be forwarded for consideration to the Treasury; PRO, CO 188/26 ff. 11–14,

Thomas Wetmore, H W Hailes, and S D Street, to Smyth, 13 December 1819.

46 Land issued by ticket of location did not confer title until a quit rent had been paid; confusion about this matter would plague the Surveyor General's office for years. Furthermore, on 4 January 1820 a notice reprinted from the *Royal Gazette* of 24 May 1819 warned military settlers that no title would be given – and no land therefore sold – before residence of three years and 'suitable cultivation'.

47 PANB, RS 24 S28-P13, *Legislative Assembly, Sessional Records*, 1820: Petition of the Surveyor General asking an annual allowance for a clerk, 10 February 1820. RS 1, *Journal of the House of Assembly*, 10 February 1820.

48 PANB, RS 6a, *Executive Council Minutes*, vol 2, pp. 390 and 413, 22 March and 26 May 1820.

49 *Ibid*, vol 2, p. 398, 18 April 1820.

50 *Ibid*, vol 2, p. 406, 4 May 1820. On 22 May Council approved of payments of £562 8s 11d to deputy surveyors for work on laying out lots for emigrants.

51 For example: PANB, RS 21, *Provincial Secretary, Treasury Administration Records*, C4/3 f. 6032, Accounts and Returns 1820–1825, Lockwood to Smyth, 9 March 1820.

52 Wynn, *Timber Colony*, p. 36.

53 PANB, RS 336 A1; Smyth to Maitland, 17 April 1820.

54 The Overseers of the Poor continued to request employment for 'shiftless persons who are in distress'. On 2 January 1821, for instance, they reassured readers of the *Royal Gazette* by noting that 'As the prices of sawing are usually stated, the employer can lose nothing by the slowness of the operator.'

55 PANB, RS 24 1820, S28-B20, Legislative Assembly Sessional Papers, Bill to authorise and empower the Justices of the Peace for York County to levy an assessment on the inhabitants of the different parishes for the erection of a county poorhouse in Fredericton, 3 March 1820 – p. 227.

56 UNBA, MG H28, *Emigrant Society Minutes* pp. 23 and 29, March–Nov 1820.

57 *Ibid*, p. 31, 13 November 1820. PANB, RS 1, *Journal of the House of Assembly*, 20 March 1820, p. 253. PANB, RS 1, *Journal of the House of Assembly*, 20 March 1820, p. 253. Forty pounds were

to be warranted by Council on 6 June 1820 for a road to Cardigan. PANB, RS 6a, *Executive Council Minutes*, vol 2, p. 416, 6 June 1820.

58 *Royal Gazette*, 26 September 1820.
59 UNBA, MG H28, *Emigrant Society Minutes*, p. 31, 13 November 1820.
60 *Royal Gazette*, 7 March 1820.
61 *Royal Gazette*, 30 January 1821. On 19 February that year the Sergeant Major of the 74th also advertised for the owner of a stray pig.

9 A Man of Respectable Appearance
1 NBM, Marriage Register, Saint John, 1810–1828. See also *Acadian Recorder*, 3 June 1820.
2 NA UK, CO 188/24 f. 75, 11 September 1818.
4 NA UK, CO 188/23, Smyth to Bathurst, 18 May 1818.
5 *Royal Gazette*, 22 March 1820.
6 NA UK, CO 188/25, Smyth to Bathurst, 12 October 1819 and 26 May 1820.
7 NA UK, CO 188/25, f. 141, H H Carmichael, Lockwood's Instructions, 29 May 1820.
8 NA UK, CO 188/25, Smyth to Bathurst, 13 October 1819.
9 PANB, RS 637/2c/1, Surveyor General's General Correspondence. In her *The Loyalists of New Brunswick*, p. 235, Esther Clark Wright noted that in 1819 a Crown grant of 300 acres or less carried fees of £11 13s 4d, of which the Lieutenant Governor received £4 1s 8d; the Provincial Secretary, £3 7s 6d; the Attorney General (Wetmore), £1 10s 10d, the Surveyor General (Lockwood), £2; and the Auditor General, 13s 4d.
10 NA UK, CO 193/3 f18. (PANB, RS 536), Mr T Baillie's Memoranda and Papers 1825–1833.
11 PANB, RS8 Legal Papers, Cases and Proceedings, Identification Case 1/3 – Estate of Anthony Lockwood, a Lunatic, 1823 (F7897).
12 NA UK, 1CO 188/26, Smyth to Bathurst, 10 March 1820.
13 PANB, RS8, Legal Papers, Identification Case 1/3, Estate of Anthony Lockwood, a Lunatic, 1823, 10 June 1823. F7897.
14 PANB, RS6a, *Executive Council Minutes*, vol 3, p. 3; and RS7, Draft *Executive Council Minutes*, p. 2997, 22 May 1821. Copy at F1689.
15 NA UK, CO 188/26, Lockwood to Bathurst, 19 July 1820.
16 Acheson, *Saint John*, p. 19.

17 [Anon], 'Canada's First Chartered Bank', *Monthly Review: The Bank of Nova Scotia*, May 1956, 1–4.
18 *Royal Gazette*, 5 July 1820.
19 PANB, RS 6a, *Executive Council Minutes*, vol 2, p. 415, 2 June 1820. Copy at PANB F1688.
20 PANB, RS 6a, *Executive Council Minutes*, vol 2, p. 440–41, 22 July 1820.
21 PANB, RS 656/H3-203.1-7 (1820).
22 NA UK, CO 188/26 f. 21, Smyth/Bathurst, 4 March 1820; and PANB, RS6a, *Executive Council Minutes*, vol 2, p. 434, 27 September 1820.
23 PANB, RS 6a, *Executive Council Minutes*, vol 2, p. 437, 5 October 1820.
24 PANB, RS 6a, *Executive Council Minutes*, vol 2, pp. 440–41, 26 October 1820.
25 On 23 December 1820 he presented a bill to Council for £37 12s 9d for this work. It was authorised for payment under the terms of the recent act to encourage emigration, *Executive Council Minutes*, 23 December 1820.
26 His bill for this work, presented with a report to Council on 23 December, amounted to £92 12s 6d. This was referred for a bill of particulars. He was evidently assisted in this work by Philip Palmer, father of Lockwood Acalus, who completed a survey of the road from Gaspereau River to Cape Tormentine at this time; PANB, RS 656/IE #33-5 WE, Gaspereau to Cape Tormentine, 2 November 1820, Philip Palmer.
27 PANB, RS 7, Draft *Executive Council Minutes*, vol 26, p. 4088 [F1696].

10 Noises Off – Loyal Dancing
1 *The Examiner*, 22 March 1812.
2 Flora Fraser, *The unruly queen: the life of Queen Caroline*, p. 66.
3 PAC Douglas Papers, Douglas to Horton, 6 Sept 1825.
4 PANB, RS 8, Surveyor General, Lockwood to Smyth, 15 November 1819.
5 *Royal Gazette*, 15 Feb 1820.
6 New Brunswick, *Journal of the Legislative Council*, vol 2, pp. 606, 627–630, 10 February and 14 March 1820.
7 *Royal Gazette*, 4 April 1820.
8 PANB, RS 6a, *Executive Council Minutes*, vol 2, p. 399, 18 April 1820.

9   PANB, RS 13/2/30, 'Proclamation of Loyalty', 19 April 1820.

10 PANB, RS 6a, *Executive Council Minutes*, vol 2, p. 399, 19 April 1820.

11 *Royal Gazette*, 19 December 1820. Napoleon François Joseph Charles Bonaparte, Duke of Reichstadt (20 March 1811–22 July 1832) was the son of Napoleon Bonaparte and his second wife, Marie Louise of Austria. He was styled as His Majesty the King of Rome, and when a small child was briefly the second Emperor of the French, after the abdications of his father in 1814 and again in 1815.

12 William Wordsworth, 'To Toussaint L'Ouverture', 'Sonnets dedicated to Liberty', no 8, *The Poetical Works of William Wordsworth*, London: Edward Moxon, 1837, vol 3, p.182.

13 PANB, RS2 *Journal of the Legislative Council,* vol 2, pp. 674 and 683, 10 March 1821 and 6 February 1822.

14 The House of Assembly granted £800 for Emigrant Settlement. On 21 June 1821 Council directed that fifty per cent of this be applied to the Nerepis-Oromocto road in addition to thirty per cent warranted by Council. The fund for Emigrant Settlement was also used to pay Deputy Surveyor Layton's fee for laying out 172 lots.

15 NA UK, CO 188/27 f. 3, Smyth to Bathurst, March 1821.

16 PANB, MC 10, Smyth Papers, will, 1823–24.

17 NA UK, CO 188/27, Bathurst to Smyth 21 September 1821. When Shore took his place, Smyth specifically noted to Bathurst that the quorum was now complete. PANB, RS 336/A1.

18 *Royal Gazette*, 27 March 1821.

19 NA UK, CO 188/27, Smyth to Bathurst, 28 March 1821.

20 Short items like this continued to pepper the pages of the *Gazette*. On 7 August, for instance (dated St Andrews 24 July) a plot in that town measuring 160 x 130 feet, owned by C Campbell, MLA, manured with seaweed in the fall, was said to have produced 2 tons 4 cwts of clover and grass. Proof, said the report, 'that our land only requires proper cultivation, to be equally productive with that of our neighbours.'

21 PANB, RS160, *York County Minutes*, p. 379. Copy at F836.

22 PANB, RS387 B/1, *York County Jail, Records*, Annual Returns, 1791–1866.

23 PANB, RS 6a, *Executive Council Minutes*, vol 3, p. 70, 6 June 1822; NBM, Chipman Papers, S38-1, F 33 #4.

24 Quoted by the *Royal Gazette* of 16 October 1821.

25 The toasts offer a useful guide to the priorities of the Loyalist establishment of the colony. George the Fourth ('God Save the King') was followed by the Duke of York and the Army ('Duke of York's March'); the Duke of Clarence and the Navy ('Rule Britannia'); the Royal family ('Britons Strike Home'); the Revered Memory of our Late King George the Third ('Dead March in Saul'); 'Church and State' ('Union March'); the United Kingdom – May she ever preserve her present exalted state among Nations ('Roast Beef of old England'); New Brunswick and her Sister Colonies in North America – May they ever flourish under the powerful protection of the Parent State ('New Brunswick March'); the Fair Daughters of this Land ('New Brunswick Waltz'); the City of Saint John and Prosperity to the Trade and Fisheries of British North America ('City March'); the several Provincial Institutions for the Education of Youth ('Hope though Nurse of fond Desire'); Success to the Institution which reared this Building; and may the fear of God, along with the loyal feelings which gave rise to our present Meeting, be ever inculcated within its wall ('All's Well'); the Militia of New Brunswick – May it become our bulwark in time of need ('New Brunswick troop'); the Agricultural Society of New Brunswick – May the industry of the Farmer be crowned with success ('speed the Plough'); the Duke of Wellington, the First Captain of the Age ('see the Conquering Hero comes'); the Governor in Chief, and Army under his command in British North America ('Dalhousie's Grand March'); the Memory of William Pitt and all Patriot Statesmen ('Death of Wolfe'); the Memory of Nelson, Abercromby, and Fallen heroes of the British nation ('Major Andre's Farewell'); Britain's Glory – Ships, Colonies, and Commerce (no tune).

26 *Royal Gazette*, 16 October 1821.

27 Street was an authentic hero of the Revolutionary War, having fought with great courage in an action at Machias, Maine, before being captured and

imprisoned at Boston. After five months, showing great resourcefulness, Street had escaped back to Saint John. But he had not receive the promotion he felt he merited then or later, believing that his English – as opposed to North American – birth was held against him. Granted land at Burton on the Saint John River, Street had called his estate, somewhat optimistically, Elysian Fields, but he was much too combative a figure to adopt the leisurely 'aristocratic' pose of a landed squire. Among the first lawyers to be admitted to the New Brunswick bar in 1785, thereafter he followed a successful legal and a turbulent political career. Elected to the Assembly in 1795, Street was prominent in the early struggle to assert the powers of the elected body in the face of the assumed rights of the first lieutenant governor, Thomas Carleton, and his council.

28 *Royal Gazette*, 27 Nov 1821.

11 A House of Brick

1 See William Franklin Bunting, *Freemasonry in New Brunswick; 'Biographical Sketches' passim*, and *History of St John's lodge, F & A M of Saint John, New Brunswick: together with sketches of all masonic bodies in New Brunswick, from AD1784 to AD1894*.
2 PANB, RS 656/IF #11 and #12, /17S #52. NBM, Map Tray 3/8 and 3/45.
3 PANB, RS7 *Crown Lands*, vol 25, p. 4090, Lockwood to Smyth, 10 November 1821. Copy at F1696.
4 NA UK, CO 188/27, Lockwood to Bathurst, 27 November 1821.
5 *Royal Gazette*, Regulations for granting licences to cut pine timber on the vacant Crown lands, 14 April 1820.
6 NBM, MC 1804, Jarvis Collection, Box 1 File 4/9, Ed Boyd to Carline Boyd, 9 April 1822.
7 NA UK, CO188/28, Smyth to Bathurst, 28 March and 21 June 1822.
8 NAC, George Bliss Collection, MG24 B, 23, W Hill to Sir Howard Douglas, 16 June 1827.
9 Lilian M Beckwith Maxwell, ed, *The old grave-yard, Fredericton, New Brunswick: epitaphs*, p. 12.
10 Note by Bill Acheson, January 2009.
11 PANB, RS 107 RNA/C 13/4/1, Surveyor General's Cash Book 1819–1824.
12 CO 188/28 f. 217, A Lockwood junior

to Robert John Wilmot, 30 May 1822. Wilmot adopted the name Wilmot-Horton in 1823.
13 NA UK, ADM1/4854, 187285, Petition of Mr Anthony Lockwood, Master of the Royal Navy, 29 March 1822.
14 PANB, RS 387 B/1, *York County Jail Records, Annual Returns*, Sketch of Jail lot; and RS 6a, *Executive Council Minutes*, vol 3, pp. 63–4, 17 May 1822.
15 PANB, RS 6a, Executive *Council Minutes*, vol 3, p. 65, 27 May 1822; and RS 656/ID #19-4 KE, surveyed plan of Buctuche Indian Reserve, minuted 'Approved in Council, 18 March 1823'.
16 PANB, RS 8, Executive Council Papers, Provincial Secretary's General Correspondence, 1822, Hugh Johnston Sr and Thomas Millidge to William F Odell, Saint John, 11 June 1822. Copy at F7853.
17 NA UK, CO 188/28, Lockwood to Bathurst, 2 July 1822.
18 NA UK, ADM106/3517, Lockwood to George Smith, 20 November 1822.
19 *Royal Gazette*, 26 July 1821. *From the Acadian Recorder*: The Grand Canal in the state of New-York. See also 13 August, from *City Gazette* 8 August 1822: letter from 'A MERCHANT'.
20 *Royal Gazette*, August 20 1822. From the *Saint John Gazette* 15 August: 'A numerous and respectable ...' The committee elected consisted of: Chipman, Hugh Johnston, Thomas Millidge, Thomas Heaviside, Charles Simmonds, and Lauchlan Donaldson. Zalmon Wheeler's name was added a few days later.
21 NA UK, CO 188/28 f. 70, Smyth to Bathurst, 3 September 1822, and Chipman, Milledge, etc, to Smyth, 'A new commercial relations', 28 August 1822.
22 *Royal Gazette*, 10 Sept 1822, from the *New Brunswick Courier*, 31 August 1822; and PANB, RS6a, *Executive Council Minutes*, vol 3, p. 163, 26 May 1823.
23 PANB, RS 6a, *Executive Council Minutes*, vol 2, p. 337, 22 June 1819.
24 NA UK, CO 188/28, Le Poer Trench to Bathurst, 12 June 1822.
25 PANB, MC10/2 #12, Smyth papers. Unless a specific date is given, passages have been conflated from several letters where the need for sequence is not required.
26 PANB, MC 10/2 #13, Smyth papers;

shipping bill; the organs and plate shipments were both insured on 14 Aug 1822 for £300.

27 PANB, RS 336/A/30, J Saunders to Smyth, 12 October 1822.

28 NA UK, WO 54/564, Return for New Brunswick, 1 April 1828. On 25 October 1817 he was appointed a clerk in the Barrack department of the Ordnance, and was employed as Dalhousie's clerk. After his appointment to Fredericton, he was transferred to the Ordnance department for his pay on 25 December 1822.

29 PANB, Saunders papers, reel 3, Henry Charles Saunders to John Saunders, 13 July [1847]; photofile P4/2/41.

12 The Perfect Storm

1 NBM, S38-1, F37, Chipman Papers, and PANB RS6a, Executive Council Minutes, vol 3, pp. 165–171, 31 May 1823. Affidavit of Thomas Emerson, Surgeon, Fredericton, sworn before Wm F Odell, May 31 1823.

2 PANB, RS 7, Draft Executive Council Minutes, vol 6, p. 3338, 4 January 1823. Committee of Council (Fredericton): AL [then crossed out], Chief Justice, G Shore, S D Street, p. 3337.

3 PANB, RS 1, Journal of the House of Assembly, 1823, p. 1, 5 February 1823.

4 PANB, RS 637 2C/2 Lockwood to Smyth, 18 February 1823; and PANB, RS 7, Draft Executive Council Minutes, vol 6 p. 3382, 24 February 1822. Copy at F1689.

5 PANB, RS 1, Journal of the House of Assembly (1823 f. 36v), 26 February 1823.

6 PANB, RS 1, Journal of the House of Assembly (1823 f. 75), 15 March 1823.

7 PANB, RS 1, Journal of the House of Assembly, 24 March 1823.

8 PANB, RS 1, Journal of the House of Assembly, f. 105, 27 March 1823.

9 Those present being Lockwood, John Saunders, Ward Chipman, John Murray Bliss, Samuel Denny Street, and George Shore. A letter confirming the death by Alexander Boyle, MD, was presented by Saunders.

10 PANB, RS 6a, Executive Council Minutes, vol 3, p. 151, 27 March 1823.

11 PANB, RS 8, Provincial Secretary, General Correspondence, 1823. 'Fredericton Province of New Brunswick, 1 April 1823.'

12 NA UK, CO189/12, Chipman to Bathurst, 9 September 1823.

13 NBM, S38-1, F 39, Chipman Papers, Chipman to Dalhousie, 3 April 1823; PRO, CO188/29 Chipman to Bathurst, 1April 1823. See also PRO, CO189/12, Bathurst to Chipman, 5 June 1823.

14 PANB, RS 7, Draft Executive Council Minutes, vol 6, p. 3475, 1 April 1823.

15 PANB, MC 10/1, D/CB 6/15 and 6/16a (7), procession order for Smyth's funeral, and oration by the Reverend James Somerville; Dictionary of Canadian Biography, s.v. 'Somerville'.

16 PANB, MC 10/2 #21 and #25, Draft inscription, and Shore to J G Smyth.

17 NA UK, CO 188/29 f. 73, For Leonard to Chipman, 2 May 1823.

18 Royal Gazette, 30 July 1822.

19 NA UK, CO188/29, Billopp with Black and Jarvis to Bathurst, 8 April 1823.

20 Transcribed in the Royal Gazette, 22 April 1822.

21 PANB, RS339/A/2a ff. 6526 and 6527.

22 PANB, RS6a, Executive Council Minutes, vol 3, pp. 1579, 30 April and 1 May 1823.

23 NA UK, CO189/12, Chipman to Bathurst, 9 September 1823.

24 NA UK, CO189/12, Bathurst to Chipman and to Billopp, 5 June, 12 and 14 July 1823.

25 NAC, MG24-A3, Sir H Douglas Letter Books Box 2/1, pp. 73-74, Douglas (Fredericton) to Bathurst, 16 November 1824.

26 Fredericton Royal Gazette, 11 March 1823.

27 PANB, RS 55 1823, Lockwood, Anthony (lunacy), Minutes of Court of Chancery, 'Be it as prayed', signed Ward Chipman, 7 June 1823.

28 PANB, RS8 Legal Papers, Identification Cases, 1/3 Lockwood. Copy at F7897.

29 NBM, S38-1, F37 #2-4, Chipman Papers, Proclamation by George Leonard, Sussex Vale, 24 May 1823, and Leonard to Odell, 24 May 1823.

30 NBM, S38-1, F37 #6, Chipman Papers, Lockwood to Millidge, 27 May 1823.

31 NBM, S38-1, F37 #5, Chipman Papers, Chipman to Leonard, 26 May 1823.

32 NBM, S38-1, F39 #17, Chipman Papers, Chipman to Dalhousie, 26 May 1823.

33 NBM, S38-1, F37 #8, Chipman Papers, Chipman to Paddock, 28 May 1823.

34 NBM, S38-1, F37 #24, Chipman Papers, Minette for Lockwood to Ward

Chipman, unsigned, marked D [28 May 1823].

35 PANB, RS6a, *Executive Council Minutes*, vol 3, pp. 165–171, 31 May 1823. The second affidavit of Robert C Minette was sworn before W F Odell, 31 May 1823, and the affidavits of Robert C Minette and John Robinson were signed before Wm T Odell, JP. Also in NBM, Chipman Papers S38-1 F 37 #10, pp. 9–11.

36 NA UK, CO 188/29 f. 82, Chipman to Bathurst, 6 June 6 1823.

37 NAC, MG24-A3, Sir H Douglas Letter Books Box 2/1, pp. 61–62, Douglas to Bathurst, 20 October 1824.

38 NBM, S38-1, F37 #11, Chipman Papers, Lockwood to 'His Honour The President', dated 'Steam Boat', and 'Fredericton – In the Council Committee Room', 30 May 1823.

39 PANB, RS6a, *Executive Council Minutes*, vol 3, pp. 165–173, 31 May and 1 June 1823.

40 NBM, Chipman Papers, S38-1 F 37 #10, pp. 9-11, Affidavit of Robert Minette, sworn before Odell, 1 June 1823. An anonymous and undated note in the Colonial Office records asserted that Lockwood had 'declared that the government had devolved upon him[self]'. NA UK, CO188/29 f. 83.

41 NBM, Chipman Papers S38-1 F 37 #10, pp. 12–13, Affidavit of Edward W Miller, Sheriff, sworn 2 June 1823 before William J Odell, JP, York County.

42 NBM, Chipman Papers S38-1 F 37 #13, Lockwood to Slason, dated from the Jail of Fredericton 1 June 1823, 8.15 [pm?].

43 PANB, RS6a, *Executive Council Minutes*, vol 3, 2 June 1823.

44 NBM, S38-1, F37 #7, Chipman Papers, Leonard to Chipman, [transcribed by his daughter E Leonard], 28 May 1823.

13 Never to Hope Again

1 NBM, Chipman Papers, S38-1, F 37, June 2, 1823. Harriet Lockwood to Ward Chipman.

2 PANB, RS 690, Writ of Lunatico Inquirendo, 2 June 1823; and PRO, CO 188/29 f. 81, Chipman to Bathurst, 6 June 1823.

3 PANB, RS 55, 1823 Lockwood, Anthony (lunacy), Petition of Edward W Miller to Chipman, 2 June 1823.

4 NBM, RS 55, 1823 Lockwood, Anthony (lunacy), 'Know all Men by these presents . . .', 7 June 1823.

5 PANB, RS55, and RS8, Legal Papers, Identification Case 1/3, Lockwood, Request for Care and Custody of Anthony Lockwood, 7 June 1823; Minute signed by Harriet Lockwood, 7 June, and Inventory of the Real and Personal Estate and Income of Anthony Lockwood Esq. Copy at F7897. His house, barn and land was assessed at £800, with the 'windmill lot in Fredericton' worth £200 and his 'church lots of land in Fredericton' at £170. His livestock 'cattle, hogs, etc' were assessed at £82; his sleighs, gig, and cart at £35; various harness, saddles, etc, at £30; the grand pianoforte at £100 with the organ and harpsichord being worth another £40; mathematical instruments, £40; stationery, £50; wine, £50; household furniture, £300; plate, £40; provisions, stores, etc, £30. The half fees of the Surveyor General's Office amounted to £250 per annum, the income paid him by the British government as Surveyor General £150, and his half-pay as Master RN added a final £100.

6 NA UK, CO 188/29 f. 235, Shore to Bathurst, 19 May 1823. The ostensible reason for his presenting a curriculum vitae was concern that he might be displaced from his current positions as Clerk of the Supreme Court. Shore was the obvious choice, Chipman told Bathurst, because he had 'formerly held this office under the appointment of the late Lieutenant Governor, and had discharged the duties of it with much credit to himself, satisfaction to Individuals and advantage to the Public, and I have accordingly given to him a temporary appointment to this office until His Majesty's Pleasure shall be known, more especially as I was given to understand that Your Lordship had on a former occasion recommended Mr Shore to the Lords Commissioners of His Majesty's Treasury for the confirmation of his appointment to that Office by the late Lieutenant Governor, which recommendation had not been successful by reason that Mr. Lockwood's appointment to it by their Lordships had taken place a few days before.' f. 81, Chipman to Bathurst, June 6, 1823. PANB, RS 55 1823, Lockwood, Anthony (lunacy), Bond, George Shore, 5 June 1823; 'Know all Men by these presents . . .', 5 June 1823, and Chipman to George Shore, 6 June 1823.

7 NBM, Chipman Papers, S38-1, F 34, George Shore to Chipman, 14 June 1823 and Chipman to Shore 18 and 22 June. As a result Chipman set Shore to work determining how many days work would be required to set the record straight, and how much it would cost.

8 On 8 December 1823 John Saunders, son of Judge John Saunders, wrote to his father from Lincoln's Inn with the advice that the post of Surveyor General would probably not be filled until Sir Howard Douglas reached Fredericton, and the suggestion that his father obtain a letter from Shore to be transmitted by Douglas to Bathurst. Shore should say that 'he had exercised the office of Surveyor General for two years and been turned out, though he had come into it at a time when it was in a state of almost hopeless confusion ... and had only after the most painful and laborious application been able to bring things into any order so that unless his appointment was confirmed he and his family must be reduced to want.' UNB Archives: Saunders Papers, John Saunders (son)/John Saunders (father), Lincoln's Inn Fields, 8 December 1823.

9 NBM, Chipman Papers, S38-1, F 37 #15, Lockwood to W F Odell, 4 am Morning 15 July 1823, Jail. On 17 January 1824 the Grand Jury reported on another visitation of the York County jail 'agreeable to that part of the charge given by the Court, and found it in a most Re[t]ched State, not only wanting repair but very filthy and dirty particular that part where persons are confined.' They were 'informed by the Sheriff that three private families was living in a part of the Gaol on rent from the said Sheriff beside the Gaoler's family w[h]ich he said was his own property, and that he had a write [sic] so to do. The Jury [do not] think that the Sheriff nor any other person has a write to rent any part of a publick building to his or their benefit where the County is taxable to build or keep the same in repair.' This was the third time the Grand Jury had visited the jail, and it was to return again on 10 June 1824, when they reported: 'The back Dungeon requires to be ceiled [sic] with three inch plank, and secured with iron bars ... The Privies in their present state are quite Offensive ... some person ought to be employed to wash out the rooms .

.. The Jail appears to be occupied with Private families to the great inconvenience of the Jailor.' PANB, RS 160 A1b, pp. 454 and 468-9, York County, General Sessions, 17 January and 10 June 1824.

10 PANB, RS55 1823, Anthony Lockwood, 16 August 1823.

11 NA UK, CO 188/29 ff. 111-126, Chipman to Bathurst, 11 October 1823; NA UK, CO 188/29 ff. 305-6, Anthony Lockwood junior to Bathurst, 17 March 1824.

12 NBM, Chipman Papers, S38-1, F 37 #53, Lockwood to Chipman, 9 August 1823.

13 NBM, Chipman Papers, S38-1, F 37 #16(1), Thomas Wetmore to Lockwood, 10 September 1823.

14 NBM, Chipman Papers, S38-1, F 37 #16(2), Lockwood to Chipman, 22 September 1823.

15 NBM, Chipman Papers, S38-1, F 37 #17, Lockwood to Wetmore, 27 September 1823, Signed Rec and Sur Genl.

16 NBM, Chipman Papers, S38-1, F 37 #19, Wetmore to Lockwood, 28 September 1823.

17 NA UK, CO 188/29 f. 273, Anthony Lockwood to Bathurst, October 18, 1823, Fredericton.

18 NA UK, CO 188/29 f. 129, Chipman to R Morton Wilmot, November 27, 1823, Saint John.

19 NBM, Chipman Papers, S38-1, F 37 #21, Lockwood to Chipman, 19 January 1824, 6 o'clock [pm?], 13:00, and 20 January at 9 o'clock.

20 NA UK, CO 188/29 ff. 305-6, Anthony Lockwood junior to Bathurst, 17 March 1824.

21 PANB, RS 6, Executive Council Minutes, vol 3, ff. 189, 191, 11 and 21 February 1824.

22 NA UK, CO 188/29 ff. 305-6, Anthony Lockwood junior to Bathurst, 17 March 1824. If there was want, it was probably in the Lockwood family. On 23 December 1823 Anthony Lockwood junior advertised in the Fredericton Royal Gazette that 'he is requested and authorized to solicit and receive Subscriptions for the New-York ALBION Newspaper, by its Editor: those who wish the above paper will therefore apply at the Surveyor-General's.' This was a serious fall from wealth, even if he were still able to use

as his address the office of the Surveyor General, and the situation of the Lockwood family was to be further reduced as a result of Chipman's death.

23 NAC, MG24-A3, Sir H Douglas Letter Books Box 2/1, p. 7, Douglas (in London) to Bathurst, 20 March 1824.

24 NAC, MG24-A3, Sir H Douglas Letter Books Box 2/1, p. 5, Douglas (in London) to Bathurst, 16 March 1824.

25 UNB Archives: Saunders Papers. Judge John Saunders to John Saunders, 27 October 1824.

26 NA UK, CO193/3 f. 18, (PANB, RS 536) Thomas Baillie's Memoranda & Papers: 1825–33.

27 *Ibid*, Baillie to Douglas, 21 November 1824; NBM Chipman Papers, S38-1 F 34 #37, List of grant plans missing from the Surveyor-General's office, nd; Douglas conveyed Baillie's recommendation that a sum of £300 be provided to hire an assistant to redraft the 'erroneous Plans produced by his insane Predecessor', NAC, MG24-A3, Sir H Douglas Letter Books Box 2/1, p. 89, Douglas (Fredericton) to Bathurst, 28 November 1824.

28 PANB, RS55 1823, Anthony Lockwood, 16 January and 6 April 1824.

29 *Royal Gazette*, 20 April 1824, p. 2. The sale was advertised of 'Household Furniture, Books, Mathematical Instruments, Carts, Gigs, Sleighs, Saddles and Bridles, Harness, Ploughs, Slate for covering a House, several Church Lots on advantageous Leases, the Wind-Mill Lot, which is real Estate, and that well known House and Lot, a part of which was occupied as a Surveyor-General's Office, and many other valuable articles well worth the attention of the public'.

30 NA UK, ADM 11/2, Memorandum of Services: Anthony Lockwood, *c*.1833. The idea that the Lockwoods might in fact have lost their home in the great Mirimichi fire of October 1825 ignores the house sale the previous May. Over £26,794 of property was destroyed in Fredericton alone, and the former Lockwood home was well placed to be ignited by sparks flying across the river, but it was no longer their home. The Lockwoods did not make a claim to the Relief Committee, and it is virtually certain they would have done so had they had any justification. PANB,

RS660 A and D, Report of the Commissioners for ascertaining the losses occasioned by the late fires in New Brunswick, and Fire Relief Committee Records.

31 PANB, RS55 1823, Anthony Lockwood, Petition of Anthony Lockwood to the Honourable John Murray Bliss, 17 April 1824.

32 NAC, MG24-A3, Sir H Douglas Letter Books Box 2/1 p. 43, Douglas to Bathurst, 26 September 1824. In the light of Lockwood's vote in favour of admitting spectators to the deliberations of the Legislative Assembly, it is not difficult to imagine what would have been his reaction to a piece of political theatre that occurred in the first days of February 1825 when a 'Tavern-Keeper', William Miller, tried to remain 'within the bar of the house' to hear Douglas's address. He was ejected by the Sergeant-at-Arms 'with much reluctance', and when the two subsequently met in a public store Miller 'accosted him . . . in a most insulting and abusive manner'. Upon hearing his complaint, the Sergeant-at-Arms was ordered to take Miller into custody. He was brought to the bar of the Council chamber and the members resolved that there had been a breach of privilege. Miller was consigned to the jail to consider his transgression, and two days later, on the 9th was brought again to the bar, where 'upon his knees' he asked 'pardon of the Council as ordered' and was discharged with costs. (PANB, RS 2, *Journal of the House of Assembly*, 4-9 February 1825.)

33 NAC, MG24-A3, Sir H Douglas Letter Books Box 1/1-4 Despatches, Bathurst to Dalhousie, 6 November 1824.

34 NAC, MG24-A3, Sir H Douglas Letter Books Box 2/1, pp. 48, 68, 74 and 89, Douglas (Saint John) to W Odell and to Bathurst, 30 September 1824, to George Shore, 16 October 1824, to John Robinson, 17 November 1824, and to Bathurst 28 November 1824.

35 NAC, MG24-A3, Sir H Douglas Letter Books Box 2/1, pp. 73–74, Douglas to Bathurst, 16 November 1824.

36 A medical board made up of a surgeon, J B Gibson, Thomas Emerson, surgeon, and someone simply recorded as Woodford, MD, advised on 20 May 1825 that Lockwood was 'at this present time in the perfect possession of his intellectual faculties and capable of

taking charge of and managing his own
affairs', although they also warned that
they could not 'form a correct opinion
as to how permanent, or of what
duration, this restoration may be,
conceiving that in his peculiar case there
can be no security against relapse.'
PANB RS8 Legal Papers, Identification
Cases, 1/3 Lockwood, Lockwood to
Douglas, 2 March 1825. Copy at
F7897; and RS55 1823, Anthony
Lockwood, 20 and 28 March, 6 and 11
April, and 20 May1825, Emerson and
Slason to Douglas, 22 October 1825.

37 PANB, RS55 1823, Anthony
Lockwood, In Chancery, in the matter
of Anthony Lockwood, Esq, late a
lunatic, 12 and 14 November 1825.

38 He asked that the latter be paid him in
London, but fourteen years later the
faithful Jedediah Slason was still
requesting that the administration of the
pension be simplified by allowing it to
be paid without waiting for the
certificates to cross the Atlantic showing
that Lockwood was still alive. NA UK,
CO188/34 ff. 169–170, Lockwood to
Wilmot Horton, 25 January 1826; and
PANB, RS 8, Legal Cases, Estate of
Anthony Lockwood, Lunatic, Slason to
the King, Bond, 25 August 1836.

39 NA UK, ADM 6/153, Lockwood to
Admiralty, 6 February 1826.

40 NA UK, ADM 6/153, Admiralty to
Navy Board, 18 August 1827; the
certificate was dated 1 August 1827.
Burrows lived at 10 Montague Street.

41 *Royal Gazette*, 25 April 1826, p. 3.

42 His youth may have helped him fit into
New Brunswick society. He was more
likely to find companions among the
junior officers of the garrison and other
local young men. On the surface he
appears to have been more of a joiner
than his father. His participation in the
Philomathean Society is consistent with
social ease. He was later a member of
the Methodist church in Fredericton.
When the doubtless half-hearted
attempt to allow him to succeed his
father as Surveyor General came to
nothing, he continued to work in his
father's old office, being shown in the
1851 census as employed in what had
by then become the Crown Lands
Office. That did not prevent him
working with the family's friend Minette
in completing a survey in Saint John
county in October 1827, and he was

listed as Deputy City Surveyor, Saint
John, under Minette. In 1826 he
published his Map of New Brunswick.
(PANB, MPG 1/620, 'A Map of New
Brunswick compiled from actual surveys
and from Documents in the Surveyor
General's office by Anthony Lockwood,
Junr, Late Assistant Surveyor General of
the Province, published as the Act
directs by Anthony Lockwood, London
and New Brunswick, March 27, 1826.)
His family connection with the former
Surveyor General would most likely
have helped him in this career, but there
is no reason to think he was not good
at the job. In 1828 he became a
Freemason, joining Minette's own
lodge. (Anthony Lockwood junior
joined the Saint John's Lodge on 3 June
1828; A J B Milton, 'Loyalist Masons in
the Maritimes', p. 98.) He married a
Martha, probably Martha née Evans,
and had at least four children. An
advertisement in the *Royal Gazette*, 20
March 1833, offers for sale or let by the
'subscriber, T R Robertson' a 'com-
modious cottage with good barn and
Garden attached, at present occupied by
A Lockwood, Esquire.'
The outline of his life suggests that the
ill-luck that had dogged his father left its
mark on him, even if his father's mental
collapse had no genetic component that
might have passed to his son. Between
1825 and 1830 he was the plaintiff in
six cases brought before the Supreme
Court of New Brunswick, and the
defendant in another two. (PANB, RS
42, Supreme Court Original Jurisdiction
Case Files, 1825–30, s.v. Lockwood.)
Martha died 13 March 1834, aged 34.
Left with a young family to raise on his
own, Anthony junior appears to have
floundered. A daughter, Maria M, was
given up for adoption by Joseph Gaynor
whom Anthony junior probably knew
through the Methodist church. Maria M
was to marry a W M S Evans of
Moncton on 15 August 1853. Their
second son, James Adolphus, died of
scarlet fever on 28 May 1836, and is
buried with his mother in the Old
Loyalist Burial Ground, Fredericton.
(Fredericton *Royal Gazette*, 1 June
1836 and 24 August 1853; Lilian M
Beckwith Maxwell, ed, *The old grave-
yard, Fredericton, New Brunswick:
epitaphs*, York-Sunbury Historical
Society, Busy East Press, 1938.)

There is unconfirmed reference to Anthony's being involved with a brewery on the north side of the St John river in 1840, but whether as an investor or employee is not said. (Lilian Maxwell, ed, *The old grave-yard, Fredericton*, p. 45.) On 10 March 1849 he advertised in *The Headquarters* 'that he continues to give instruction in music, on his usual terms. Mr Lockwood would also be pleased to take any orders for tuning pianos, or any other matter in the way of his profession. Mr Lockwood's residence is at St Joseph Burt's, King Street, immediately opposite the Infant School.' The choice of the word 'profession' suggests that he was presenting himself as a professional musician. (*The Headquarters*, 10 March 1849, p. 3. He was also believed to be lodging with the family of Nicholas Walter, a Saint John bookbinder.) Perhaps it was during this period that he played the organ at the Methodist Church in Fredericton.

By the time of the 1861 census Anthony junior was living in Fredericton with his daughter Marion Evans, aged twenty-nine, her son William, aged four, listed as Methodists, and an Emilia Wright, Baptist, who was nineteen and was probably a servant, although she could have been Anthony's mistress. Anthony himself was listed as Church of England and remained a Clerk in the Crown Lands Office. He was living in Charlotte Street by the census of 1871. The evidence for his wife's maiden name being Evans is only the choice of that name for their daughter, and there is no evidence of what if any connection there was between his wife's family and the man who married his daughter Maria M.

43 Greater London Record Office.
44 NA UK, ADM 1/4863, Harriet Lockwood to the Admiralty Secretary, 14 April 1831.
45 An affidavit signed by James Phillips, of Bethnal House, Surgeon, declared on 12 March 1849 that 'Mr Anthony Lockwood is now and for some time past has been insane and is under my medical care ... the said Anthony Lockwood is unfit and incapable of managing his business or affairs or to take care of himself.' This affirmation was made under the terms of an act passed under William IV as a substitute for a legal oath. It was necessary for Lockwood to claim his Navy pension annually and each year he was required to provide a certified declaration, signed by himself, that he was still alive. These declarations were sworn and signed in the Justice Room of London's Guildhall before a JP. During Anthony's periods of confinement he was probably taken to the Guildhall by keepers.

46 Anthony Lockwood, described as 'master, RN' and son of Richard, 'Sergeant, Royal Artillery', was married at St Dunstan's, Stepney; his bride, another Harriet, Harriet Teran, a widow, daughter of William Johnson, a labourer. She signed the register with her mark and the marriage was witnessed by a Fanny Turner, also signing by mark, and an Ithiel Price. General Registry, St Catherine's House; Births, Deaths and Marriages, England and Wales, 1849, Stepney, vol 11, p. 301. According to the 1841 census, a Henry Lockwood, aged 73, 'Royal Navy Newfoundland' and born 'Kent Newfoundland', was head of household at 15 Whitehorse Terrace, Stepney, living with Harriet, described as his wife (24), and their children Henry (10), Elizabeth (2), Alfred (six months), and son-in-law Frank Johnson. A Harriet Eliza Lockwood, aged nine months, recorded as the daughter of Henry Lockwood, 21 Harbour Square, had died 'of a decline' in Stepney on 5 September 1837. Present at the death was the wife of a member of the board of the Mariner's Church. General Register Office, Stepney District, Mile End Old Town Sub-district, Middlesex, 1837/115, Harriett Eliza Lockwood (St Catherine's House, Stepney 11/396).

47 The 1851 census shows that its inhabitants were generally artisans or of the 'respectable' working class: a coal dealer, a 'milliner at home', an auctioneer, a milkman, a clerk at a coal wharf, a retired mariner, a housekeeper, a railway contractor (a euphemism for navvy), a labourer, a tailor, a laundress, a carpenter, a stay maker, a brush maker, a shipwright, a Metropolitan Police constable, a coal dealer, an excise [officer] superannuated, a tailoress, a milliner, a cloak maker, a publican's widow, a grocer. Yet it was a long way in every sense from that seat of government.

48 In the 1851 census (Ratcliff district) Anthony's name and other personal details are fused with Henry's. He is named as Henry, described correctly as master RN, but as Surveyor General of Newfoundland, which is also given as his place of birth. Was he capable of giving information about himself? More likely this was the garbled version of someone else in the household or a casual census-taker. It is possible that Anthony's father was stationed for a time in Newfoundland and that the birthplace is correct, but more likely that Lockwood's antecedents were only approximately known, and it would be easy to confuse Newfoundland with New Brunswick. Other members of the household in 1851, were Harriet's daughter Elizabeth, aged ten; a son Alfred aged six months; John Johnson, described as 'son-in-law', a 'mathematical instrument maker' aged twenty-six; and Queeny Beagley, a servant, aged eighty-four.

There are several questions here. An Emily, listed on the St Dunstan's, Stepney, baptismal record as daughter of Anthony Lockwood and Harriet, was baptised on 23 January 1850. Little Alfred, meanwhile, was baptised at St Dunstan's, Stepney, on 5 January 1851, evidently Harriet's second child of that name. His father, officially Anthony, is described as a 'master mariner' in the baptismal register – perhaps a version of 'master, RN'. Given Anthony's state of health his sexual capacity is doubtful. An Alfred Lockwood was later buried at St Dunstan's on 4 February 1855, aged four. Meanwhile, a Henry Lockwood, described as the child of Anthony and Harriet, had been baptised at St Mary, Stepney, on 25 January 1850. He then vanishes from the record, presumably dying in infancy.

The relationship with John Johnson does suggest a link with Lockwood's professional past, when he had much to do with his surveying instruments. Perhaps the Lockwoods and Johnsons

were close families. It seems likely that John was Harriet's brother, like the Frank Johnson of the 1841 census, who appears to be a different person since John would have been only sixteen ten years earlier – hardly old enough to be a son in law. If in 1851 he really was Anthony's son-in-law he may have been married to either the deceased Sarah or Marina. There are surviving Guildhall affidavits from 1838–1854, inclusive, containing a signed affirmation in his own varying hand that he was indeed alive. In 1854 he provided two affidavits, on 2 January and 1 July. It was plainly a major enterprise to transport him to Guildhall. Near the end, on 1 April 1851, he began to sign himself simply 'Anthony Lockwood RN' and drop reference to his New Brunswick offices (PANB, RS 13/2/17/b Certificates verifying Anthony Lockwood to be alive, 1840–1854).

49 UKHO, LP57 L613-4, Lockwood to Beaufort, 12 November 1849.

50 General Register Office, Stepney District, Ratcliff sub-district, County of Middlesex 1855/306, Anthony Lockwood.

Reflections: The Theatre of Life

1 Listed in the bibliography as parts of the collections of the National Library of Scotland, Cochrane papers 2316 folio 9r; the Public Archives of New Brunswick; the United Kingdom Hydrographic Office; and the Vaughan Library, Acadia University, Wolfville, Nova Scotia.

2 NAC, MG24-A3, Sir H Douglas Letter Books Box 2/1, p.112, Douglas to Telford, 24 March 1825.

3 NAC, MG24-A3, Sir H Douglas Letter Books Box 2/1, pp. 215-19, Douglas to Robinson, 18 Dec 1825.

4 *Considerations*, 1831, 29.

5 See *Report*, Government of Canada, Dec 1875, and 'The Chignecto Canal' report by the Economic Research Corp, Fredericton, 1960.

Bibliography

Primary Sources

VAUGHAN LIBRARY, ACADIA UNIVERSITY, WOLFVILLE, NOVA SCOTIA
Country Harbour, NS.

BARBADOS ARCHIVES
Parish Records
PR   St Michael, RL 1/66.
PR   St Michael, RL 1/70.
PR   St Michael, vol 6, 268.
Record Books
RB   1/251/164.
RB   1/254/264.
RB   1/255/12.
RB   1/264/84-85.
RB   2/2.
RB   2/235, Index.
RB   4 (1807), Index.

BRITISH LIBRARY

Maps SEC8 (480)   Anthony Lockwood, A survey of Culebra or Passage
                     Island, 1811 [Admiralty Chart].
Maps 70525 (9)   Anthony Lockwood, Mouth of the River Saint John,
                     J Walker sculpt. Two nautical miles.

CUMBRIA RECORDS OFFICE, CARLISLE
St Nicholas Parish Records.

LIBRARY AND ARCHIVES OF CANADA

MG23-F1	DesBarres Series 5 Correspondence 1761–1894 (Film A-2083, originals the property of Mrs David Micklem Langleys, Great Waltham, Chelmsford, Essex, England).
MG24-A3	Box 1 (1-4) Douglas Papers, Despatches. Box 2 Douglas Papers, Correspondence, despatches and related papers of Sir Howard Douglas, 1816–1859 (new reference: R2455-0-4-E).
MG24 B23	George Bliss Collection (new reference: R2561-0-2-E).

NATIONAL ARCHIVES OF SCOTLAND

GD45	Papers of the Maule Family, Earls of Dalhousie (NAC A536-538).
GD45	3/540-611 Personal journals, papers and accounts of the Earl of Dalhousie 1816–1836.
NA7100	Sir Alexander Forrester Inglis Cochrane.

NATIONAL ARCHIVES, UK, PUBLIC RECORD OFFICE

ADM 1	Admiralty In-Letters:
1/110	From Flag Officers, Channel Fleet: 1798, nos 351–544.
1/223	From Commanders-in-Chief, Channel Islands (Guernsey), 1805–1807.
1/326	From Commanders-in-Chief, Leeward Islands, 1805.
1/327	From Commanders-in-Chief, Leeward Islands, 1806.
1/329	From Commanders-in-Chief, Leeward Islands, 1808.
1/330	From Commanders-in-Chief, Leeward Islands, 1809.
1/331	From Commanders-in-Chief, Leeward Islands, 1810.
1/333	From Commanders-in-Chief, Leeward Islands, 1812.
1/335	From Commanders-in-Chief, Leeward Islands, 1814.
1/505	From Commanders-in-Chief, North America: 1814, nos 1–140.
1/509	From Commanders-in-Chief, North America: 1815, nos 127–316.
1/510	Letters from Senior Officers, Halifax, 1816–1817.
1/511	Letters from Senior Officers, Halifax, 1818–1820.
1/2498	From Captains, Surnames S: 1798, nos 201–392.
1/3523	From the Hydrographer of the Navy (Alexander Dalrymple, later Thomas Hannaford Hurd) 1808–1809.

1/3737	From the Transport Board, 1798 Sept–1799 Mar.	
1/4822	From Promiscuous Sources: Surnames L, 1804.	
1/4824	From Promiscuous Sources: Surnames L, 1805, nos 202–335.	
1/4826	From Promiscuous Sources: Surnames L, 1806, nos 201–372.	
1/4828	From Promiscuous Sources: Surnames L, 1807, nos 151–358	
1/4833	From Promiscuous Sources: Surnames L, 1810, nos 1–198.	
1/4839	From Promiscuous Sources: Surnames L, 1813, nos 2–250.	
1/4841	From Promiscuous Sources: Surnames L, 1814, nos 1–250.	
1/4842	From Promiscuous Sources: Surnames L, 1814, nos 251–523.	
1/4846	From Promiscuous Sources: Surnames L, 1816, nos 251–469.	
1/4848	From Promiscuous Sources: Surnames L, 1817, nos 201–461.	
1/4849	From Promiscuous Sources: Surnames L, 1818, nos 1–150.	
1/4850	From Promiscuous Sources: Surnames L, 1818, nos 151–326.	
1/4851	From Promiscuous Sources: Surnames L, 1819.	
1/4854	From Promiscuous Sources: Surnames L, 1822.	
1/4863	From Promiscuous Sources: Surnames L, 1831.	
1/5125	Petitions and a related instruction from George III to Admiral Howe, 1797.	
1/5348	Court Martial *Jason*, 25 February 1799.	
ADM 6	Admiralty: Service Records, Registers, Returns and Certificates.	
6/153	Masters' Passing Certificates, statements of service, &c, L, *c.*1800–1850.	
ADM 11/2	Survey of Masters' Services, nos 3–249, 1833–1835.	
ADM 12	Admiralty: Digests and Indexes.	
ADM 36	Admiralty: Ships' Musters (Series I).	
36/5973	*Lenox*, 1762 Sep–1763 Feb.	
36/11522	*Iphigenia*, 1795 Sep–1796 Sep.	
36/12344	*Duke*, 1796 Sep–1797 Feb.	
36/13155	*Jason*, 1797 Sep–1798 Sep.	
ADM 37	Admiralty: Ships' Musters (Series II).	

37/5973	*Examiner*, 1814 Oct–1817 Sept.
37/8608	Yard Muster Book, Barbados.
ADM 42	Admiralty Yard Books.
42/2118	Barbados pay lists, 1813.
42/2121	Barbados: lists of persons entered dead or discharged, 1809 to 1816.
ADM 45/34/294	Anthony Lockwood, Master, who died: 25 January 1855. Notes on executor's application for money owed by the Royal Navy.
ADM 51	Admiralty: Captain's Logs.
51/1138	*Iphigenia*, 1794 June 2–1796 Sept 10.
51/1197	*Duke*, 1796 Aug 22–1797 Aug 31.
51/1203	*Jason*, 1797 Jan 1–1797 Dec 31.
51/1429	*Crescent*, 1799 Apr 22–1802 Mar 31.
51/2067	*Examiner*, 1815 July 1–1816 July 31.
ADM 52	Master's Logs
52/2893	*Crescent*, 1799 Apr 22–1801 July 26.
52/4484	*Examiner*, 1815 Mar 20–1815 Oct 5.
ADM 103	Navy Board Registers of Prisoners of War.
103/476	Britons released from France, 1798.
ADM 106	Navy Board: Records, Papers relating to Masters.
106/1560	In-Letters, Promiscuous letters, L, 1805–1810.
106/1693	In-Letters from Masters, 1808–1831, 'L'.
106/1698	In-Letters from Masters, 1808–1831, 'O'.
106/1987	In-Letters, Antigua, 1809–1812.
106/3517	1781–1823.
ADM 160	Admiralty: Records of Naval Ordnance Departments and Establishments.
160/42	Entry book of In-Letters, 1798 June 20–1799 Dec 31.
ADM 196/1/168	Officers Time of Service: Anthony Lockwood, Master.
ADM 344	Chart of West Coast of Europe.
CO 43	Colonial Office Records: Canada, formerly British North America.
43/56	Letters from Secretary of State: Offices and Individuals, 1817, Sept 24–1818.
43/58	Letters from Secretary of State: Offices and Individuals, 1819, Feb 9–Nov 12.
CO 188	Colonial Office: New Brunswick Original Correspondence.
188/2	Secretary of State, 1785–1817.

	188/22	Secretary of State, 1816.
	188/23	Secretary of State, 1817.
	188/24	Secretary of State, 1818.
	188/25	Secretary of State, 1819.
	188/26	Secretary of State, 1820.
	188/27	Secretary of State, 1821.
	188/28	Secretary of State, 1822.
	188/29	Secretary of State, 1823.
	188/30	Secretary of State, 1824.
CO	189	Colonial Office: New Brunswick Entry Books,1769–1867 (parts 6–9 transferred to the Canadian National Archives).
	189/12	Letters from Secretary of State, Despatches, covering dates 1819 May 8–1830 Mar 31.
CO	193/3	Mr T Baillie's Memoranda and Papers. 1825–1833 (PANB RS 536 F1565)
CO	217	Colonial Office: Nova Scotia and Cape Breton Original Correspondence.
	217/101	Despatches, Offices and Individuals, 1818.
CO	384	War and Colonial Department and Colonial Office: Emigration Original Correspondence.
	384/4	Secretary of State, North America, Settlers, A-L, 1819.
MPG	1/620	A Map of New Brunswick compiled from actual surveys and from Documents in the Surveyor General's Office by Anthony Lockwood, junr, late assistant Surveyor General of the Province.
RGO		Royal Greenwich Observatory.
	13/3	Records of the Board of Longitude.
	13/29	Board of Longitude Papers: Inventions.
	14/4	Minutes of the Board of Longitude.
T	28	Treasury: Various Out-letter Books.
	28/3	America, 1797–1823.
	28/15	Naval and Military Departments, 1817–1818.
	28/48	Secretaries of State, Home, Foreign and Colonial, 1817–1820.
T	29	Treasury Board: Minute Books.
	29/171	1819, March.
WO	10	War Office:
	10/73–87	Artillery muster books and pay lists, 1759–1762.
	10/102	Artillery muster books and pay lists, 1765 Additional.

WO   54   Ordnance Office and War Office: Entry Books and
                    Registers.
      54/564   Returns of People Employed by Place: Foreign,
                    1828.

NATIONAL LIBRARY OF SCOTLAND

Cochrane Papers   Personal and family correspondence of Sir Alexander
                    and Sir Thomas Cochrane, 1786–1854, chiefly
                    letters addressed to the latter.
      2296   Private letter book of Sir Alexander, 1806–1807.
      2316   Folio 9r, Sketch, Anthony Lockwood, work clearing
                    wrecks in Carlisle Bay.
      2322   Letter books containing copies of letters to the
                    Admiralty, 1807–1809.
      2349   Private letter book of Sir Alexander, 1814–15.
      2399   Rough journal of Sir Thomas, 1845.

NEW BRUNSWICK MUSEUM

Chipman   Hazen, Hugh T (b.1870). Collection of Ward
                    Chipman papers.
      S38-1, F 34   Land grants, council meetings; Surveyor General's
                    Office, 1823.
      S38-1, F 37   Correspondence, etc, re Anthony Lockwood, 1823–
                    1824.
Ganong Collection, Box 12 #3, 'Cartography'.
Jarvis   Jarvis Collection, MIC-Loyalist FC LFR.J3F3C6, M-
                    1963.
Marriage Register, Saint John, 1810–1828.

PUBLIC ARCHIVES OF NEW BRUNSWICK

H2-203.29   A Lockwood, Mouth of the River St John [1818].
H3-203.1   Stephen James' 200 Acre Lot ('with 10 per cent') nr
                    Otter Lake, St John Co, next to St Andrew's Church
                    Land [c.1820].
MC   10   Smyth Papers, 1804–1823.
MC   1428   Fredericton *Royal Gazette*.
MC   2713   Saint George (steamer) fonds, 1830–1832.
      MS1   Steamer 'Saint George' Records:
                    A. Accounts and receipts, 1830–1832 (35 items).
                    B. Statement of Receipts and Expenditures, 11 June–
                    26 November 1831 (1 item).

MS2		Receipts for Goods and Services, Steamer 'John Ward', 1830–1831 (2 items).
MPG620		'A Map of New Brunswick compiled from actual surveys and from Documents in the Surveyor General's office by Anthony Lockwood, Junr Late Assistant Surveyor General of the Province, published as the Act directs by Anthony Lockwood, London and New Brunswick, March 27, 1826'.
R-203.1		Return of Survey Grant of Shag Rock [St John Harbour] to Governor and Trustees of Madras School in New Brunswick [c.1820].
RS 1		Journal of the New Brunswick House of Assembly (F5).
RS 2		Journal of the Legislative Council of the Province of New Brunswick.
RS 6a		New Brunswick Executive Council, Minutes and Orders.
	vol 2	1807–1821.
	vol 3	1821–1833.
RS 7	vols 1–6	New Brunswick Executive Council, Draft Minutes and Orders in Council, 1813–1821. Pagination unbroken by volumes (F1688–1689).
	vol 16	Crown Lands and Forests, Petitions, 1819–1843 (F1696).
RS 8		Executive Council Records.
	Estates, A1	Administration of Anthony Lockwood's Estate (F7850).
	Legal Papers, Cases and Proceedings.	
		Identification Cases 1/3 – Estate of Anthony Lockwood, a Lunatic, 1823 (F7897).
	Lighthouses, 1812–1833 (F7899).	
	Provincial Secretary, General Correspondence, 1823.	
RS 13		Correspondence of Provincial Secretary – Executive Council Records (each year is a file).
	13/2	General Correspondence.
	13/2/17	Re: Anthony Lockwood.
	13/2/17/a	Correspondence, 1822.
	13/2/17/b	Certificates verifying Anthony Lockwood to be alive, 1840–1854.
RS 21		Provincial Secretary: Treasury Administrative Records.
	A1	Correspondence: 1789–1835.

	C4/2	Requests for Warrants, 1919–20.
	C4/3	Accounts and Returns, 1820–1825.
	H1819–1823	Treasury Documents laid before the Executive.
RS 24		Legislative Assembly, Sessional Records, 1786–1978.
RS 42		Supreme Court Original Jurisdiction Case Files, 1784–1836.
RS 55B 1823		Equity: Lockwood, Anthony (Lunacy).
RS 107 RNA/C13/4/1		Surveyor General's Cash Book, 1819–24.
RS	336/A	Records of Lieutenant Governor, George Stracy Smyth, Correspondence.
	336/A 1	Letterbook, 3 December 1817–2 May 1825 – including letters from Sir Howard Douglas.
	336/A 2	1812–1819. Primarily copies of correspondence with the Earl of Bathurst regarding the war of 1812.
	336/A 3	Correspondence 1820–1823.
RS	387/B	York County Jail Records, Annual Returns, 1791–1866.
RS	541	Provincial Secretary: Lighthouse Administration Records.
	541	Brier Island, 1815–1830.
RS	637/2c	Records of the Surveyor General, 1784–1912: Correspondence, Anthony Lockwood.
	637/2c 1	General 1819–1823.
	637/2c 2	To George S Smyth, 1819–1823.
RS	541	Provincial Secretary – Lighthouse Administration.
	541	Brier Island, 1815–1830.
	541	Reports on the State of Lighthouses, 1815.
RS	656	Crown Lands, Maps and Plans.
RS	660	Records of the Mirimichi Fire Relief Committee
	660/A	Fire Relief Committee Records.
	660/D	Report of the Commissioners for ascertaining the losses occasioned by the late fires in New Brunswick, Fredericton: King's Printer, 1826.
RS 690		Commission of Anthony Lockwood, Surveyor General (1823).

PUBLIC ARCHIVES OF NOVA SCOTIA

Churches	Saint George's – Halifax (microfilm 15070).
Index of Deeds, volume 1, 1749–1867 (Microfilm 17811).	
Maps	F209, WM 1819, Wentworth Taylor.
MG 20	Societies and Special Collections, Collections of the

	Nova Scotia Historical Society.
679 No 1	Rev Kennedy B Wainwright, 'Admiral Sir Alexander Cochrane, GCB and Landed Proprietors of Shubenacadie'.
RG1	Bound volumes of Nova Scotia Records, 1624–1867.
141	Provincial Secretary's letter Book, 1814–1818 (microfilm 15273).
193	Executive Council Minutes, 1816 (microfilm 15290).
2141/2A	Executive Council Minutes, 1819 (microfilm 15313).
305	Letters of the House of Assembly 1815–1818 (microfilm 15386).
RG 20	Land Petitions.
Series A	Land Papers – Anthony Lockwood, 1817 (microfilm 15720).
RG 31	Treasury Papers.
	Series 106 volume IV, 1815, Lighthouse Papers.
RG 47	Deeds.

Vertical Map Case III, 209. Sketch map of the road from Hammond's Plain to Salmon River.

Scottish National Archives

SNA, GD45/3/540-611 (NAC A536), Dalhousie Journals, 10 September 1818.

United Kingdom Hydrographic Office

207 Ag 1	Caribbean Sea: West Indies: Puerto Rico, vicinity: Culebra (Passage) Island. Survey plan by Anthony Lockwood, Master, RN, showing coastline, limited hydrography and remarks about anchorage.
249 Ag2 pt 1	Caribbean Sea: West Indies: Leeward Islands: Virgin Islands. Survey, by Anthony Lockwood, ordered by Admiral, Sir Francis Laforey, showing coastline, hydrography and topography, includes site of shipwreck.
249 Ag2 pt 2	Caribbean Sea: West Indies: Leeward Islands: Virgin Islands. Survey, by Anthony Lockwood, ordered by Admiral, Sir Francis Laforey, showing coastline, hydrography and topography. Annotated on reverse: 'Lockwoods Virgin Islands'.
250 Ag	Caribbean Sea: West Indies: Puerto Rico, vicinity: Culebra (Passage) Island. Survey plan by Anthony

Lockwood, Master, RN, showing coastline, limited hydrography and remarks about anchorage. Annotated: 'Received 1814'. Scale: 2 inches to 1 mile.

260 Ag1 Pt 3   Caribbean Sea: West Indies: Leeward Islands: Guadeloupe: Les Saintes (Saints). Survey plan, by Anthony Lockwood, showing coastline, hydrography, topography and fortifications. Includes remarks and anchorage site of Statira (?). Annotated: 'No13' and 'Saints, Lockwood'. Scale: 5.5 inches to 1 mile.

263 Ag2   Caribbean Sea: West Indies: Leeward Islands: Virgin Islands. Chart, published by Robert Blachford, surveyed by Anthony Lockwood, ordered by Admiral, Sir Francis Laforey, showing coastline, hydrography, topography, known shipwrecks and island populations. Survey census details slave and animal stock levels.

274 Ag1 1808   Caribbean Sea: West Indies: Windward Islands: Barbados: Carlisle Bay: Bridgetown. Survey plan, Anthony Lockwood, Master Attendant, showing coastline, hydrography, topography, fortifications and remarks. Scale: 6 inches to 1 mile.

314 Ag 2   Caribbean Sea: West Indies: Leeward Islands: Guadeloupe, vicinity: Îles des Saintes (Saints). Survey, ordered by Rear Admiral Sir Alexander Cochrane, KB, prepared by Anthony Lockwood, Acting Master Attendant, showing coastline, hydrography, topography, fortifications and remarks. Scale: 5 inches to 3 miles.

784 Press 51c   United Kingdom: English Channel: Channel Islands: Guernsey and Sark. English MS survey (incomplete) of 'A General Chart of the Islands of Guernsey, Sark, Herm and Jethou Surveyed by Anthony Lockwood, Maritime Surveyor, Guernsey, 5 July 1806', showing coastline, detailed hydrography, limited topography, Base Line and triangulation stations, leading lines and remarks. Scale: 3 miles (10.3 inches).

I40/2 Shelf Db   United Kingdom: England, SW Coast: Cornwall: Falmouth. English MS survey, untitled and unassigned, of Carrick Roads, showing coastline, detailed hydrography, buoyage, anchorage and mooring shackles with remarks and reference. Annotated: 'By Mr Lockwood (see l1)'. Scale: 10 inches to 1 mile.

L1 Shelf Od*   United Kingdom: England, S Coast: Cornwall: Falmouth. English MS tracing, unassigned, of a combination of three superimposed surveys of Falmouth, attributed to Lieutenant McKenzie [sic] (black), Lieutenant Manderson (red) and Mr Lockwood (yellow), showing coastline and detailed hydrography. Scales: 6 and 7 inches to 1 mile.

L56 Shelf Hy   Europe, W Coast: Spain: Galicia: Ria da Coruna and Ria de Betanzos. English MS 'Plan of Corunna Ferrol and Intermediate Bays in 3 sheets Survey'd by order of Rear Admiral Cochrane by A Lockwood, late Master of HM Ship Malta, 1804', 'No 1', showing detailed coastline, hydrography, leading lines, anchorages, townships, fortifications and remarks. Annotated in red: '(only one sheet found August 1883)'and in pencil: 'Received 2 November 1804' with monogram (illegible). Scale: 1 mile (3.25 inches).

M17 Shelf pr   United Kingdom: English Channel: Channel Islands: Guernsey. English MS survey of 'A Series of Triangles formed on Island of Guernsey in Year 1805. A Lockwood (signature)', showing limited coastline, triangulation stations with base line, remarks and list of calculations.

Q69 Shelf Ag2   Caribbean Sea: West Indies: Netherland Antilles: Curacao: Willemstad, vicinity. English MS 'Plan of Curacoa [sic] Harbour by Antony Lockwood, Master of HMS Crescent', showing detailed coastline and hydrography, limited topography, township, fortifications and references. Annotated in pencil: 'North taken from (?) Plan of Entrance by J L March'. Scale: 6 inches to 500 fathoms (approx).

V97 Ag2   South America, N Coast: Venezuela, N Coast: Lesser Antilles: Netherlands Antilles: Curacoa: Willemstad harbour, by Ant[hon]y Lockwood, showing coastline, hydrography, some soundings in red (drying heights) and settlements. Scale: 64/10 =1'.

A284 Ah1   North America, E Coast: Canada: Nova Scotia, N Coast: Pictou, by A[urthu]r [sic] Lockwood. Shows cl, hy, top and np. Annotated on reverse. Scale: 2.85 inches to 4 mile.

B18 Ah2   North America: Canada, E Coast: New Brunswick: Bay of Fundy: Mouth of the River St John. Published by A Lockwood 28 February 1818. Shows cl, hy, ancs, top, rems and np. Scale: 4.2 inches to 2 miles.

B797 3k   North America: Canada, E Coast: Nova Scotia, E Coast: Halifax Harbour, by Lockwood. Shows cl, hy, ancs, top, rems and np. Pencil annotations. Scale: 2.5 inches to 1 nm.

D611 Part2 Ah4   North America: Canada, E Coast: Nova Scotia: Harbour of Halifax. 'A Sketch of Backhouse's Chart'. Plan of Herring Cove to Sandwich Point at sc: 1.4 ins to 200 fathoms. Shows cl, hy and rems by Edw[ard] Fairfax London 3 September 1815. Annotated in pencil; 'a Copy 8 December A Lockwood'. Annotated on reverse; 'No 20'. No scale.

LP57   Letters Prior to 1857. 12 Nov. 1849, A Lockwood to Admiral Beaufort (Hydrographer), giving a list of his surveys, etc, carried out between 1801 and 1819, written in a very shaky hand.

University of New Brunswick Archives

MG H28   Minutes of the Fredericton Emigrant Society.
Sir H Douglas Letter Books.
Saunders Papers.

Whitehaven, Cumbria, Town Library

The Monumental Inscriptions of the Church & Churchyard of St James, Whitehaven.
Trinity Churchyard Register.

Periodicals

Acadian Recorder	Canadian newspaper – Nova Scotia.
Annual Register	English newspaper – London.
The Bridgetown Mercury	Barbados newspaper.
Colonial Journal	Canadian newspaper – Ontario.
The Examiner	English newspaper.
Halifax Journal	Canadian newspaper – Nova Scotia.

The Headquarters	Canadian newspaper – New Brunswick.
Royal Gazette: New Brunswick	Canadian government newspaper – New Brunswick.
Nova Scotia Royal Gazette	Canadian government newspaper – Nova Scotia.
The Star	Canadian newspaper – New Brunswick – Saint John.

SECONDARY SOURCES

Acheson, Thomas William (b.1936), *Saint John: the making of a colonial urban community*, Toronto: University of Toronto Press, 1993 (*c*.1985).

Anonymous, *Advice to the officers of the British navy*, London: the Author, 1785.

Anonymous, *Celebration of the centennial anniversary of the introduction of Freemasonry into the province of New Brunswick, July 1, 1884*, 1884?

Anonymous, 'Canada's First Chartered Bank', *Monthly Review: The Bank of Nova Scotia*, May 1956.

Armstrong, John Russell (b.1848), *The Exchange Coffee House and St John's first club: a paper read before the New Brunswick Historical Society, 30th April, 1907*, 1907?

Baillie, Thomas (1796–1863), *An account of the province of New Brunswick: including a description of the settlements, institutions, soil, and climate of that important province: with advice to emigrants*, Printed for J G & F Rivington, 1832.

Barnett, Cleadie B, *Beginnings*: Coffin, John, http://homepages.rootsweb.ancestry.com/~nbpast/family/begin/C–13.htm .

William Franklin Bunting, *Freemasonry in New Brunswick; 'Biographical Sketches'*, Saint John, New Brunswick: MacMillan, 1895.

Bunting, William Franklin, *History of St John's lodge, F & A M of Saint John, New Brunswick: together with sketches of all Masonic bodies in New Brunswick, from A. 1784 to A. 1894*, J & A McMillan, 1895.

Campbell, P F, 'St Ann's Fort and the Garrison', *Journal of the Barbados Museum and Historical Society*, XXXV, 1, March 1975.

Cobbett, William, *Rural Rides*, 1830.

Cowan, Helen I, *British immigration before Confederation*, Canadian Historical Association, 1968.

Crossman, Evelyn de Blois, *Millidge Ancestors*, [private publication] 1980.

Dawson, Llewellyn Styles, *Memoirs of Hydrography. Including brief biographies of the principal officers who have served in HM Naval Surveying Service, between the years 1750 and 1885* 2 pt, Eastbourne: Henry W Keay, [1883].

Day, Sir Archibald, *The Admiralty Hydrographic Service 1795–1919*, HMSO, 1967.

Dobrée, Bonamy, *see* Manwaring.

Dugan, James, *The Great Mutiny*, New York, 1965.

Edwards, Bryan, *The History, Civil and Commercial, of the British West Indies*, 6 volumes, London, 1819.

Ells, Margaret, compiler, *Calendar of the Official Correspondence of the Legislative Papers of Nova Scotia, 1802–1815*, Public Archives of Nova Scotia; no 3, 1936.

Evans, Geraint Nantglyn Davies (b.1935), *Uncommon Obdurate: The Several Public Careers of J J W Desbarres*, Peabody Museum, 1969.

Fingard, Judith, 'Sir John Wentworth', *Dictionary of Canadian Biography*, vol 5.

Fraser, Flora, *The Unruly Queen: the life of Queen Caroline*, London: Macmillan, 1996.

Gesner, Abraham (1797–1864), *New Brunswick: with notes for emigrants: comprehending the early history, an account of the Indians, settlement, topography, statistics, commerce, timber, manufactures, agriculture, fisheries, geology, natural history, social and political state, immigrants, and contemplated railways of that province*, Simmonds & Ward, 1847.

Gibson, John Frederic, *Brocklebanks, 1770–1950*, Liverpool: H Young, 1953.

Gosset, W P, The *Lost Ships of the Royal Navy, 1793–1900*, London: Mansell, 1986.

Graves, Donald E, *Merry Hearts Make Light Days: The War of 1812 Journal of Lieutenant John Le Couteur, 104th Foot*, Ottawa: Carleton University Press, 1993.

Gray, Charlotte (b.1948), *Canada, a portrait in letters, 1800–2000*, Anchor Canada, 2004.

Gray, Hugh, *Letters from Canada: written during a residence there in the years 1806, 1807 and 1808; shewing the present state of Canada ...* Printed for Longman, Hurst, Rees, and Orme, 1809.

Hannay, James (1842–1910), *History of New Brunswick*, J A Bowes, 1909.

Heinl, Robert Debs (b.1916), *Written in blood: the story of the Haitian people, 1492–1971*, Houghton Mifflin, 1978.

Hurd, Captain Thomas Hannaford, *Plan du Port de Falmouth, de la*

Rivière d'Helford, et de la Côte jusqu'à Manacle Rock. Levé en 1806 par la Capitaine T Hurd, Paris, 1825.

James, Admiral Sir William M, *The Naval History of Great Britain*, 6 volumes, London: Harding, Lepard and Co, 1826.

Kee, Robert, *The green flag: the turbulent history of the Irish National Movement*, Delacorte Press, 1972.

Laffin, John, *Jack Tar: the story of the British sailor*, London: Cassell, 1969.

Laws, Lt Col M E S, *Battery Records of the Royal Artillery, 1716–1859*, Royal Artillery Institute, Woolwich, 1952.

Lockwood, Anthony, *A brief description of Nova Scotia with plates of the principal harbors: including a particular account of the Island of Grand Manan*, London: Printed for the author by G Hayden and sold by Cadell and Davies, 1818.

Lockwood, Anthony, *Mouth of the River Saint John*, J Walker sculpt, 1818.

Lockwood, Anthony, *Report on the projected canal across the istmus [sic] that divides Nova-Scotia and New-Brunswick: explored and levelled in the autumn of 1819, by order of His Excellency Major-General George Stracey Smyth, lieutenant-governor of the province of New-Brunswick*, printed by George K Lugrin, 1820.

Lewis, Michael, *Spithead: An Informal History*, London, 1972.

Dr George MacBeath and Captain Donald F Taylor, *Steamboat Days: An Illustrated History of the Steamboat Era on the St John River*, based on the notes of Captain C C Taylor (1868–1941), St Stephen, New Brunswick: Print'N Press Ltd, 1982.

Macgregor, John (1797–1857), *Historical and descriptive sketches of the maritime colonies of British America*, London: Longman, Rees, Orme, Brown, and Green, 1828.

Mackenzie, Murdoch Jr, *A Treatise of Maritime Surveying . . .*, London: Edward & Charles Dilly, 1774.

MacNutt, W Stewart (1908–1976), *The Atlantic Provinces: the emergence of colonial society, 1712–1857*, McClelland & Stewart (*c.*1965).

Mahan, Alfred Thayer, *Types of Naval Officers Drawn from the History of the Royal Navy*, Boston: Little, Brown and Co, 1901.

Mann, John (1798–1891), *Travels in North America: particularly in the provinces of Upper & Lower Canada and New Brunswick, and in the states of Maine, Massachusetts [sic] and New York*, preface by William Arthur Spray (b.1938), Saint Anne's Point Press, 1978 (originally published Glasgow: A Young, 1824).

Manwaring, George Ernest, and Bonamy Dobrée, *The Floating Republic*, London, 1966.

Marshall, John, *Royal Navy Biography, or, Memoirs of the Service of all
    ...*, 4 volumes with supplements, London, 1835.

Maxwell, Lilian Mary Beckwith, ed, *The old grave-yard, Fredericton, New
    Brunswick: epitaphs*, York-Sunbury Historical Society, Busy East
    Press, 1938.

—————————, *An outline of the history of central New Brunswick to the
    time of Confederation*, York-Sunbury Historical Society, 1984.

Milton, A J B, *Loyalist Masons in the Maritimes*, Canadian Masonic
    Research Association [papers read before the Association], 1974.

Morriss, Roger, *The Royal Dockyards During the Revolutionary and
    Napoleonic Wars*, Leicester, 1983.

National Library of Scotland, *Catalogue of Manuscripts acquired since
    1925. Volume 2, Manuscripts 1801–4000, Charters and other
    formal documents 901–2634*, Edinburgh: Her Majesty's Stationery
    Office, 1966.

New Brunswick, *Journal of the New Brunswick House of Assembly*, 22
    March 1817–7 March 1826, Fredericton: King's Printer, 1817,
    1818, 1822 and 1823.

New Brunswick, *Journal of the Legislative Council of the Province of New
    Brunswick*, vol 2 (1817–1830), Fredericton: King's Printer, 1831.

New Brunswick, *Report of the Commissioners for ascertaining the losses
    occasioned by the late fires in New Brunswick*, Fredericton: King's
    Printer, 1826.

Nova Scotia, House of Assembly, *Journals and proceedings of the House of
    Assembly of the Province of Nova Scotia*, Queen's Printer, 1816.

Owen, Hugh (b.1925), *The Lowther Family: eight hundred years of 'A
    family of ancient gentry and worship'*, foreword by the Earl of
    Lonsdale, Chichester: Phillimore, 1990.

Parry, Sir William Edward (1790–1855), *Journal of a voyage for the
    discovery of a North-West passage from the Atlantic to the Pacific:
    performed in the years 1819–20, in His Majesty's ships Hecla and
    Griper under the orders of William Edward Parry, RN, FRS, and
    commander of the expedition*, London: J Murray, 1821.

Pivka, Otto von (b.1935), *Navies of the Napoleonic Era*, Newton Abbot:
    David and Charles, 1980.

Pope, Dudley, *Life in Nelson's Navy*, G Allen & Unwin, 1981.

Poyer, John, *History of Barbados from the first discovery of the island
    1605 till the accession of Lord Seaforth*, London: Frank Cass, 1971
    (1808).

Raddall, Thomas (1903–1994), *Halifax: Warden of the North*, Doubleday,
    1965.

Ralfe, James (*fl* 1820–1829). *The naval biography of Great Britain:*

consisting of historical memoirs of those officers of the British Navy
who distinguished themselves during the reign of . . . George III, 4
volumes, London, 1828.

Raymond, William Odber, 'New Brunswick: General History, 1758–1867',
in Canada and its provinces: a history of the Canadian people and
their institutions by one hundred associates, general editors: Adam
Shortt and Arthur G Doughty, T and A Constable . . . for the
Publishers Association of Canada, 1913–1917.

Raymond, William Odber, Winslow Papers, AD1776–1826, Riverton, NJ:
Gregg Press, 1972.

Robinson, Adrian Henry Wardle (b.1925), Marine Cartography in Britain.
A history of the sea chart to 1855, etc, Leicester: Leicester University
Press, 1962.

Rodger, N A M (Nicholas) (b.1949), The Command of the Ocean: A
Naval History of Britain, 1649–1815, London: W W Norton &
Company, 2005.

Rollin, Charles, The Ancient History by Charles Rollin, 8th edition,
Edinburgh: Apollo Press, 1789–1790.

Ryan, Anthony, 'An Ambassador Afloat: Vice Admiral Sir James Saumarez
and the Swedish Court', in The British Navy and the Use of Naval
Power in the Eighteenth Century, Jeremy Black and Philip
Woodfine, eds, Humanities Press International, Atlantic Highlands,
New Jersey, 1988.

Spray, William A, The Blacks in New Brunswick, Fredericton: Brunswick
Press, 1972.

Squires, W Austin (William Austin) (1905–1978), History of Fredericton:
the last 200 years, City of Fredericton, 1980.

Donald F Taylor, Captain, Steamboat Days, see Dr George MacBeath.

Taylor, Eva Germaine Rimington (1879–1966), Mathematical Practitioners
of Hanoverian England, 1714–1840, Cambridge University Press,
1966.

Tracy, Nicholas, Who's Who in Nelson's Navy, Chatham Publishing, 2006.
——————, Britannia's Palette: the Arts of Naval Victory, Montreal:
McGill-Queens UP, February 2007.

Thomas, David A, A Companion to the Royal Navy, Harrap, 1988.

Thomas, Peter (1939–2007), Strangers from a secret land: the voyages of
the brig Albion and the founding of the first Welsh settlements in
Canada, University of Toronto Press, c.1986.

Turnbull, William, The Naval Surgeon, London: Richard Phillips, 1806.

Winks, Robin W, The Blacks in Canada: a history, McGill-Queens UP,
1997.

Young, John (1773–1837), The letters of Agricola on the principles of *vegetation and tillage: written for Nova Scotia and published first in the Acadian recorder*, Halifax, NS?: sn, 1822.

Young, Murray (b.1922), *The Colonial Office in the early nineteenth century*, published for the Royal Commonwealth Society by Longmans, 1961.

Webb, Paul, 'Construction, repair and maintenance in the battle fleet of the Royal Navy, 1793–1815', *The British Navy and the Use of Naval Power in the Eighteenth Century*, Jeremy Black and Philip Woodfine, eds, Humanities Press International, Atlantic Highlands, New Jersey, 1988.

Whalen, James M (b.1939), 'New Brunswick poor law policy in the nineteenth century', University of New Brunswick, Dept of History, MA Thesis, 1968.

Whitelaw, Marjory, *The Dalhousie Journals*, 3 volumes, Oberon Press, c.1978–1982.

Wordsworth, William, *The Poetical Works of William Wordsworth*, vol 3, London: Edward Moxon, 1837.

Wright, Esther Clark (b.1895), *The Loyalists of New Brunswick*, Moncton, 1955.

Wynn, Graeme (b.1946), *Timber colony: a historical geography of early nineteenth century New Brunswick*, Toronto: University of Toronto Press, 1981.

Index

Mitchell, John, 120
Moore, Sir Graham, 80, 228
Morris, Charles, Surveyor General of
    Nova Scotia, 62, 84, 89–92
Mulgrave, Henry Phipps, 1st Earl of,
    39, 54
mutiny, 8–15, 159, 222

Napoleon (Napoleon Bonaparte), 25,
    39, 55, 58, 163–4, 170, 218
National Assembly, 6
Navy Board, 5, 9, 19–27, 36–7, 46–8,
    51–7, 61, 77–81, 91–2, 96, 115,
    212–14, 222
Navy, British Royal , 4–9, 15–31, 36–7,
    40, 43, 46–8, 51–60, 63, 66, 81, 96–
    8, 100–1, 104–5, 115, 118–20, 141,
    149, 183, 213–14, 217; purser, 5
navy, French, 53
Neales, surgeon, 10
Needham, Mark, 159
Nelson, Clause, 66
Nelson, Vice Admiral Lord Horatio,
    29–30, 66, 137
Netherlands, 16
New Brunswick, 3, 16, 21, 44, 60, 62,
    65, 67–70, 73–4, 78–9, 82–4, 88–92,
    and passim
New Brunswick, Bank of, 153, 183,
    213
New Brunswick Central Society for
    Promoting the Rural Economy of the
    Province, 144; Central Agricultural
    Society, 143, 155, 165
New Brunswick, College of, 121, 138,
    160, 179, 194; and see King's College
New Brunswick, emigrants, 102–4,
    111–18, 122–3, 126–35, 140, 143–7,
    153–4, 164, 170, 179, 183; Emigrant
    Society, 123, 129–31, 140–6, 155,
    166, 174; and: Irish, 112–14, 146,
    160–2, 169–70, 179, 187–8; Welsh
    118, 121–4, 127, 129, 146–7, 156,
    232–4
New Brunswick geography: Allen's
    Creek, 133; Alwington Manor, 117;
    The Barony, 117; Bartibog, 179; Bay
    de Verte Canal, 186, 227; Cape
    Tormentine, 145, 227; Cardigan,
    115–16, 121–4, 128–9, 135–6, 140,
    145–6, 155–6; Chaldiac, 191;
    Chaleur, 154, 185; Charlotte county,
    New Brunswick, 111, 154, 167;
    Chebuctouche, 192; Cheney Island,
    65, 76; Chignecto, 124–5, 131–3,
    191–2, 219; Duck Island, 76; Fort
    Howe, 108, 119, 179; Fort

Nashwaak, 118; Fredericton, 3, 84,
    89, 92 and passim (Avery's Tavern,
    122; Barracks, 119–20, 189; Christ
    Church Cathedral, Fredericton, 138,
    194–5; Jerusalem Coffee House, 123;
    Methodist Church, 152, 183; Streets,
    120); Gagetown, 116; Gaspereau
    River, 145, 154; Grand Falls, 119;
    Grand Lake, 117; Grand Manan
    Island, 65, 68–70, 73, 76–9, 83–4,
    224, 226; Green Island, 76;
    Hammond River, 154; Hillsborough,
    179; Hopewell, 179; Kennebecasis,
    117; Keswick river, 122; Kingsclear,
    132, 159; Kingston, 160, 179; Lake
    George, 135; Lincoln, 120; Loch
    Lomond, 154; Long Reach, 116;
    Magaguadavic River, 111; Maryland
    Hill, 172–4; Maugerville, 116–18,
    154, 173, 178; McLeod's Inn,
    Fredericton, 121; Memramcook, 59,
    191; Murre Ledge, 76, 79;
    Nashwaksis Stream, 121; Nerepis,
    117, 135–6, 145, 154, 159, 165;
    Newcastle, 166; Northumberland
    Strait, 124, 154, 219;
    Northumberland County, 170;
    Norton, 100; Oromocto, 117, 136,
    145, 154; Otter Hole, 154; Partridge
    Island, 78–9, 88, 132;
    Passamaquoddy Bay, 73, 76, 83, 119;
    Prequ'ile, 135; Quaco, 135;
    Queensbury, 180; Restigouche River,
    146, 154; Restook, Kent parish, 190;
    Richibucto, 153–54, 192; Ross
    Island, 65; Saint John, 3, 63, 65, 73–
    4, 76, 79, 83, 88–9, 97–8, and
    passim (Trinity Church, 138, 148;
    Cody's, see Exchange Coffee House;
    St Andrew's Kirk, 74, 107, 148, 178;
    Exchange Coffee House, 137;
    Market Square, 111, 120, 137, 150);
    Saint John river, 56; Scovil's Inn,
    Gagetown, 116; Shag Rock, 154;
    Sheffield, 154, 166; Shepody, 135; St
    Ann's Point, 118; St; Croix River, 83;
    St; Andrews, 119, 135–8, 142, 154,
    178, 191, 219; Sussex Vale, 106–8,
    161, 194–5, 199–201, 210;
    Tantramar Marsh, 125; Tay creek,
    121; Taylor's Inn, Maugerville, 116;
    Washadamoac, 117; White Head
    Island, 76; Wolves, 65, 73; Worden's
    Inn, Long Reach, 116; York County,
    113, 119–20, 129, 139, 146, 172,
    204
New Brunswick government, 102–3:

Paddock, Adino junior, 104
Paddock, Dr Thomas, 190, 200
Pagan, William, 107–8
Pains and Penalties Bill, 1820, 163
Palmer, Acalus Lockwood, 125
Palmer, Philip, 125
Palmer, Sarah Ayer, 125
Parker, Admiral Sir Peter, 29
Parry, Captain William, 96
Parslow, Mr, storekeeper, 75
Pechell, Captain George Richard
    Brooke, 71
Pepys, Samuel,
Perdix, 3
Pergami, Bartolemeo, 157
Peters, Charles J, 173
Phillips, Colonel, 130
Philomathean Society, 181
Pickard, David, 130
pitch, 50
Pitt, William the Younger, 4
plays: *A Female Convict's Address to
    her Infant*, 140; *Fortune's Frolics*, 43;
    Lovers' Vows, 43; *The Child of
    Nature*, 43; *The Irishman in London*,
    43; *The West Indian*, 43; *The
    Entertainment of the Spoilt Child*, 43
Pole, Hon William Wellesley, Admiralty
    Secretary, 40, 53
poorhouse, 113, 146
Portugal, Tagus, 13
Powell, Miss, 136–7
Poyer, John, 41
Presbyterian church, 107, 148–9, 178;
    and see Kirk, 74, 166
Prince Edward Island, 63, 66, 71, 100,
    154, 226–7; Cape West, 227
prisoner, 13–16, 29, 40, 66, 114, 164,
    172, 204, 208
publications: *Address to the Island of
    Barbados*, in the *Bridgetown
    Mercury* by AZ, 41; *Advice to
    Officers of the British Navy*,
    Anonymous, 1785, 21; *Agricola
    Letters*, 91, 117, 123, 142–3; *Ancient
    History*, Charles Rollin, 1789, 144;
    Brief Description of Nova Scotia,
    1818, Anthony Lockwood, 37, 43,
    63, 83–5, 88–91, 97, 115, 126, 153;
    Frankenstein, Mary Shelly, 1818, 88;
    *Historical and descriptive sketches of
    the maritime colonies of British
    America*, John McGregor, 1828, 141;
    History of Barbados, John Poyer,
    1808, 41; *Memoirs of Hydrography*,
    Llewellyn Styles Dawson, 37; *Mouth
    of the River Saint John*, Anthony

Lockwood, 1817, 83; *Rural Rides*,
    William Cobbett, 143; *The Deserted
    Village*, Oliver Goldsmith, 108; *The
    Naval Surgeon*, William Turnbull,
    20; *The Atlantic Neptune*, Joseph
    Frederick Wallet Desbarres, 1778,
    55, 58, 64; *Travels*, John Mann,
    1824, 112; *Treatise on Maritim[e]
    Surveying*, 24Quakers, 87

Quota Acts, 4

Rafter, William, Lt, 43
Rainsford, Andrew, councillor, 106,
    150
Rainsford, Andrew junior, 150–2
Ralfe, James, 22
Ramsey, Colonel, 29
Reichstadt, Duke of, 164
Republican, 158, 196
Revere, Paul, 178
Reynolds, William, Saint John
    bookseller, 177, 182, 206, 209–10
Riboleau, Lieutenant, 13
Richards, Captain John, 79
Ricketts, George Points, Governor, 41
Ring, Jarvis, 130
Robinson, Beverley, 107, 178
Robinson, F P, 179
Robinson, Frederick, 167
Robinson, John, 121–3, 130–2, 160–
    61, 172, 202
Ross, Captain Sir John, 81–2, 89, 97
Royal College of Physicians, 214
Russia, Borodino, 55
Ryan, John, 89
Ryan, Michael, 89

Saint John City Council, 141
Saumarez, Admiral Sir James, 26–37,
    53, 72
Saumarez, Thomas, 106
Saunders, John junior, 92, 103, 106,
    189, 193
Saunders, John senior, Judge, 100, 117,
    129, 160–1, 207
Saunders, Richard, 181
Saxe-Coburg-Saalfeld, Prince Leopold
    of, 158
school, 4, 105, 131, 135–8, 159, 166,
    191, 195, 219; Madras schools, 138,
    154, 171, 188
Scotland, 4, 22–4, 48, 91, 111, 142–4,
    153, 162, 178
Segee, Captain James, 116
Selby, Captain, 35
Seymour, Vice Admiral Lord Hugh

theodolite, 23, 70, 76
Thomas, 18
Thomas, John Tull, 45
Thoms, Richard, 90
Tidbald, Mr, 40
timber, 49–50, 84, 100–5, 111, 118,
    127, 132, 136, 139–50, 154, 165–7,
    179–84, 219; tropical woods, 49–50;
    masts, 101
Tomkinson, pianomaker, 188
tools, 76
Toone, Mr, 28
Toussaint L'Ouverture, 7
Tracy, John, secretary, 52
tradesmen, 45, 69, 75
Trench Sir Robert Le Poer,
    commandant of the 74th regiment,
    106, 119, 123, 129, 138, 168, 187
triangles, chain of, 26, 33
Trinity House, 12, 23, 79–80, 96, 214
Troughton, Edward, optician, 81
Turnbull, William, 20
Turner, J, 63, 72, 76, 226

Uniacke, Richard, 173
United States, 8, 22, 30, 39, 42, 55–8,
    61, 63, 66, 80, 83, 87, 97–102, 105–
    16, 123–7, 130, 136–9, 159, 165,
    178,181, 186, 214, 218–19
United States geography: Albany, 3;
    Boston, 112, 137; Connecticut, 183;
    Fort Edward, 3; Hudson River, 116,
    185; Massachusetts, 87; New
    Orleans, 164; New England, 57, 60;
    New York, 112, 124, 133–4, 137,
    181; Onondago Falls, 3;
    Pennsylvania, 87; Philadelphia, 112,
    164, 181; Rhode Island, 56;
    Washington, 57, 164, 178; White
    House, 57

Van Horne, Gabriel, innkeeper, 178
Vernon, Joseph, Receiver of Fees, 95
Vienna, 58, 164

Wallace, Michael, 67, 167
Warren, Admiral Sir John Borlase, 22,
    55–7
Washington, George, 178
Waterloo, 58, 120, 122
Watkins, Captain Frederick Barlow, 16
Wellington, Duke of, 119
Wentworth, John, Surveyor General of
    Woods, 60–1, 100–1, 147, 167
Wentworth, Frances, 60

West Indies, 7, 15, 18–22, 38–41, 44,
    47, 53, 91, 99, 219; Antilles, 165;
    Aruba, 20; Barbados (Bridgetown,
    39–53, 61, 87–91, 98, 148–9, 152,
    177 – careenage, 39, 50; Carlisle Bay,
    15, 39–40, 45, 50; St Ann's Fort, 39;
    St Michael's church, 43, 74;
    Needham Point, 50; Speightstown,
    41); Bonaire, 20; Cartagena, 165;
    Curaçao, 15–17, 20; Demerara, 19;
    English Harbour, Antigua, 46–7, 51;
    Guadeloupe, 53; Havana, 8, 16, 49;
    Jamaica, 3, 4, 7–8, 15–19, 75, 164
    (Kingston, 8, 19; Montego Bay, 19;
    Port Royal, 3, 8, 15–17; Salt River,
    19; Spanish Town, 19); Martinique,
    40, 50–3; Saint-Dominique, 6–8, 38–
    41 (Artibonite, 7; Gulf of Paria, 49;
    Jeremie, 7; Haiti, 9, 164, 180;
    Marmelade, 7; Môle St Nicolas, 7;
    Petit Riviere, 8; Port-au-Prince, 7; St
    Marc, 8); Saintes, 53, 54, 59; St
    Vincent, 19; Tortola, 54–6; Trinidad,
    48–50, 68, 165; Vera Cruz, 16
Wetmore, George, 172–4
Wetmore, George (Miss) 172
Wetmore, Thomas, Attorney General,
    104, 107, 121, 128, 130–2, 144,
    150, 160, 166–7, 173, 178, 208–9
Wheeler, Zalmon, 148–9, 183–6, 205
White, Commodore Charles, 51–3
William IV, 60
William the Conqueror, 30
Williamson, General Adam, 7–8
Willis, Reverend Dr Robert, 148, 167
Wilmot, Robert (Wilmot-Horton),
    Parliamentary Under Secretary of
    State for the Colonies, 184, 209
Winslow, Edward, 108–10, 173
Wodehouse, Captain the Honourable
    Philip, 73, 228
Wolsey, Cardinal, 198
Woodford, MD, 241
Woolaston, Dr, inventor, 81–2
Woolford, John Elliot, 189
Wordsworth, William, 164
Wright, Esther Clark, 138

yellow fever, 7, 15–16, 19–20
York, Duke of, 118, 236
Yorke, Charles Philip, First Lord of the
    Admiralty, 1810–12, 54
Young, Admiral, 22
Young, John, 90, 142
Young, William, 90